Augusta Foote Arnold

THE SEA-BEACH AT EBB-TIDE

*A Guide to the Study of the Seaweeds
and the Lower Animal Life found
between Tide-marks*

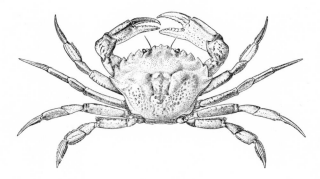

with more than 600 illustrations

DOVER PUBLICATIONS, INC., NEW YORK

Published in Canada by General Publishing Company, Ltd., 30 Lesmill Road, Don Mills, Toronto, Ontario.
Published in the United Kingdom by Constable and Company, Ltd., 10 Orange Street, London WC 2.

This Dover edition, first published in 1968, is an unabridged and unaltered republication of the work originally published in 1901 by The Century Company.

Standard Book Number: 486-21949-6

Library of Congress Catalog Card Number: 68-20554

Manufactured in the United States of America
Dover Publications, Inc.
180 Varick Street
New York, N. Y. 10014

And hath been tutor'd in the rudiments
Of many desperate studies.
SHAKSPERE.

PREFACE

THIS volume is designed to be an aid to the amateur collector
and student of the organisms, both animal and vegetable,
which are found upon North American beaches.   In it are
described many invertebrates and some of the more notable varieties of seaweeds, and each individual is given its proper place in
the latest classification.

The technicality of classification or scientific grouping may
at first seem repellent, but it in reality makes the study of these
objects more simple; and a systematic arrangement has been
adopted in the belief that it is the easiest as well as the only satisfactory way of becoming familiar with the organisms described.
Without it a very confused picture of separate individuals would
be presented to the mind, and a book like the present one would
become a mere collection of isolated scraps of information.   Morphology, or the study of structure, has been touched upon just
enough to show the objects from the biologist's point of view and
to enable the observer to go a little beyond the bare learning of
names.

Scientific names have been used from necessity, for the plants
and animals of the beach are so infrequently observed, except by
scientific people, that but few of them have common names;
and, as a matter of fact, the reader will find that a scientific name
is as easily remembered as a common one.   Technical phrase-
ology has, however, been avoided as much as possible, even at the

v

expense of conciseness and precision ; where it has been used, care has been taken to explain the terms so that their meaning will be plain to every one. A general glossary has been omitted, but the technical terms used have been indexed. The illustrations will bear the use of a hand-glass, and this will often bring out details which cannot well be seen by the unaided eye.

The systematic table of the marine algæ, as given in Part I, and followed in the text, will be of use to collectors who wish to make herbaria. In order to name and group specimens such a guide is necessary. Should specific names lead to embarrassment, many of them can be neglected, for the names of genera are often a sufficient distinction.

Since so many species of invertebrates are found on the beach that a complete enumeration of them is impracticable, only the most conspicuous ones have been selected for description in Part II; but the attempt has been made to designate the various classes and orders with sufficient clearness to enable the collector to identify the objects commonly found on the shore, and to follow the subject further, if he so desires, in technical books.

It is hoped that this book will suggest a new interest and pleasure to many, that it will encourage the pastime of collecting and classifying, and that it will serve as a practical guide to a better acquaintance with this branch of natural history, without necessitating serious study. Marine organisms are interesting acquaintances when once introduced, and the real purpose of the author is to present, to the latent naturalist, friends whom he will enjoy.

Grateful acknowledgment is here made to the following persons who have kindly assisted and advised the author and have also extended valued courtesies to her in the preparation of this book : Smith Ely Jelliffe, M.D., Ph.D. ; Herbert M. Richards, A.B., Ph.D., Professor of Botany in Barnard College ; Marshall A.

Howe, A.B., Ph.D.; the Rev. George A. Holst; the Long Island
Historical Society of Brooklyn for the use of its fine herbarium,
containing the collections of Mr. John Hooper, Mr. A. R. Young,
and others, from which most of the illustrations of algæ in this
book were photographed; Miss Toedtleberg, Librarian of the Long
Island Historical Society; Miss Ingalls, in charge of the Museum
of the Long Island Historical Society; Dr. Theodore Gill; James
A. Benedict, Ph.D., Assistant Curator of Marine Invertebrates
in the Smithsonian Institution; Miss Mary J. Rathbun, second
Assistant Curator of Marine Invertebrates in the Smithsonian
Institution; Miss Harriet Richardson; and especially to Mr. John
B. Henderson, Jr.

Thanks, also, are due to Messrs. Macmillan & Co. for permission to use cuts from the "Cambridge Natural History," Parker
and Haswell's "Zoölogy," and Murray's "Introduction to the
Study of Seaweeds"; to Swan Sonnenschein & Co. for the use of cuts
from Sedgwick's "Student's Text-book of Zoölogy"; to Wilhelm
Engelmann for a cut from "Die natürlichen Pflanzenfamilien"
of Engler and Prantl; to Little, Brown & Co. for permission to
reproduce illustrations from Agassiz's "Contributions to the
Natural History of the United States"; to Henry Holt & Co. for a
cut from McMurrich's "Invertebrate Morphology"; to Houghton,
Mifflin & Co. for cuts from the "Riverside Natural History"
and Agassiz's "Seaside Studies in Natural History"; to the Com-
monwealth of Massachusetts for the use of illustrations from
Verrill's "Report upon the Invertebrate Animals of Vineyard
Sound and the Adjacent Waters," Gould's "Invertebrata of
Massachusetts" (ed. Binney), and certain fisheries reports; and
to the United States government for illustrations taken from
Bulletin 37 of the Smithsonian Institution and from reports of the
United States Fish Commission.

CONTENTS

PART I

MARINE ALGÆ

PART II

MARINE INVERTEBRATES

CONTENTS

MARINE INVERTEBRATES (*Continued*)

INTRODUCTION

In vain through every changeful year
  Did nature lead him as before;
    A primrose by a river's brim,
    A yellow primrose was to him,
  And it was nothing more.

At noon, when by the forest's edge
  He lay beneath the branches high,
    The soft blue sky did never melt
    Into his heart; he never felt
  The witchery of the soft blue sky.
                          WORDSWORTH.

To him who in the love of Nature holds
Communion with her visible forms, she speaks
A various language.
                  BRYANT.

INTRODUCTION

I

SIGNS ON THE BEACH

THE sea-shore, with its stretches of sandy beach and rocks, seems, at first sight, nothing but a barren and uninteresting waste, merely the natural barrier of the ocean. But to the observant eye these apparently desolate reaches are not only teeming with life; they are also replete with suggestions of the past. They are the pages of a history full of fascination for one who has learned to read it.

In this history even the grains of sand have a part. Though so humble now, they once formed the rocky barriers of the shore. They stood as do the rocks of to-day, defiant and seemingly everlasting, but the fury of the sea, which knows no invincible adversary, has laid them low. Every coast-line shows the destructive effects of the sea, for the bays and coves, the caves at the bases of the cliffs, the buttresses, stocks, needles, and skerries, are the work of the waves. And this work is constantly going on.

Even a blind man could not stand long upon a shingly beach without knowing that the sea was busily at work. Every wave that rolls in from the open ocean hurls the pebbles up the slope of the beach, and then as soon as the wave has broken and the water has dispersed, these pebbles come rattling down with the currents that sweep back to the sea. The clatter of the beach thus tells us plainly that as the stones are being dragged up and down they are constantly knocked against each other; and it is evident that by such rough usage all

1

angular fragments of rock will soon have their corners
rounded off and become rubbed into the form of pebbles. As
these pebbles are rolled to and fro upon the beach they get
worn smaller and smaller, until at length they are reduced to
the state of sand. Although this sand is at first coarse, it
gradually becomes finer and finer as surely as though it were
ground in a mill; and ultimately it is carried out to sea as
fine sediment and laid down upon the ocean floor.[1]

The story of the sands is not only one of the conflict of the sea
and rocks; it is also a story of the winds. It is the winds that
have rescued them from the waves and driven them about, sifting
and assorting them, arranging them in graceful forms, and often
heaping them up into dunes which, until fastened by vegetation,
are themselves ever moved onward by the same force, sometimes
burying fertile lands, trees, and even houses in their march.
The sands, moreover, are in turn themselves destructive agents,
to whose power the many fragments which strew the beach and
dunes bear ample witness. The knotty sticks so commonly seen
on the beach are often the hearts of oak- or cedar-trees from
which the tiny crystals of sand have slowly cut away their less
solid outer growth. Everything, in fact, upon the sands is
" beach-worn," even to the window-glass of life-saving stations,
which is frequently so ground that it loses its transparency in a
single storm.

The beach is also a vast sarcophagus holding myriads of the
dead. " If ghosts be ever laid, here lie ghosts of creatures innumerable, vexing the mind in the attempt to conceive them."
And there are certain sands which may be said to sing their
requiem, the so-called musical sands, like the " Singing Beach "
at Manchester-by-the-Sea, which emit sounds when struck or otherwise disturbed. On some beaches these sounds resemble rumbling,
on others hooting; sometimes they are bell-like and even rhythmical. The cause of this sonorous character is not definitely
known, but it is possibly due to films of compressed gases which
separate each grain as with a cushion, and the breaking of which

[1] Huxley.

causes, in the aggregate, considerable vibrations. Such sands are not uncommon, having been recorded in many places, and they exist probably in many others where they have escaped observation. They may be looked for above the water-line, where the sand is dry and clean.

We have to do, however, in this volume, not with the history of the past, nor with the action of physical forces, but with the life of the present, and to find this, in its abundance, one must go down near the margin of the water, where the sands are wet. There is no solitude here; the place is teeming with living things. As each wave retreats, little bubbles of air are plentiful in its wake. Underneath the sand, where each bubble rose, lives some creature, usually a mollusk, perhaps the razor-shell *Solen ensis*. By the jet of water which spurts out of the sand, the common clam *Mya arenaria* reveals the secret of its abiding-place. A curious groove or furrow here and there leads to a spot where *Polynices heros* has gone below; and the many shells scattered about, pierced with circular holes, tell how *Polynices* and *Nassa* made their breakfast and their dinner. Only the lifting of a shovelful of sand at the water's edge is needed to disclose the populous community of mollusks, worms, and crustaceans living at our feet, just out of sight.

Even the tracks and traces of these little beings are full of information. What may be read in the track of a bird on the sand is thus described by a noted ornithologist:

Here are foot-notes again, this time of real steps from real feet. . . . The imprints are in two parallel lines, an inch or so apart; each impression is two or three inches in advance of the next one behind; none of them are in pairs, but each one of one line is opposite the middle of the interval between two of the other line; they are steps as regular as a man's, only so small. Each mark is fan-shaped; it consists of three little lines less than an inch long, spreading apart at one extremity, joined at the other. At the joined end, and also just in front of it, a flat depression of the sand is barely visible. Now following the track, we see it run straight a yard or

more, then twist into a confused ball, then shoot out straight
again, then stop, with a pair of the footprints opposite each
other, different from the other end of the track, that began
as two or three little indistinct pits or scratches, not forming
perfect impressions of a foot. Where the track twisted there
are several little round holes in the sand. The whole track
commenced and finished upon the open sand. The creature
that made it could not, then, have come out of either the
sand or the water; it must have come down from the air—a
two-legged flying thing, a bird. To determine this, and, next,
what kind of bird it was, every one of the trivial points of the
description just given must be taken into account. It is a
bit of autobiography, the story of an invitation to dine, ac-
ceptance, a repast, an alarm at the table, a hasty retreat. A
bird came on wing, lowering till the tips of its toes just
touched the sand, gliding half on wing, half afoot, until the
impetus of flight was exhausted; then folding its wings, but
not pausing, for already a quick eye spied something inviting;
a hasty pecking and probing to this side and that, where we
found the lines entangled; a short run after more food; then
a suspicious object attracted its attention; it stood stock-still
(just where the marks were in a pair), till, thoroughly
alarmed, it sprang on wing and was off.[1]

Following the key further, he draws more conclusions. The
tracks are not in pairs, so the bird does not belong to the perch-
ers; therefore it must be a wader or a swimmer. There are no
web-marks to indicate the latter; hence it is a three-toed walking or wading bird. It had flat, long, narrow, and pointed wings
because it came gliding swiftly and low, and scraped the sand
before its wings were closed. This is shown by the few scratches
before the prints became perfect. A certain class of birds thus
arrests the impetus of flight. It had a long feeling-bill, as shown
by the little holes in the sands where the marks became entangled; and so on. These combined characteristics belong to one
class of birds and to no other; so he knows as definitely as

[1] Elliott Coues.

though he had seen the bird that a sandpiper alighted here for a brief period, for here is his signature.

It is plain that tracks in the sand mean as much to the naturalist as do tracks in the snow to the hunter, and trails on the land to the Indian who follows his course by signs not seen by an untrained eye.

The tide effaces much that is written by foot and wing, but sometimes such signs are preserved and become veritable "footprints on the sands of time." In the Museum of Natural History in New York is a fossil slab, taken from the Triassic sandstone, showing the footprints of a dinosaurian reptile now extinct, which, in that long ago, walked across a beach—an event unimportant enough in itself, but more marvelous than any tale of imagination when recorded for future ages. From such tracks, together with fragments of skeletons, the dinosaur has been made to live again, and its form and structure have been as clearly defined as those of the little sandpiper of Dr. Coues.

II

COLLECTING

IT has been said that everything on the land has its counterpart in the sea. But all land animals are separate and independent individuals, while many of those of the sea are united into organic associations comprising millions of individuals inseparably connected and many of them interdependent, such as corals, hydroids, etc. These curious communities can be compared only to the vegetation of the land, which many of them resemble in outer form. Other stationary animals, such as oysters and barnacles, which also depend upon floating organisms for their food, have no parallel on the land.

The water is crowded with creatures which prey upon one another, and all are interestingly adapted to their mode of life. Shore species are exceedingly abundant, and the struggle for life is there carried on with unceasing strife. In the endeavor to escape pursuers while they themselves pursue, these animals have various devices of armature and weapons of defense; they have keen vision, rapid motion, and are full of arts and wiles. One of the first resources for safety in this conflict is that of concealment. This is effected not only by actual hiding, but very generally by mimicry in simulating the color of their surroundings, and often by assuming other forms. Thus, for instance, the sea-anemone when expanded looks like a flower and is full of color, but when it contracts becomes so inconspicuous as to be with difficulty distinguished from the rock to which it is attached. Anemones also have stinging threads (nematophores), which they dart out for further defense.

The study of biology has great fascination, and the subject seldom fails to awaken interest as soon as the habit of observation is formed. Jellyfishes, hardly more dense than the water and almost as limpid, swimming about with graceful motion, often illuminating the water at night with their phosphorescence, showing sensitiveness, volition, and order in their lives, cannot fail to excite wonder in even the most careless observer. Not less interesting are the thousands of other animals which crowd the shores, lying just beneath the surface of the sand, filling crevices in the rocks, hiding under every projection, or boldly— perhaps timidly, who shall say?—lying in full view, yet so inconspicuous that they are easily passed by unnoticed.

To find these creatures, to study their habits and organization, to consider the wonderful order of nature, leads through delightful paths into the realms of science. But even without scientific study the simple observation of the curious objects which lie at one's feet as one walks along the beach is a delightful pastime.

The features which separate the classes and the orders of both the plant and the animal life are so distinctive that it requires but very superficial observation to know them. It is easy to discriminate between mollusks, echinoderms, and polyps, and to recognize the relationship between univalves and bivalves, sea-urchins and starfishes, sea-anemones and corals. The equally plain distinctions between the branched, unbranched, tubular, and plate-like green algæ make them as easy to separate.

The pleasure of a walk through field or forest is enhanced by knowing something of the trees and flowers, and in the same way a visit to the sea-shore becomes doubly interesting when one has some knowledge, even though it be a very superficial one, of the organisms which inhabit the shore.

ROCKY SHORES

Rocky shores furnish an abundance and great variety of objects to the collector. The seaweeds here find places of attachment, and the lee and crevices of the rocks afford shelter to many animals which could not live in more open and exposed places. The rock pools harbor species whose habitat is below low-water mark and which could not otherwise bear the alternation of the tides.

The first objects on the rocky beach to attract attention are the barnacles and rockweeds. They are conspicuous in their profusion, the former incrusting the rocks with their white shells, and the latter forming large beds of vegetation; yet both are likely to be passed by with indifference because of their plentifulness. They are, however, not only interesting in themselves, but associated with them are many organisms which are easily overlooked. The littoral zone is so crowded with life that there is a constant struggle for existence,—even for standing-room, it may be said,—and no class of animals has undisputed possession of any place. Therefore the collector should carefully search any object he gathers for other organisms which may be upon it, under it, or even in it, such as parasites, commensals, and the organisms which hide under it or attach themselves to it for support. Let the rockweed (*Fucus*) be carefully examined. Among the things likely to be found attached to its fronds are periwinkles (*Littorina litorea*), which simulate the plant in color, some shells being striped for closer mimicry. Sertularian hydroids also are there, zigzagging over the fronds or forming tufts of delicate horny branches upon them. Small jelly-like masses at the broad divisions of the fronds may be compound ascidians. Calcareous spots here and there may be polyzoans of exquisite form, while spread in incrusting sheets over considerable spaces are other species of *Polyzoa*. Tiny flat shelly spirals are the worm-cases of *Spirorbis*. A pocket-lens is essential to enable one to appreciate the beauty of these minute forms. Under the rockweeds are many kinds of crustaceans; perhaps there will also be patches of the pink urn-like egg-capsules of *Purpura* at the base of the fucus.

Various kinds of seaweed abound in the more sheltered parts of the rocks, and among them will be found amphipods and isopods, many of which are of species different from those of the sandy beaches. Here, too, is the little *Caprella*, imitating the seaweed in form, and swaying its lengthened body, which is attached to the plant only by its hind legs. On the seaweeds, as well as in the tide-pool, may be found beautiful hydroids, and on them the curious little sea-spiders (*Pycnogonidæ*), animals which seem to be all legs.

Mollusks, and other classes as well, differ in different latitudes. On the rocks of the Northern shores *Littorina* and *Purpura* shells are very abundant, the latter in various colors and beautifully striped. Limpets are also plentiful, but are not as conspicuous, since they have flat, disk-shaped shells. When their capture is attempted, they must be taken unawares and pushed quickly aside, else they take such a firm hold of the rock that it is difficult to dislodge them. Near low-water mark under ledges will perhaps be found chitons, which are easily recognized by their oval, jointed shells. On the California coast in like localities will be found the beautiful *Haliotis, Acmæa*, and chitons. Every stone that is lifted will disclose numbers of little amphipods (*Gammarus*), which will scuttle away on their sides to other shelter; worms will suddenly disappear into the mud, and perhaps a crab, here and there, having no alternative, will make a stand and fight for his liberty. Flat against the stone and not easily perceived may be a chiton, a planarian worm, or a nudibranch. And just below the water's edge are sea-urchins and starfishes, which grow in numbers as the eye becomes accustomed to the search.

The rock pools are natural aquaria, more interesting by far than any prepared by man. The possibilities of these little sea-gardens are beyond enumeration. The longer one studies them the more one finds. In them all classes of seaweeds and marine invertebrates may be found and their habits watched. The great beauty of these pools gives them an esthetic charm apart from the scientific interest they excite. Perhaps one may find here a sponge, and removing it to a shallow vessel of sea-water can watch the currents of water it creates. Several sponges of the same species placed in contact will at the end of two days be closely united. If the sponges are of different species they will not coalesce.

In the clefts and crannies of the rocks are various fine seaweeds, often of the red varieties, sea-anemones, hydroids, polyzoans, crustaceans, mollusks, and ascidians. Crabs will be snugly ensconced under projecting surfaces. Most species are more plentiful at the lowest-water mark, and many are found only at this point and below.

On sandy shores the greater part of the inhabitants live under the surface. Many give evidence of their presence by the open mouths of their burrows, and some distinctly point out these places by piles of sand or mud in coils at the opening. Some tubicolous worms have their tubes projecting above the surface. The tubes of *Diopatra* are hung with bits of shells, seaweeds, and other foreign matter. Some mollusks announce themselves by spurting jets of water or sending bubbles of air from the sand. The majority of the underground species, however, give no sign of their presence on the surface, and must be found by digging. Many of them go deep into the sand, and in searching for worms the digger must be quick and expert, or he will lose entirely or cut in two many of the most beautiful ones, which retreat quickly and to the extremity of their holes at the least alarm. One can be a rambler on the sandy beach for a long time without being aware of the many beautiful objects which inhabit the subsurface of the sand. The curious crab *Hippa* will disappear so quickly into the sand that one is hardly sure he has really seen it. The vast number of worms will surprise any one who searches for them by their variety, their beautiful color, and their interesting shapes. Here again a glass is requisite to appreciate the delicacy and beauty of their locomotive organs, their branchiæ, and so on. The most common of the gasteropod mollusks on sandy shores are *Nassa obsoleta*, *Nassa trivittata*, and *Polynices* (*Lunatia*) *heros*. The last are detected by the little mounds of sand which they push before them as they plow their way just below the surface. On more southern beaches, *Fulgur*, *Strombus*, and *Pyrula* are the common varieties. *Olivella*, *Oliva*, and *Donax*, also inhabitants of sandy beaches, will quickly disappear when uncovered by the waves, being rapid burrowers. Most of the many dead shells on the beach will be found to be pierced with a round hole, which is

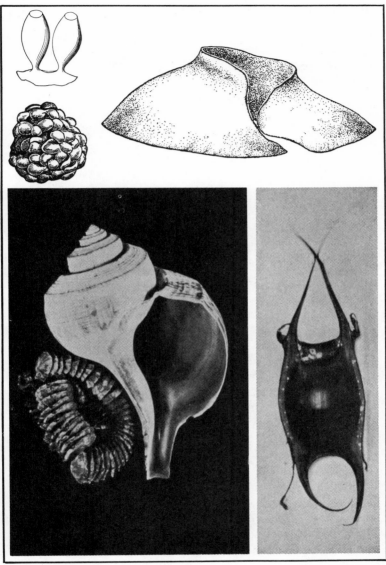

PLATE I.

Egg-capsules of Purpura lapillus.   Egg-case of Polynices heros.
Egg-capsules of Buccinum undatum.   Egg-case of the skate.
Fulgur canaliculata (whelk) and egg-cases.

drilled by the file-like tongue, or lingual ribbon, of *Polynices*, *Urosalpinx*, or *Nassa*, which thus reach the animal within and suck out its substance. Another similar species is *Polynices* (*Neverita*) *duplicata*, which extends to the Gulf of Mexico, while *P. heros* is not commonly found below Hatteras. Crustaceans are abundant on the sandy beach over its whole breadth. Some of the sand-crabs live above tide-mark. Among these is the fleet-footed *Ocypoda*, which is interesting to watch. Often they go in numbers to the water's edge and throw up mounds, behind which they crouch like cats, watching for whatever prey the tide may bring up. When unable to outrun a pursuer they rush into the surf and remain there until the danger is past. The wet sand is often thickly perforated with the burrows of the sand-hoppers (*Orchestia*). These often rise about the feet as do grasshoppers in the fields.

Hippa talpoida is a remarkable crab, somewhat resembling an egg. It is not likely to be seen unless searched for by digging at the water's edge. It burrows so rapidly that one must be quick to catch it after it is exposed by the shovel. In some places the tests of "sand-dollars" are common. The living animal may be found buried just below the surface at extreme low-water mark.

The sea-wrack drifted in lines along the shore will repay careful examination, for here will be found many things belonging to other shores and deep water. It is often alive with sand-hoppers, which hop away while one searches for less common things. Often the most delicate seaweeds, numerous small shells, worms, polyzoans, etc., will be found there.

The surface of the sand-beach is strewn with remains of many species, usually beach-worn, but interesting nevertheless as examples of species one would like to find in better condition, but good specimens of which elude ordinary search or are unobtainable except by dredging.

Egg-cases form another class of objects which are often gathered with no idea of their identity. Of these the most common are the long strings of saucer-like capsules which contain the eggs of the mollusk *Fulgur*, those having square edges being the egg-cases of *F. carica*, and those having sharp edges those of *F. canaliculata*. Collar-like sandy rings contain the eggs of *Polynices* (*Lunatia*), which are cemented together in this shape. The boys of Cape Cod call them "tommy-cod houses." Cylindrical piles of little capsules, sometimes called "ears of corn," hold the eggs of *Chrysodomus*. The irregular masses of small hemispherical capsules are those of the common whelk (*Buccinum*). The so-called "Devil's pocket-books" are the egg-cases of the skate.

MUDDY SHORES

On muddy shores the eel-grass (*Zostera marina*) grows abundantly, giving an appearance of submerged meadows. It is one of the very few flowering plants which live in salt water. In summer its little green blossoms may be seen in grooves on the leaf-like blades. Many animals live on and among eel-grass. Found upon it is the delicate gasteropod mollusk *Lacuna vincta*, and its eggs in little rings; the iridescent *Margarita helicina*, and *Nassa*, with its bright-yellow eggs in small gelatinous masses; also little worms (*Spirorbis*) in tiny flat spiral shells, compound ascidians in jelly-like masses, clusters of shelly or horny polyzoans, isopods, planarian worms, and so on. Scallops (*Pecten*) will be found at the base of the plants, and the common prawns are very numerous, swimming freely about. Mud flats and shores are the homes of many mollusks, especially of *Nassa obsoleta*,—which is the most abundant shell of any considerable size from Cape Cod to the Gulf of Mexico,—and of vast numbers of the tiny *Littorinella minuta*, which serve as food for fishes and aquatic birds. Clams and worms of all varieties are also abundant.

There are many varieties of mud-crabs, of which the most common are the "fiddlers," which honeycomb the banks and the surface of salt-marshes with their burrows. The common edible crab *Callinectes hastatus* is plentiful in bays and estuaries. The sluggish spider-crabs hide beneath the surface of the mud and in decaying weeds and eel-grass. Hermit-crabs are plentiful here as well as elsewhere. *Panopeus* is a sluggish crab found in shallow water and in all sorts of hiding-places along the shore. It may often be found in dead shells, and, in the South, in holes in the banks. This genus is represented by a number of species, some of which are quite pretty.

On the piles of wharves and bridges may often be found beautiful tubularian hydroids in large tufts just below low-water mark, branched hydroids looking like little shrubs, polyzoans, sea-anemones, mollusks, and ascidians. The species peculiar to these localities are the boring mollusk *Teredo navalis*, or shipworm, the boring isopod *Limnoria lignorum*, and the boring amphipod *Chelura terebrans*, all of which penetrate the wood and are most destructive.

The animals and plants of tropical beaches and coral reefs are so various and abundant, so curious and beautiful, as to make a description or even an enumeration of them in a brief space difficult. The collector is bewildered and excited when he first views the profusion of the wonderful forms there found.

It is not generally known that a fine species of "stony coral" is common from Cape Cod southward, growing in clear water as an incrustation on rocks, and developing little spires as it advances in age. This species, the *Astrangia danaë*, is especially interesting, since it will live in a dish of clear sea-water, and the polyps will expand, showing a very close relationship to the sea-anemone. With care in changing the water this coral will live for days, and may be examined in its expanded condition with a lens of moderate power.

The most favorable time for collecting on any beach is at the lowest tide, many objects being then uncovered which do not appear higher up on the beach. At the spring-tides, which occur twice a month, at the period of the new and that of the full moon, the ebb is especially low, and affords an opportunity to search for forms whose habitat is below ordinary low-water mark. During storms deep-water forms are often torn from their beds and cast upon the beach. Shore-collecting at these times is often very interesting.

EQUIPMENT FOR COLLECTING INVERTEBRATES

The equipment for collecting upon sandy beaches is a shovel, a sieve, and a net. Numerous trials should be made with the shovel from about half-tide mark to as deep as one cares to wade, and the sand raised should be carefully searched for shells, crustaceans, and worms. By washing out the sand in the sieve the smallest specimens, which might otherwise escape notice, may be secured. On a rocky beach a strong knife and a net are sufficient. It is well to have a number of homeopathic vials for small specimens, which will be injured by contact with larger forms, and jars for holding the general collection.

PRESERVING INVERTEBRATES

To preserve specimens, they should first be placed in a weak solution of alcohol, the strength of which should be increased gradually until the animal is entirely free from water and is hardened throughout. If the alcohol becomes colored and sediment falls to the bottom of the jar, the animal is degenerating, and the alcohol should be changed. Specimens for transportation can be packed by wrapping each one in a bit of cheese-cloth and then placing them together in a large receptacle. Care should be taken to keep the fragile specimens separate. Sand-dollars possess a pigment which discolors and soon vitiates alcohol, and consequently these should be separated from the other forms and placed where the alcohol may be changed from time to time as appears necessary. The homeopathic vials containing small specimens may be put into the can without injury to the other specimens. Special cans of various sizes, with handles and screw covers, are made for naturalists. One of these cans is a convenient receptacle for carrying the alcohol to the station and for receiving the collection for transportation. Careful notes should be made on the spot of the conditions under which the species are found. One is likely to forget details if this is delayed until one reaches home. Labels should be used, giving name when known, or a number when the name is not known, corresponding with the note-book. Names written with lead-pencil on a slip of paper will not be defaced by or injure the alcohol. Collections when arranged permanently should be placed in glass jars, the species being kept separate.

COLLECTING AND PRESERVING SEAWEEDS

To collect seaweeds one must search for them on rocks, in tide-pools, in the sea-wrack upon the beach, on piles of wharves, on eel-grass, and on the surface of incoming waves. It is well to follow the receding tide and take advantage of its lowest ebb (especially of that of the spring-tides, as mentioned above) to search the extreme limit of the beach in the short time it is exposed. Many of the red seaweeds are found there.

The equipment for collecting consists of a basket, two small tin pails, one small enough to be carried within the other, a staff with an iron edge at one end and a small net at the other, and a pocket-lens. Rockweeds (*Fucus*) or other coarse gelatinous sea-weeds should be put into the basket. The pails, half filled with sea-water, will receive the other specimens, fine and delicate algæ being put into the smaller pail. It is well to have a second small receptacle for *Callithamnion* and *Griffithsia*, if one can be further burdened. *Desmarestia* should be kept apart, if possible, since it discolors and decomposes other algæ; it should also have the earliest attention when the time comes for mounting, and salt water should be used for floating it upon the mount, otherwise the beauty of the specimen will be impaired.

Besides its use as a support, the staff is needed to dislodge specimens from the rocks, and the net to secure those that are floating just out of reach. When possible, it is desirable to secure the whole plant, including the holdfast, and to gather several plants of the same species, since they vary with age and other conditions, and it is also well to have duplicates for exchange. It is particularly desirable to obtain plants which are in fruit. Each specimen as it is taken should be rinsed in the sea-water to free it from sand.

Collections should be mounted as soon as convenient, and

especial care in this respect should be taken with red algæ, as they decompose quickly. The requisites for mounting are blotters, pieces of muslin, two or more smooth boards, weights, a basin, and several shallow dishes containing water. Fresh water has a strong action on the color and substance of seaweeds, and specimens should not be left in it for any length of time.

Lift a specimen from the general collection, and in a basin of deep water carefully wash off all superfluous matter; then place it in shallow water and spread it out, trimming it judiciously, so that when mounted it will not be too thick and the characteristics be hidden. Specimens are more interesting and their species more easily determined when laid out rather thin, showing their branching and fruit. After the specimen is thus prepared, place it in a second shallow dish of water. It should now be perfectly clean. Float it out into the desired position, spreading it well, letting some parts show the details of the branching, and other parts the general natural effect of the mass. Run under it a rather heavy sheet of white paper, and lift it carefully from the water. If raised from the center, it is easier to let the water subside evenly and gradually without disarranging the parts. Some collectors find it better to float the specimen in water deep enough to allow the left hand to be placed under the sheet to raise it. Lay the sheet on a plate, and with a needle or forceps rearrange any of the delicate parts which have fallen together. A few drops of water placed on any portion will usually be sufficient to enable one to separate the branchlets or ultimate ramifications. A magnifying-glass will be useful in this work.

Cover a blotter with mounted specimens, spread over them a piece of cotton cloth, and on this place another blotter, upon which lay more mounted specimens and a cloth. Proceed in this way until all the specimens are used. Lay the pile of blotters between boards, and on them place the weights. The weights should not be very heavy. Judgment must be used in assorting the specimens, those that are fine being placed together. Those that are coarse and likely to indent the blotters should be placed between separate boards. In this way a flat surface and an even pressure will be obtained. The blotters and cloths should be changed twice each of the first two days, then the cloths should be removed and the specimens left in press for a week, the blotters being changed daily. Be sure that the specimens are perfectly dry before placing them in the herbarium. Label each specimen with the name and the date and place of collection.

There are some seaweeds which cannot be treated in the above manner. *Fucus* if placed in fresh water soon becomes slimy. It is so full of gelatine that it soon destroys blotters; therefore it is well to hang it up for several hours and then place it between newspapers, which should be frequently changed, and as the plant becomes pliable it should be arranged in proper position.

Those specimens which do not adhere to paper in drying should be secured with gum. When it is impossible to mount specimens at the time they are collected, they can be preserved by drying; afterward they can be soaked and mounted in the usual manner. To dry the plants, lay them separately upon boards without pressing out the sea-water, and leave them in an airy, shaded place until thoroughly dry; then pack them loosely into boxes and label, giving date and locality. Blotters or driers can be obtained at botanical-supply stores at thirty-five cents per quire.

HOW TO ARRANGE A HERBARIUM

The standard herbarium-paper is sixteen by eleven and a half inches. The sheets are single, white, smooth, and quite heavy. These, together with folded sheets of yellow manila paper, called genus-covers, are the only requisites. It is desirable to have also a case of shelves protected by glass doors. The shelves should be twelve by eighteen inches, and four to six inches apart. They are more convenient when made to slide like drawers.

The different species of one genus are gummed on one or more of the white sheets and placed within the folded manila paper, which serves as a cover. Each specimen should be signed with its name, place, and date of collection, thus:

C. rubrum. Bar Harbor. Aug. 12, 1899,

the generic name being indicated by its initial capital letter and the specific name written in full. To this are often added the

name of the collector and some interesting comment. On the
lower left-hand corner of the genus-cover is written the generic
name in full and the species of that genus which the cover contains, thus:

$$Ceramium \begin{cases} C.\ rubrum \\ C.\ strictum \\ C.\ diaphanum \end{cases}$$

The genera of an order are then placed within a cover and labeled
in the same way, the legend then having the name of the order
on the left and the genera on the right of the bracket, thus:

$$\begin{matrix} Rhodymeniaceæ, \\ \text{suborder} \\ Ceramieæ \end{matrix} \begin{cases} Callithamnion \\ Griffithsia \\ Ceramium \end{cases}$$

When the order is a large one the genera are distributed through
as many covers as may be necessary. The covers are then
arranged on shelves in the regular order of their classification,
and each shelf is labeled with the order it contains. Herbarium-
sheets cost at retail one dollar per hundred. Genus-covers cost
at retail one dollar and eighty cents per hundred.

III

CLASSIFICATION

THE first great biological division is into kingdoms, namely, the animal kingdom and the vegetable kingdom. Then by classification the vast number of existing animals and plants are grouped so as to give each individual a definite place. By this system a beautiful order is established, which enables the student to find any particular animal or plant he may wish to study, and also to know its general characteristics from the name of the group to which it belongs.

In broad generalization, objects of wide dissimilarity are recognized as belonging to the same kingdom, as do trees and grasses, or as do birds and fishes. Certain trees or grasses and certain birds or fishes have such points of resemblance that they plainly show that they belong to subdivisions. The most untutored people recognize these distinctions, but the naturalist goes further and finds points of distinction which the casual observer overlooks.

The animal kingdom has a varying number of divisions, called *branches, subkingdoms,* or *phyla.* Some late authors have admitted twelve divisions, and have given them the name *phyla.* Each phylum is composed of a group of animals with a plan of structure which is common to themselves, but differs from that of the animals of all other phyla.

The higher animals begin with the twelfth phylum, namely, the *Chordata,* or vertebrates. These animals have a spinal column, or series of vertebræ, while the lower animals, or invertebrates are without a spinal column, and depend for stability

upon muscles or coriaceous or calcareous coverings. The vertebrates are first represented in the fish-like forms. Bilateral symmetry, however, or the uniform arrangement of parts on each
side of a central axis, exists in several groups which are below
the vertebrates, the first pronounced example being found in
worms. Groups lower than worms have their organs arranged
around a central axis or radiating from it, and were once all
classed as *radiates*.

An animal is classified in accordance with its morphology,
anatomy, histology, and embryology. Morphology determines
its general shape, the position of its limbs, eyes, and mouth, and
the covering of its body; anatomy, the arrangement of its internal
organs, such as the position of its heart, lungs, stomach, etc.;
histology, the character of the tissues of the body; and embryology, the method of the development of the animal from the
embryo to maturity. It is only after these exact discriminations
have been made that the groups are arranged. Owing to the
greater accuracy resulting from histology and embryology
(methods which have been employed only in later years), many
changes in classification have been made, and as science advances
will continue to be made.

The primary groups are based on broad general characteristics,
but their divisions and subdivisions are determined by closer
distinctions. Animals having shells differ from those having a
cartilaginous or those having a crustaceous covering, and are
placed in different groups. Yet mollusks having a single or a
double shell, having spiral or flat forms, living on land, in fresh
water, or in the sea, while differing from one another, are all of
one group. Lobsters and crabs, although both have crustaceous
coverings, are very unlike; and again, there are many species of
both lobsters and crabs.

To group individuals, noting resemblances as well as differences, a system of classification has been arranged with the following divisions:

Kingdom, Phylum, Class, Order, Family (or Suborder), Genus,
Species.

ANIMAL LIFE IN ITS LOWEST FORMS

THE biological division, or discrimination, between animal and vegetable life, is based on the manner of assimilating food. Plants feed upon mineral substances, or, in other words, assimilate inorganic matter, while animal life requires for its support vegetable or some other organic matter. Animal as well as vegetable life in its lowest forms begins with one-celled organisms, which are called respectively *Protozoa* (first animals) and *Protophyta* (first plants). Both of these divisions are composed mostly of microscopic objects, and, together with other minute forms of life of the marine species, constitute a great part of the *plankton*, or free-floating organisms of the sea. These minute organisms seem like connecting-links between the two kingdoms. They were claimed by both botanists and zoölogists until the use of the microscope made close observation of minute structure possible.

Among the small animalcules of the phylum *Protozoa* are some which are familiar to all by name, such as the *Infusoria*, which are most interesting creatures to examine in a drop of water under the microscope. A more tangible example of the *Protozoa* are the *Foraminifera*. *Foraminifera*, like diatoms, have a shell-like covering, and these shells, among the most plentiful of which are those of the genus *Globigerina*, fall, as do those of diatoms, in immense numbers to the bottom of the ocean, and form respectively what are known as *Globigerina* and diatomaceous ooze. In course of time the sedimentary strata become fossilized; thus, the stone of which the city of Paris is built consists of fossilized foraminifers, and the pyramids of Egypt are built of nummulites, another genus of *Foraminifera*. It is estimated that an ounce of this deposit contains four millions of these protozoans, so it is impossible to conceive the numbers of once living animals represented in the tombs of the Pharaohs. Telegraph-cables raised from the depth of two miles bring the message to naturalists that the bottom of the ocean at that depth is composed of little else than the calcareous shells of *Foraminifera*.

Many of the lower animals resemble plants in form. Hydroids and polyzoans are often gathered and preserved as seaweeds. Corals, sea-anemones, and holothurians are curiously like plants. For a time the confusion about the division of animals and plants was partly owing to this resemblance of forms, and the theory of the animal nature of corals was for a long time considered to be refuted by the testimony of a naturalist who declared that he had seen them in bloom. Later this class of animals was believed to occupy an intermediate sphere and partake of the characteristics of both kingdoms. The name zoöphyte, meaning "animal-plant" or "mingled life," was adopted because of these resemblances and was formerly applied to these forms only. To-day it has a broader application. There is still a neutral class, called *Protista*, comprising organisms which have not yet been classified as plants or animals.

V

DISTRIBUTION OF ANIMAL LIFE IN THE SEA

ALL living things which inhabit the sea have their appointed boundaries, and the localization of marine life is as distinct as is that of terrestrial life. Each kind of beach has forms of life peculiar to itself. Those animals which inhabit rocky shores or stony beaches or sand or mud may be looked for anywhere under similar physical surroundings. They are, however, modified by climatic conditions, and in wide ranges differ in genera and species. The rocky coast of Maine has a class of sea-urchins and starfishes which are different from those which live on the rocky shores of the northern Pacific coast, yet they are all easily recognized as belonging to the same family, and a description of typical forms is a sufficient guide to the recognition of their relationships.

A bathymetrical division defines the classes of animals according to the depth of water in which they live. Those which live near the shore are *littoral* species, those of the broad sea are *pelagic*, while those living at great depths are *abyssal*.

Their modes of life are distinguished by other terms. Those which float at or near the surface and are carried about by the currents, like the jellyfishes and the minute organisms mentioned elsewhere, are *plankton*. Strong swimming animals which move about at will are *nekton*. Those which are fixed, like oysters, sponges, etc., and those which crawl on the bottom, like crabs, echinoderms, etc., are *benthos*.

Again, geographical divisions are named, in recognition of climatic influences. The *boreal* fauna and flora on the Atlantic coast extend from Cape Cod northward; the *American*, from Cape Cod to Cape Hatteras; the *West Indian*, from Cape Hatteras southward. On the Pacific coast the divisions, without definite names, are from the Isthmus to Acapulco, Acapulco to the Gulf of California, Cape Lucas to the Strait of Fuca. These divisions merge at indefinite lines, but the above limits are generally accepted as the points of broad division.

The shore or littoral fauna is especially abundant and comprises more species that are curious in form and beautiful in color than the others. The invertebrates of the deep sea are mostly transparent and of a blue or violet tint, while the fishes are gray or bluish above and white beneath, which renders them inconspicuous to their enemies.

VI

SOME BOTANICAL FACTS ABOUT ALGÆ

THE vegetable world is separated into two great divisions: *thallophytes*, or plants having no distinction of leaf or stem, and *cormophytes*, or plants which have leaves and stems. All thallophytes that live in the water and are nourished wholly by water are called *algæ*.

A second great division of plants is into *cryptogams*, or those that have no flowers, and *phanerogams*, or those that have flowers, by means of which seeds are produced and successive generations of plant life continued.

Thallophytes and *cryptogams* comprise the lowest and simplest vegetable organisms. Algæ belong to both these divisions; to the first because they have neither stems nor leaves, and to the second because they have no flowers.

The lowest forms of algæ are microscopic in size, each individual being a single cell; but in the ascending scale they attain curious and beautiful shapes, some growing to a gigantic size and in forms that resemble shrubs and trees. The green surface commonly seen on the shady side of trees, on stone steps, and in other damp places is one of the species of algæ which consist of a single cell. This plant or cell divides, and the separate divisions divide and subdivide again and again, and in time the aggregate number is great enough to spread over a comparatively large surface, and thus become visible to the naked eye. This plant, the *Pleurococcus vulgaris*, is a fresh-water alga. The *Protococcus nivalis*, or red snow, described on page 33, is a closely allied species. The green and blue-green scums and slimes on brackish ditches and on the stones and woodwork of wharves are also species of the lowest orders of algæ and increase by cell-division. Many of them are in colonies incased in gelatinous matter. These, together with plants of a little higher order, though still of low organization, the *Confervaceæ*, form a large part of the green vegetation between tide-marks.

The vegetative body of a thallophyte is a *thallus*, and corresponds to stem and leaf. It is also called a *frond*. What corresponds to the root of flowering plants is in algæ a disk or conical expansion of the base of the plant. It is simply a hold-fast by which the frond attaches itself to any submerged material. The algæ which grow on sandy shores and on corals have hold-fasts which branch like fibrous roots and penetrate porous substances in all directions; but this is only for greater stability, and is an adaptation to the habitat. Holdfasts do nothing for algæ other than the name implies, whereas real roots absorb the nourishment upon which plants live. Algæ are nourished by the substances held in solution by the water which surrounds them.

Algæ are the lowest and simplest in organization of all plants, because they are composed of but one class of cells, such as in flowering plants are called the *parenchyma*, or soft cells, these being the ones which compose the pulp of the leaf. In the lowest orders of algæ single cells constitute individual plants, as in *Pleurococcus;* but in the higher forms, such as *Sargassum*, they arrange themselves in such a variety of combinations as to resemble plants which have leaf and stem. The botanical distinction is that in leaf and stem there would exist the woody and the vascular cells as well as the parenchyma cells.

Beginning with plants composed of a single cell, the next development is into filamentous plants, which are single thread-like rows of cells, as in *Cladophora*. In *Ulva* is seen the earliest type of an expanded leaf. The cells are here arranged in a horizontal surface of plate-like or ribbon-like shape.

In *Ulva* there is a double layer of cells. The layers separate in *Enteromorpha*, giving a hollow or tubular form. In *Monostroma* a double layer is opened or torn apart, giving a frond with a single layer of cells.

The stem-like forms of certain algæ are composed of cylindrical cells which combine or grow in a longitudinal direction chiefly. Sometimes the cells are arranged evenly, in which case the stem seems articulated, as in some species of *Ceramium*. Again, they are irregularly placed, so that the stem appears solid.

The highest types of algæ in the differentiation of parts, or vegetative forms, are to be found in the *Fucaceæ*, of the brown seaweeds; the highest in the reproductive development, in the red class.

Reproduction by cell-division, in which the organism itself breaks up into two or more individuals, is called *vegetative reproduction*. Higher forms reproduce by spores, or germ-cells, which give rise to new individuals on germination.

The substance of an alga is more or less firm, according as the vegetable mucus or gelatinous matter it contains has more or less consistency; it is *membranaceous* when the gelatine is scant and glossy, *gelatinous* when it is abundant and fluid, and *cartilaginous* when it is hard.

Some algæ are annuals; a few are perennials, and cast off and renew their laminæ every season. Many plants present quite a different appearance at different seasons of the year, and so are often difficult to identify. Those which form spores throw off these isolated cells, which sink or are washed to positions where they germinate and begin their cycle of life. Many of the spores begin their growth at once, without regard to season, so the species is ever present.

NAMING OF PLANTS

THE real or technical names of plants, which at first appear long and unpronounceable, are in reality simple when the system of naming is understood. Every plant has a *generic* and a *specific* name. The generic name is analogous to the surname of a person, such as *Smith* or *Jones*. The specific name is analogous to the Christian name of a person, such as *John* or *James*. The specific name never stands alone, and would have as little designating character as John —— or James ——.

This is called the *binomial* (two-name) *nomenclature*. It was introduced by Linnæus, and greatly simplified the system of naming. The rule in scientific nomenclature is that all names must be Latin or Latinized. This gives a universal language by which scientists of all countries understand one another.

The names of classes (the highest groups) and subclasses are adjectives or adjective nouns, expressing the most prominent characteristic of the class or subclass. Thus the four subclasses of the class *Algæ* are:

Cyanophyceæ (subclass of blue-green algæ).

Chlorophyceæ (subclass of grass-green algæ).

Phæophyceæ (subclass of dusky-brown or olive-green algæ).

Rhodophyceæ or *Florideæ* (subclass of red algæ).

Orders are, with few exceptions, the names of genera with the termination *-aceæ*, as:

Ulvaceæ, from the genus *Ulva*.

Ectocarpaceæ, from the genus *Ectocarpus*.

Gigartinaceæ, from the genus *Gigartina*.

Suborders, or groups between orders and genera, terminate in
-*eœ*. Names of genera are nouns or words taken as nouns. They
are derived from any source,—from prominent or peculiar characteristics, from localities, or from names of botanists,—or they
may be wholly arbitrary. Personal generic names are divested
of titles and take a final *a*, or, in many cases, for euphony, *ia*.
Thus, *Ulva* is the Latin for "sedge"; *Ectocarpus* is from two
Greek words meaning "fruit outside"; *Corallina* means "coral-
like"; *Grinnellia* is named for Mr. Henry Grinnell.

The specific names are commonly adjectives, but sometimes
they are nouns, and occasionally are the names of the botanists
who first described the plants, in which case the name terminates
in -*i* or -*ii*. The specific name always follows the generic name,
thus:

Ectocarpus Hooperi, a species of *Ectocarpus*, first described by
Mr. Hooper.

Grinnellia Americana, a species, peculiar to America, of a genus
named for Mr. Grinnell.

Griffithsia corallina, a species resembling coral, and belonging
to a genus named for Mrs. Griffiths.

With regard to the four subclasses mentioned above, it should
be said that algæ are strictly classified in accordance with their
methods of reproduction; but since allied species have, with few
exceptions, the same color, the classification by colors is generally
adopted as convenient and sufficiently precise.

Familiar, or, in technical language, "vulgar," names are very
generally given to land plants, and especially to flowers; but seaweeds are less in sight than flowers are, and so, save in a few
instances, have not been named except by the man of science.
To remember the scientific names will not be found difficult, for
without effort or special pains to acquire the new vocabulary,
the names, like those of new personal friends, will insensibly
become fixed in the memory.

In the body of this work each of the groups (class, subclass,
order, etc.), in the classification of both animals and plants, is
indicated by a special kind of type.

VIII

DISTRIBUTION OF ALGÆ

THE eastern coast of North America has been divided into four sections, which correspond to the distribution of the algæ which are characteristic of each section. The boundary-lines are not precise, since some species of each section extend beyond the defined limits; but arctic forms are not generally found south of Cape Cod, nor can tropical varieties be expected north of Cape Hatteras. On the intervening coast, however, there are some species common to both sections. The divisions are: (1) Greenland to Cape Cod; (2) Cape Cod to Cape Hatteras; (3) Cape Hatteras to Cape Florida; (4) the Florida Keys and the shores of the Gulf of Mexico.

On the Pacific coast such distinct lines of demarcation do not exist, there being no such natural barriers as are formed on the eastern coast, first by Cape Cod, and, second, by the stretch of sand-beach which extends from New York to Charleston, and which divides sharply the climatic varieties.

The whole shore is again divided laterally into three distinct belts, called the *littoral*, the *laminarian*, and the *coralline* zones. The first or littoral zone covers the space between tide-marks. Vegetable life in this zone is subjected first to exposure to the sun and air, and even to desiccation, and then to entire submergence at constantly recurring periods. The rockweeds (*Fucus*), which are so plentiful in this zone, are very gelatinous, nature having apparently provided the gelatine to protect the cells of the plant from the effects of the alternating extreme conditions. *Fucus* and *Enteromorpha* predominate in this zone.

30

The laminarian zone extends from low-water mark to the depth of fifteen fathoms. The *Laminariaceæ* and the beautiful red algæ (*Florideæ*) grow here.

The third or coralline zone extends to the depth of about fifty fathoms. The algæ of this zone, the nullipores, are incrusted with a deposit of lime which gives them the appearance of corals; and, singularly enough, the corals, which are animal forms, simulate plant life.

Again, algæ have special habits and demand certain climates and seasons for their growth. Algologists register the place where a specimen is found, and in this way localities have been pretty well determined. However, great exactness has not been reached, and the collector is ever watchful to find an alga in some undiscovered home within the given range. Although algæ grow from extreme high-water mark to the depth of fifty fathoms, almost every variety may be found on the beach, those growing in deep water being frequently torn off and washed ashore by the waves. The heaps of sea-wrack will often reward one who examines them carefully for deep-water species. Sea-weeds are most abundant on rocky shores, particularly where there are stratified rocks with crevices, which afford shelter from the waves. Rock pools often contain beautiful varieties of the more delicate species. Red algæ will sometimes be found on the shady side of these pools. Sand-beaches are unfavorable to the growth of seaweeds, but fronds which have been carried long distances by the currents will frequently be found on such shores.

IX

SOME PECULIAR AND INTERESTING VARIETIES OF ALGÆ

THE species of seaweeds that are known and classified are said to number several thousands. These plants, which have neither vessels for the conduction of fluids, nor fibers, consisting simply of the first vegetable element, the cell, have, notwithstanding this limitation, assumed a great variety of forms. In size they vary from one one-thousandth of an inch in diameter, the smallest green plants known, to those which exceed in length the height of the tallest trees and form dense submarine forests, which in places make comparatively deep water impassable for boats. In texture they vary from a jelly- to a paper- and a leather-like consistency. In color they have all the shades of green, brown, and red.

DIATOMS AND OTHER MINUTE ALGÆ

Among the smallest algæ are diatoms. They are microscopic in size, but exist everywhere in both salt and fresh water, and are infinite in variety as well as in numbers. They have a silicious, shell-like covering, which divides and subdivides in their reproductive growth, forming varied shapes which are exceedingly beautiful and interesting to examine under the microscope. In vast numbers they float on the surface of the sea, and, together with other minute free-floating organisms, form the basis of food-supply for fishes. Their indestructible shells fall to the bottom of the sea, forming large deposits, which in time become fossilized. The city of Richmond, Virginia, is built upon a fossiliferous bed of diatoms, which measures twenty to eighty feet in depth and several miles in length.

Associated with diatoms, in fresh water, are desmids, which are green in color and resemble the diatoms except in having a cartilaginous instead of a silicious covering. Another minute organism, *Pyrocystis noctiluca*, is luminous and is said to produce the beautiful phosphorescent effects seen in tropical seas. *Trichodesmium* is a little alga which periodically occurs in great numbers, giving the water a red appearance, as in the Red Sea, which is said to derive its name from this circumstance.

RED SNOW

In the high latitudes of the arctic regions, also on snowy mountains at altitudes where all vegetable life is supposed to be extinguished, there sometimes appears a redness on the surface of the snow, which in some cases extends for many miles. At a certain place in Greenland the color was so vivid that an arctic voyager named the locality the Crimson Bluffs.

The strangeness and almost sudden appearance of this color in the snow have been so unaccountable to uninformed observers that it has been ascribed by them to the falling of bloody snow and has been regarded with superstition. The redness is caused by the growth of one of the smallest of plants, the *Protococcus nivalis*. It is a simple one-celled alga containing protoplasm and endochrome (red coloring-matter). It grows by cell-division, the cell dividing into four, eight, or sixteen parts on a quaternary scale. Each part acquires a new covering while within the mother cell, and when it emerges it is a complete individual and ready to repeat the process. Only a few hours are required for its growth and development; hence its increase is rapid, and it requires but a little time to make itself manifest in those places where the conditions are favorable to its existence.

THE SARGASSO SEA

When the voyager reaches a certain region of the North Atlantic, called the Sargasso Sea, he sails into a vast undulating marine prairie. Farther than the eye can reach is spread a yellowish-brown vegetation which covers the water as grass covers the plain. Sometimes these weeds are so thick as to impede navigation, and, seen from a little distance, seem substantial enough to walk upon. At other times, according to seasons and conditions of storm and wind, they are divided into strips or into island-like masses, with spaces of clear water between. If the sailor did not know the special conditions existing here he might suppose he had come upon dangerous shallows; or were the waters less turbulent he might dream that he was floating among the water-weeds of an inland lake.

This vast acreage of vegetation, as large as the continent of Europe, lying southwest of the Azores and extending between the Canary and the Cape Verde Islands, was first reported by Columbus, and takes its name from the floating plant of which it is composed, the *Sargassum bacciferum*, a species of the order *Fucaceæ*, commonly known as gulfweed. Columbus's sailors took fright at the marvelous appearance and wished to turn back, thinking they had reached the end of the navigable ocean. They thought, if land were beyond, it was guarded by shoals, and that the weeds concealed dangerous rocks. Columbus threw out two hundred fathoms of line, but did not reach bottom, and continued on his course for fifteen days before emerging into clear water. From that day to this the Sargasso Sea has attracted the attention of all navigators. It is especially interesting to scientists. The physicist finds there the phenomenon of the ocean currents holding in a vortex this immense mass of seaweed, the zoölogist finds a great pasture in whose protecting shelter are living and breeding countless numbers of marine animals, and the botanist is puzzled because the source of this species of plant is clouded with doubt.

According to one theory, the plants are dislodged by the tempests from terrestrial beds and carried by the Gulf Stream into the huge eddy; but since there does not exist enough of the attached plants of this species to supply the vast accumulation, another and more generally accepted theory is that the gulfweed lives also a pelagic life and adapts itself to the conditions of the

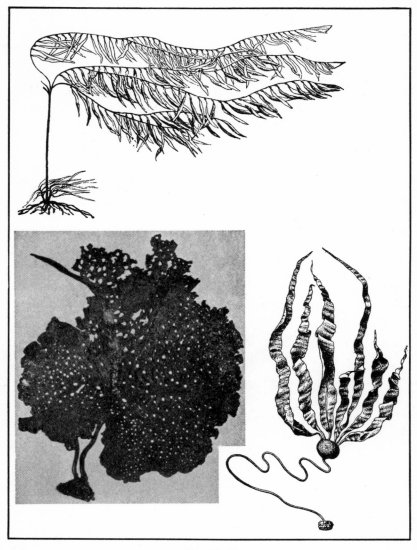

PLATE II.

Macrocystis pyrifera.

Agarum Turneri.   Nereocystis Lütkeana.

floating state, thus dispensing with the disk-like root, as it needs no holdfasts, and propagating solely by lateral and axillary ramification.

There are said to be one hundred and fifty species of *Sargassum*, but *S. bacciferum* alone constitutes the beds of the Sargasso Sea. The plant is the most highly differentiated of any seaweed, in that it more nearly approaches the true leaf and stem, and is described botanically as follows: Frond furnished with distinct, stalked, nerveless leaves and simple, axillary, stalked air-vessels. The integument is leathery, and the color brown of varying shades. The most striking peculiarity is the abundance of globular cells. These berry-like air-bladders give the plant buoyancy enough to support the weight of its innumerable guests. (Plate XVI.)

THE LAMINARIACEÆ

In the laminarian zone, described above, grow the *Laminariaceæ*, an order of brown seaweeds, some of whose genera grow to enormous size, and in some places form dense submarine forests. Darwin speaks of the good service rendered by these plants to vessels navigating stormy coasts, where often they act as natural breakwaters, and again as buoys designating dangerous rocks near the shore on which they grow. The seaweeds belonging to this order, commonly known as oarweeds, tangle, devil's-apron, and sea-colander, are frequently seen twelve to twenty feet in length, and others are measured by fathoms. One of the giant plants is *Nereocystis Lütkeana*, which occurs on the northwest coast. It has a stalk, sometimes three hundred feet in length, which bears on its extremity a barrel- or cask-shaped air-vessel, six or seven feet long, from the surface of which a tuft of fifty or more forked laminæ grows to a length of thirty or forty feet. The stem which anchors this immense frond is so small that the Aleutian Indians use it for fishing-lines. The sea-otter makes his home on its huge air-vessel, and the plant is called by the Russians the "sea-otters' cabbage."

But the longest of all known plants is the alga *Macrocystis*. Its thin naked stem, the diameter of which seldom exceeds one quarter of an inch, is reported by one author to be seven hundred feet in length, by another fifteen hundre feet. It is terminated by a lamina fifty feet long, resembling a pinnatifid leaf, each leaflet of which, at its point of division on the stem, expands into an air-vessel as large as an egg. These air-vessels sustain the immense frond which floats on the surface of the water, its leaflets depending in a vertical position from the stem. *M. pyrifera*, the only species, is found in the Southern oceans and on the Pacific coast of North America.

Lessonia, another genus, resembles a palm-tree. It grows erect to a great height and has a stem like the bole of a tree. It branches in a forking manner and has depending from its branches laminæ two or three feet long. The large stems from which the laminæ have been torn by the storms, and which have been cast ashore on the Falkland Islands, as described by Sir Joseph Hooker, resemble driftwood, as they lie in piles three or four feet high and extending for many miles.

Agarum and *Thalassiophyllum* are arctic genera, but they are found within our limits, the former in the North Atlantic. It has a simple but enormous leaf-like frond. The latter, which is found on the North Pacific coast, has a compound frond. Both are characterized by their fronds being perforated throughout with holes, giving them the name of sea-colander.

X

USES OF ALGÆ

WATER covers two thirds of the surface of the earth, and algæ, with a very few exceptions, constitute the whole vegetation which exists in that enormous area. They have, therefore, an important part to perform in the economy of nature. Algæ do not, like land plants, derive their nourishment from the soil to which they are attached, but from substances held in solution by water. In their growth they effect changes in the water analogous to those effected by land plants in the air; that is, they change so-called impurities in the water into materials essential to animal life. The function of plants is that of transforming or manufacturing inorganic matter, which they assimilate, into organic matter (such as starch, albumen, sugar), which forms their own structure and which is the food essential to animals. In this process, plants inhale carbonic acid gas which animals breathe out, and exhale oxygen which animals breathe in. Plants feed on mineral substances and furnish vegetable food, thus keeping up the balance of life.

Fresh-water algæ have a like economic value. The green surface on stagnant pools is a vegetable growth whose function is to assimilate the matter which makes the pool offensive. A submerged district soon becomes covered with scum, or minute plants (*Sphæoplea annulina*), which grow with great rapidity, using up the materials of the decaying vegetation, and in great measure counteracting the ill effects, in the atmosphere, of such decay. When the waters subside, the plants shrivel up and appear like thin paper covering the ground. This ephemeral substance soon disappears, without giving evidence of its nature in dust or gases, its body seeming to be a machine which transmutes, but does not hold, the substances on which it grows.

Algæ, as has been said above, grow in definite zones, and each zone has also a definite animal life which finds there its food. Darwin says: "In all parts of the world a rocky and partially protected shore perhaps supports in a given space a greater number of individual animals than any other station." And speaking of the *Laminariaceæ*, he adds: "I can only compare these great aquatic forests of the southern hemisphere with the terrestrial ones in the intertropical regions. Yet if in any country a forest was destroyed I do not believe nearly so many species of animals would perish as would here from the destruction of the kelp." The same may be said of the Sargasso Sea, where millions of living creatures make their home. In every kind of marine fauna there are species which derive, if not the whole, at least a part of their nourishment from the seaweeds.

The vegetation in the narrow boundary of the three zones is palpably inadequate to supply the needs of the animal life which exists in deeper waters. But over the broad area of the ocean there exists a vast number of pelagic, free-floating algæ, which, although microscopical in size, are almost infinite in numbers. In illustration of this it has been estimated that, although they are not especially numerous in the Sargasso Sea, yet if all the seaweed there were gathered into one mass and the free-floating algæ into another, the bulk of the latter would exceed that of the former. The pelagic flora consists of *Diatomaceæ*, *Protococcaceæ*, *Peridinieæ*, and others. Undoubtedly it is on these pastures that fishes feed, as well as other organisms which in turn are food for fishes.

Fucus and *Laminaria* constitute the kelp from which iodine is obtained, and were at one time the source of the potash of commerce. *Fucus vesiculosus* is a constituent of a medicine used as a cure for obesity. *Chondrus crispus*, commonly known as Irish moss, was a few years ago generally used as an article of diet. *Porphyra vulgaris* (laver) is used by the Chinese for soups. *Rhodymenia palmata* (dulse) is an article of food in Ireland and Scotland. *Gracilaria spinosa* is used by birds, allied to the swallows, for making their nests—the edible nests found in large numbers on the islands of the Indian Archipelago, especially in the caves on the shores of Java, and gathered and sent to China, where they bring large prices and are used in making the famous birds'-nest soup. *Gracilaria lichenoides,* also a species of the Eastern seas, is the source of agar-agar, a preparation used in laboratories as a culture-medium for bacteria. Fossil diatoms are ground and used for polishing-powders. Seaweeds are everywhere used by farmers on the coasts as fertilizers.

XI

COLLECTING AT BAR HARBOR

THE beautiful coast of Maine is a particularly good field for shore-collecting. The rocky coast harbors the boreal fauna and flora which depend upon such physical conditions, and the shores at Bar Harbor are typical of those found elsewhere in northern New England. The rocks give shelter from the beating surf, while life has exposure to the cold, pure waters of the arctic current. Everywhere along the shore, rock pools are to be found. These are perhaps the most fascinating of all spots to the collector. They are veritable gardens of the sea, where species flourish which naturally belong to deeper water, but which find in such pools conditions suitable to their existence.

At Bar Harbor one well-known and frequently visited rock pool is found in Anemone Cave. Entering a field at Schooner Head, one turns to the right and follows the rocky shore for two or three hundred feet. It is difficult to take this short walk without being constantly diverted and delayed by the various attractions one meets, such as the tide-pools, the barnacles which in places whiten the rocks, the periwinkles, the purpura shells, and the curious algæ; but at last one arrives at a cavern under an overhanging rock. Here is a large tide-pool which at first sight displays only a beautiful scheme of color. It is carpeted with a bright-pink alga, *Hildenbrandtia rosea*, which incrusts the basin of the pool.

Interspersed with the pink are patches of a deep-red color, having a velvety appearance, which are formed by another crustaceous alga, *Petrocelis cruenta*. The water of the pool is of crystal clearness, and as one gazes into it one object after another comes into view, until one is filled with astonishment at the number of beautiful objects the pool contains. The little green balls, one half of an inch to one inch in diameter, which look like small green tomatoes scattered on the stones, are *Leathesia difformis,* an alga which cannot be mistaken for any other. Bunches of *Corallina officinalis,* which resembles coral, as the name indicates, are abundant. This alga should be examined with a magnifying-glass. It is covered with calcareous matter, and its peculiar form of growth is beautiful and interesting.

The fronds of the laminarian *Alaria esculenta* are tiny here, while just outside the cave they are to be seen several feet in length, beating against the rocks in the swash of the waves. Thorny sea-urchins (*Strongylocentrotus drobachiensis*) make green spots which look like tufts of moss. Yellow and green sponges in little cones are spread over small surfaces. Starfishes and ophiurans are plentiful. The *Purpura lapillus* and *Littorina litorea* and *rudis* (periwinkles), so plentiful on this coast, are present. The *Mytillus* and the *Saxicava* and the *Acmœa testudinalis* are also to be found. A green crab (*Carcinus mœnas*) is snugly hidden in a dark nook on the shady side of the pool, and many small crustaceans scuttle away from under stones as they are lifted. The collector is always anxious for uncommon, or rather less plentiful, species, and here are found two specimens of nudibranchs, or naked mollusks, *Æolis* and *Dendronotus.* The *Chiton ruber,* a jointed mollusk, was also found here, and five species of sea-anemones were counted. As this is a favorite hunting-ground, the anemones have not been left to attain full growth; but there are very many small ones which at first are not distinguishable, as they retract their tentacles at the slightest disturbance of the water and are then quite inconspicuous. After a little time of quiet watching they will be seen putting out their tentacles and expanding their beautiful flower-like forms. It is useless to try to capture them uninjured, so tightly do they adhere to the rocks, and the difficulty of preserving them in an expanded form is so great that amateur collectors had better leave them undisturbed to beautify the pool.

It was hard to resist robbing this rock pool, where the author in half an hour counted twenty different species, and finally left, feeling that its treasures were not half discovered; but collecting should be done elsewhere, and this pool be guarded as a gem to be admired and not to be despoiled.

This pool in Anemone Cave, although so very attractive, is surpassed in beauty and interest by pools on Porcupine Island, at the base of the cliff. This place is somewhat difficult of access, and the timid will not undertake the descent to it; but the enthusiastic collector, who overlooks small obstacles, will be repaid by a visit to this spot, where all the treasures of Anemone Cave are multiplied many times over. These pools are resplendent with large anemones, hydroids, nudibranchs, mollusks, echinoderms, crustaceans, and algæ. *Alaria esculenta*, several feet in length, is beaten to a fringe against the rocks, and *Agarum Turneri*, the sea-colander, is also found here, together with beautiful specimens of *Rhodymenia palmata*, which is so plentiful that it reddens the rocks.

A *Metridium marginatum*, the most common sea-anemone of this coast, was taken here which measured six inches in diameter. This creature threw out so many of the processes used for defense that it seemed at first as though it were covered with some seaweed; but the worm-like movements of these threads, which measured six inches or more in length, soon disclosed their nature.

On the more accessible shores of Porcupine Island are found the naked mollusks (nudibranchs) *Æolis* and *Dendronotus*. Clinging sideways to the rocks just above high-water mark are many shells of *Littorina rudis*. They are fastened to the rocks by a glutinous deposit along the outer lip, and the peculiar exposure of the open end, as well as the position above tide-mark, indicates that this animal is undergoing transformation into a land species. *Littorina palliata* is abundant on the rockweeds (*Fucus*); some of the specimens are banded with yellow, and all closely simulate the seaweed on which they cling. Beautifully banded specimens of *Littorina litorea* are also plentiful. Among other shells which are abundant here as well as elsewhere on this coast are *Purpura lapillus, Acmæa testudinalis, Buccinum undatum, Mya arenaria,* and *Mytillus edulis*.

Under the rockweeds in small pools and crevices are the polyzoans *Bugula turrita* and *Membranipora pilosa*, and the hydroids *Sertularia pumila* and *S. argentea*.

The seaweeds *Rhodymenia palmata* (dulse) and *Desmarestia* are plentiful; also beautiful worms, crustaceans, and starfishes.

A very interesting beach is found a few hundred feet south of Otter Cliffs, to which an easy descent is made if one follows a pathway leading to it through a grove adjacent to the drive. Here one will be interested in the study of numerous and beautiful rock pools.

Sea-urchins (*Strongylocentrotus drobachiensis*) seem to carpet some of them, having the appearance of mossy tufts. Beautiful pink and purple starfishes (*Asterias vulgaris*), brittle-stars (*Ophiopholis aculeata*), sea-cucumbers (*Pentacta frondosa*), sea-anemones, and crabs are abundant. If one lifts a stone the little crustaceans *Orchestia* and *Gammarus* will hurry away, and very likely an interesting worm or a nudibranch will be found. It is also most interesting to watch the barnacles, which are below the surface, reaching out their curled, feather-like feet in regular rhythmic grasping motions. The common mussels (*Mytillus edulis*), which in places blacken the shore, are beautiful under examination, and the silky network or byssus which forms the anchorage should be observed.

The rocks are hung so plentifully with *Ascophyllum nodosum* (rockweed) that its beauty is likely to be passed over unnoticed. On the *Ascophyllum* is growing in tufts *Polysiphonia fastigiata ;* other seaweeds, *Rhodymenia palmata, Chordaria flagelliformis, Desmarestia aculeata, Corallina officinalis,* and *Ceramium,* are so abundant that one forgets to value them at the moment. Higher up on the beach the rocks are spotted with papery sheets, which, floated out in water, prove to be the beautiful purple *Porphyra*. A fine, dark colored, hairy scum on the rocks is *Bangia fusco-purpurea*. Sometimes one finds here fronds of *Laminaria* which have been washed ashore. Various green algæ are abundant. Even if not collecting, it is well to carry a small tin pail to the beach and float out pieces of the algæ in order to observe carefully, if but for a moment, the beautiful forms they have in their natural state. Watched for a few minutes in a pail of water animals disclose curious and surprising forms and habits which are difficult to watch leaning over a pool.

Most of the various species mentioned above are common along the whole shore, and may be looked for at almost any point where the water is free from contamination. At the sand-beach are found species which do not inhabit the rocky shore, as the sand-dollar (*Echinarachnius parma*), *Polynices* (*Lunatia*) *heros*, *Mya arenaria*, and others. After a storm various deep-water forms are washed upon this beach. *Laminaria digitata*, six feet long, is found here sometimes under these circumstances. *Chordaria flagelliformis*, resembling long switches of hair, floats from the rocks near the shore. To the left, on the rock under the overhanging ledge, is a tide-pool which one would hesitate to deface by touching a single specimen. So crystal-clear is the water, so brilliant the *Hildenbrandtia*, so lovely the *Corallina*, that all seem placed there to excite admiration.

But most of all one should obtain the permission of the owner to visit Rodicks Weir. Here is an immense natural aquarium, full of living wonders. On a clear day, sunlight penetrates to the bottom, and at low tide the whole contents of the weir are clearly seen as one floats through the inclosed water-spaces. On the bottom are sea-urchins, many of them with sticks or stones on their backs, which the animals have placed there in the endeavor to conceal themselves; starfishes feeding; and great numbers of whelks (*Buccinum undatum*). Cuttlefishes dart rapidly about, and skates, sculpins, and other fishes display their curious forms. Very likely a giant jellyfish (*Cyanea arctica*) is entangled in the brush, so that one can examine at short range its wonderful and beautiful parts. Other jellyfishes may be closely scrutinized.

The alga *Polysiphonia violacea* floats in long feathery tufts from the stakes.

On the eel-grass are to be found *Lacuna vincta* and the delicate iridescent little shells of *Margarita helicina*.

Every tide brings different species of the ocean fauna to temporary imprisonment in this inclosure, so that it is difficult to say what one may not chance to find in this interesting place.

PART I

MARINE ALGÆ

SEAWEED

When descends on the Atlantic
　　　The gigantic
Storm-wind of the equinox,
Landward in his wrath he scourges
　　　The toiling surges,
Laden with seaweed from the rocks;

From Bermuda's reefs; from edges
　　　Of sunken ledges
In some far-off, bright Azore;
From Bahama and the dashing,
　　　Silver-flashing
Surges of San Salvador;
　　．　　．　　．　　．　　．　　．

Ever drifting, drifting, drifting
　　　On the shifting
Currents of the restless main;
Till in sheltered coves, and reaches
　　　Of sandy beaches,
All have found repose again.

LONGFELLOW.

I

BLUE-GREEN SEAWEEDS
(CYANOPHYCEÆ)

GRASS-GREEN SEAWEEDS
(CHLOROPHYCEÆ)

TABLE SHOWING THE CLASSIFICATION OF THE BLUE-GREEN
SEAWEEDS DESCRIBED IN THIS CHAPTER

Class
ALGÆ

Subclass
Cyanophyceæ
(Blue-Green Seaweeds)

Order	Genera	Species
NOSTOCACEÆ	*Spirulina* *Oscillaria* *Calothrix* *Lyngbya*	*L. majuscula* *L. ferruginea*

BLUE-GREEN SEAWEEDS

THE minute algæ, which form patches of purple color on rocks, slimy layers or spots on wharves, bluish-green slime on mud, emerald-green films on decaying algæ, blue-green slime on brackish ditches, and so on, are various species of the subclass **Cyanophyceæ.** The prevailing color of these plants is blue-green, but some are purple, brown, or pink. Some of them are gelatinous in texture and shapeless, others have more definite forms; but all are too small to classify without the aid of a powerful glass, and are not of special interest except to the botanist.

GENERA *Oscillaria* and *Spirulina*

The genus *Oscillaria* is so named from an oscillating movement which these filamentous plants show when viewed under the microscope. They are very delicate blue-green threads occurring singly, or in loose or felt-like floating masses, or like slime or scum, on mud or woodwork. In *Spirulina* the filaments are spirally twisted like a corkscrew and also have a vibrating movement. *Spirulina* is often found growing with *Oscillaria,* and forms purple patches on wharves.

GENUS *Calothrix*
(" *Beautiful hair* ")

Filaments one tenth of an inch long, terminating in transparent hair-like points, occasionally branching. The plant grows in fine tufts or like a fringe on algæ or in patches on rocks. Sometimes it forms a spongy layer, again a velvety stratum. The color varies in different species; it may be bright green, brownish-green, or dark bluish-purple. The genus is very common, and the plants are often found on the bottoms of boats.

Genus *Lyngbya*
(Named for Hans Christian Lyngbye, a Danish botanist)

L. *majuscula*, mermaid's-hair. The filaments are curled or crisped, long, thick, and tenacious, matted together at the base, and blackish-green. The species grows in tufts on eel-grass and algæ, and is often found floating free. It is common in summer everywhere south of Cape Cod and on the Pacific coast.

L. *ferruginea* or *æstuarii*. In this species the filaments are thin, soft, and without stability (flaccid), so that they lie flat like a thin stratum. They are verdigris-green in color, and are found in brackish pools and ditches and on muddy shores near the sea.

TABLE SHOWING THE CLASSIFICATION OF THE GRASS-GREEN
SEAWEEDS DESCRIBED IN THIS CHAPTER

Class
ALGÆ

Subclass
Chlorophyceæ
(Grass-Green Seaweeds)

Orders	Genera	Species
	Ulothrix	
CONFERVACEÆ	*Chætomorpha*	*C. melagonium* *C. ærea* *C. linum*
	Cladophora	*C. arcta* *C. rupestris* *C. gracilis*
	Ulva	*U. lactuca* *U. latissima*
ULVACEÆ	*Enteromorpha*	*E. clathrata* *E. compressa* *E. intestinalis* *E. lanceolata*
	Monostroma	

Group **Siphoneæ**

VALONIACEÆ	*Chamædoris* *Anadyomene*	*C. annulata* *A. flabellata*
DASYCLADACEÆ	*Acetabularia* *Dasycladus* *Cymopolia*	*A. crenulata* *D. occidentalis* *C. barbata*
UDOTEACEÆ	*Penicillus*	*P. dumentosus* *P. capitatus* *P. Phœnix*
	Udotea	*U. flabellata* *U. conglutinata*
	Halimeda	*H. tuna* *H. tridens* *H. opuntia*
CODIACEÆ	*Bryopsis* *Codium*	*B. plumosa* *C. tomentosum*
CAULERPACEÆ	*Caulerpa*	*C. prolifera* *C. Mexicana* *C. plumosa* *C. Wurdemanii*

51

GRASS-GREEN SEAWEEDS

"THERE can hardly be a more fascinating group of plants than this, whether to the strictly scientific botanist or to the more catholic lover of nature. The green algæ are among the most widely diffused of plant forms. They grow practically in every place where enough moisture, together with light and air, is to be had. Between tide-marks on almost every coast, floating on the surface of the deep sea, covering damp earth, walls, palings, and tree-trunks, sticking to the surface of leaves in the moist atmosphere of tropical forests and jungles, and inhabiting almost every river, brook, pond, ditch, or casual pool of rain-water in all quarters of the globe, are members of this ubiquitous group to be found." [1]

The grass-green seaweeds are more simple in structure, and therefore are lower in order, than the red or brown algæ. They are among the lowest of all plants, many of them being minute single cells. They abound in fresh as well as in salt water, and in this respect differ from the other groups, the red and the brown algæ being almost exclusively marine plants.

As one approaches the shore, the attention is often attracted by the green mantle which covers everything overflowed by the tides. This consists largely of the confervoid algæ, which are very abundant and are found almost everywhere. They are dense tufts of fine thread-like plants, often matted at the base; sometimes they are sponge-like, floating masses.

The **Ulvaceæ**, the plants next higher in order, are the first which assume ribbon- and leaf-like expansions, and usually first engage the attention of the collector.

[1] Kerner.

In the green algæ are found the extreme forms of one-celled plants. In *Pleurococcus* the cell is microscopic in size. In the **Siphoneæ** the plant still consists of a single cell, but it attains large dimensions and develops into forms resembling, in outward appearance, leaf, stem, and root (see *Caulerpa*).

Other plants consist of single rows of cells, called filaments (**Confervaceæ**), or of cells arranged in layers or flat surfaces, called membranes (**Ulvaceæ**).

ORDER **CONFERVACEÆ**

The silkweeds. This order is characterized by cylindrical cells strung end to end, forming threads or filaments, branched and unbranched. The plants inhabit both fresh and salt water, and are very abundant and widely distributed. They grow in dense tufts, often matted at the base.

Genus *Ulothrix*

A yellow-green, unbranched, decumbent, soft, hair-like fleece on the surface of rocks, extending indefinitely. This genus differs from *Chætomorpha* in the character of its filaments, which are soft and gelatinous in *Ulothrix,* but bristle-like and wiry in *Chætomorpha.*

Genus *Chætomorpha*

The frond is filiform; the filaments are coarse, rigid, and unbranched. In some species the filaments grow straight and in tufts from a definite base; in others they are twisted together and are prostrate. Often they are found floating in masses. In *C. tortuosa* the filaments are as fine as human hair, but rigid, and so closely interwoven as to resemble a layer of wool on the rocks. The cell-divisions give a striped appearance to the filaments when dry.

C. melagonium. This species is dark green, with filaments erect, coarse as a double bristle, and wiry; five to twelve inches long. It is found in rock pools from Boston northward. It does not adhere to paper in drying, and loses its color if immersed in fresh water. (Plate III.)

C. ærea. Yellowish-green, with filaments erect and less rigid than in *C. melagonium*, which it otherwise resembles; tufts three to twelve inches long; cell-divisions very marked. This species is found in rock pools from Cape Cod to New York Bay.

C. linum. Bright green; filaments coarse, rigid, twisted together, and prostrate. It is found floating in masses and forming strata on rocks and gravel from New York northward. It is thought by some that this, as well as *C. picquotiana,* which it closely resembles, is not a true species, but consists of the mature plants of the species *C. melagonium* and *C. œrea,* which have become detached from their holdfasts and have continued to grow. (Plate III.)

GENUS *Cladophora*
("*Branch-bearing*")

Frond filiform, branched. There are many species of *Cladophora,* which differ from one another in their branching, color, and size. They abound on rocks at low-water mark, in tide-pools, in muddy ditches, and on wharves. They are especially characterized by being so profusely branched as to form tufts or spherical masses, by which the collector can easily distinguish the genus.

C. arcta. Bright, glossy green; filaments fine, erect, much branched, two to eight inches long; tufts dense, more or less entangled, and in bunches, giving a starry effect. The species is common on rocks near low-water mark from New York northward. The plants vary slightly in appearance with the season. (Plate III.)

C. rupestris. Dark green; filaments straight, rigid, tufted; branches crowded; many branchlets flattened against the filaments, so that the alga somewhat resembles grass; five to ten inches long. The cell-divisions show plainly. Plants of this species do not adhere to paper in drying. They are found on rocks at low-water mark, and are common on the northern New England coast. (Plate III.)

C. gracilis. Bright yellow-green; filaments very fine, loosely tufted, three to twelve inches long, soft, silky, much branched; branches rather short, and branchlets more or less curved and arranged in a comb-like manner. It grows on wharves, in muddy pools, and on eel-grass. (Plate IV.)

ORDER **ULVACEÆ**

The plants of this order are, with few exceptions, formed of celled surfaces and show the earliest type of an expanded leaf. The cells form thin membranes, which sometimes are broad surfaces of no definite shape, sometimes are narrow and ribbon-like, or they may be simple or branched tubes. When the membrane

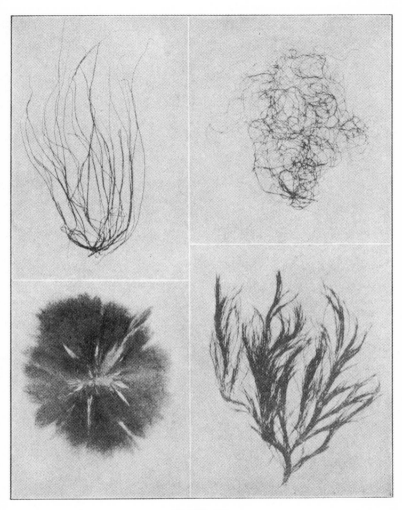

PLATE III.

Chætomorpha melagonium.   Chætomorpha linum.
Cladophora arcta.   Cladophora rupestris.

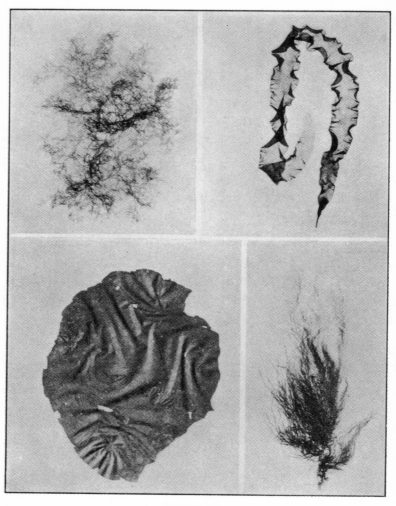

PLATE IV.

Cladophora gracilis.　　　　　　Ulva lanceolata.
Ulva lactuca, var. rigida.　　　　Enteromorpha clathrata.

consists of a single layer of cells it is *Monostroma* ("one layer"); when it consists of a double layer it is *Ulva;* when the layers separate, the thallus becomes hollow, and it is then *Enteromorpha.* These plants are mostly a brilliant grass-green in color, are silky in texture, and are attached by a small disk to rocks and stones. They abound everywhere, and are commonly known as *green laver.*

GENUS *Ulva*

Frond a thin, silky, flat membrane, sometimes leaf-like, again an extended surface of no definite shape. These are the largest green algæ. They are common everywhere.

U. lactuca, the sea-lettuce. Frond a flat membrane of various shapes, sometimes orbicular, again deeply incised, often ribbon-like; margin always much waved or ruffled. In the variety *rigida* the frond is oval in outline, not very large, and quite firm or rigid. The species is found on rocks exposed to the action of the waves. (Plate IV.)

U. latissima. Frond a flat, expanded membrane of indefinite shape, but general outline oval, never ribbon-like ; attains a size of twelve to twenty-four inches; often deeply lobed, very waved, often perforated with holes; membrane brilliant green, thin, smooth, glossy. It grows apart or in tufts, and is found everywhere, in all stages of growth. It is the largest species of *Ulva*, and is very common on muddy shores.

GENUS *Enteromorpha*

Fronds tubular, simple or branched, sometimes inflated. The tubes vary in size in different species and also in the same species, some being fine like a hair, others large, and flat or inflated. The genus is widely distributed and very abundant. Species of *Enteromorpha* grow on the bottoms of ships, and in nautical language are called *grass.*

E. clathrata. Fronds thread-like, tubular, branched, and branches beset with numerous fine branchlets; densely tufted, soft. Common everywhere. (Plate IV.)

E. compressa. Fronds long, slender, branched, tufted; branches simple, compressed, extending from main central branch, obtuse at ends, but attenuated at base. The species is very abundant everywhere, and is a useful plant for the aquarium. (Plate V.)

E. intestinalis. Single, long, inflated tubes or sacs, obtuse at the apex, very attenuated at the base; fronds often crimped and twisted, resembling an intestine, whence the name. (Plate V.)

E. lanceolata. Formerly called *Ulva Linza.* Frond narrow, ribbon-like, six to twelve inches long, one inch to two inches wide; blunt or pointed at apex, tapering at base; attached by a disk; edges much ruffled; bright green, soft, thin.

Genus *Monostroma*

This genus resembles *Ulva*, but is more delicate since it has but one layer of cells, as its name implies. The frond is usually sac-like at first, then breaks apart, leaving a thin, semi-transparent membrane of no definite shape.

GROUP SIPHONEÆ

The distinct and peculiar character of this group is that in each individual the whole plant consists of but one cell. There are many genera, some of which are plants of elaborate form and considerable size, but always the one cell expands and branches without dividing the elongated cavity with septa, or plates of division. In **Caulerpa** the stability of the plant is secured by numerous fibrils which emanate from the interior of the cell, forming a spongy network of interlacing filaments. In other orders the branches gain support from incrustation, from interlacing, and from cohering on the edges.

ORDER VALONIACEÆ

The algæ of this order are found only in tropical or subtropical waters. Their holdfasts resemble fibrous roots and penetrate the sand or coral on which they grow.

Genus *Chamædoris*

C. annulata. When young this alga consists of an annulated tube formed of a single cell. The annular constrictions occur at short intervals, giving it the appearance of being jointed. It grows to the height of two to three inches, when it ceases to lengthen and produces a dense mass of filaments, forming a head or spherical tuft one inch or more in diameter. It is bright grass-green in color, rather rigid and tough, and when mature is thinly coated with carbonate of lime. The holdfast is a tuft of fibers. The species is found at Key West and is a native of the West Indies.

PLATE V.

Enteromorpha compressa.   Enteromorpha intestinalis.
Enteromorpha intestinalis.   Anadyomene flabellata.

PLATE VI.

Acetabularia crenulata.   Dasycladus occidentalis.
Penicillus dumentosus.   Udotea conglutinata.

GENUS *Anadyomene*

A. flabellata. Frond composed entirely of branching filaments, which unite and form an undulating, rigid membranaceous surface, which seems like a network of veins. The species grows in bunches on short stems in the fissures of tidal rocks, and at first view resembles young *Ulva.* It is a very curious and beautiful alga, and should be examined with a glass. It is one inch to four inches in diameter when full-grown. (Plate V.)

ORDER **DASYCLADACEÆ**

This order also inhabits only tropical or subtropical seas. It is placed in this group, although only the main axis is unicellular. The one-celled axis is surmounted or encircled by whorls of minute filaments or branchlets (*ramuli*), which protrude through small holes and are either persistent or deciduous. In the latter case the fallen filaments leave disk-like scars on the stem.

GENUS *Acetabularia*

A. crenulata. This little alga resembles a mushroom of the *Agaricus* variety or gilled species, and so is easily identified. It is thinly incrusted with lime and is found on rocks and coral, within tide-marks, on the Florida reefs. When full-grown the stipe is two to three inches long and the cap one half of an inch in diameter. (Plate VI.)

GENUS *Dasycladus*

Fronds destitute of calcareous matter, soft, cylindrical or club-shaped; single unicellular axis, beset with fine filaments or ramuli.

D. occidentalis. Frond club-shaped, one to two inches high, one half of an inch or less in diameter; covered with whorls of fine filaments, making the fronds almost spongy; substance soft but tough; dark green. These plants have been compared to foxes' tails. They grow in bunches on rocks between tide-marks. (Plate VI.)

GENUS *Cymopolia*

C. barbata. Frond branched, dividing regularly in pairs; thickly incrusted with lime. Annular constrictions at short intervals give the branches the appearance of strings of beads. Each section is covered with pores or scars of fallen ramuli. The branches terminate in tufts of fine filaments.

ORDER **UDOTEACEÆ**

GENUS *Penicillus*

The merman's shaving-brush, characteristic of coral reefs.

P. dumentosus. Holdfast much branched, like a fibrous root, and penetrating deep into the coral or sand; stem short, thick, more or less flattened, sometimes hollow, covered with velvety scurf; top covered with loosely spreading tuft of soft filaments three to six inches long, which branch repeatedly in pairs (dichotomous); color deep green. When old, these plants are incrusted with a thin, porous layer of carbonate of lime. (Plate VI.)

P. capitatus. Holdfast a dense mass of fibers two or more inches long; stipe one to five inches long, one fourth to one third of an inch in diameter, usually cylindrical, sometimes wider at top than at base, sometimes flattened; thickly incrusted with lime, which is smooth and often polished; top a dense, spherical mass of filaments one to two inches in diameter; filaments branching dichotomously, and rigid from incrustation of lime.

P. Phœnix. Stipe cylindrical, one to three inches long, one fourth of an inch in diameter, thickly incrusted with lime, smooth; capitulum or head ovoid, and composed of filaments which are incrusted with lime and coherent, forming many distinct, flat, wedge-shaped, level-topped, spreading laminæ. This species is found at Key West.

GENUS *Udotea*

U. flabellata. Short, flattened stem, expanding into a broad, fan-shaped, smooth frond, concentrically zoned; margin wavy; thickly incrusted with lime. Abundant at Key West.

U. conglutinata. Deeply descending root; stem expanding into fan-shaped frond; entire, lobed, or irregularly torn; slightly incrusted with lime. The frond is composed of longitudinally parallel, adherent filaments, which are visible, giving a striated, rough surface. (Plate VI.)

GENUS *Halimeda*

This genus resembles the corallines externally, and is abundant on coral reefs. It appears as if formed of separate parts, resembling a series of heart- or kidney-shaped segments strung together. The plants are more or less incrusted with lime. The branching holdfast grasps particles of sand, and with them forms a solid ball.

H. tuna. Articulations roundish or half kidney-shaped, one half to three quarters of an inch broad; frond flat, smooth, and thinner than most species; bright green; somewhat flexible. (Plate VII.)

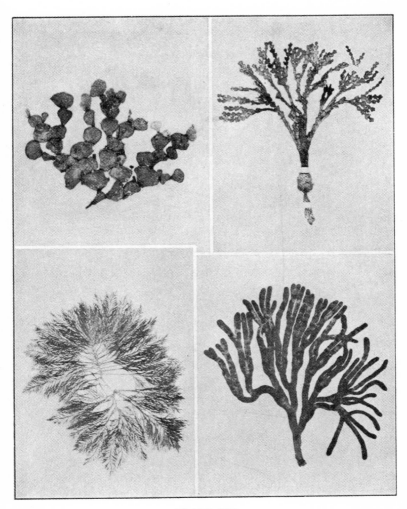

PLATE VII.

Halimeda tuna.   Halimeda tridens.
Bryopsis plumosa.   Codium tomentosum.

PLATE VIII.

Caulerpa Mexicana.   Caulerpa Wurdemanii.
Caulerpa plumaris.   Caulerpa paspaloides.

H. tridens. Fronds solitary, erect; base composed of confluent articulations; above divided into numerous branches of articulations, which are all flat, and in one plane giving a fan-shaped outline; middle joints wedge-shaped; upper ones divided into three lobes, frequently bearing articulations at the summit of each lobe; thinly incrusted with lime; color bright green. (Plate VII.)

H. opuntia. Articulations kidney-shaped, flat, rather thin; margins scalloped; irregularly branched and spreading; dense tufts.

ORDER **CODIACEÆ**

GENUS *Bryopsis*

(" Moss-like ")

There are said to be about twenty species of this genus. They are distinguished by the manner of branching, but are not very definitely marked. All are erect, one-celled, branching stalks, and are feather-like in appearance.

B. plumosa. Fronds branched twice or more; branchlets or pinnules tapering as they rise on the stalk, giving a triangular outline; stalk naked below; plants a vivid dark green in color, two to six inches long, growing in tufts on wharves and stones at low-water mark and in tide-pools. It is common along the whole Atlantic and Pacific coasts. It is well to use salt water for mounting this alga, since the green coloring-matter or granular endochrome with which it is filled easily escapes. (Plate VII.)

GENUS *Codium*

C. tomentosum. This is called the commonest seaweed in the world. It is abundant in every latitude, yet it does not appear on the eastern coast of North America. It is found on the gulf coast of Florida and is plentiful on the Pacific coast. The fronds are often a foot long, composed of closely packed, club-shaped branches dividing in a forking manner, and densely covered with fine filaments which give them a soft, sponge-like texture. (Plate VII.)

ORDER **CAULERPACEÆ**

GENUS *Caulerpa*

(From two Greek words meaning " stem " and " creep ")

Caulerpa is the only genus of its order, but it contains about a hundred species, many of which resemble mosses, ferns, or cacti. Each plant is composed of a single cell, however much it may be ramified. The frond consists of a prostrate stem, from the lower side of which root-like fibers or holdfasts descend into the hard sand or coral, and from the upper side leaf- and branch-like secondary fronds arise. These plants grow luxuriantly in tropical waters, extending over large surfaces, and are the chief food of turtles. (Plate VIII.)

C. prolifera. Frond or lamina flat and leaf-like, two to four inches long, one half to three quarters of an inch wide, either simple or once forked; margin entire. Similar laminæ spring from the surface or from the edge or base of the different leaf-like portions. Laminæ rise from the upper side of the creeping, rooting stem. Its substance is somewhat horny and translucent.

C. Mexicana. Prostrate, creeping stem, with rootlets or holdfasts below, and leaf-like fronds above; fronds simple or with one or two branches deeply cut in narrow lobes nearly to the center. The species abounds at Key West. (Plate VIII.)

II

OLIVE-GREEN AND BROWN SEAWEEDS
(PHÆOPHYCEÆ)

TABLE SHOWING THE CLASSIFICATION OF THE OLIVE-GREEN
AND BROWN SEAWEEDS DESCRIBED IN THIS CHAPTER

Class
ALGÆ

Subclass
Phæophyceæ

(Olive-Green and Brown Seaweeds)

Orders	Genera	Species
ECTOCARPACEÆ	*Ectocarpus*	*E. littoralis* *E. siliculosus* *E. viridis* *E. tomentosus*
SPHACELARIACEÆ	*Sphacelaria* *Cladostephus*	*S. cirrhosa* *S. radicans* *C. verticillatus*
RALFSIACEÆ	*Ralfsia*	
ENCŒLIACEÆ	*Punctaria* *Asperococcus* *Phyllitis*	*P. latifolia* *P. tenuissima* *P. plantaginea* *A. echinatus* *P. fascia*
DESMARESTIACEÆ	*Desmarestia* *Arthrocladia*	*D. viridis* *D. aculeata* *D. ligulata* *A. villosa*
DICTYOSIPHONACEÆ	*Dictyosiphon*	*D. fœniculaceus*
ELACHISTACEÆ	*Elachista*	
CHORDARIACEÆ	*Chordaria* *Mesoglœa* *Leathesia* *Myrionema*	*C. flagelliformis* *M. virescens* *M. divaricata*

62

Orders	Genera	Species
LAMINARIACEÆ	*Chorda*	*C. filum*
	Alaria	*A. esculenta*
	Agarum	*A. Turneri*
	Laminaria	*L. longicruris*
		L. saccharina
		L. digitata
	Macrocystis	
	Nereocystis	
	Lessonia	
	Thalassiophyllum	
DICTYOTACEÆ	*Dictyota*	*D. fasciola*
		D. dichotoma
	Zonaria	*Z. lobata*
	Taonia	*T. atomaria*
	Padina	*P. pavonia*
	Haliseris	*H. polypodioides*
CUTLERIACEÆ	*Cutleria*	*C. multifida*
FUCACEÆ	*Himanthalia*	*H. lorea*
	Fucus	*F. vesiculosus*
		F. serratus
		F. furcatus
		F. ceranoides
	Ascophyllum	*A. nodosum*
	Phyllospora	*P. Menziesii*
	Cystoseira	*C. expansa*
	Halidrys	*H. osmunda*
	Sargassum	*S. vulgare*
		S. Montagnei
		S. bacciferum

OLIVE-GREEN AND BROWN SEAWEEDS

THIS subclass contains some of the most remarkable of the seaweeds. It is especially notable for the diversity of its plant forms, which range from filaments to plants which appear to have stems and leaves (*Sargassum*). The species vary in size from very small fronds to those of immense size (the *Laminariaceæ*). It includes *Fucus* (the rockweeds), a very conspicuous genus, which furnishes fully three fourths of the vegetable covering of the tidal rocks in the localities in which it grows.

ORDER **ECTOCARPACEÆ**

This order comprises many species of branched, filamentous plants, some of which are of hair-like fineness and form beautiful feathery tufts of brownish or olive-green color. They resemble, except in their tawny color, the green alga *Cladophora*.

The name is derived from Greek words meaning "outside" and "fruit," the spores of the plants being borne on the branches.

The species are determined by the arrangement of the spores, according as they are in the pod-like branches, in groups, or in cases on stalks. Since these differences are not perceptible to the naked eye, it is impracticable to describe many species, or for the amateur collector to try to separate them.

Genus *Ectocarpus*

E. littoralis. Filaments fine, in dense tufts, interwoven, six to twelve inches long; pod linear in the substance of the branches; color olive-green. This is the most common species of *Ectocarpus*, and grows abundantly everywhere, appearing like large, fine, dull-green plumes. (Plate IX.)

E. siliculosus. Tufts loosely entangled at the base, free and feathery above, of indefinite length; spores in pod-like forms at the ends of the branches. Common on the larger algæ and on wharves.

E. viridis. Tufts a little more loose and expanding than in *E. siliculosus;* spores in pods at the base of the branches. (Plate IX.)

E. tomentosus. Fine filaments, densely interwoven into rope-like, spongy masses, two to four inches long; yellowish-brown; pods on stalks. Found in summer growing on *Fucus.*

ORDER **SPHACELARIACEÆ**

Genus *Sphacelaria*

S. cirrhosa. Olive-brown; branched, feathery filaments, one half of an inch to two inches long. Each branch ends with an oblong, swollen cell containing a dark granular mass which gives it a withered appearance. These cells can be seen with a strong pocket-lens. It forms dense, globe-like tufts on *Fucus.*

S. radicans. Filaments one half of an inch to one inch high; branches few and hairy. It forms a dense, grass-like covering, of indefinite extent, on the under side of muddy rocks. Found on the New England coast.

Genus *Cladostephus*

C. verticillatus. Fronds bristle-like, dividing regularly; covered with whorls of branchlets set close to the stems, each whorl overlapping the previous one, giving the plant a spongy appearance. (Plate IX.)

ORDER **RALFSIACEÆ**

Genus *Ralfsia*

The species of this genus are brown, leathery, crustaceous expansions of indefinite form, one inch to six inches in diameter, resembling lichens. They appear on rocks in shallow, exposed pools.

ORDER **ENCŒLIACEÆ**

Genus *Punctaria*

Dotted-weeds. Fronds pale olive-green, membranaceous, leaf-like, with short stem; covered with spores which appear like dots.

P. latifolia. Frond pale green, four to twelve inches long, one inch to five inches wide, leaf-like, and tapering suddenly to a short stalk; much waved on margin; substance soft and thin; dotted with spores. In the young plants fine hairs emerge from the dots, but disappear later, and the fronds become darker and more rigid. Found in summer on rocks and on other algæ on the Long Island and New England coasts.

P. tenuissima. Fronds smaller and more slender than in *P. latifolia;* thin and delicate. Found on eel-grass and *Chorda filum.*

P. plantaginea. Fronds dark brown, leathery, leaf-like, blunt or wedge-shaped on top; dense clusters of hairs on the dots; six to twelve inches long, one inch to one and a half inches wide.

Genus *Asperococcus*

This genus differs from *Punctaria* in having a tubular instead of a flat frond. (Plate IX.)

A. echinatus. Resembles *Enteromorpha* in being tubular; compressed or inflated; obtuse at the apex; attenuated at the base. It differs from *Enteromorpha* in being olive in color, and in being covered with small oblong dots of darker shade. When the plant is young the dots are hairy. It grows in clusters, two to eighteen inches long, one half of an inch to one inch wide. Common along the New England coast.

Genus *Phyllitis*

P. fascia. Fronds light olive-green, leaf-like, three to six inches long, one fourth to one half of an inch wide; margin entire, slightly waved; contracted at base to short stalk; attached by disk. This species grows in bunches on rocks and stones at low-water mark, and is very common everywhere. (Plate X.)

ORDER DESMARESTIACEÆ

(Named for M. Desmarest, a French naturalist)

Genus *Desmarestia*

D. viridis. Filaments cylindrical, about as thick as a bristle; branches opposite, in pairs, at intervals on the main stem. The branches branch again and continue to be disposed in the same manner. All are long and ultimately become very fine. The color is olive-green, becoming verdigris-green when exposed to the air for a short time or placed in fresh water. The species grows in deep tide-pools and below low-water mark, forming fine, feathery plumes, often a yard long, which give submerged rocks the appearance of a luxuriant garden. (Plate X.)

D. aculeata ("spiny"). Fronds cylindrical at base, flattened above; branches long and straight, arranged alternately, when young beset with pencils of fine hairs, often one half of an inch long, which, later, fall off, leaving alternate spines along the edges of the flattened branches. It

PLATE IX.

Ectocarpus littoralis.
Cladostephus verticillatus.

Ectocarpus viridis.
Asperococcus bullosus.

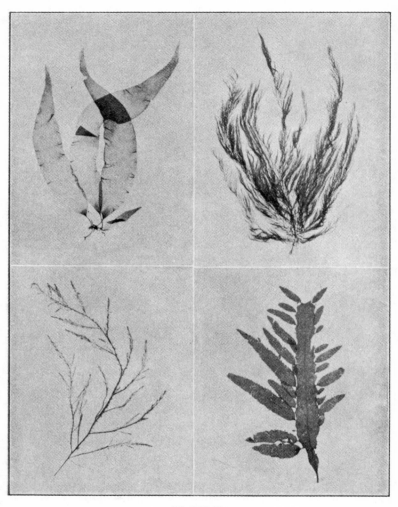

PLATE X.

Phyllitis fascia.   Desmarestia viridis.
Desmarestia aculeata.   Desmarestia ligulata.

grows from one foot to six feet in length, below low-water mark, and is found washed ashore. It is an attractive plant in the spring, but is brown and coarse when old. Common everywhere. (Plate X.)

D. ligulata. Fronds two to six feet long, pinnate, having a flat main stem one half of an inch or more wide, with opposite flat branches; leaflets arranged along the edges of the branches, pointed at each end, and bordered with forward-pointing spines. It is found washed ashore, in abundance, in California, but is not found on the Atlantic coast. (Plate X.)

Genus *Arthrocladia*

A. villosa. Olive-brown filaments, resembling fine, knotted threads, each knob having a whorl of delicate filaments. It grows from six inches to three feet long, in deep water. It is rare, but is occasionally found on the New England coast.

ORDER **DICTYOSIPHONACEÆ**

Genus *Dictyosiphon*

D. fœniculaceus. Fronds filiform, bristle-like, branching into delicate, hair-like branches; yellowish-brown. It resembles *Chordaria flagelliformis*, but is much finer. (Plate XI.)

ORDER **ELACHISTACEÆ**

Genus *Elachista*

The plants of this genus are small, olive-colored, unbranched, hair-like filaments, growing in dense, radiating tufts, one half of an inch in height, on *Fucus*. They are interesting to the microscopist, but not to the collector.

ORDER **CHORDARIACEÆ**

(" Cord-like ")

Genus *Chordaria*

C. flagelliformis (" whip-like "). Firm, leathery, somewhat elastic, slimy strings, six to twenty-four inches long, and twice as thick as a bristle; branches mostly undivided, short or long, irregularly placed on the main axis, and curving inward at the top of the frond; main axis not extending as far as the branches; blackish in color; attached by a disk to stones and shells; solitary or in bunches. It is common along the New England coast. (Plate XI.)

Genus *Mesoglœa*

M. virescens. Soft, slimy filaments, with branches and branchlets; olive-green. (Plate XI.)

M. divaricata. Fronds two to twenty-four inches high; branching irregularly, and generally without definite main axis; branches flexuous, solid at first, later hollow; branchlets short and wide-spreading. Common from Cape Cod southward; abundant in Long Island Sound. (Plate XI.)

Genus *Leathesia*

This singular alga resembles a tuber and cannot be mistaken for any other plant. Its fronds are gelatinous, fleshy balls, one half of an inch to two inches in diameter, at first solid, afterward lobed and hollow. It grows singly or in bunches on algæ and on sand-covered rocks, and is found in summer on every coast. The common species is known as *L. difformis* or *L. tuberiformis.*

Genus *Myrionema*

Minute algæ which grow on other plants and which appear like dark spots, or, at first, like stains, on *Ulva, Enteromorpha,* and small red algæ. These spots, which to the naked eye appear like decay, show, under the microscope, a jelly-like substance full of beaded filaments.

ORDER **LAMINARIACEÆ**

The plants of this order have large and coarse fronds (some attaining an immense size), with stems, branching root-like holdfasts, and expanded leaf-like laminæ. They are leather-like, not articulated, olive-green or brown in color, and sometimes yellow and semi-transparent. They grow in deep water and are found washed ashore. Sometimes small plants are found in deep tidepools at low-water mark. Some species are perennial. In these instances the stems only survive, and the laminæ are reproduced annually. The new growth takes place at the apex of the stem. The old lamina is pushed off, but is held on the summit of the new growth until the latter has matured.

In the genus *Chorda* the fronds are cylindrical; in *Agarum*

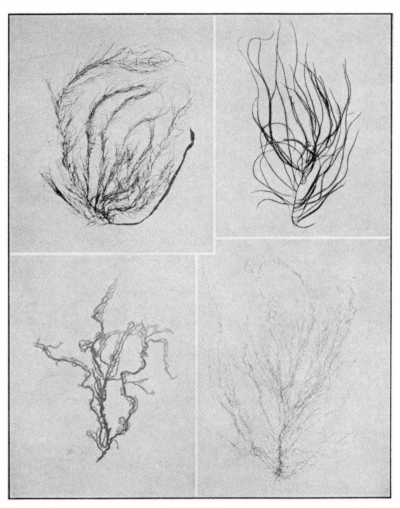

PLATE XI.

Dictyosiphon fœniculaceus.   Chordaria flagelliformis.
Mesoglœa virescens.   Mesoglœa divaricata.

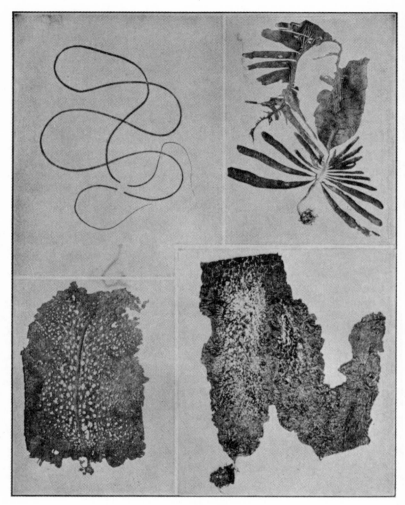

PLATE XII.

Chorda filum.   Alaria esculenta.
Agarum Turneri.   Laminaria saccharina.

the laminæ are perforated; in *Alaria* there are wing-like leaflets below the laminæ.

The *Laminariaceæ* and *Fucaceæ* are the seaweeds used in making kelp. For this the algæ are burned, and the ash is then separated into its different mineral constituents and used for various manufacturing purposes.

Genus *Chorda*

C. filum. Entire frond cylindrical, divided internally by transverse septa; one fourth to one half of an inch in diameter, tapering at each end; ordinarily one to twelve feet long, but sometimes attaining a length of forty feet. When young the frond is covered with fine, transparent hairs; later it is brown and leather-like. The growth takes place at the base, just above the disk-like holdfast, and at the apex it is constantly dying off. The species is common on Northern shores, at and below low-water mark. Often it is in masses which seem like meadows of waving grass under water. Various small algæ and many zoöphytes are to be found on the fronds. (Plate XII.)

Genus *Alaria*

This genus is readily distinguishable by the fact that it has leaflets below the lamina. It is found north of Cape Cod.

A. esculenta. Stem compressed, four to twelve inches long, one fourth to one half of an inch wide, and running like a midrib through the lamina; lamina one to ten feet long, two to ten inches wide, frequently torn and ragged; margin wavy; leaflets three to eight inches long and without midrib, growing on both sides of the stem, below the lamina. The spores are produced in the leaflets in the autumn. This is an edible alga and is used as food in Scotland and Ireland, where it is called henware, badderlocks, murlins, and so on. (Plate XII.)

Genus *Agarum*

The sea-colanders.

A. Turneri. Stem two to twelve inches long, round below, flattened above, and extending like a midrib through the lamina; lamina one foot to four feet long, with holes over the whole surface; margin wavy. The perforations in the lamina are produced by conical hollow papillæ which cover the young frond and which at length burst, leaving a hole which enlarges as the plant expands. This species is found from Cape Cod to Greenland.

There are other species, which differ from this one in the size of the perforations, the shape of the lamina, and the prominence of the midrib. Harvey describes the plant as an arctic genus growing ten to twelve feet long. (Plate XII.)

Genus *Laminaria*

The plants of this genus are all làrge, varying from one foot to twelve feet or more in length. They are of wide geographical range, and are more numerous in species than any others of the order. They are commonly known as oarweeds, tangle, devil's-aprons, sole-leather, kelp, sea-furbelows, and so on.

L. longicruris ("long-stalked"). Stem six to twelve feet long, one to two inches thick, slender and solid at base, hollow and inflated at the middle, contracted at the top; attached by a strong, branching, root-like holdfast; color light brown. The large, single, leaf-like lamina, usually shorter than the stem, is five to twenty feet long, two to three feet broad, with much waved and folded margin, outlined with two rows of depressed spots. The spores form a band in the center of the blade. Found from Cape Cod northward and on the Pacific coast.

L. saccharina, the sea-tangle. This species differs from *L. longicruris* in having a short, solid stem and narrow, ribbon-like lamina. Stem three inches to four feet long; lamina three to thirty feet long, six to eighteen inches wide, with central band of depressed spots; margin much waved; color olive-green, semi-transparent. It is named from the saccharine matter, called *mannite,* which it contains. Found on northern shores of the Atlantic and the Pacific oceans. (Plate XII.)

L. digitata ("fingered"). Stem one to five feet long, thick, round, and solid; lamina oval at base, leathery, smooth, brown, deeply cleft into segments of unequal breadth. It is named from the hand-like form of the lamina. This species is found in Long Island Sound, but is not common south of Cape Cod. The stem is used by fishermen for knife-handles. Pieces of it, placed on the blades while green, contract in drying and become solid. (Plate XIII.)

For the genera *Macrocystis, Nereocystis, Lessonia,* and *Thalassiophyllum,* see the Introduction, pages 35, 36.

ORDER **DICTYOTACEÆ**

Genus *Dictyota*

D. fasciola. Fronds olive-brown, expanded, membranaceous, erect, flat; many times forked narrow branches; grows in tufts six to ten inches long, matted at the base.

D. dichotoma. Same as *D. fasciola,* except that the divisions of the forked frond are one eighth to one half of an inch wide. Found in tide-pools in Southern waters. (Plate XIII.)

Genus *Zonaria*

Z. lobata. Thallus flat, fan-shaped, but not so rounded as in *Padina pavonia,* twelve or more inches in height, cleft irregularly into many

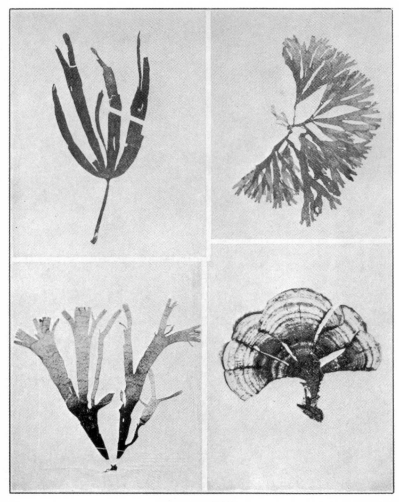

PLATE XIII.

Laminaria digitata.   Dictyota dichotoma.
Taonia atomaria.   Padina pavonia.

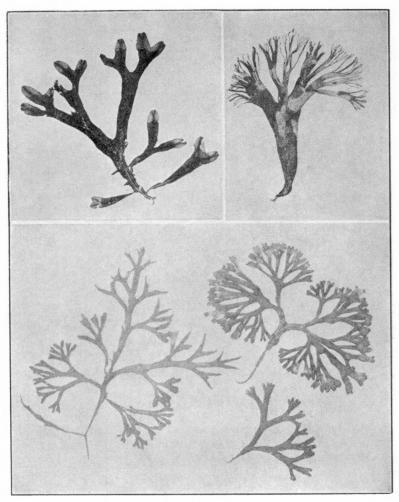

PLATE XIV.

Haliseris polypodioides.   Cutleria multifida.

Fucus vesiculosus.

narrow lobes, the clefts extending nearly or quite to the base; olive-green, with concentric zones of darker color; edges thin and bordered with a dark line. Found in southern California and in tropical and subtropical seas.

Genus *Taonia*

T. atomaria. Spreading, fan-shaped frond; clefts irregular and not extending to the basal stem; spores arranged in dark wavy lines and spots on the frond, giving it a mottled appearance and beautiful gradation of color. Found in tropical seas. (Plate XIII.)

Genus *Padina*

P. pavonia, the peacock's-tail. Frond broadly fan-shaped; substance between membranaceous and leathery; powdery on the outer surface; deeply and variously cleft or entire; several laminæ emanating from a stalk-like base; each lamina fan-shaped; concentric lines numerous; variegated in zones. This beautiful alga is always regarded as a prize. It is found on stones at low-water mark, and is not uncommon south of Charleston, South Carolina, but is more luxuriant in tropical seas. (Plate XIII.)

Genus *Haliseris*

The sea-endive.

H. polypodioides. Fronds flat, forked, notched on lower part; divisions about one quarter of an inch wide; distinct midrib; olive-green; grows in tufts. It is found in North and South Carolina, and is abundant on the Florida Keys. (Plate XIV.)

ORDER CUTLERIACEÆ

Genus *Cutleria*

C. multifida. Frond erect, flat; branches in a forking manner; ultimate branches fine and short, and with branchlets on the tips. This species resembles *Taonia.* It is found in Southern waters. (Plate XIV.)

ORDER FUCACEÆ

Genus *Himanthalia*

H. lorea, the sea-thong. A cup-shaped base, from the center of which arises a flat, strap-like frond one fourth to one half of an inch wide and two to twenty feet long, branching dichotomously (or by forking), and dotted with pits, or conceptacles, in which the spores are formed. Found in the extreme North.

Genus *Fucus*

The rockweeds. The plants of this genus grow in thick bunches, and are found in great abundance between tide-marks. The plants are attached by sucker-like disks to the rocks, from which they hang like fringe when the tide recedes; when it rises they float and sway in the water in beautiful bouquet-like forms. In color they are brown or olive-green, in texture thick and leathery, but they sometimes expand into thin membranes. They are many times forked in the same plane, which produces a flat thallus. They often have a distinct midrib. The air-vessels, whose function it is to float the plant, are disposed along the midrib, usually in pairs.

The species are named according to the divisions of the frond, and the disposition, or presence, of the air-bladders and the *conceptacles*, or spore-chambers.

The conceptacles congregate in particular portions of the frond and give its surface a roughness which is very perceptible; such portions are then known as the *receptacles*. In *Fucus* this usually occurs on the bulbous extremities of the branches. Under the microscope a section of one of these little pointed spots shows a spherical cavity filled with a beautiful arrangement of *paraphyses*, or threads, some of which hold spores, while others protrude through a small opening in the outer membrane. Conceptacles are peculiar to the order **Fucaceæ**. In them spore-production is carried on in a manner as complicated as is the formation of seeds in flowering plants. Although rockweeds are such a conspicuous feature of sea-shore vegetation, two species only, *Fucus vesiculosus* and *Ascophyllum nodosum* (formerly called *Fucus nodosus*), are common on the Atlantic coast, and these do not occur south of New York, owing to the fact that a long stretch of sand-beach extends beyond that point.

F. vesiculosus. Midrib distinct through all the forked branches; margin entire, often wavy; air-vessels spherical or oblong, usually in pairs along the midrib; receptacles on terminal branches, which are swollen and filled with gelatinous matter, heart-shaped or forked, in oblong or pointed divisions; frond tough and leathery, often two feet long. (Plate XIV.)

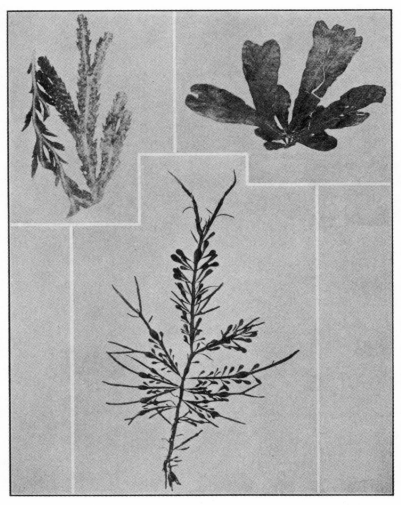

PLATE XV.

Fucus serratus.   Fucus ceranoides.
          Ascophyllum nodosum.

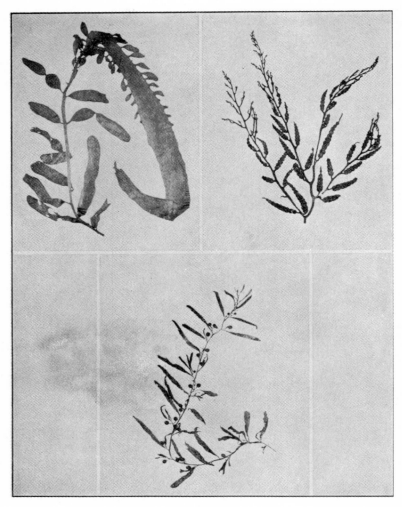

PLATE XVI.

Phyllospora Menziesii.   Halidrys osmunda.
           Sargassum vulgare.

F. serratus. Frond distinctly toothed or serrated along the margin; midrib conspicuous through the main axis and forked branchings; no air-vessels. This species is rare on the Atlantic coast. (Plate XV.)

F. furcatus. Frond narrow, tough, without air-vessels; regular forked branching; midrib distinct below, inconspicuous above; receptacles long, narrow, not inflated. Found from Boston northward.

F. ceranoides. Frond flat, rather membranaceous, or less leathery than in the preceding species; repeatedly forked; midrib not running through every division; no air-vessels. (Plate XV.)

GENUS *Ascophyllum*

A. nodosum. This species, formerly called *Fucus nodosus*, is next to *Fucus vesiculosus* the most common rockweed. Frond one to five feet long, dark brown, strap-like, leathery; width of main stems one fourth of an inch or more, and uniform throughout; large, single, oblong air-vessels distend the frond at intervals. Branches of various length emerge from the sides of the main stem. Ovoid or ellipsoidal branchlets or receptacles, single or in groups, occur at intervals along the sides of both stem and branches. These fall off after a time and are found in quantities in tide-pools. (Plate XV.)

GENUS *Phyllospora*

P. Menziesii. Branching holdfast; short stem which immediately divides into strap-like branches; branches edged with leaves varying in length, rounded at top, narrow, stalked at base; leaves placed at intervals, or crowded together, and interspersed with air-vessels which are often tipped with leaflets; stems expand at summit into leaf-like laminæ and are edged with leaflets at the base; plant often one hundred and twenty feet or more in length; tough and leathery in substance. Very common on the California coast. (Plate XVI.)

GENUS *Cystoseira*

C. expansa. Frond long, slender, repeatedly branched; air-vessels ellipsoidal and "chained" together in the lower half of the branches. The plant grows in deep water, and shows iridescent colors when seen through the water. It is found on the California coast.

GENUS *Halidrys*

H. osmunda, the sea-oak. Frond flat, alternately toothed or indented below; branched apex, bearing air-vessels like long-stalked pods; substance leathery. Found on the coast of southern California. (Plate XVI.)

GENUS *Sargassum*

Sargassum is distinguished by its differentiation into stem and leaf, resembling in outward appearance the higher plants. It is a tropical and subtropical genus, and has one hundred and fifty species. Two of these, *S. vulgare* and *S. Montagnei*, are found as far north as Cape Cod. See Introduction, page 34.

S. vulgare. Stems cylindrical; branches alternate; leaves long, narrow, toothed, with short stalk and midrib; minute dark spots on its surface; air-vessels small balls resembling berries set on stalks and usually tipped with a long point; receptacles small, twig-like forms in the axils of the leaves; color olive-brown; plant one foot to three or more feet long. Common in Long Island Sound. (Plate XVI.)

S. Montagnei. This species resembles *S. vulgare*, but is more slender in all its parts, and the receptacles are more elongated. From south of Cape Cod.

S. bacciferum. Particular interest attaches to this species from the fact that it is the one which forms the floating vegetation of the Sargasso Sea. It grows attached on the Florida Keys and in the West Indies. Specimens are sometimes carried by the currents northward, and are found washed ashore. It differs from *S. vulgare* in the leaves, which are thicker, more attenuated, and sharply toothed, and in having a greater number of air-vessels. A branch of this species brought from the Sargasso Sea had air-vessels so numerous and closely set that it resembled a bunch of small grapes.

III

RED SEAWEEDS
(RHODOPHYCEÆ or FLORIDEÆ)

TABLE SHOWING THE CLASSIFICATION OF THE RED SEAWEEDS DESCRIBED IN THIS CHAPTER

Class
ALGÆ

Subclass
Rhodophyceæ or Florideæ
(Red Seaweeds)

Orders	Suborders	Genera	Species
NEMALIONACEÆ			
	HELMINTHOCLADIEÆ	{ *Nemalion*	*N. multifidum*
		{ *Liagora*	
	CHÆTANGIEÆ	*Scinaia*	*S. furcellata*
	GELIDIEÆ	*Gelidium*	*G. corneum*
GIGARTINACEÆ			
		Chondrus	*C. crispus*
		Gigartina	{ *G. mamillosa*
			{ *G. radula*
			{ *G. spinosa*
			{ *G. microphylla*
		Phyllophora	{ *P. membranifolia*
			{ *P. Brodiæi*
		Sternogramme	*S. interrupta*
		Gymnogongrus	*G. Norvegicus*
		Ahnfeldtia	*A. plicata*
		Callophyllis	{ *C. variegata*
			{ *C. laciniata*
		Iridæa	

76

Orders	Suborders	Genera	Species

RHODOPHYLLIDEÆ
- Cystoclonium — *C. purpurascens* / *C. cirrhosa*
- Euthora — *E. cristata*
- Rhodophyllis — *R. veprecula*
- Rhabdonia — *R. tenera* / *R. Coulteri*
- Eucheuma — *E. isiforme*

RHODYMENIACEÆ

SPHÆROCOCCEÆ
- Gracilaria — *G. multipartita*
- Hypnea — *H. musciformis*

RHODYMENIEÆ
- Rhodymenia — *R. palmata*
- Lomentaria — *L. Baileyana*
- Champia — *C. parvula*
- Chylocladia — *C. articulata*
- Plocamium — *P. coccineum*

DELESSERIEÆ
- Nitophyllum — *N. laceratum* / *N. Ruprechteanum* / *N. punctatum*
- Grinnellia — *G. Americana*
- Delesseria — *D. sinuosa* / *D. alata* / *D. Leprieurii*

RHODOMELEÆ
- Polysiphonia — *P. fastigiata* / *P. nigrescens* / *P. parasitica* / *P. dendroidea* / *P. Baileyi* / *P. Harveyi* / *P. Olneyi* / *P. fibrillosa* / *P. violacea* / *P. urceolata* / Var. *formosa* / *P. variegata* / *P. Woodii*
- Laurencia — *L. pinnatifida*
- Dasya — *D. elegans* / *D. plumosa*
- Bostrychia — *B. rivularis*
- Rhodomela — *R. subfusca* / *R. Rochei* / *R. larix* / *R. floccosa*
- Chondria — *C. dasyphylla* / *C. tenuissima* / *C. striolata*

Orders	Suborders	Genera	Species
			C. americanum
			C. Pylaisœi
		Callithamnion	*C. Baileyi*
			C. seirospermum
			C. byssoideum
			C. floccosum
		Griffithsia	*G. Bornetiana*
			P. serrata
		Ptilota	*P. elegans*
			P. densa
			P. hypnoides
	CERAMIEÆ	*Spyridia*	*S. filamentosa*
			C. rubrum
			Var. *proliferum*
			Var. *secundatum*
		Ceramium	*C. strictum*
			C. diaphanum
			C. fastigiatum
			C. tenuissimum
			Var. *patentissimum*
		Microcladia	*M. Coulteri*
			M. borealis

CRYPTONEMIACEÆ

GLOIOSIPHONIEÆ	*Gloiosiphonia*		*G. capillaris*
GRATELOUPIEÆ	*Halymenia*		*H. ligulata*
	Grateloupia		*G. Cutleria*
	Prionitis		*P. lanceolata*
			P. Andersonii
DUMONTIEÆ	*Pikea*		*P. Californica*
	Halosaccion		*H. ramentaceum*
RHIZOPHYLLIDEÆ	*Polyides*		*P. rotundus*
SQUAMARIEÆ	*Peyssonnelia*		*P. Dubyi*
	Petrocelis		*P. cruenta*
	Hildenbrandtia		*H. rosea*
CORALLINEÆ	*Corallina*		*C. officinalis*
	Melobesia		

BANGIACEÆ

Bangia		*B. fusco-purpurea*
Porphyra		*P. vulgaris*
		P. laciniata

RED SEAWEEDS

IN **Rhodophyceæ**, known also as **Florideæ** and **Rhodospermeæ**, algæ attain their highest development. This is marked by the mode of reproduction, which, more nearly than in the other subclasses, resembles that of flowering plants. The fronds, however, are not as large and do not as closely resemble stem and leaf as do some species of the brown algæ.

The species of this subclass are very numerous, and the variety in their fronds, their delicate texture, and their colors, which vary from pink to purple, make them the most attractive of the seaweeds. They grow mostly in deep water, but are often found washed ashore, and many grow just below low-water mark and on the shady side of tide-pools.

In the simplest species the frond consists of branched cell-rows. In some of these the filaments are so fine that a pocket-lens is required to determine the differences in branching and fully to appreciate the beauty of the plant (*Callithamnion*). Some have a cell-surface. In *Delesseria* the membrane assumes the outline of a foliage-leaf. *Dasya*, which is an abundant variety, is especially beautiful in its feather-like appearance. The corallines are singular in that they are incrusted with lime and resemble corals.

ORDER **NEMALIONACEÆ**

SUBORDER **HELMINTHOCLADIEÆ**

GENUS *Nemalion*

The threadweeds.

N. multifidum. Frond six to twelve inches long, cylindrical, solid, cord-like, elastic, tough, shiny, very gelatinous; branches repeatedly in a wide-forking manner; sometimes a branch will divide into several parts at the same point; color dark brown or purple. It is found, in summer only, from Long Island Sound northward, growing on smooth rocks which are exposed to the action of the waves.

GENUS *Liagora*

Fronds filamentous; branching regularly in a forking manner to the very top, forming thick bunches; slightly incrusted with lime, yet somewhat viscid. It is found in Florida and California, and abounds in tropical waters.

SUBORDER **CHÆTANGIEÆ**
GENUS *Scinaia*

S. furcellata. Frond cylindrical, one eighth of an inch in diameter, tapering at base, sometimes constricted at intervals, regularly and several times forked, ending in short divisions; branches of same length, giving a level top; two to four inches high; lake-red. When pressed the axis is visible, giving the appearance of a flat frond with a midrib. This species is found in summer only, washed ashore from Cape Cod southward and on the California coast. It is not common. (Plate XVII.)

SUBORDER **GELIDIEÆ**
GENUS *Gelidium*

G. corneum. Frond flat and horny, one inch to four inches high, narrow, erect, branched several times in the same plane; ultimate branchlets club-shaped, or swollen at the tips with masses of spores; color purple-red. It grows in tufts on mud-covered rocks, and on algæ at low-water mark. The typical form is found in Florida and on the Pacific coast. Smaller plants are found all along the Atlantic shore. It is an extremely variable plant, and is often difficult to distinguish on this account. (Plate XVII.)

ORDER **GIGARTINACEÆ**
GENUS *Chondrus*

Carrageen or Irish moss.

C. crispus. Frond begins with flattened stem, which divides and subdivides many times in a broad-forked, fan-like manner; varies greatly in length and breadth of divisions, also in size and color, according to conditions of its habitation. In shallow tide-pools it is pale and

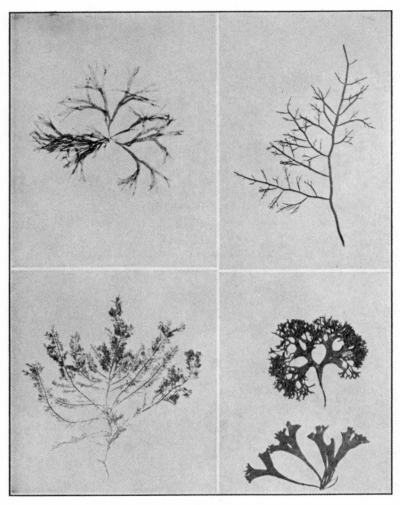

PLATE XVII.

Scinaia furcellata.
Gelidium Coulteri.

Gelidium corneum.
Chondrus crispus.

PLATE XVIII.

Gigartina mamillosa.
Gigartina spinosa.

Gigartina radula.
Gigartina microphylla.

stunted; but under the shelter of rocks, in deep water, it grows in dense masses and is a dark purplish-red or reddish-green. Often it appears iridescent when seen through the water, with the sun shining on it. It is firm and leathery in substance. It is an edible alga, and was formerly very generally used for culinary purposes. At Hingham, Massachusetts, large quantities are gathered as an article of commerce. It is a beautiful and very common plant found from New York northward. (Plate XVII.)

Genus *Gigartina*

Of the species of this genus but one is found on the eastern coast; on the Pacific coast there are several, and they are large and conspicuous.

G. mamillosa. Frond three to six inches high, one inch to two inches broad, flat, leathery, gelatinous; forking near the base, then dividing and subdividing in the same plane; segments more or less wedge-shaped and with a tendency to roll inward; covered with numerous small nipple-like protuberances which contain the spores. These projections distinguish this genus from *Chondrus*, which it otherwise resembles, and with which it grows. The color is dark purple. It is found from Boston northward. (Plate XVIII.)

G. radula. Frond flat and thick; rising from a short stem and widening to several inches; sometimes tapering to the top, sometimes blunt or divided, sometimes cleft on the sides, but usually simple; covered with wart-like projections; color dark, livid red. It is found on the Pacific coast at all seasons, growing on rocks between tide-marks. Large specimens are one foot to three feet long and six to ten inches wide. (Plate XVIII.)

G. spinosa ("thorny"). Frond thick, leathery; surface rough and spiny; form variable, the divisions sometimes emanating from a broad, flattened base, or again branching from a main axis; all covered with the protruding processes peculiar to the genus; color dark red, brown, or purple. It is found on the California coast. (Plate XVIII.)

G. microphylla ("small-leaved"). Plant rises from short, flat stem, and rapidly expands into a flat, wide, thin frond which is simple or divided into two or three segments, each of which tapers into a long, pointed apex; thickly covered with long, slender spines, and on its edges bearing small, thin leaflets; color brownish-red. It is abundant on the California coast. (Plate XVIII.)

Genus *Phyllophora*

Leafweed. Fronds cylindrical; branched stalks which expand into rigid, membranaceous, simple or cleft, wedge-shaped laminæ; laminæ bear leaflets on their edges or on their surface; spores in masses form projections on the surface, or are on stalks at the summit; color dark red. Found washed ashore from New York northward.

P. membranifolia. Several stems rise from same disk; branches expand into wedge-shaped, cleft or forked laminæ; lobes bear on the summit other laminæ or leaflets divided in the same manner.

P. Brodiæi. Stem less branched and leaf-expansions broader and larger than in *P. membranifolia;* laminæ wedge-shaped and deeply lobed. (Plate XIX.)

Genus *Sternogramme*

S. interrupta. Frond a thin membrane repeatedly forked, widely spreading, divisions one fourth to one half of an inch wide; fertile plants have the spores arranged in an interrupted line through the center of the segments resembling a midrib; frond two to eight inches high; bright red. It is found on the California coast. The illustration shows a plant on which the hydroid *Sertularia pumila* is growing. (Plate XIX.)

Genus *Gymnogongrus*

G. Norvegicus. Frond two to four inches high, thin but leathery in substance, flat, narrow, divided in a regular forking manner; spreading ends of terminal forks obtuse; axils rounded; spores form spherical masses in the upper segments, and project on both sides like hemispheres. It resembles a simple form of *Chondrus crispus*, but is more delicate. The color is red or purple. This species is found in deep tide-pools from New York northward. (Plate XIX.)

Genus *Ahnfeldtia*

A. plicata. Frond coarse, stem-like filaments, stiff, wiry, irregularly and profusely branched; sometimes regularly forked and upper segments equal; entangled; six to eight inches long; tufts several inches in diameter; dark purple or black. Specimens long exposed on the beach are faded to white. It is very common from New York northward. (Plate XIX.)

Genus *Callophyllis*

C. variegata. Deeply cleft, wide-spreading, flat, membranaceous frond; all parts notched more or less angularly; color dark to bright red; spores form hemispherical warts on surface. Some varieties differ from this one in having long and narrow, and others in having short and broad segments. It is a beautiful and common alga on the Pacific coast, resembling *Euthora* of the eastern coast. (Plate XX.)

C. laciniata. Frond deeply cleft; segments wedge-shaped. It is found on the Pacific coast. (Plate XX.)

Genus *Iridæa*

Frond rises from stalk and widens into a flat, thick, leathery, oval expansion, one to two feet long, and one to three inches broad;

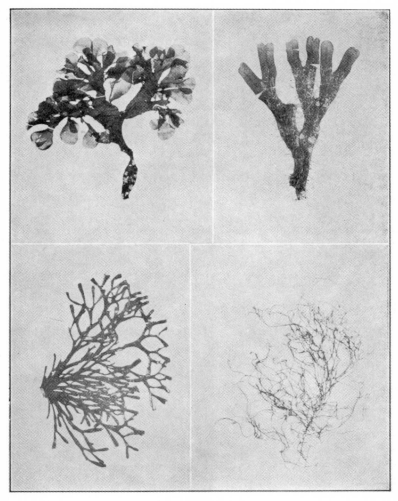

PLATE XIX.

Phyllophora Brodiæi.   Sternogramme interrupta.
Gymnogongrus Norvegicus.   Ahnfeldtia plicata.

PLATE XX.

Callophyllis variegata.　　　　Callophyllis laciniata.
Iridæa.　　　　　　　　　　　Cystoclonium cirrhosa.

simple or lobed; surface sometimes roughened by collections of spores in dots; dark red, often glittering in the water with blue and purple tints. It is found on the Pacific coast. (Plate **XX**.)

SUBORDER **RHODOPHYLLIDEÆ**

GENUS *Cystoclonium*

C. purpurascens. The translucent, fleshy, juicy main stem, one eighth of an inch or less in diameter, runs through the whole plant; irregularly branched all around main stem; branches again branch in same manner; branches attenuated at the base, and taper to a long point; smaller branches distended in places by spores into bladder-like swellings, hence the name; color rose-red to dark purple; plants exposed on the beach often faded to orange and white; six to eighteen inches long. It grows on rocks between tide-marks as well as in deep water. With the exception of *Ceramium rubrum*, this is the most common red alga on the eastern coast from New York northward. It differs from *Rhabdonia* in having bladdery branches; otherwise it is easily mistaken for it.

C. cirrhosa. Ends of branches terminate in spirals like tendrils; otherwise identical with *C. purpurascens.* (Plate **XX**.)

GENUS *Euthora*

E. cristata. Frond one inch to five inches high, membranaceous, broadly spreading; divisions wide and numerous, ultimately becoming fine like minute branchlets, each one of which, under a glass, shows a notch in the tip. This beautiful, bright-red alga is found in abundance north of Cape Cod. It differs from *Delesseria alata* in having no midrib or veins. It grows in deep water on stones, shells, and algæ. (Plate **XXI**.)

GENUS *Rhodophyllis*

("Rosy leaf")

R. veprecula. Frond two to five inches long, one fourth of an inch to one and one half inches broad, membranaceous, forked; margin covered with leaflets which are in turn edged with minute branchlets; color deep red. It is found on the northern New England coast. (Plate **XXI**.)

GENUS *Rhabdonia*

("A wand")

R. tenera. Frond six to eighteen inches long, cylindrical, fleshy, translucent, juicy; irregularly and profusely branched, branches longest at the base, erect, tapering at both ends, numerous branchlets; sometimes the main stem runs through the plant, sometimes it is lost in the branching; spore-masses sometimes form knotty bunches on the side of branches. It resembles a large *Cystoclonium purpurascens*. It is characteristic of Long Island Sound, and is not found north of Cape Cod, but common from there southward along the whole Atlantic coast. (Plate XXI.)

R. Coulteri. This species is common on the Pacific coast, and differs from *R. tenera* in having a more pronounced leading stem, and branches shorter and crowded at the top of the frond.

Genus *Eucheuma*

E. isiforme. Frond grows in tufts a foot or more in diameter; stems branch in all directions from a central point, and taper gradually to the end; secondary branches spread to all sides; all branches swollen at intervals and armed with several spines spreading from a conical base; color dark red, becoming on exposure orange or yellow, and at length semi-transparent and horn-like; substance firmly cartilaginous. Abundant at Key West.

ORDER **RHODYMENIACEÆ**

Suborder **SPHÆROCOCCEÆ**

Genus *Gracilaria*

G. multipartita ("many times divided"). Frond four to twelve inches long; starting from a short, cylindrical stem, it flattens and broadens as it rises, dividing in an irregular, forking manner, or cleft into palmate segments which broaden as they rise, and which divide in the same manner; often cleft or branched on the edges; conical spore-masses scattered over the frond during July and August; dingy purple in color. The plant is variable and sometimes is difficult to determine. It is common from Cape Cod southward. A narrow variety is most abundant in Long Island Sound. In Florida and on the California coast there are broad varieties which may be mistaken for *Rhodymenia*. (Plate XXI.)

Genus *Hypnea*

H. musciformis ("moss-like"). Frond six to twelve inches long; main stem running through, thick below and tapering to the size of a bristle; much and irregularly branched, especially at the base; branches wide-spreading in every direction, and longest at the base; branches branch again in the same manner; all parts beset with short, horizontal spines; color purplish-red. A characteristic feature, by which the plant can easily be distinguished, is that the ends of the long branches are naked and are turned over like a hook, or nearly twisted. It is found washed ashore, often in large, intricately twisted tufts, from Cape Cod southward and on the Pacific coast.

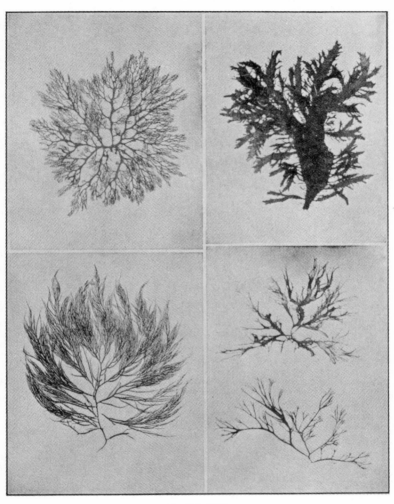

PLATE XXI.

Euthora cristata.   Rhodophyllis veprecula.
Rhabdonia tenera.   Gracilaria multipartita.

PLATE XXII.

Rhodymenia palmata.   Rhodymenia palmata.
Lomentaria Baileyana.   Chylocladia articulata.

GENUS *Rhodymenia*
(" Red membrane")

R. palmata ("hand-shaped"). The plant commonly known as dulse. Frond rises from a disk in a short cylindrical stem which spreads into a thin, broad, fan-shaped membrane six to twelve inches long and four to eight inches wide at the top; deeply and irregularly cleft into many wedge-shaped segments; margin usually entire, but often with leaflets; ends of segments indented, showing where divisions will ultimately occur; color dark purplish-red. It grows on rocks and on algæ below low-water mark, and is common on the New England and California coasts. This is an edible alga, and, like *Chondrus crispus*, is an article of food in seaports. (Plate XXII.)

GENUS *Lomentaria*

L. Baileyana. Fronds two to five inches high; grows in tufts; filaments tubular, irregularly branched; branchlets often all on one side; branches and branchlets curved or arched, and tapered at both ends; color brownish-red. It is found washed ashore from Cape Cod southward. (Plate XXII.)

GENUS *Champia*

C. parvula. Frond two to six inches long, irregularly branched; grows in tufts; filaments hollow and constricted, so that they appear somewhat like a string of beads; color brownish-purple. It is found washed ashore from Cape Cod southward. (Plate XXIII.)

GENUS *Chylocladia*

C. articulata. Frond filamentous, three to twelve inches long, hollow, constricted at intervals; branches emanate from constricted joints; has the appearance of a series of pink, delicate, oval sacs. (Plate XXII.)

GENUS *Plocamium*

P. coccineum ("scarlet"). Frond a flat, semi-cartilaginous main stem one eighth of an inch, or less, wide, three to eight inches long, with alternate branches of unequal length emanating from the edges; branches have alternate branchlets arranged in groups of three or four in a row; branchlets have pinnulæ on the upper side, like the teeth of a comb (this peculiarity in branching makes the genus easy to identify); color dark lake-red. It is not found on the eastern coast, but is plentiful in California. (Plate XXIII.)

GENUS *Nitophyllum*

N. laceratum. Frond expands from narrow base and divides almost at once into long, narrow, strap-shaped segments; minute leaflets, showing a dot or spore-cluster, occur at intervals on the margin; plant six to eight inches long; thin and silky in texture. Abundant on the California coast. (Plate XXIII.)

N. Ruprechteanum. Frond one foot to two feet long, spreading from narrow base and dividing by forking into deep-cut, broad, straplike lobes; top divisions rounded; traversed lengthwise by parallel veins; margin of the older parts bordered with a narrow frill of thin ruffled membrane which sometimes extends also over parts of the surface of the frond; substance somewhat rigid; color dark red to purple. It is found on the California coast. (Plate XXIV.)

N. punctatum. Frond six to twenty inches long and of the same width, dividing in a forking manner; crowded at top; when in fruit, covered with dark dots; substance thin and silky; color rose-pink. It is found on the California coast. (Plate XXIV.)

Genus *Grinnellia*

(Named for Mr. Henry Grinnell of New York)

G. Americana. Frond a delicate membrane, rose-red or purplish in color, leaf-shaped, four to eight inches long, one inch to four inches wide, tapering at both ends; margin entire, but much waved; a line of darker color through the center resembles a midrib; masses of spores form dots or specks irregularly over the whole surface; grows from a disk and short slender stem in bunches on shells and stones in deep water. It is found washed ashore from Cape Cod southward, and is luxuriant in New York Bay, where it can be found at any season, but is in perfection in August. (Plate XXIV.)

Genus *Delesseria*

D. sinuosa. Delicate, leaf-like membrane. with midrib and veins, much indented and resembling in general outline an oak-leaf; four to eight inches long, two to four inches broad; short stem; color dark red, often flecked with green. It grows in bunches in deep water, and is easily distinguished, since it is the only alga having a midrib and veins, and resembling the leaf of a tree. It is found washed ashore from Cape Cod northward. (Plate XXIV.)

D. alata ("winged"). Frond rises from short stem, which flattens and divides irregularly into many branches and appears like a midrib, all bordered with narrow membrane one eighth of an inch to one inch wide; frond two to four inches long; color light red or pink. It is found on the shore from Cape Cod northward. (Plate XXV.)

D. Leprieurii. Frond one inch to two inches long, very narrow, with delicate midrib, forked, constricted at intervals; branches start from constricted points; thin and delicate; color purple. It is found in tidal rivers near New York, and is common on the southern coast. (Plate XXV.)

Suborder **RHODOMELEÆ**

The genera included in this suborder are easily distinguished when in fruit by the spore-cases, or cystocarps, which appear

PLATE XXIII.

Champia parvula.
Plocamium coccineum.

Champia parvula, magnified.
Nitophyllum laceratum.

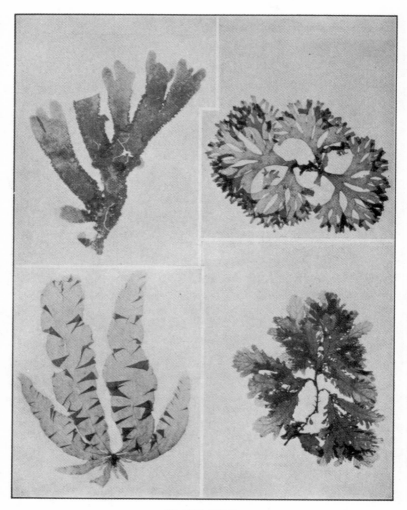

PLATE XXIV.

Nitophyllum Ruprechteanum.   Nitophyllum punctatum.
Grinnellia americana.   Delesseria sinuosa.

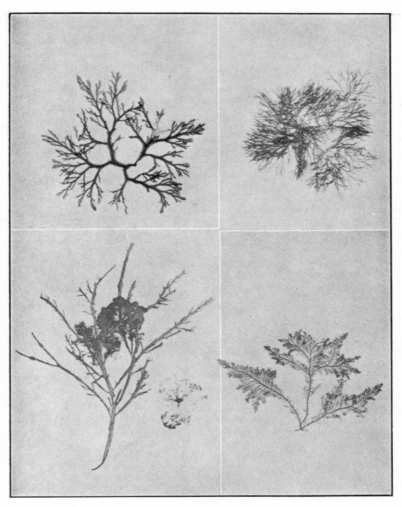

PLATE XXV.

Delesseria alata.
Polysiphonia fastigiata (on Ascophyllum).

Delesseria Leprieurii.
Polysiphonia parasitica.

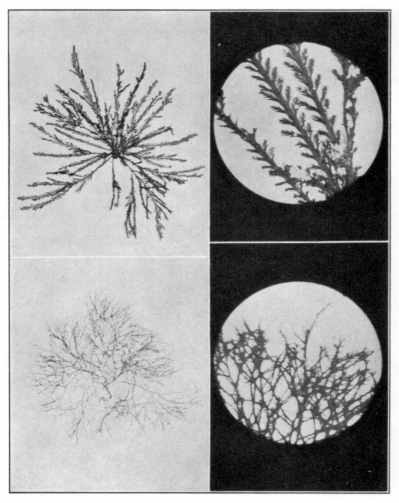

PLATE XXVI.

Polysiphonia dendroidea.　　　　Polysiphonia dendroidea, a piece magnified.
Polysiphonia Harveyi.　　　　　Polysiphonia Harveyi, a piece magnified.

like little balls, either adherent to the branches, or raised on short stalks. It is the largest group, and contains many of the most beautiful of the red algæ.

GENUS *Polysiphonia*

(" Many tubes ")

A filament of *Polysiphonia* appears, when seen under the microscope, like a bundle of filaments made up of a central tube, or axis, surrounded by a number of other tubes. It is by the number of these parts, called siphons, which vary in number from four to twenty, that the species is determined. In some plants the siphons are surrounded by a layer of cells, called corticating or bark cells, which give the filaments a solid, uniform appearance. In others the siphons are naked, and the filaments then seem striped or banded with color. It is difficult, without a microscope, to be sure of the classification. There are, however, other characteristics which separate many of the species, and some of these are described below. Two hundred species of *Polysiphonia* have been named by algologists. The plants are plentiful on all shores, especially in warm, shallow waters. Some species are perennial, but most of them are annuals and disappear in winter.

P. fastigiata. This species grows on *Ascophyllum nodosum* in a globular tuft, and appears like a dark-brown ball, one inch to three inches in diameter. The frond is a dense mass of rigid filaments branching many times in a forking manner and at broad angles. The ends are of nearly equal length, giving the plant a spherical shape. It is common from New York northward at all seasons, and is easily recognized by its general form and place of growth. Egg-shaped cystocarps, or spore-cases, occur in the ends of the terminal filaments. (Plate XXV.)

P. nigrescens. Frond three to twelve inches long, rigid below, soft above; main stem thick as a bristle, but not always easy to distinguish; branches alternate and densely branched at the ends; siphons twelve to sixteen in number; filaments banded; color black or very dark brown. (Plate XXVII.)

P. parasitica. Frond one inch to three inches long; branched in a pinnate or feather-like manner; filaments flat; all branches and branchlets emanating from the edges and on the same plane, giving a flat frond; color reddish-brown; resembles a fine *Ptilota plumosa;* cystocarps on short stalks. It is found on the California coast. (Plate XXV.)

P. dendroidea. This is a variety of the species *P. parasitica.* Frond four to five inches long; main branches placed at irregular intervals, but the secondary branches at regular intervals and alternate; branches set at acute angles, giving the plant a slender appearance; color black or dark brown. It is common on the California coast. (Plate XXVI.)

P. Baileyi. Frond three to six inches high, flat; branches emanate from edges of the flat stems; main branches wide-spreading and irregularly placed, secondary branches regular and alternate; branchlets one eighth to one half of an inch long, covered on the edges and around the top with incurved ramuli; branchlets broken off near the base of the branches in mature plants; branchlets usually uniform in length, but occasionally one is longer and branches like the primary stem; color black. Common on the California coast.

P. Harveyi. Frond two to six inches high; grows in globose tufts, and has a bushy aspect; branches stiff and wide-spreading; stems and branches beset with simple or branched spine-like branchlets; color dark brown, or black when dry; does not collapse when taken from the water; cystocarps on short stalks; siphons four in number. It grows on eel-grass and algæ, and is common in Long Island Sound and northward. (Plate XXVI.)

P. Olneyi (dough-balls). Fronds two to five inches high, densely tufted; soft filaments of hair-like fineness, much branched, and spreading; when in fruit covered with tiny balls or cystocarps; siphons four in number. It is common from Cape Cod to New York.

P. fibrillosa. Frond four to ten inches high, rather robust below; main stem quickly lost in a number of prominent stems and spreading branches; irregularly and profusely branched, becoming ultimately very fine; numerous branchlets covered with colorless fibrils in hairy tufts, which give it a misty appearance; fibrils so delicate that they do not show well in dried specimens, but a distinct feature by which to recognize the species in the young plant; color light to dark brown; cystocarps adherent to branchlets or on short stalks; siphons four in number; main branches only corticated. It is common in summer on stones and on eel-grass, at low-water mark, from Cape Cod to New York. (Plate XXVII.)

P. violacea. Fronds six to twenty-four inches high, pyramidal in general outline; main axis with long, wide-spreading branches at the base; branches rather robust and naked below, but numerous and becoming very fine and tufted at top; cystocarps adherent or on short stalks; siphons four in number; main stems corticated; ultimate branchlets show articulations; color brownish-red. It is common from New York northward. (Plate XXVII.)

P. urceolata. Frond three to ten inches high; main stem bristle-like; branches naked below, divided and subdivided above; branches with short branchlets set at a wide angle and often recurved; siphons four in number; shows articulations; color deep red. Name refers to cystocarp, which resembles a pitcher. The plant grows in loose tufts, and is common from New York northward and on the California coast.

Variety *formosa.* Filaments soft and finer than in *P. urceolata;* branches long and flexuous; articulations five to ten times longer than broad; color bright red. It grows in tufts sometimes a foot long, and is found only in the spring.

P. variegata. Fronds four to ten inches high; filaments thick as a bristle below, and branched in a forking manner to the very top; divided at long intervals below, at the top becoming of hair-like fineness

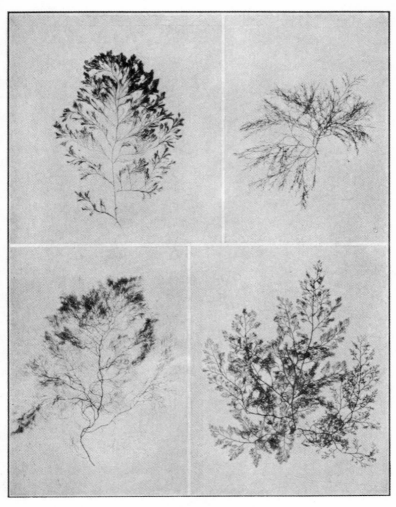

PLATE XXVII.

Polysiphonia nigrescens.   Polysiphonia fibrillosa.
Polysiphonia violacea.   Polysiphonia Woodii.

PLATE XXVIII.

Laurencia pinnatifida.   Dasya elegans.
Dasya plumosa.   Dasya plumosa, magnified.

and dividing rapidly, forming a densely tufted mass, which collapses when taken from the water; color purple-brown; when mounted, silky in appearance; filaments banded; siphons six in number. It forms purple tufts on woodwork and on eel-grass from Cape Cod southward.

P. Woodii. Fronds four to six inches high; branches flat, long, wide-spreading, emanating from the edges in one plane; younger branches show articulations; ultimate branchlets inclined to curve inward; color light brown. Found on the California coast. (Plate XXVII.)

GENUS *Laurencia*

L. pinnatifida. Frond flat, thick, leathery; main stem with opposite, or alternate, branches of about the same size and character as itself; all pinnatifid, or cut on the edges into branchlets, some of which are again divided; color bright purple, often unevenly faded. It is found on the Pacific coast. (Plate XXVIII.)

GENUS *Dasya*

Chenille-weed.

D. elegans. Fronds from six inches to three yards long; main stem and branches cylindrical, and all densely clothed with a fine, hair-like fringe, which gives the plant the appearance of chenille; cystocarps on stalks along the branches; color pink or lake-red. Out of water it seems like a mass of purple jelly. It is found at or just below low-water mark from Cape Cod southward, and is very plentiful in New York Bay. (Plate XXVIII.)

D. plumosa. A species found on the California coast. The fringe covering the stems consists of minute leaflets instead of hairs, as in *D. elegans.* (Plate XXVIII.)

GENUS *Bostrychia*

B. rivularis. Fronds one inch high; color dark purple; branches fine and irregularly bent. It grows where the water is not very salt, and is found in patches on submerged logs near New York. Common from Charleston, South Carolina, southward. (Plate XXIX.)

GENUS *Rhodomela*

R. subfusca. Frond six to eighteen inches long; main stem cylindrical, and branching widely on all sides; branches longest at base and gradually shortening to the top of the stem; branches naked below, but at the ends profusely branched, forming tufts of branchlets. It is a perennial plant, and changes in aspect with the season. When mature it is stiff and coarse, and when dry it is quite black. Common from New York northward.

R. Rochei. This species resembles in form *R. subfusca,* but is much finer and more delicate. In spring it is a soft, fine, feathery, and beautiful alga of a red-brown color. It is found washed ashore, or in deep tide-pools, south of Cape Cod. (Plate XXIX.)

R. larix. Frond cylindrical, robust, six to fourteen inches high; branches of unequal length standing out horizontally all around the main stem; clusters of branchlets growing spirally around stem and branches. Found on the northern California coast. (Plate XXIX.)

R. floccosa. Frond four to ten inches high; less robust than *R. larix ;* stem and branches flat and divided in one plane; branches alternate; ultimate branchlets somewhat incurved; color black. In fertile plants the terminal branchlets are gathered in a mass. Found on the California coast. (Plate XXIX.)

Genus *Chondria*

Plants of this genus are distinguished by having the ultimate branches attenuated at the base.

C. dasyphylla. Frond four to eight inches high; general outline pyramidal; branches alternate on main stem; stem and branches covered with short, club-shaped (blunt at top, attenuated at base) branchlets; cystocarps, or spore-cases, adherent to branchlets or on short stalks; color light or dull brown. It grows in tufts, and is common from New York to Cape Cod. (Plate XXX.)

C. tenuissima. This species is similar to *C. dasyphylla*, but is more slender, and the branchlets taper at both ends instead of being club-shaped.

C. striolata. A species similar to *C. tenuissima.* The branchlets bear secondary branchlets, and the cystocarps are on short stalks. It is plentiful in Long Island Sound.

Suborder CERAMIEÆ

Genus *Callithamnion*

These are very beautiful and delicate plants, growing in small, soft, silky tufts, bright red in color, with darker dots along the much-branched filaments. There are many species, and they are common on the northern shores of both oceans; but the different species are not easy to distinguish with the naked eye, and so but a few of them are described below. The special characteristics by which the genus may be recognized are: fronds filamentous, of cobweb fineness, one inch to six inches long, much branched, and closely crowded at the top; brilliant red color.

C. americanum. Frond three to six inches long, densely tufted; filaments of extreme fineness; main branches alternate; much branched; main and secondary branches have pairs of branched ramuli along the

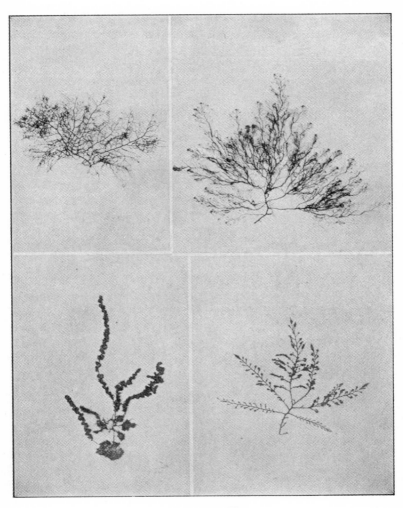

PLATE XXIX.

Bostrychia rivularis.
Rhodomela larix.

Rhodomela Rochei.
Rhodomela floccosa.

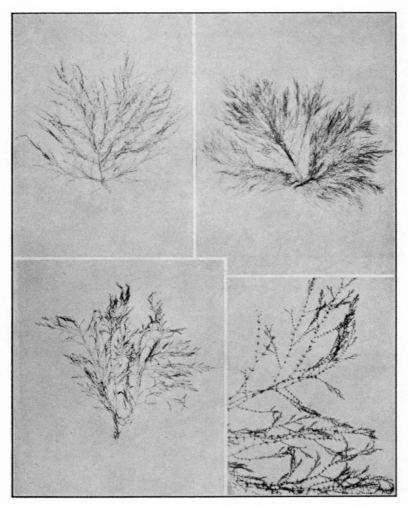

PLATE XXX.

Chondria dasyphylla.
Callithamnion Pylaisæi.

Callithamnion americanum.
Callithamnion Pylaisæi, a piece magnified.

branches; color rose-pink. It grows on wharves and on algæ below low-water mark, and is a common and beautiful species. It is found (but only in the spring) from New York northward, and is abundant in Long Island Sound. (Plates XXX, XXXI.)

C. Pylaisæi. Fronds three to six inches long, more robust and darker in color than in *C. Americanum;* main and secondary branches alternate, decompound, all bearing at short intervals short opposite branchlets, which in turn are covered with ramuli. It is found in spring on wharves and on algæ from Boston northward. (Plate XXX.)

C. Baileyi. Fronds one inch to three inches long, with main stem as thick as a bristle, and running to the top of the frond; branches around the main stem longer at the base than at the apex, giving the plant a pyramidal outline; branches also have a main stem and short branches beset with branchlets; shrub-like in aspect; color purplish-red. Common in summer from New York to Cape Cod.

C. seirospermum. Frond two to five inches high, pyramidal in out-line; has main stem and alternate lateral branches; branches have secondary branches beset with delicate, erect branchlets; hair-like in fineness. It is common from Cape Cod southward, and is plentiful in Long Island Sound. (Plate XXXI.)

C. byssoideum. Fronds one inch to three inches long; filaments very delicate; main branches many times divided; secondary branches long; many branchlets; rose-colored. It grows in globose tufts, and is common in Long Island Sound. (Plate XXXI.)

C. floccosum. Fronds three to six inches long, hair-like in fineness; flaccid; main branches sparingly branched below; numerous alternate branches above; all clothed with short, simple branchlets; color dark brownish-red. The plant is so exceedingly fine that it is difficult to dis-tinguish the divisions. It grows on eel-grass and on algæ below low-water mark, and is found from New York to Cape Cod. (Plate XXXI.)

GENUS *Griffithsia*

(Named for Mrs. Griffiths, an English algologist)

These are among the most beautiful of seaweeds, because of their brilliant color and exceedingly delicate structure. They grow in deep water, and specimens cast ashore are usually torn and imperfect, but they may often be gathered from deep tide-pools, and sometimes are found growing on eel-grass. If placed in fresh water they discharge their coloring-matter and quickly decompose.

G. Bornetiana. Fronds two to five inches high; filaments jointed, the divisions being long and pear-shaped, growing shorter as they near the top; repeatedly forked; very soft and fragile. It grows in tufts, resembling corals; attains perfection in July, and disappears later in the summer. Found from Cape Cod southward, washed ashore after storms. (Plate XXXII.)

Genus *Ptilota*

Feather-weed.

P. serrata. Fronds three to six inches long, dark red in color, cartilaginous; flattened main stem with opposite, flattened branches, one of which is minute, so that it appears like alternate branching; branches also have lateral branchlets and pinnulæ, looking like feathers or ferns; all branching in one plane, making a flat frond. It is found in the drift on the beach after a storm, and is common from Cape Cod northward, and also on the California coast. (Plate XXXII.)

P. elegans. Narrower and more delicate than *P. serrata*, otherwise it has the same essential features. It is common in summer from New York northward, growing on cliffs, under *Fucus*, near low-water mark, and it is also found washed upon the beach. (Plate XXXII.)

P. densa. Frond three to twelve inches high, one eighth of an inch wide, flat, cartilaginous; has leading stem with flat alternate branches; branches simple or branched again; edges of whole plant beset with notched, curved pinnulæ alternating with smaller feather-like pinnulæ, giving a dense edge to all parts of the frond. It is found on the California coast. (Plate XXXIII.)

P. hypnoides. Flat, cartilaginous main stem, much branched, and all beset with pinnulæ. It differs from *P. densa* in having the alternate pinnulæ straight and club-shaped, instead of toothed and curved, and the plant is not so dense and compact. Found on the California coast. (Plate XXXIII.)

Genus *Spyridia*

S. filamentosa. Fronds four to eight inches long; filaments as thick as bristles, irregularly and repeatedly branched; young branches show articulations and seem to be striped; all branches clothed with short, very delicate, transparent filaments, which give the plant a hazy appearance; color purplish-red, which becomes brown when dried; does not collapse when taken from the water. It grows in tufts below low-water mark, and is found in the drift on the beach from Cape Cod southward. (Plate XXXIII.)

Genus *Ceramium*

The pitcher-weed. This genus is easily recognized by the ends of the filaments, which are forked and incurved, resembling minute pincers or claws. The filaments are also more or less distinctly banded. It is widely distributed.

C. rubrum, red ceramium. This is a very common and robust species, found everywhere, and growing on everything. It is variable in appearance, becoming quite coarse when old, the incurving, claw-like ends, which are characteristic of the genus, being less pronounced. It branches by repeated forking, and, under the microscope, shows a bark-

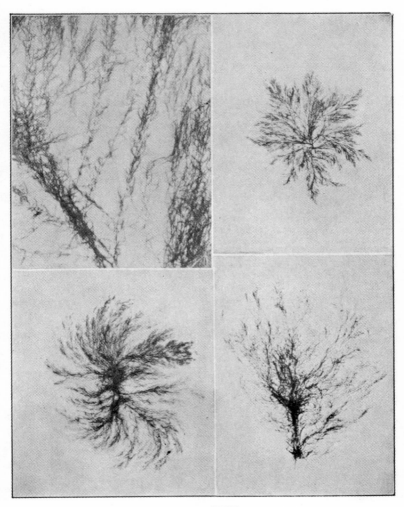

PLATE XXXI.

Callithamnion americanum, a piece
   magnified.
Callithamnion byssoideum, var.
   fastigiatum.

Callithamnion seirospermum.
Callithamnion floccosum.

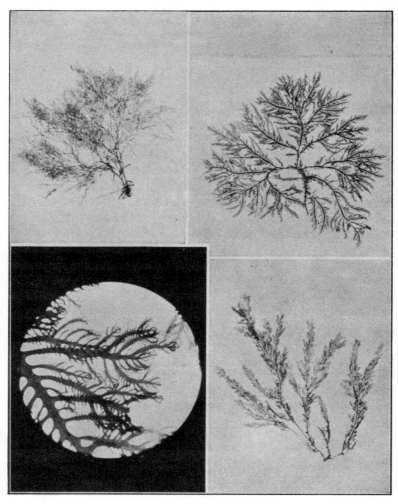

PLATE XXXII.

Griffithsia Bornetiana.   Ptilota serrata.
Ptilota serrata, magnified.   Ptilota elegans.

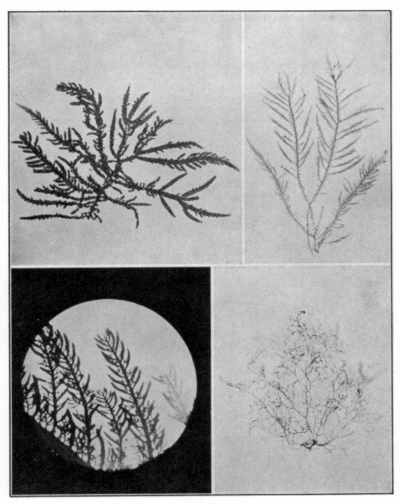

PLATE XXXIII.

Ptilota densa.
Ptilota hypnoides, magnified.

Ptilota hypnoides.
Spyridia filamentosa.

PLATE XXXIV.

Ceramium rubrum, var. proliferum.   Ceramium rubrum, top of frond magnified.
Ceramium diaphanum.   Ceramium tenuissimum, var. patentissimum.

like layer of cells over the whole surface, which make the ring-like bands on the filaments less conspicuous.

Variety *proliferum.* Fronds beset on all sides with simple or forked branchlets. (Plate XXXIV.)

Variety *secundatum.* Branchlets generally arranged on one side of the filaments, or secund.

C. strictum ("straight"). Brown or purplish-red filaments of hair-like fineness, growing in tufts two to six inches high, branching in narrow forks more and more closely as they reach the top of the frond. There are no principal branches, the filaments being of about the same diameter and regularly dividing in a forking manner throughout. The filaments are banded, the red rings being relatively very narrow. The white interstices at the base are several times longer than broad, but shorten gradually until at the top they are of equal length with the red bands. This species is common from Cape Cod to New York.

C. diaphanum. This species has comparatively stout leading branches, with secondary alternate branches which are finer than the main stems and divide in a forking manner throughout, and ultimately become very fine. The color is brown or purplish-red, distinctly banded. It grows on eel-grass and algæ, and is found from Cape Cod to New York. (Plate XXXIV.)

C. fastigiatum. Filaments of hair-like fineness and of about same size throughout; branched in regular forking manner throughout, the divisions being wide and distant at the base, but gradually becoming closer and narrower as they reach the top; the upper segments about equal, giving a level top and regular outline in mounted specimens; the terminal forks erect, or less incurved than in other species; small points or branchlets emanate from some of the nodes or joints between the bands of color; tufts globe-shaped, two to five inches high; color lake-red. This species grows on mud-flats and mud-covered rocks as well as on algæ and eel-grass.

C. tenuissimum. Fronds two to four inches high, densely tufted; the forked divisions very wide or open; color rose-pink.

Variety *patentissimum.* Fronds small; the forked divisions distant and very wide open. A mounted specimen appears somewhat like network. The species is common in Long Island Sound. (Plate XXXIV.)

Genus *Microcladia*

M. Coulteri. Cylindrical, slightly flattened main stem; branches set uniformly and alternately, short at the base, gradually lengthening as far as the center, and from there diminishing to the apex of the stem, giving a leaf-like outline. The same mode of branching and the same outline are repeated in the branches. The ultimate divisions are like forked divisions, and are somewhat incurved. The plant is six to eight inches high, and in color is of many shades of red and pink. It is found in abundance on the Pacific coast at all seasons. (Plate XXXV.)

M. borealis. Branches and branchlets placed on one side of arched main stems; secondary branches curved in opposite direction and bearing branchlets, also divided on one side only; color dark brown. It is found on the northern Pacific coast. (Plate XXXV.)

ORDER **CRYPTONEMIACEÆ**

Suborder **GLOIOSIPHONIEÆ**

Genus *Gloiosiphonia*

(" Viscid tube")

G. capillaris. Frond six to ten inches high, solitary or in tufts; main stem cylindrical, solid above, hollow below; from about an inch above the base densely beset with short, wide-spreading branches arranged evenly and all around the stem; branches again branched in the same way; branches and branchlets attenuated at base and apex; soft, tender, juicy; shrinks much in drying. The species is easily recognized by its delicate gelatinous substance, tapering branchlets, and brilliant red color. It is found in early summer in tide-pools on the New England coast.

Suborder **GRATELOUPIEÆ**

Genus *Halymenia*

H. ligulata. Frond membranaceous, repeatedly and regularly divided in a forking manner; the larger divisions one half of an inch wide and growing very narrow at the top; four to five inches high, spreading in a fan-shape; color rose-red. It is found at Key West.

Genus *Grateloupia*

G. Cutleria. Frond coarse, flat, variable; either simple, long, and narrow, or short and broad, tapering at both ends, or blunt at the apex, or deeply cleft into many segments; sometimes with leaflets along the edges; height two to three feet; color reddish-brown; in fading, changes to purple and green, and may be variegated. When simple, the plant resembles *Iridæa.* Found on the northern California coast.

Genus *Prionitis*

P. lanceolata. Frond narrow, flat, smooth; leathery stems, which branch irregularly and sparingly from the edges; branches bordered with lance-shaped leaflets; color dark brownish-red; plant ten or more inches high, and varies considerably. (Plate XXXV.)

There are other species, among them **P. Andersonii** (Plate XXXVI); all are easily distinguished by the lance-shaped leaflets. Common on the Pacific coast.

Suborder **DUMONTIEÆ**

Genus *Pikea*

P. Californica. Divisions of frond thick, narrow, cartilaginous; central axis one eighth of an inch to one inch wide, three to four inches high, thickly set with similar branches irregularly placed; all bordered

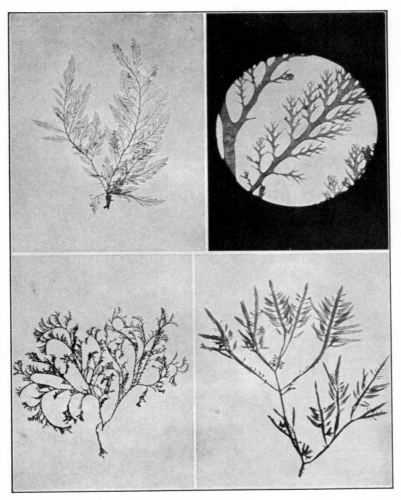

PLATE XXXV.

Microcladia Coulteri.
Microcladia borealis.

Microcladia Coulteri, magnified.
Prionitis lanceolata.

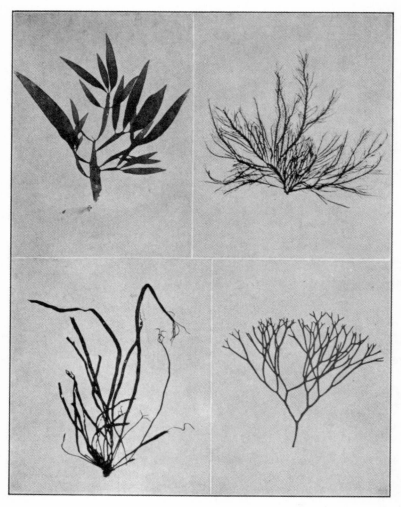

PLATE XXXVI.

Prionitis Andersonii.　　　　　　Pikea Californica.
Halosaccion ramentaceum.　　　　Polyides rotundus.

with numerous forward-pointing branchlets, which in turn have spine-like ramuli of various lengths; frond flat, broadly spreading; dark red. It is common at all seasons on the California coast. (Plate XXXVI.)

Genus *Halosaccion*

H. ramentaceum. Fronds brownish-purple, six to fourteen inches long, coarse and cartilaginous, cylindrical, hollow, compressed, attenuated at the base; more or less covered with simple or forked hollow branches half the size of the main stem. In exposed pools the plants are short and densely branched; in sheltered places they are larger and more delicate in texture. They are common on the northern New England and northern California coasts. (Plate XXXVI.)

SUBORDER RHIZOPHYLLIDEÆ

Genus *Polyides*

P. rotundus. Frond three to six inches high, cylindrical, cartilaginous, repeatedly forked, ends obtuse; spore-masses form numerous lighter-colored excrescences on the upper divisions of the frond; dark red. Common from New York northward, in deep pools and washed ashore. (Plate XXXVI.)

SUBORDER SQUAMARIEÆ

Genus *Peyssonnelia*

P. Dubyi. Frond completely adherent to the rock or stone on which it grows; color dark purple; somewhat calcareous; redder and thicker than next species. It is found at low-water mark or in deep water on the northern New England and northern California coasts.

Genus *Petrocelis*

P. cruenta. Frond closely adherent, forming dark-purple velvety patches of indefinite outline on rocks and stones. Common north of Cape Cod.

Genus *Hildenbrandtia*

H. rosea. Forms continuous pink incrustations of considerable extent on stones and rocks at low-water mark. Common everywhere.

SUBORDER CORALLINEÆ

The genera of this suborder are characterized by a calcareous or stony incrustation of the fronds, which gives them the appearance of corals. Most of the species are tropical.

Genus *Corallina*

(" Coral-like ")

C. officinalis, common coralline. Frond grows from a disk in tufts more or less dense. The plant is rigid, and seems like jointed, branched coral. The articulations are cylindrical at the base, wedge-shaped and flattened above. Branches emanate from the top of the articulations. The color varies from reddish-purple to gray-green, and is often bleached white when exposed to the sun. Common in tide-pools and on rocks at low-water mark from New York northward. (Plate XXXVII.)

Genus *Melobesia*

This genus will attract attention, although it cannot be gathered. It is a thin, brittle, scaly substance of indefinite form, which expands horizontally and resembles a lichen. It forms brown and pink crusts on other algæ and on rocks, stones, and shells.

ORDER BANGIACEÆ

Genus *Bangia*

B. fusco-purpurea (" brown-purple "). Fine, hair-like, unbranched, dark-purple filaments, one inch to six inches long. It grows in large patches on rocks and woodwork, floating free, but falling into soft, silky, fleece-like masses when left by the tide. Common on northern shores. (Plate XXXVII.)

Genus *Porphyra*

(" Purple dye ")

This plant, except in color, is like the green alga *Ulva.* In color it is purple of various shades. The species are named from variations in the outline of the frond. They are found everywhere, and throughout the year. The plants are edible, being the laver of commerce, eaten principally by the Chinese, who make them into soup.

P. vulgaris. Frond a broad, thin membrane of purple color, three to twelve inches across; margin much waved; sometimes attached at the center, often widely expanded and folded, sometimes deeply lobed. (Plate XXXVII.)

P. laciniata. Differs from *P. vulgaris* in being divided into narrow segments or into wavy, ribbon-like forms. (Plate XXXVII.)

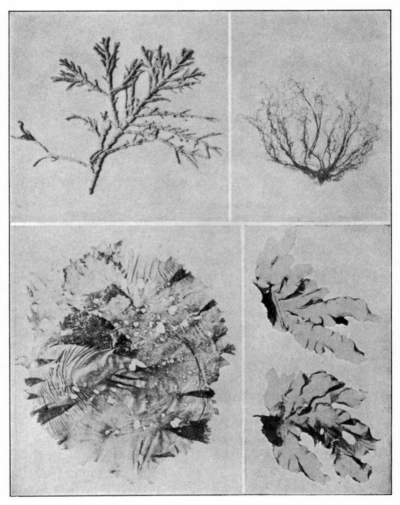

PLATE XXXVII.

Corallina officinalis.   Bangia fusco-purpurea.
Porphyra vulgaris.   Porphyra laciniata.

PART II

MARINE INVERTEBRATES

I
PORIFERA
(SPONGES)

TABLE SHOWING THE CLASSIFICATION OF THE SPONGES
DESCRIBED IN THIS CHAPTER

Phylum and Class

PORIFERA

Subclass

Calcarea

Order	Families	Genera	Species
HETEROCŒLA			
	SYCONIDÆ	*Grantia*	*G. ciliata*
		Leucosolenia	*L. botryoides*

Subclass

Non-Calcarea

Order	Families	Genera	Species
CHONDROSPONGIÆ			
	SUBERITIDÆ	*Suberites*	*S. compacta*
		Polymastia	*P. robusta*
		Cliona	*C. sulphurea*
CORNACUSPONGIÆ			
	DESMACIDONIDÆ	*Esperiopsis*	*E. quatsinoensis*
		Microciona	*M. prolifera*
	HETERORRHAPHIDÆ	*Tedania*	
	HOMORRHAPHIDÆ	*Halichondria*	*H. panicea*
	SPONGIDÆ Subfamily EUSPONGINÆ	*Chalinopsilla*	*C. oculata*
			C. arbuscula
		Euspongia	*E. officinalis*
			Var. *adriatica*
			Var. *mollissima*
			Var. *rotunda*
			Var. *dura*
		Hippospongia	*H. equina*
			Var. *cerebriformis*
			Var. *meandriformis*
			Var. *elastica*
			H. canaliculata
			Var. *gossypina*
			Var. *flabellum*
	SPONGIDÆ Subfamily STELOSPONGINÆ	*Hircinia*	*H. campana*

SPONGES

THERE are many animals which consist of but one cell. These are called *Protozoa*, and comprise the *Infusoria* and other microscopic organisms. The animals next higher in the scale are *Metazoa*, or multicellular animals, and the first group of this subdivision is **Porifera,** the sponges, the lowest of the many-celled animals.

For a long time sponges occupied a disputed ground between the animal and vegetable kingdoms. Aristotle was the first to point out that a sponge is not a plant. The assertion was doubted and combated, but at last the animal nature of the sponge was established. Sponges were then believed to be colonies of one-celled animals, but finally it was decided that they were individuals with cells of different kinds that performed functions analogous to those of higher organisms.

The sponge, as commonly seen, is only the skeleton or framework, so to speak, of the living animal. In its natural state it is a very different-looking object. Its entire surface is covered with a thin slimy skin, usually of a dark color, which is perforated with holes corresponding to the apertures of the canals. The organic portion of the sponge is a soft, jelly-like substance composed of three layers—the external (*ectoderm*), the internal (*endoderm*), and the middle (*mesoderm*). The external layer is composed of flat cells. The endoderm has cylindrical cells, each one of which has a flagellate hair. The main mass of the body, the mesoderm or middle layer, is made up of cells having various functions, some being concerned in the formation of framework, some in digestion, and some in reproduction.

The framework is secreted in the mesoderm, and in different

101

genera consists respectively of a horny or silicious or calcareous substance, or of the first two of these substances combined. The sponge of commerce has the first kind and is composed entirely of exceedingly fine flexible fibers of a horny substance called *spongin*. In other species the spongin is intermixed with spicules of silica, or of carbonate

Various forms of sponge-spicules.

of lime, in various shapes. In the sponges, so much valued as curiosities, called "Venus's flower-basket" and "glass-rope sponge," the framework is composed of silicious spicules alone.

The spicules have a great variety of shapes, being rod-like, knobbed, three-pointed, six-pointed, anchor-like, etc., and are a feature in the classification of sponges.

The sponge is traversed throughout by a canal system, consisting of a series of tubes through which water circulates, carrying air and food to the animal. The exterior of the sponge has numerous small pores and a comparatively few large openings. The fine pores are inhalent, taking in and straining the water of its coarser floating material, and then passing it through perforations in their sides into sacs lined with peculiar cylindrical cells having flagellate hairs, each hair having a collar at its base. These cells, called *choanocytes*, resemble independent animals of the *Protozoa*, known as *flagellate Infusoria* or *Choa-*

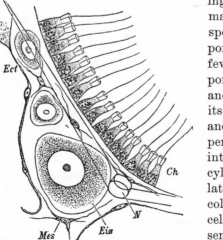

To illustrate choanocytes (*Ch*): section of a calcareous sponge. *Ect*, ectoderm; *Mes*, mesoderm; *N*, calcareous spicule; *Eiz*, ovum.

noflagellata. They take in and digest food and eject excrement from the area inclosed by the collar. The cilia (hairs) by their constant movement create currents which keep the water in motion. Water, then, is taken through the pores into the first or incurrent canals; thence it is passed into the ciliated chambers, and thence into the excurrent canals, and out through large passages terminating in large openings called *oscula*, or craters. The canal systems vary. In some species they become quite complex.

Sponges vary greatly in shape, size, color, surface, rigidity, canal systems, and skeleton. They are cake-shaped, tubular, digitate, palmate, cup-shaped, vase-shaped, cone-shaped, spherical, hemispherical, pedunculate, etc., their shapes depending upon whether their growth is uniform or is excessive in a horizontal or in a vertical direction. When they grow evenly in both directions massive uniform shapes arise. If lateral growth predominates, broad, low, and incrusting shapes result. When there is an excess of vertical growth the forms are digitate;

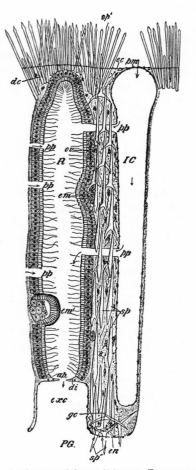

Canal system of *Sycon gelatinosum*. Transverse section through the wall of a cylinder (parallel with the course of the canals), showing one incurrent canal (*IC*) and one radial (*R*) throughout their length; *sp*, triradiate spicules; *sp'*, oxeate spicules of dermal cortex (*dc*); *sp''*, tetraradiate spicules of gastral cortex (*gc*); *ec*, ectoderm; *en*, endoderm; *pm*, pore-membrane; *pp*, prosopyle; *ap*, apopyle; *di*, diaphragm; *exc*, excurrent passage; *PG*, paragastric cavity; *em*, early embryo; *em'*, late embryo. (The arrows indicate the course of the water through the sponge.)

but if vertical growth is not greatly in excess and is restricted to the marginal part, cup-shaped forms result, and tubular forms when lateral growth is particularly restricted. In some varieties tubular masses coalesce; sometimes flat forms unite in intricate compressed folds. Differences in rapidity of vertical growth make undulations more or less marked, producing lobes and protuberances. Sometimes narrow vertical growth is retarded and horizontal growth predominates, forming various shapes on apparent stems.

Many of the horny sponges are colored, in shades of yellow, brown, red, and violet; some are black.

Sponges are divided into two classes, the **Calcarea** and **Non-Calcarea.** The former have calcareous skeletons, which make them hard and rigid; the latter have skeletons of spongin-fiber or of silicious spicules, or of the two combined.

All sponges, with the exception of one family (the *Spongillidæ*, which live in fresh water), are inhabitants of the sea, and live at various depths. The sponges of commerce belong to the *Non-Calcarea* and are all confined to the genus *Spongia*. In this genus the skeleton is more or less flexible, being composed of spongin. They are shallow-water species, are confined to seas where the waters are of comparatively uniform high temperature, and flourish best when protected by reefs and islands.

There are fisheries for sponges in the waters of the West Indies, the Bahamas, on the southern and western coasts of Florida, and in the Mediterranean and Red seas. Those of the Mediterranean surpass in quality the sponges of our coasts.

Five species of commercial sponges are taken from Florida waters. They are graded by the trade in the order of their importance, as the "sheepswool," "yellow," "grass," "velvet," and "glove." The fishing for sponges is done from small boats, two persons manning each boat. One man sculls, while the other, using a water-glass, scans the bottom. The water-glass is a box with a pane of glass on the bottom. If the glass is held below the surface and the face is placed in the box, the observer is enabled to see with some distinctness the bottom at a considerable depth in these clear waters. The sponges are dragged up by hooks—a primitive method which restricts the fishing to shallow water, the fishing here being in water not deeper than thirty feet, but usually three to twenty feet. The sponges are "killed" by being exposed on the beach for several days; they are then placed in "crawls," or pens, where they are washed by the action of the waves for about a week; then, if clean, they are dried, assorted, strung on cords, pressed and baled for shipment. The sponge-fisheries are of considerable value, and much attention is being given to the subject of artificial propagation. It is thought that such beds could be subjected to the regulations which govern oyster-beds. Already the planting of sponges has been shown to be practicable. The living sponge is cut to pieces, and the cuttings are placed in favorable localities. Pieces planted in Florida waters attain a marketable size in one year.

Sponges reproduce by eggs formed in the mesoderm. The eggs escape as ciliated spheres and swim about until they find a place on which to attach themselves. As soon as they become fixed they grow with much rapidity into mature individuals.

Some species seem to prefer association with other animals and live as commensals with crabs. The crab *Dromia* is always concealed under a sponge, which grows upon its back. Spider-crabs are often overgrown with sponges as well as seaweeds. In this case, however, the crab finds and plants the sponge himself. *Aplysella violacea* overgrows worm-tubes. Many sponges afford shelter to numerous small animals which bore into their bodies for protection, no animal seeming to feed upon the sponge.

Sponges may be found in tide-pools, on the under side of stones, on seaweeds, and so on. A small bright-red incrusting sponge with irregular lobe-like branches is common on the New England coast; a thin yellow incrusting sponge also is found on the under side of stones. *Grantia ciliata*, a small urn-shaped species, having a large aperture at the summit, is found in tide-pools.

Perhaps the most singular in habit of any sponge is *Cliona sulphurea*, the boring-sponge, a common species found from Cape Cod to South Carolina and abundant in Long Island Sound. It is bright sulphur-yellow in color, grows in irregular masses of considerable size and fine texture, and has low wart-like prominences. It lives on shells spreading over both surfaces, at first forming little burrows, but eventually penetrating the shell in every direction, honeycombing and at last completely destroying it by absorption. Sometimes it settles upon living shells and greatly irritates the animal, which constantly secretes new lime to cover the perforations in its shell.

These sponges are an important factor in the economy of the sea, as they disintegrate dead shells, which would otherwise accumulate in vast quantities.

SUBCLASS **CALCAREA**

Genus *Grantia*

G. ciliata. Small, urn-shaped or oval, with large aperture at the summit, surrounded by a circle of projecting spicules. It is found in tide-pools and on piles of wharves from Rhode Island northward.

Genus *Leucosolenia*

L. botryoides. Tubular, branched. Occurs in the same places as *Grantia ciliata.*

SUBCLASS **NON-CALCAREA**

Genus *Suberites*

S. compacta. Elongated, compressed masses, sometimes in several lobes; attached by one edge; texture fine, firm, compact; surface smooth; color bright yellow. It grows on sandy bottoms, and is common in shallow water south of Cape Cod. (Plate XXXVIII.)

Genus *Polymastia*

P. robusta. When young it forms yellowish-white incrustations over shells and stones; later it grows into long, slender, round, tapering, finger-like projections. Found on the northern New England coasts in deep water.

Genus *Cliona*

C. sulphurea, the boring-sponge. Irregular massive form of firm texture; surface covered with scattered low wart-like prominences about one eighth of an inch in diameter; bright sulphur-yellow. It destroys, by absorption, vast quantities of dead shells.

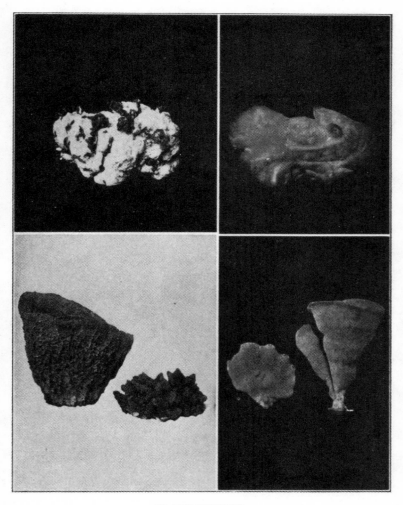

PLATE XXXVIII.

Halichondria panicea.   Suberites compacta.
Hircinia campana.   Esperiopsis quatsinoensis (found
                                 on the sea-beaches of Alaska).

PLATE XXXIX.

Microciona prolifera.   Chalinopsilla arbuscula.

Chalinopsilla imitans.   Euspongia officinalis, var. tuba.   Chalinopsilla oculata.

Genus *Microciona*

M. prolifera. When young this species forms bright-red incrustations over shells and stones; later it rises into irregular lobes and tubular prominences. When fully developed it is profusely branched in a forking manner. The branches are more or less flattened, and often are palmate at the ends. It grows in clusters six inches in diameter, of a dark orange-red color. When dry it is grayish-brown, brittle, and bristly. It is found from Cape Cod to South Carolina, and is abundant in Long Island Sound. (Plate XXXIX.)

Genus *Tedania*

Irregular, uneven, pale-yellow masses spreading over seaweeds; oscula scattered irregularly over the surface; texture close.

Genus *Halichondria*

H. panicea, crumb-of-bread sponge. It resembles the crumb of bread, and is found cast up on all beaches. (Plate XXXVIII.)

Genus *Chalinopsilla*

C. oculata, the finger-sponge. Stem stout, more or less flattened, dividing at the upper end into branches which vary in form and thickness, being finger-like or more or less compressed lobes; oscula scattered over the smooth, undulating surface; texture rather hard, but delicate; color, when living, dull orange-red; when the animal matter is removed, white. The species is found in shallow and deep water from New York to Labrador. Common in Massachusetts Bay. (Plate XXXIX.)

C. arbuscula. Profusely branched in a forking manner from close to the base; branches slender; clusters six to eight inches high and about the same in breadth; color buff or gray when living, yellowish-white when free from animal matter; texture finer and more delicate than that of *C. oculata*. It is found in shallow water from Cape Cod to North Carolina, and is abundant in Long Island Sound. (Plate XXXIX.)

Genus *Euspongia*

E. officinalis. This is one of the commercial sponges and is known as the "glove-sponge." It is the one of least marketable value, having inferior elasticity and becoming brittle with age; yet a Mediterranean sponge of the same species, variety *adriatica*, is of the finest quality and greatest value. This singular fact demonstrates that the quality of sponges depends largely upon physical conditions. *E. officinalis* has an average height of five to six inches. It grows on rocky bottoms in shallow water on the east coast of Florida. This species has a number of varieties of various forms; some are dome-shaped, others tubular, rotund, flabellate, etc. The surface is covered with fine tufts and is generally free from ridges. On the sides are numerous small apertures, and one or more large oscula occur on top.   The color of the living sponge is black. (Plates XXXIX, XL.)

E. officinalis, variety *adriatica.*   More or less globose; sometimes attached by a broad base, sometimes by a short stem ; latter form more or less club-shaped; oscula scattered over upper surface.   Found in the West Indies and the Mediterranean.   (Plate XL.)

E. officinalis, variety *mollissima,* the Levant toilet-sponge. Generally cup-shaped; oscula on inner side of cup or on upper flat surface; very soft and elastic.

E. officinalis, variety *rotunda.*   Usually massive; attached by a broad base ; sides vertical; oscula large and conspicuous on top, or small in longitudinal rows on the sides.   In the young this variety may have a conical form with only one orifice, but later it has several oscula. Its rotundity of form increases with the number of large orifices, but in the adult stages the form varies, some being conical, while others have the top divided into radiating ridges.

E. officinalis, variety *dura.*   Irregular, massive, horizontally expanded, with conical process on upper surface.

Genus *Hippospongia*

H. equina.   Some of the sponges of this species are massive, spherical, and attached by a small base ; others are horizontally expanded or cake-shaped ; some have a depression in the upper surface and become cup-shaped.

H. equina, variety *cerebriformis.*   Massive, circular, cake-shaped, often depressed in the center, producing a cup-shape, attached by broad base; surface broken up by parallel longitudinal ridges having many tufts.   Cup-shaped forms predominate, and have a more or less rough surface.   This is one of the species known as grass-sponges.

H. equina, variety *meandriformis,* the velvet sponge.   The surface of this variety has a protruding flattened cushion of fiber which slightly resembles the convolutions of the brain-coral.   Sometimes these cushions are extended into long pencils.   The oscula are large and ragged on the edges; the shape is irregular.   The average size is seven to eight inches in diameter. (Plate XL.)

H. equina, variety *elastica* (variety *agaricina,* Hyatt), the yellow sponge.   This is the second grade of commercial sponge, corresponding to the Zimocca sponge of the Mediterranean.   It is found growing with the " sheepswool" in a depth of two to twenty feet, and is abundant. It is massive and cake-shaped.   The whole surface is a network covered with numerous small, fine cones. (Plate XL.)

The variety *dura* is classed with this species, which it resembles in appearance, though it is harder in texture.

H. canaliculata.   Massive, frondose ; more or less horizontally expanded ; bears finger-like processes of varying development on the upper surface.

H. canaliculata, variety *gossypina,* the sheepswool sponge.   This is the highest grade of the commercial bath-sponge.   It is called "sheepswool" because, perhaps, of its irregular shaggy surface.   It is covered with tufts, the larger oscula occupying the intervening depressions.

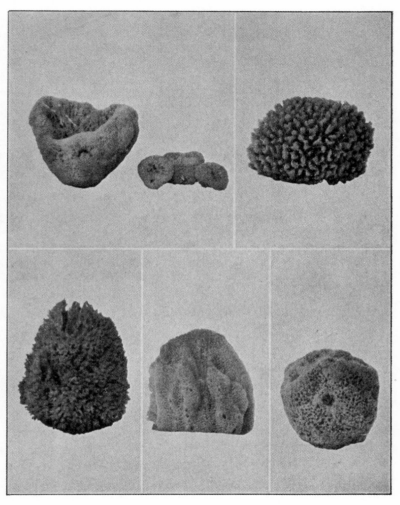

PLATE XL.

Euspongia officinalis, var. adriatica.   Hippospongia equina, var. meandriformis.
Hippospongia canaliculata,   Hippospongia equina, var. elastica.
    var. gossypina.   Euspongia officinalis.

Sometimes these are very numerous, the whole interior being cavernous; again, the structure is more dense, with fewer large openings and more of the small ones between the tufts; again, the depressions are filled up so that the surface has fewer tufts. When living, the color is shining black. This is the best sponge found on the American coast, and although of coarser texture than the best Mediterranean sponges, it is more durable and quite as elastic. (Plate XL.)

H. canaliculata, variety *flabellum* (*Spongia graminea,* Hyatt). This is one of the species of sponges of the third commercial grade, which bear the trade-name of " grass-sponge." The shape is cone-like, with either a flat or a funnel-shaped top. The oscula re on the upper surface. The sides are fluted with deep furrows which contain the small incurrent apertures.

Genus *Hircinia*

H. campana. The normal variety is vase-shaped, but the species varies greatly in form. Some varieties have branches. When living, its color is black. It is found at Key West in four to forty feet depth. (Plate XXXVIII.)

II
CŒLENTERATA
(POLYPS)

CŒLENTERATA

Classes

HYDROZOA

(Zoöphytes, small Jellyfishes, and a few Corals)

SCYPHOZOA

(Large Jellyfishes)

ACTINOZOA

(Sea-anemones and most of the Stony Corals)

CTENOPHORA

(Comb-jellies)

CŒLENTERATA

THE animals included in the phylum **Cœlenterata** were once all called *zoöphytes*, or animal plants, because of their resemblance to vegetable forms. The name *Cœlenterata* is derived from two Greek words meaning " hollow" and "intestine," and it describes the anatomical structure of each member of the group. They are commonly known as polyps. In the simplest forms the parts which perform the different functions cannot be distinguished one from the other, and even in higher forms there is but little differentiation. Shakspere's description of old age applies to them : "Sans teeth, sans eyes, sans taste, sans everything."

Nevertheless, this very low order of animals has, like the higher orders, such a diversity of form and habit as to require classification. Some of them are stationary, and of these some branch like plants ; some move about by the aid of tentacles, some move by means of vibrating cilia, and others move by the contraction and expansion of the soft body.

Cuvier included them in his *Radiata*, a class comprising all the animals whose parts diverge or radiate from a central axis. Recent classification has divided the radiate animals into several classes. This arrangement of parts is obviously quite different from that of bilateral symmetry, or the disposal of parts on each side of a longitudinal axis. The type of radiate structure is shown in polyps. The body is a sac, in the center of which is another sac or axis. This is the digestive cavity. Vertical partitions extend from the central to the outer sac, forming distinct divisions or chambers. The number of divisions varies with the different species and also with the age of the animal. Other partitions start from the outer sac, and extend toward the central axis, but do not unite with it. These partitions, called *mesenteries*, are always in definite multiples, varying in different species, new divisions growing between the first partitions in regular order. On the inner edge of these partitions the eggs of the animal are formed, which, when mature, drop into the chambers and pass through openings into the inner sac, or digestive cavity, and out of the mouth into the water.

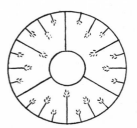

Diagram of radiate structure.

The animals are classed according as the eggs are formed on all or on special partitions, those being of the highest order where a limitation and constancy of function is maintained. The upper surface of the body has hollow tentacles, each one of which opens into one of the chambers and extends outward. All parts of the animal communicate, and whatever enters the mouth circulates through the whole structure; and when assimilation is completed the residue returns by the same road and is expelled through the mouth. This structure is common to all polyps; but there are great differences in their texture, some being soft and some horny, while others deposit a calcareous skeleton (corals). Some grow in colonies, like the hydroids and corals, and are stationary, others are free and independent; some have but few, others have many tentacles; and they differ widely in size, form, and color.

Hydroids, sea-anemones, corals, sea-fans, starfishes, and sea-urchins are different examples of the radiate structure. They are not, however, all of them polyps.

The *Cœlenterata* are divided into four classes : **Hydrozoa,** which include the colonies of zoöphytes which resemble seaweeds, the small jellyfishes which are born of these colonies, and the *mille-pores*, which are colonies of zoöphytes which secrete a stony instead of a horny skeleton, yet differ in some respects from other stony corals; **Scyphozoa,** large jellyfishes, many of which do not have the double form of development; **Actinozoa,** the sea-anemones and the different forms of stony corals, including sea-fans, sea-pens, etc.; **Ctenophora,** the jellyfishes commonly known as comb-jellies.

TABLE SHOWING THE CLASSIFICATION OF THE HYDROZOA
DESCRIBED IN THIS CHAPTER

Class
HYDROZOA

Order LEPTOLINIÆ

(Branched colonies or shrub-like communities of hydroids ; some permanently fixed, others liberate swimming-bells)

Suborders	Divisions	Genera and Species
ANTHOMEDUSÆ *(Zoöids not covered by protective sheath ; umbrella of medusæ strongly arched ; egg-sacs in manubrium)*	**TUBULARIANS** *(Without polyp-cups)*	*Clava leptostyla* *Hydractinia polyclina* *Coryne mirabilis* *Sarsia* *Eudendrium ramosum* *Tubularia indivisa* *T. Couthouyi* *Parypha crocea* *Corymorpha pendula* *Hybocodon prolifer* *Pennaria tiarella* *P. gibbosa* *Bougainvillea superciliaris*
LEPTOMEDUSÆ *(Zoöids covered with cup-like sheaths ; umbrella of medusæ thin and not very convex ; egg-sacs in line of radial canals)*	**CAMPANULARIANS** *(Polyp-cups stalked)*	*Obelia commissuralis* *Eucope diaphana* *Oceania languida* *Clytia poterium* *C. bicophora*
	SERTULARIANS *(Polyp-cups sessile)*	*Sertularia pumila* *S. argentea* *S. cupressina*
	PLUMULARIANS *(Polyp-cups on one side of branches only)*	*Aglaophemia struthioides* *Plumularia falcata*

Family
GERYONOPSIDÆ   *Tima formosa*

Family
ÆQUOREIDÆ   *Zygodactyla groenlandica*

116

Order **TRACHYLINÆ**

(No fixed zoöphyte stage; always free-swimming medusæ)

Suborders

TRACHYMEDUSÆ

(Tentacles spring from margin of umbrella; manubrium long; gonads in connection with radial canals)

Trachynema digitale

NARCOMEDUSÆ

(Tentacles spring from midway between summit and margin of umbrella; manubrium short; gonads in connection with manubrium)

Order **HYDROCORALLINA**

(Skeleton of carbonate of lime)

Millepora alcicornis

Order **SIPHONOPHORA**

(Pelagic free-swimming colonies; exhibit extreme polymorphism of zoöids)

Nanomia cara
Physalia arethusa
Vellela limbosa

Cœnosarc (" common flesh ") : The fleshy axis, or organized living bond, by which the zoöids are organically united to one another. It consists of three layers : ectoderm, endoderm, and mesoderm.

Ectoderm (" outside skin ") : The outside one of the three organized layers of which every hydroid is composed.

Endoderm (" inside skin ") : The innermost layer.

Gonangium (" seed-vessel ") : The external horny receptacle within which the gonophores are developed.

Gonophore (" seed-bearing ") : A generative zoöid.

Hydranth (" water flower ") : A nutritive zoöid.

Hydrorhiza (" water-root ") : The part of the colony which fixes it to other bodies, like a root.

Hydrosoma (" water-body ") : The entire hydroid colony.

Hydrotheca (" water-receptacle ") : The cup-like, horny receptacle which protects the hydranth.

Mesoderm (" middle skin ") : A layer which lies between the ectoderm and the endoderm.

Nematophore (" thread-bearing ") : The name of peculiar bodies developed in certain genera from definite points ; characteristic of plumularians.

Perisarc (" around flesh ") : The transparent, chitinous shell, or unorganized outer membrane of horny consistency, which covers to a greater or less extent the soft parts of the colony.

Zoöid (" animal form ") : One of the animals which form the colony.

CLASS **HYDROZOA**

SEAWEED-LIKE ZOÖPHYTES AND SMALL JELLYFISHES

THE hydroids have been called the nurses of jellyfishes. From casual observation these two forms would not be associated together, for the shrub-like organisms, which so much resemble plants that they are often collected and preserved as seaweeds, suggest only vegetable life. Examined with a glass, however, they disclose their animal nature. Along the stems, arranged in various ways, are small cups, from which protrude the numerous moving tentacles of the little polyps living within them.

Hydroids are colonies of associated animals living a communal life. The multitude of individuals composing the colony are invested with a horny covering, the *perisarc*, which in some genera assumes a tree-like form. Through these stems and branches runs a fleshy tube, a thread of animal substance, which connects in one living whole the zoöids, or individuals of the community. There is division of labor, as in other communities: some of the zoöids obtain the food for the colony, and have tentacles around their open mouths; others have no mouths, but reproduce the species, and at certain stages of development liberate swimming-bells, or small jellyfishes (medusæ).

The typical hydroid colony is attached by a kind of creeping stem from which arises a vertical axis, which gives off short lateral, alternate branches bearing zoöids at their ends. There is often more complex branching. The zoöids in certain genera (tubularians) are uncovered; in others (sertularians) they are incased in a glassy, cup-like, horny sheath.

Three kinds of zoöids, polyps, or hydranths—as they are indiscriminately called—are attached to the stem. Those having an

119

open end and a crown of tentacles are the nutritive individuals. Small, club-like dilations are immature zoöids. The *blastostyles*, or reproductive zoöids, are long, cylindrical, mouthless, and covered. At maturity the cover is ruptured, and the medusæ have the appearance of a pile of thin saucers attached by the middle of the convex side. When at length these saucers are set free as little medusæ, or jellyfishes, the convex side of each saucer, or swimming-bell, is called the *ex-umbrella ;* the concave, under side, the *subumbrella.* From the center of the subumbrella projects the *manubrium,* or stomach of the animal. At the free end of the manubrium is a four-cornered mouth. From the attached end of the manubrium four tubes or canals diverge, and, extending through the animal, open into a circular canal which runs around the margin of the umbrella. When the medusa is as above described, it has reached the highest point in its development.

When the medusa has matured, it lays eggs, known as *planulæ.* These are spherical bodies covered with cilia (hairs), by means of which they swim about for a time; but they finally attach themselves to some object, there to grow and develop into hydroid colonies. The cycle of life is thus completed. This process is known as *alternation of generation,* or *metagenesis,* one life-history containing two quite different forms of being. The term of life of an individual is one year, the zoöphyte stage beginning in the autumn and the medusa stage in the spring.

Some medusæ, besides reproducing by means of eggs, multiply by budding, small medusæ growing on the manubrium or on the margin of the umbrella. *Sarsia* and *Lizzia* sometimes increase by budding.

The *Hydrozoa* are not all of the above type. In the sertularians the zoöids perish on the stem and have no medusa life, their reproductive element giving rise to the hydroid form without metamorphosis. The *Trachylinæ* have no hydroid life, being always free-swimming medusæ; others, the *Siphonophora,* live a hydroid life which is unattached, the colony floating on the ocean ; the millepores secrete calcareous skeletons and always remain fixed, reproducing by budding.

Hydroids are very abundant, but are comprised in the few groups mentioned: namely, those which live only in the fixed colonial state; those which have alternation of generation, being first hydroids and then swimming-bells, or medusæ; those which live always in the medusa state, the eggs of the jellyfish developing at once into other medusæ; and the *Siphonophora*, or those which have a floating colonial state, the hydroid never being attached, but floating at large and capable of locomotion, some of the colony having the function of propulsion.

Hydroids are particularly interesting as exemplifying the close resemblance that may exist in outward appearance between animal and vegetable life and as illustrations of communal life and of the alternation of generation. A few examples of different types are given below.

ORDER LEPTOLINIÆ

The members of this order agree in all essential particulars being branched colonies having two principal forms of zoöids, the nutritive and the reproductive. Some genera attain the length of several inches, or even feet; others are very small tufts growing on shells and seaweeds. The cup may completely inclose the zoöid and be close to the stem (sessile), as in sertularians; it may be on the end of a short stalk, as in campanularians; or it may not reach above the base of the zoöid, as in tubularians. The genera are based upon these differences in the perisarc.

The hydroids, like all other classes, exist in such great variety that it would be impracticable to describe here the many named species; but to recognize the genera is simple. A long tubular pedicel without a cup is characteristic of the tubularians; the campanularians have an arborescent form and bell-shaped cups on stalks; the sertularians have sessile cups; and the plumularians have a feather-like form, with zoöid-cups on one side only of the branches.

The beautiful and varied structure of these "animal plants" is most interesting, and to be fully appreciated they should be seen in life and examined with a glass. Some species are confined to deep water, but many are littoral and to be found in tide-pools, in the chinks and crannies of rocks, under stones, and under the hanging *Fucus*. The horny skeletons of large varieties are frequently washed ashore, and in their tangled masses smaller living species often may be found.

THE TUBULARIANS

This division is characterized by zoöids borne on long, slender stems which are sometimes simple and small, sometimes branching and eight to ten inches long. The zoöid has two rows of tentacles, the central one being sometimes on a kind of proboscis. The reproductive zoöids are in bunches, sometimes below the outer row of tentacles, sometimes between the two rows. The perisarc does not cover the zoöid. In color they are commonly red or yellow.

GENUS Clava

C. leptostyla. This species is found growing on *Fucus*, on the under side of stones at low-water mark, and in tide-pools, where it often covers several feet of the surface of the rock with a delicate velvet-like carpet. It is red in color and is, apparently, a soft and tender species, but it thrives on the most exposed beaches. The colonies are cylindrical tubes about one quarter of an inch in height, rising from a creeping stem (*hydrorhiza*). Each tube is surmounted by a zoöid with fifteen to thirty tentacles, which is constantly changing form by its contractions. Below the tentacles are reproductive buds arranged in clusters. Common from Long Island Sound northward. (Plate XLI.)

GENUS Hydractinia

H. polyclina. The soft, pinkish covering often seen on shells inhabited by hermit-crabs. This association of two different kinds of animals is known as *commensalism*, and is a partnership formed for the benefit of one or both the individuals. In this case the mossy appearance of the hydroid conceals the shell, while the stinging-cells with which it is invested are weapons of defense against the enemies of the crab and also help to paralyze its prey. In return for these favors the colony is moved about, thereby obtaining perhaps better oxygenation. Originally it was thought that *Hydractinia* lived only on the shells occupied by hermit-crabs, and that the nomadic life was essential to its existence ; but this is not the case, for it is also found growing on rocks in tide-pools. These colonies arise from a creeping stem, which forms a horny, root-

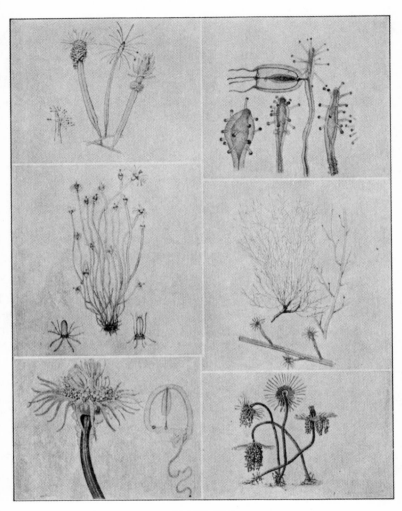

PLATE XLI.

Clava leptostyla.
Tubularia indivisa.
Hybocodon prolifer.

Coryne mirabilis.
Eudendrium ramosum.
Tubularia Couthouyi.

like network over a surface and develops at intervals projecting points on which the zoöids live. Each colony consists of feeding members, of reproductive members, and of a third kind which seems to have a protective function. These last are more slender than the others, and are without tentacles, but are armed with lasso- or stinging-cells. The colonies are of different sexes, the male being lighter in color than the female colonies. The eggs develop into planulæ, which swim about for a while and then give rise to other colonies. It is found from New Jersey northward, and is very abundant in Long Island Sound.

Colony of *Coryne*, natural size.

Genus *Coryne*

C. mirabilis. A hydroid about one inch high, growing in patches and appearing like tufts of moss on rocks between tide-marks. When highly magnified it shows club-shaped tubes with pedicels, terminating in zoöids, scattered over the swollen ends. The medusa-bud is larger than the others and is lower on the tube. It liberates a swimming-bell, which is called *Sarsia*. (Plate XLI.)

Sarsia

S. mirabilis. This medusa of *Coryne* is from one quarter to three quarters of an inch in diameter when full-grown. Its umbrella is nearly hemispherical, and from the center hangs a manubrium. From the margin of the umbrella hang four very long tentacles. The shape of its body and the length of its tentacles and proboscis are constantly changing as it moves in the water. These little medusæ are very plentiful in the spring and summer, and swim rapidly in all directions near the surface of the water.

Genus *Tubularia*

T. Couthouyi. This species is found in the same places as *Parypha crocea*. The stem is three to six inches long, and is inclosed in a horny sheath, which is more or less ringed or jointed, or it may be smooth throughout. The head, when the tentacles are expanded, measures one and a half inches in diameter. It has a proboscis covered with tentacles, disposed in series, which grow successively shorter, the last being merely papillæ. The medusa-buds hang in clusters between the outer tentacles and the proboscis. The animal grows in bunches of five to ten tubes, which spring from a creeping, tangled stem. (Plate XLI.)

Genus *Parypha*

Sarsia, the free medusa of *Coryne*.

P. crocea. This is one of the most beautiful of the tubularians. It has a large, drooping head on a stem three to four inches long. It is bright red in color, and from the center of the circle of tentacles the reproductive zoöids hang in a cluster, like a bunch of grapes. It does not liberate swimming-bells. It is found in bunches on piles of wharves and bridges, in brackish water, on the eastern coast as far south as Charleston, South Carolina.

Corymorpha pendula. See Plate XLII.

GENUS *Hybocodon*

H. prolifer. One of the largest tubularians, somewhat resembling *Parypha crocea*. It is deep orange in color, and the head is erect on a long stem. The reproductive zoöids are in a cluster in the center of a double row of tentacles, and resemble a basket of fruit. It grows singly, or in groups of two or three, in shaded tide-pools, which are protected from the surf, and in which the water is very pure. It is found on the Massachusetts coast, but is not common. This species liberates swimming-bells. (Plate XLI.)

GENUS *Pennaria*

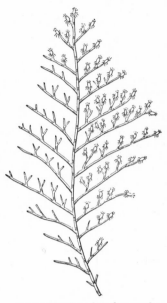

Pennaria tiarella; a branch, natural size.

P. tiarella. The branches are arranged alternately and at right angles to a central stem or axis; they taper, being shortest at the top and bottom of the stem. The zoöids are red in color, and are arranged along the upper side of branches at considerable intervals. The stems are black and beaded, being constricted at intervals. The zoöids have two rows of tentacles, the upper ones on a small proboscis. From the lower part of the proboscis deep, bell-shaped bodies, which eventually become swimming-bells, are developed. The species is found on rocks and eel-grass along the whole eastern coast.

P. gibbosa. A species similar to *P. tiarella*, found on the coast of Florida.

GENUS *Bougainvillea*

B. superciliaris. This hydroid is found in tide-pools on the New England coast, growing in clusters, about two inches high, attached to rocks or to mussel-shells. The stem is very slender, and branches. It is red in color. The medusæ which it liberates are found in great numbers in the spring. The tiny swimming-bells are nearly globular. The tentacles are long, are arranged in four clusters on the margin, and extend in every direction. The manubrium is yellow and short, and the mouth is concealed by four clusters of short tentacles. On these oral tentacles

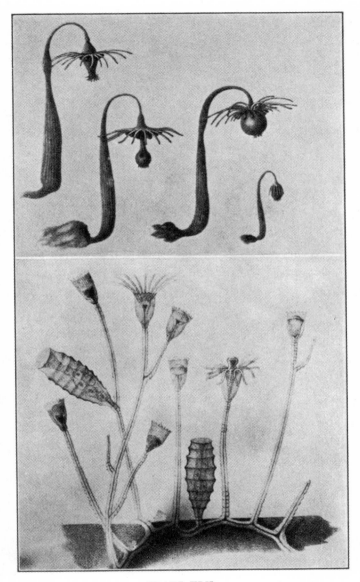

PLATE XLII.

Corymorpha pendula.
Clytia bicophora.

PLATE XLII, A.

Obelia longissima.

Clytia poterium.   Sertularia pumila.

the eggs of the animal are produced. In its habits it is sluggish, often remaining in one position for several days.

THE CAMPANULARIANS

The hydroids which have an open, bell-shaped cup at the termination of a short, stalk-like stem, or branchlet, are mostly campanularians. This division embraces jellyfishes of different families. Many medusæ cannot be referred with certainty to the hydroids from which they sprang, and the medusa-buds of many of the hydroids have not been noted.

GENUS *Obelia* (Plate XLII, A)

O. commissuralis. This is a delicate, much-branched hydroid, five to six inches long, found at low-water mark in tide-pools, attached to stones and seaweeds, along·the rocky shores from Nova Scotia to South Carolina. Its branches are arranged spirally and spread nearly at right angles to the main stem, and the main branches subdivide in a similar manner. Every interval of the stem has a slight curve, and at the base of every branch there are four or five rings. The ultimate branches, or pedicels, bear at their ends bell-shaped cups which have even edges, but are twelve-sided and slightly incurved. The pedicels are ringed for the whole length. The reproductive cups on short ringed pedicels are larger than the others, and occupy the angles of the branches. These cups are constricted and again expanded at the apex, forming an urnlike top.

GENUS *Eucope*

E. diaphana. This species is often abundant on the fronds of *Laminaria* washed ashore, and also on *Rhodymenia* and *Fucus*. It has a creeping base, zigzag in form, but keeping a straight course, and in its branching often forming a network over the surface of the flat fronds. At each angle of the creeping stems rises a pedicel about an inch high, which inclines in the direction of the stem and terminates in a zoöid-cup similar in form to that of *Obelia*. The medusa which this hydroid liberates is called *Thaumatias diaphana*. The swimming-bell is very shallow and thin, turning inside out at almost every pulsation. The tentacles are numerous and rigid like stiff hairs. This little medusa is very active and is abundant. The species is found from Long Island Sound northward.

GENUS *Oceania*

O. languida. This medusa is one inch in diameter and one half of an inch high, and is so delicate and transparent that it is hardly visible except in its outlines. In its early stages it is nearly spherical and has no tentacles; later the disk flattens and has from thirty-two to thirty-six tentacles and numerous eye-spots. When disturbed it flattens its disk and folds together, leaving its tentacles sprawled in every direction. It is very languid in its movements, and often remains in one position for hours. These medusæ are found only in the hottest hours of the day, but are very plentiful then, shoals of them often stretching for miles, and so thick as to touch one another. Their habitat is the New England coast.

Genus *Clytia*

C. poterium. This hydroid is found creeping over seaweeds in tide-pools from Long Island Sound northward. The main stem is prostrate, or root-like, running over the body to which it is attached. The stems rise as do the tubularians. The sterile zoöids are on single stems about one quarter of an inch high. The stems are faintly ringed for their entire length, and at the top have a distinct ring, on which rests an open, bell-shaped cup, which is smooth around the rim. The reproductive zoöids are on very short pedicels, and the cups are long and cylindrical, with a wavy outline. (Plate XLII, A.)

C. bicophora. This species is found in the same places as the preceding, and is of about the same size. The long stems are more or less ringed and sometimes branched. The edges of the cups are notched. The medusa-buds are urn-shaped and ringed, and are on very short pedicels. (Plate XLII.)

THE SERTULARIANS

The sertularians are distinguished by the horny cup, which is sessile—that is, set directly against the stem instead of being raised upon a stalk. They are among the most common objects of the beach, and, like the plumularians, are often mistaken for plants by the amateur collector and are gathered and pressed as seaweeds. They are found everywhere along the coast. They zigzag over the fronds of seaweeds or hang in fringes upon them, as well as upon rocks, stones, and shells. They well repay close examination with a glass. Every open cup bears a wreath of tentacles, which makes the branch a spray of stars. This is not an inappropriate comparison, for besides their starry shape some species emit a phosphorescent light.

Genus *Sertularia*

S. pumila. The most abundant of all the hydroids on the northeast coast is this species, which is found in profusion upon *Fucus* and other seaweeds, and mingled with them upon the rocks. It is easily distinguished from the campanularians because its zoöid-cups are close against the stems (sessile) instead of on stalks or pedicels. The stem creeps

Sertularia argentea.

PLATE XLII, B.

Sertularia cupressina.

PLATE XLIII.

Plumularian hydroid.   Aglaophemia struthioides.
Aglaophemia struthioides, magnified.   Plumularia falcata.

over the fronds of seaweeds, often crossing and recrossing in a tangled mass. At short intervals the upright, straight branches rise to one inch or one and a half inches in height, and are more or less branched. All except the creeping stems are close set on each side, with cylindrical zoöid-cups which turn outward at the ends. The cups of the reproductive zoöids are not sessile; they are much larger than those of the nutritive ones and are urn-shaped. (Plate XLII, A.)

S. argentea. This is a beautiful species, common from New Jersey northward. It has a profusion of silvery branches on a dark stem. The colonies are often a foot or more long, and the branches at the top and bottom of the stem are shorter and fewer than those in the middle of the colony. The zoöid-cups are nearly cylindrical, pressed closely to the stem, nearly opposite or subalternate to one another, and end in pointed tips. The medusa-bud is urn-shaped, with two horns at the top. (Plate XLII, B.)

S. cupressina, the sea-cypress. This species is similar to *S. argentea*, but the main stem is thicker and longer, and the branches less crowded and less subdivided. The branches are arched or drooping, instead of straight, and gradually decrease in length at some distance from the lower and upper parts of the stem, giving a spire-like apex, the stem often continuing into a bare, branchless extremity. The zoöid-cups are tubular, not much narrowed or divergent above, and two-lipped on the margin. It is found from New Jersey northward. (Plate XLII, B.)

THE PLUMULARIANS

These hydroids are feather-like in the manner of branching, short lateral branches being arranged on each side of a long central stem. In some species the stems are naked below and resemble quills. The zoöid-cups are only on one side of the short branches. (Plate XLIII.)

GENUS *Aglaophemia*

A. struthioides, the ostrich-plume. This species, which is found on the Pacific coast, is perhaps the most beautiful of the hydroids. It varies in size and color, but always suggests a small ostrich-plume. The zoöid-cups are arranged in a single row on one side of each short branch, and the main stem has a joint between each of the branches, which are placed quite close together. The rims of the cups have sharp-pointed teeth, and from the top emerge three tubular projections, which are called *nematophores*, and are supposed to be degenerate zoöids. At intervals a branch is replaced by a cylindrical body covered with nematophores, and in these the generative zoöids are developed. (Plate XLIII.)

GENUS *Plumularia*

P. falcata (Johnston), or *Hydrallmania falcata* (Hincks). This species is found on shells and rocks near low-water mark from Long

Island Sound northward. It is from four to twelve inches high. The main stem is in long spiral turns, and at intervals has spreading plumose branches. The zoöid-cups are tubular and closely pressed against one another, and are ranged in rows on one side of the branchlets; the apertures of the cups are plain and oblique. (Plate XLIII.)

FAMILY GERYONOPSIDÆ

GENUS *Tima*

T. formosa. A very delicate and transparent medusa; size one to two inches in diameter; bell conical; radial tubes four in number; manubrium long, hanging far below the disk; four frilled appendages diverging from the corners of the mouth; tentacles thirty-two; egg-sacs white and following the line of the radial tubes in undulating folds. This species is not very common; it is found on the New England coast.

FAMILY ÆQUOREIDÆ

GENUS *Zygodactyla*

Zygodactyla groenlandica.

Z. groenlandica. Medusa seven to eleven inches in diameter; disk violet-colored and transparent; margin fringed with long, fine, contractile tentacles of a darker violet color; numerous radiating tubes; egg-sacs in slightly waved plates; manubrium hanging below the line of the disk and with a thin frilled membrane depending from it. Found north of Cape Cod in July.

ORDER TRACHYLINÆ

The *Trachymedusæ* are characterized by their direct development, the egg of the jellyfish producing a medusa and not a hydroid colony.

GENUS *Trachynema*

T. digitale. Size one inch to one and a half inches in height; rose-colored; the bell thin and hard, and conical at the top. The swimming is effected by contractions of the muscular velum (the band around the inner margin of the umbrella) instead of wholly by the bell. The tentacles are long and numerous, and are curled up when moving. The manubrium is long and has four expansions at the mouth. Eight egg-cases hang in long pendent sacs from the upper part of the radial canals and reach nearly to the velum. Four garnet-colored eyes in club-shaped processes are prominent on the margin. The animal moves by jerks in straight lines.

ORDER **HYDROCORALLINA**

CALCAREOUS HYDROIDS

The genus *Millepora* ("thousand pores"), which is the type of this order, is a colony of animals, like other hydroids, which secrete calcareous instead of horny coverings. It differs from true corals in that the members of a colony perform different functions, whereas in true corals each member of a community is a complete individual. It differs also in the arrangement of the stony partitions, which in **Hydrocorallina** are the outside coverings and connecting

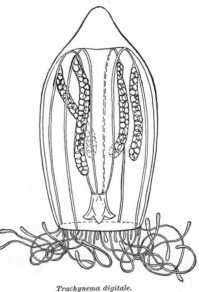

Trachynema digitale.

canals, but in true corals are vertical partitions inside the animal, between the inner and outer sacs, as explained on page 114.

GENUS *Millepora*

M. alcicornis, elk-horn coral. This beautiful coral, which is abundant in Florida and contributes to the building of the reefs, rises in broad expansions, more or less lobed, and suggests by its shape the object for which it is named. The whole mass is porous, being traversed by innumerable canals. Its surface, although smooth compared with that of other corals, is covered with very minute pores, which are of two sizes. The larger ones are the *gastropores*, or stomach-pores, in which the nutritive animal lives; it has a cylindrical body, with four knob-like tentacles and a mouth. Placed more or less irregularly around the gastropores are smaller pores, the *dactylopores* (finger-pores), from which emerge slender mouthless processes, or *dactylozoöids*, with tentacles and stinging-cells. These seem to be the guard-polyps of the community. The cups occupied by the zoöids are shallow. As one animal dies, another succeeds it and builds a horizontal partition separating the new cup from the old one. Thus the stony mass increases in size by the progress of succeeding generations of zoöids. The living animal occupies only the outer, open space. (Plate XLIV.)

ORDER **SIPHONOPHORA**

This order of hydroids consists of free-floating communities and is one of peculiar interest, since it shows in a clear manner the special function of each individual member of the colony, and illustrates better than the foregoing, perhaps, the curious forms of animal life which this class presents.

GENUS *Nanomia*

N. cara. This species is found on the New England coast. The members of the community are arranged along a hollow stem about three inches long which opens into every individual. At the top of the stem is a sac, or float; just below this is a group of swimming-bells which have no manubrium or mouth, and whose sole function is to provide locomotion for the community; and below these are three sets of zoöids, each having a triangular shield and tentacles. The tentacles are longer than the main stem. One of these last groups consists of the nutritive members, the mouths of the community, resembling manubriums of swimming-bells out of place. Each one has at the point of attachment a bunch of long, delicate tentacles having pendent knobs of lasso-cells. A second group, also with mouths, has shorter tentacles which are carried in spiral coils. The members of the third group have but one tentacle each and resemble the float at the end of the stem; presumably these drop off and produce new colonies. There are also on the lower part of the stem other reproductive members, which resemble the clusters of buds seen on

Adult *Nanomia cara.*

tubularian hydroids.   These animals are pink in color and move
through the water with a graceful swaying motion.

Genus *Physalia*

P. arethusa, the Portuguese man-of-war.   This colony is perhaps the
best-known one of the group, since it attracts much attention in Southern
waters, and is also one of the most remarkable examples of an animal
community.   The most prominent part
of the compound body is the float, an
oblong pear-shaped bag, full of air, which
floats on the surface of the water.   Its
color is bright blue, varying to rose.   On
the upper side of this air-vessel is a crest, or
sail, and from the under side depend long
tentacles, or streamers.   Some of these tentacles are covered with stinging- or lasso-
cells ; some are the feeding zoöids, with flask-
shaped bodies, and some, which look like
bunches of grapes, are the reproductive
zoöids. The tentacles in this curious cluster
are all close together and hang from one
side of the float, near the broader end.   The
longest are on the outside, which may be
called the windward side, since they serve to
keep the crest, or sail, before the wind ; and
when the wind is strong they stretch out to
a remarkable length,— forty to fifty feet,—
acting as anchors to keep the colony from
being driven ashore.   They also change its
course by raising the pointed end of the
float, thus forcing it to " come about."   These
long tentacles, ordinarily carried more or less
curled up, are in bunches of two to four, and
emerge from a common stem.   Clusters of
similar, but smaller, tentacles alternate with
the larger ones, but grow somewhat nearer
the pointed end of the float ; these are purely
locomotive organs.   Next come two smaller
sets of appendages, also of unequal size,
which are the nutritive organs of the community.   They are clustered together on a
stem like the others.   The appendages of

Physalia arethusa, Portuguese man-
of-war, one fifth natural size.

the third kind are small, resemble bunches
of grapes, and are scattered among the nutritive hydræ.   These last
are the reproductive zoöids of the community.

Genus *Vellela*

V. limbosa.   This hydroid is abundant on the Florida coast.   It has
a bright-blue, flattened, oblong, bladder-like float, four to five inches

long, which is divided into a number of concentric, communicating compartments. The margin of the float is entire, and a triangular sail extends diagonally across the top. On the under side is a single mouth on a manubrium, and surrounding it are a large number of short thread-like appendages having different functions. Some of them are feelers, others bear reproductive buds, and others have stinging-cells. Associated with *Velella* is an allied hydroid called *Porpita*, which has no sail, and in company with these two is a jellyfish called *Rataria*, which is supposed to be the offspring of one or the other of them.

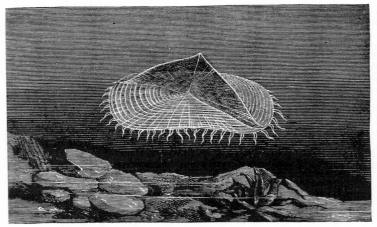

Velella limbosa.

TABLE SHOWING THE CLASSIFICATION OF THE SCYPHOZOA DESCRIBED IN THIS CHAPTER

Class

SCYPHOZOA

(Velum usually absent and tentaculocysts present ; the eggs are discharged into a gastric cavity. The type of this class is Aurelia)

Orders	Suborders	Genera	Species
STAUROMEDUSÆ *(Umbrella conical or vase-shaped ; no tentaculocysts)*		*Lucernaria*	*L. auricula*
PEROMEDUSÆ *(Umbrella conical and divided by transverse constrictions; four interradial tentaculocysts)*		*Pericolpa*	*P. quadrigata*
CUBOMEDUSÆ *(Umbrella four-sided, cup-shaped; four perradial tentaculocysts)*		*Charybdœa*	*C. marsupialis*
DISCOMEDUSÆ *(Flattened, saucer-like or disk-shaped umbrella ; radial tubes branched ; eight tentaculocysts)*	**CONNOSTOMÆ** *(Very small; marginal tentacles; short and solid; mouth square without arms)*		
	SEMOSTOMÆ *(Square mouth with four long arms; tentacles long and hollow)*	*Aurelia* *Cyanea* *Linerges* *Pelagia*	*A. flavidula* *C. arctica* *C. fulva* *C. versicolor* *L. mercurius* *P. cyanella*
	RHIZOSTOMÆ *(" Root-mouth ")* *(Mouth obliterated by growth of oral arms across it; tentacles absent)*	*Cassiopeia*	*C. frondosa*

133

CLASS **SCYPHOZOA**

THE LARGE JELLYFISHES

THERE is perhaps no marine animal which excites more wonder than the jellyfish. Its transparency, its graceful rhythmical movements, its long streaming tentacles, the variety and eccentricity of its form, and often of its color, attract attention, and one naturally desires to know something of its life-history. Jellyfishes are also called *medusæ*, because their long appendages suggest the locks of the Gorgon; *acalephs*, on account of their stinging or nettle-like properties; and sun-jellies, sea-blubbers, etc., because they float upon the surface during the warmest part of the day, when the sun is high. The name *jellyfish* is inappropriate, since the animal in no way resembles a fish except in the fact that it swims; but it is, nevertheless, the commonest name.

Jellyfishes vary in size from that of a pinhead to six or seven feet in diameter. They differ in the number, size, and position of the tentacles, the number of the radial canals, the form of the manubrium, the position of the egg-sacs, etc.; but the general plan of the internal structure is the same in all species. In shape they are compared to a mushroom. From the center of an umbrella-like top falls a central organ like the stalk of a mushroom. It is called the *manubrium* and is the mouth and stomach of the animal.

From the top of the manubrium radiate straight or branched tubes, which are connected with a canal which runs around the whole margin of the umbrella. Extending around the inner circumference of the disk in certain species (usually the hydroid medusæ), there is a horizontal shelf, called the *velum*, or veil, because it sometimes falls like a veil.

From the margin of the umbrella depend the tentacles. There are little mineral deposits, like crystals, called *lithocysts*, disposed at intervals on the margin, and known also as *marginal bodies*, which are supposed to be eyes. In some species these lithocysts are inclosed in club-shaped bodies, and they are then called *tentaculocysts*, because they are like small tentacles. These, together with the nerve-fibers, are called the sense-organs; but to what extent jellyfishes can see and feel is undetermined. This is the first appearance of sense-organs in animals. Around the concave surface of the umbrella is a muscular zone, or zone of contractile tissue, by which the animal opens and shuts the umbrella and gets its locomotive power. The *gonads*, which are conspicuous from being more opaque than the rest of the body, are the egg- or sperm-sacs. They vary in form and in position.

The jellyfish is carnivorous, feeding on small organisms such as crustaceans and even fishes. The tentacles are invested with stinging-cells, as are also the frills about the mouth, when such occur. With these stinging-cells, which are in some species so powerful as to have been compared with an electric battery, the jellyfish benumbs its prey. The stinging properties are due to nettle-like threads contained in poison-cells. When these penetrate the flesh they produce a pain similar to that of an electric shock.

The food is taken into the manubrium by the square mouth at its free end, and is there digested. It is then sent as nutritive fluid through the canal system of the body, and ejected through small pores in the canal which surrounds the margin of the umbrella.

There are two sexes. The gonads of the female contain eggs; those of the male, sperms. The contents of the gonads drop into the central cavity and pass out through the mouth. The fertilized ovum is called a *planula*, and is a transparent sphere covered with cilia, by means of which it swims about for a time. At length it attaches itself to some object, and becomes in some species a branching colony (hydroid), in other species a *strobila*. The latter, as it grows, is constricted at intervals, and at maturity resembles a pile of inverted saucers with lobed edges. Each of these saucers is finally detached, and when liberated is called an *ephyrula*, and becomes a jellyfish. Thus its cycle of life is complete. There are some species which, having no hydroid or strobila state, mature without alternation of generation (*metagenesis*).

The term of life of the jellyfish does not exceed one year. Even the giant *Cyanea* attains its immense growth in six months. It starts in the spring as an ephyrula, not more than one half of an inch in diameter, and when it dies in the autumn is often six to eight feet in diameter. The bodies of jellyfishes are ninety-nine per cent. water, and the dead ones thrown upon the beaches by the autumn storms rapidly disappear, leaving no traces behind.

The powerful stinging-cells with which the large medusæ are armed make them formidable enemies, and it is probable that some deaths by drowning are caused by swimmers encountering them and becoming paralyzed by them.

ORDER **STAUROMEDUSÆ**
(" *Cross-medusæ* ")
Genus *Lucernaria*

L. auricula. This little iridescent jellyfish, which measures about one and a half inches in diameter, is commonly found attached to eel-grass by a stalk-like projection of the top of the umbrella. Short, globe-tipped tentacles are arranged in eight clusters, each cluster on a raised prolongation of the margin of the umbrella, and in the center of each space between them is a dark kidney-shaped organ called the *anchor*. These anchors are used for holding, either for suspension or when moving from place to place. The mouth forms a slight quadrangular projection in the center of the bell-like expansion. The arm-like projections are mottled with two rows of spots, which are the ova. Although a free form and capable of moving about, *Lucernaria* is sedentary in habit. It is sometimes found free, but generally attached by its extremity to eel-grass or *Fucus*, seldom to rocks. It is constantly changing its shape. The one it most frequently assumes is that of a cup or inverted bell. It is found on the New England coast. (Plate XLIV.)

ORDER **PEROMEDUSÆ**
(" *Maimed medusæ* ")
Genus *Pericolpa*

P. quadrigata. Umbrella conical and divided by a horizontal constriction into two parts, the lower one being again divided into lobes. There are four long tentacles and four tentaculocysts. It is not found on the coasts of the United States.

ORDER **CUBOMEDUSÆ**

(" *Cube-medusæ* ")

GENUS *Charybdœa*

C. marsupialis. Umbrella square, flattened on top, and of firm consistency. Four tentacles fall from lobes on the umbrella, and four club-shaped eyes are in marginal notches. Plate-like egg-sacs follow each side of the four radial canals. The bell is one inch in diameter and about two inches in height. It is not found on the coasts of the United States.

ORDER **DISCOMEDUSÆ**

(" *Disk-medusæ* ")

SUBORDER **SEMOSTOMÆ**

GENUS *Aurelia*

A. flavidula. Size eight to ten inches in diameter ; disk gelatinous, transparent bluish-white, broad and comparatively flat, with a fringe of short tentacles of even length around the margin ; margin broken by eight notches, in each one of which is a club-like organ (*tentaculocyst*) containing calcareous spots or eyes, which are hidden by lappets or hood-like coverings ; groups of nerve-cells also lie in the marginal notches; radial canals branched; manubrium very short, with square mouth, which is surrounded by delicate membranes, or oral arms, each arm being a folded membrane tapering to a point. The edges of the membranes are covered with lasso- or stinging-cells. Four egg-sacs, or gonads, are conspicuous in horseshoe shape around the center of the disk. The gonads are pink in the males, and yellow in the females. These medusæ swim in shoals, and are common everywhere in summer. They may be said to be annual animals, for they make their appearance regularly as free-swimming medusæ in the latter part of April, when they may be seen in immense numbers near the surface when the water is smooth and the sky clear. At this time they are about an inch in diameter. They grow rapidly, and by the end of June have attained their full size. At

Aurelia flavidula, about one fourth natural size.

the end of July they are fully developed, and begin to discharge their eggs, which go into the folds around the mouth and remain there until they attain the planula stage. After the spawning period the medusæ, reduced in strength, are unable to resist the storms of the autumn, and many of them are cast ashore ; many others, in a more or less wasted condition, float near the surface, but the body is less transparent, its tissues are thickened, its tentacles gone, and general dissolution has commenced. In this condition the medusæ are frequently capsized by the air which accumulates in the empty egg-cavities, and, floating helplessly on the surface, are attacked and destroyed by swarms of small crustaceans; thus their cycle of life is terminated. It has been suggested that the destruction of the mothers, by being cast

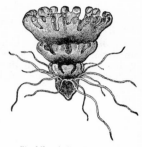

Strobila of *Aurelia flavidula*.

upon the beaches in the autumnal gales, is a provision to set free the planulæ in a position favorable to their existence ; for when liberated

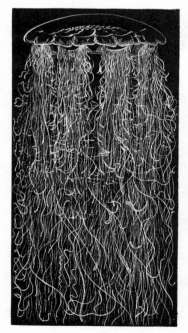

Cyanea arctica, greatly reduced in size.

they fasten upon the rocks and sea-weeds of the shore, where, during the winter months, they develop into strobilæ, which in turn free their saucer-like disks early in April.

Genus *Cyanea*

C. arctica, the sun-jelly or sea-blubber. This is the largest jellyfish known. Some individuals measure seven and a half feet across the disk and have tentacles more than one hundred feet long. Usually they are three to five feet in diameter, with tentacles thirty to forty feet long. The disk is red, the margin white and scalloped. The tentacles, of different colors, are covered with lasso- or stinging-cells, and are arranged in eight distinct, thick clusters on the margin. From the mouth hang four long and very broad, thin curtains, much folded and ruffled, whose edges at times look as if they were embroidered, because great numbers of discharged eggs are attached to them. Four egg-sacs hang from the disk near the manubrium, and eight sense-organs (tentaculocysts), in hardened coverings, lie in some of the deep incisions of the margin. *Cyanea* is usually solitary, seldom being seen in company with others. It is common on the New England coast, and is frequently found stranded on the beach, where it in no way suggests the beautiful appearance it presents when floating in the water. Like *Aurelia*, *Cyanea* has a strobila stage. It is supposed that the young remain near the bottom, for they are seldom seen, while adults are plentiful. They begin to appear in numbers at the end of summer from Cape Cod northward.

C. fulva. This species is found in midsummer south of Cape Cod and is common in Long Island Sound. Its general color is light yellowish-brown, the flowing curtains being the darkest part of the animal. It is not as large as *C. arctica*, and the lobes of the margin are deeper and more rounded.

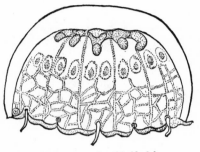

Linerges mercurius, thimble-fish.

C. versicolor. The whole disk is bluish milky-white, the flowing curtains are light brown, and the tentacles are pink. It is not so large as *C. arctica*. Found in the spring on the southern coast.

Genus *Linerges*

L. mercurius, the thimble-fish. The English name indicates the form as well as the size of this little brownish jellyfish, which is found near the Florida Keys, extending in lines for considerable distances.

Genus *Pelagia*

P. cyanella. Umbrella spherical, margin scalloped, tentacles eight in number; four long appendages ruffled on the edges hang from the mouth; size about two inches in diameter; appendages four inches long; color pink. (See next page.)

Suborder RHIZOSTOMÆ

The **Rhizostomæ**, or root-mouth jellyfishes, are very remarkable. They have no tentacles, but covering the end of the manubrium and hanging from it like tentacles are oval appendages with numerous minute funnel-like apertures, called suctorial mouths. As the manner of locomotion of jellyfishes is peculiar to themselves, so also is this many-mouthed development unique in the animal kingdom. The type of this group, described below, is found on the Florida Keys. The different species vary in diameter from three to eight inches.

Genus *Cassiopeia*

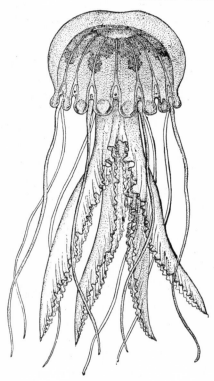

Pelagia cyanella.

C. frondosa. This species has a circular disk, on the margin of which are sixteen sense-organs (tentaculocysts), but no tentacles. The lower end of the manubrium, which in other jellyfishes is an open mouth, is closed by eight arms which emanate from it and are usually extended laterally, lying parallel to the disk. These arms are much branched, and the branches, in turn, have numerous appendages. Some of these appendages look like little polyps and have mouths surrounded by crowns of tentacles; others are ovoid bodies without external openings, but with a central cavity connected with vessels leading to the arms. The former are mouths, but the function of the ovoid bodies is not known. Although able to swim freely, *Cassiopeia* lies usually on its back, as if attached, and languidly opens and closes its disk, rarely changing its position. Its arms, extending upward, appear like the fronds of algæ. These jellyfishes are common on the Florida coast, huddled together on the sands of the coral reefs. (Plate XLIV.)

TABLE SHOWING THE CLASSIFICATION OF THE ACTINOZOA
DESCRIBED IN THIS CHAPTER

Class

ACTINOZOA

Subclass
Zoantharia

(Mesenteries numerous, usually in multiples of six; tentacles unbranched hollow cones)

Orders	Genera	Species
ACTINIARIA *(The sea-anemones. Single; no skeleton)*	*Metridium* *Rhodactinia* *Holocampa* *Sagartia*	*M. marginatum* *R. davidsii* *H. producta* *S. leucolena*
MADREPORARIA *(The stone- or reef-corals. Colonies; skeleton calcareous)*	*Oculina* *Astræa* *Meandrina* *Diploria* *Madrepora* *Astrangia*	*D. cerebriformis* *M. cervicornis* *M. palmata* *A. danaë*
ANTIPATHARIA *(The black corals)*		

Subclass
Alcyonaria or Halcyonoida

(Tentacles and mesenteries eight in number; tentacles feathered, that is, with uniform branches)

ALCYONACEA	*Alcyonium* *Tubipora*	*A. palmatum*
GORGONACEA *(The sea-fans and sea-whips. Compound, tree-like colonies, with horny axis, branching throughout)*		
PENNATULACEA *(Free, phosphorescent; colonies, with horny axis; polyps in lateral branches)*	*Pennatula*	

141

CLASS **ACTINOZOA**

SEA-ANEMONES, REEF-CORALS, SEA-FANS, SEA-WHIPS, AND SEA-PENS

THE animals of this class are divided into two subclasses, based on the following anatomical differences: In the first subdivision, which includes the sea-anemones and the reef-building corals, the polyps have numerous simple, hollow tentacles and radial partitions of the same number, both being some multiple of six. The polyps of a colony are all alike, and the hard matter they secrete is carbonate of lime. In the second subdivision, the *Alcyonaria,*—or halcyonoids, as they are commonly called,—the tentacles and radial partitions are always eight in number, and the tentacles have small symmetrical appendages or branches. The polyps of this group are often accompanied by small zoöids having no tentacles. The hard secretions are horny and elastic, as in sea-fans, sea-whips, and sea-pens, or they are extremely hard, as in *Corallina rubrum.*

SUBCLASS **ZOANTHARIA**

("Animal-flowers")

ORDER **ACTINIARIA**

SEA-ANEMONES

These curious and, at times, beautiful creatures are polyps, and are constructed on the radial system. They have a cylindrical body with a broad base and rows of hollow tentacles around the upper disk. They have a central sac, and a space between the outer and inner sacs which is divided vertically by walls called *mesenteries,* as explained on page 114. Each tentacle, however many there may be, has a corresponding chamber. The inner sac has a mouth, like a slit, at the top of the disk, opening to the outside, and it also has openings into the chambered spaces which surround it. These chambers also open into the hollow tentacles; thus a continuous circulation throughout the whole animal is established.

The food taken in at the mouth is digested in the inner sac, passes through all the chambers of the cavity as nutritive fluid, and is then expelled at the mouth again. The inner sac, or gullet, has longitudinal grooves; two of these are broad and deep, and correspond to the corners of the mouth. These are called *siphonoglyphs*. The sea-anemone is soft and contractile, and belongs to the only order of this class which does not secrete a skeleton. It has two sets of muscles, one of which extends from the base to the summit of the body and is placed on the dividing partitions. Sea-anemones are classified by the arrangement of the septa and the manner in which the muscles are placed upon them. The other set of muscles is arranged around the circumference of the column or body. Each tentacle is furnished with similar sets of muscles. The animal is sensitive, and at the least alarm contracts its body by means of these muscles, and quickly transforms itself from a beautiful, flower-like form into a shapeless, unattractive, inconspicuous mass.

The *Actiniaria* are developed from the egg. The eggs form on the edges of the inner walls (mesenteries), and when mature drop into the outer sac (gullet), and out of the mouth as ciliated spheres (planulæ). After swimming about for a time these attach themselves to rocks, and, conforming to the irregularities of the surface, secure a tight hold. The upper surface of the planula then becomes depressed and forms a gullet, and in time a complete animal is formed. The *Actiniaria* reproduce also by budding. A small protuberance or simple elevation of the body-wall appears on the side at the base, or in some species on the disk of the animal, which generally develops into a complete animal and at maturity falls away from the parent. Sometimes several anemones bud simultaneously from the same individual, and a third generation commences to bud at the same time from the immature young of the parent stock. The sea-anemones increase also by self-division. In this case a constriction is formed, which gradually deepens and forms a complete partition of the body, and two individuals exist where originally there was but one.

The *Actiniaria* are carnivorous and very voracious. They feed on small organisms and on shell-fish and crustaceans, which they suck out of their shells. To secure their prey they are armed with an abundant supply of stinging-cells on the tentacles, and also with fine stinging-threads which are ejected from pores which are distributed over the whole body.

Sea-anemones vary greatly in color and form, and when expanded suggest flowers, but do not resemble the one for which they are named. They abound on every shore, the same genus often being found in widely separated regions. They are larger and more highly colored in tropical waters. Many of the species are littoral, and are found in the tide-pools of rocky caverns, on the under side of rocks, and on the piles of wharves and bridges at low-water mark. The majority of them are attached, but are able to change their location; others, *Edwardsia* and *Cerianthus*, swim about when young, and in the adult state burrow in the sand or mud, leaving only their tentacles exposed. *Bucidium parasiticum* is parasitic on the folds of the membrane which hangs from the mouth of the large jellyfish *Cyanea arctica*. *Fenja* and *Peachia* lie on the sea-bottom, with their bodies horizontal like a worm, the mouth-end and tentacles erect.

Adamsia palliata furnishes another example of commensalism; it lives on the back of shells, commonly the whelk, inhabited by hermit-crabs. *Minyas* is pelagic; it has a float at one end, and by means of its tentacles swims about freely.

A very few species only are described below, since these polyps are unmistakable, being always columnar bodies, with the upper disk more or less crowded with tentacles, and so brilliant in coloring and beautiful in form as to attract attention if found in the expanded state; otherwise they are easily overlooked.

Genus *Metridium*

M. marginatum. This is the most conspicuous and abundant sea-anemone of the northeastern coast. It is common from New York northward, and is found near low-water mark in tide-pools, on the under side of large stones, in sheltered crevices of rocks, and on the piles of wharves and bridges. In contraction it is a broad, low cone, but when expanded is sometimes ten inches across the disk. Allied species found in Florida are eighteen inches in diameter. The column is smooth, cylindrical, and broader than long. At the top is a slightly elevated, thickened fold, and above this a deeply folded and frilled margin, with numerous fine, short tentacles, appearing like a fringe, which cover the upper side of the disk half-way to the oval mouth. The color is exceedingly variable; commonly the column is yellowish-brown, but it may be pink, white, salmon, orange, or dark brown, or striped or mottled with different colors. The disk and folds are lighter or flesh-colored, and the tentacles are of varying colors, usually grayish with tips of brighter colors. When irritated this species throws out from the column numbers of long, slender white threads (*acontia*), which are covered with minute stinging-cells. These organs of defense protect the animal from the attacks of many enemies.

Genus *Rhodactinia*

R. davidsii (Agassiz), *Tealia crassiformis* (Gosse), the thick-petaled rose-anemone. The color varies, being often bluish-green mottled with crimson, often bright cherry-red, with the thick tentacles somewhat lighter in shade, or flesh-colored. The animal is found in shallow water. It assumes various shapes, changing every few minutes. The tentacles are short, conical, and uniform in size; the column, the breadth of which is greater than its height, often has wart-like processes in longitudinal lines. The diameter of the disk is about three inches. Found from Cape Cod northward in tide-pools and on ledges covered with *Fucus*.

Genus *Holocampa*

H. producta. Its column, stretched to its full extent, is a foot in length and about an inch in diameter, but when contracted is much shorter and thicker. It has but twenty tentacles, and these have swollen tips. Rows of suckers extend the length of the column. It ranges from Cape Cod to South Carolina, and is found under rocks at low-tide mark, and also on sandy beaches, buried in the sand, with its tentacles only above the surface.

Genus *Sagartia*

S. leucolena, the white-armed anemone. It ranges from Cape Cod to North Carolina, and is common in Long Island Sound, being found at low-water mark on the under side of stones. The column is elongated, cylindrical, translucent, flesh-colored, with simple plain disk and long, slender, whitish tentacles crowded together near the margin.

ORDER **MADREPORARIA**

STONE- OR REEF-CORALS

The coral resembles the sea-anemone and is a polyp constructed on the radial plan (page 113). It lives in colonies, but, unlike the hydroid colonies, each polyp of the community is a complete organism, and in the reef-building corals all the individual polyps of a colony are alike. The home of each animal is called a *corallite*, and the aggregation of many corallites is a *corallum*.

The corallite is composed of carbonate of lime secreted by the polyp, and, broadly speaking, may be called a skeleton. The secretion forms a basal plate and radiating partitions between the mesenteries in the cavity of the animal, and also surrounds the polyp like a cup. In some species this is a solid substance; in others it is like a network through which the animal substance (cœnosarc) of the zoöids of the colony is connected, as in *Madrepora*.

The polyps reproduce by budding and by self-division (fission), in a manner similar to that of sea-anemones. The way in which the budding or the fission takes place determines the shape of the colony, or corallum, which has a great variety of forms. In some species the budding is confined to certain individuals of the colony. In this case the branched forms result. When growth takes place by fission, hemispherical masses are formed, which are often perfectly symmetrical, as in the so-called brain-corals. In *Astræa* the polyps are inclosed separately, but in *Meandrina* fission is confined to the upper half of the polyps, so that a complex polyp is formed, with several mouths opening into a common stomach, making long serpentine furrows on the corallum.

Some of the genera of the second subdivision, the alcyonarians, differ materially from the ordinary idea of corals, as their framework is of a horny and more or less flexible material (chitin). Of these are the sea-fans, sea-whips, and sea-pens. The organ-pipe coral of the same subdivision is an example of an exceedingly fragile lime structure, while the red coral, *Corallina rubrum*, the species so much used for ornamental purposes, has an exceedingly hard and stony character. The madrepore corals are called reef-builders, but not in the sense of constructors of reefs. They do not erect definite structures as bees do. It is the aggregation of the skeletons of the dead polyps, together with other agencies, which forms a reef. The coral polyps, though so minute individually, are almost infinite in numbers. It is estimated that the colonies rise one half of an inch in ten years.

Corals live at different depths in the sea. Those which form the base of the reef are the astræans, which do not live above a depth of six fathoms. They are characterized by little star-shaped spots on the corallum, the radial partitions meeting in the center of the spots, or corallites. Next above the astræans come the mæandrinas and the porites. The former have elongated openings which extend in waving furrows over the surface. The porites resemble astræans, but the pits are smaller, with fewer partitions, and the substance is more porous. Above these and capping the reefs are the beautiful branching and palmate madreporians, together with millepores, numerous varieties of sea-fans (*Gorgonacea*), and the calcareous seaweeds (nullipores), making a garden of beautiful branching forms of every shape and color.

The coral reef is as thickly inhabited by other living organisms as is the forest by birds and insects. Mollusks, worms, crabs, starfishes, and sea-urchins find resting-places there and work destruction to the coral masses, as they bore and penetrate the reef in various ways until large fragments of it are detached and either washed by the waves to places far from their foundation, or ground to sand, which, filling the interstices of the reef, adds to its solidity.

The living coral is quite different in appearance from the bleached skeletons commonly seen. The surface of the corallum is often soft and downy, from the numerous waving tentacles, and its coloring is vivid and varied. The madrepores are pink, yellow, green, brown, and purple. *Tubipora*, the organ-pipe coral, has green polyps emanating from its red tubes. White polyps in star-like form dot the branches of the red coral of commerce, *Corallina rubrum*. The whole mass of *Helipora* is bright blue, and the beautiful sea-pens are both highly colored and phosphorescent. Owing to the fact that these brilliantly colored polyps were mistaken for blossoms, the recognition of their true character was long delayed, they having been ranked as vegetables until comparatively recent times.

With few exceptions, corals do not grow in water below the temperature of 68°, hence they are inhabitants of tropical and subtropical waters. The Florida Keys are coral reefs, and the species described below are to be found there.

Genus *Oculina*

Arborescent; corallites arranged somewhat spirally on branches and widely separated; branches compact between corallites. Each bud is for a time at the apex of the branch, but finally becomes lateral, and then gives off another bud from its upper surface, and so the stem lengthens. (Plate XLIV.)

Genus *Astræa*

The star-corals. The corals of this genus are hemispherical masses covered with small star-shaped pits, or corallites. Although the diameter of an **astræa-dome may be** twelve feet or more, it has only one half or three quarters of an inch of living coral on its surface, the rest being solid matter left behind as the polyps rose in growth. The colony increases by self-division. The septa meet in the center of the corallite, making star-like pits; the surface is comparatively smooth. (Plate XLIV.)

Genera *Meandrina, Diploria*

Corallum massive, hemispherical in shape, with furrows running in irregular lines over the whole surface. The peculiar serpentine form of the corallite is produced by the animal growing in one direction, fission being incomplete, and new mouths being successively opened until a line of them extends along a common stomach.

D. cerebriformis. This species is commonly known as brain-coral or brain-stone. The hemispherical shape, together with the peculiar serpentine corallites, makes its resemblance to the human brain very noticeable and the name unusually appropriate. This species, when living, is bright yellow. (Plate XLV.)

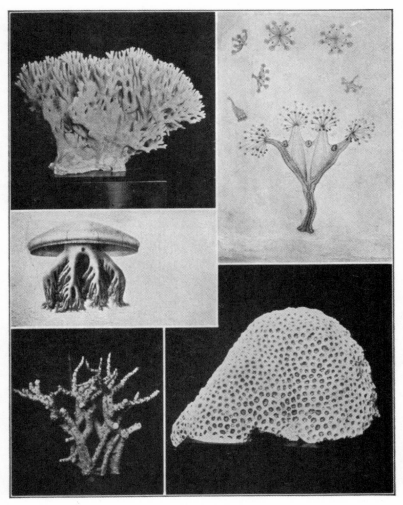

PLATE XLIV.

Millepora alcicornis.   Lucernaria auricula.
Cassiopeia frondosa.   Astræa argus.
Oculina.

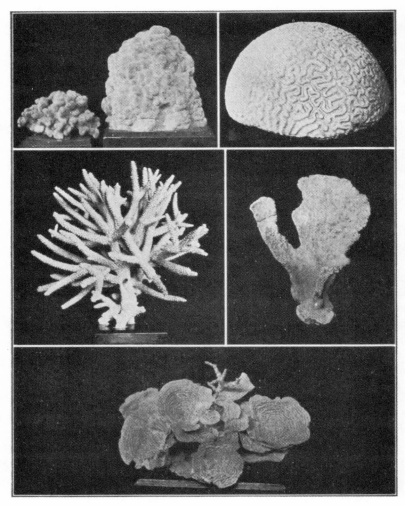

PLATE XLV.

Porites furcata and P. astræaoides.   Diplora cerebriformis.
Madrepora cervicornis.   Madrepora palmata.
                    Mycedium fragile.

GENUS *Madrepora*

Some species of these corals appear like branches, while others have flat, low surfaces or fronds; all of them are covered with innumerable small cylindrical cups. Each cup is the home of a polyp, which secretes calcareous matter around its column, and septa between its radial partitions. The corallum, when examined with a glass, looks like meshwork. Through the fine openings of the porous surface, the polyps of the colony are connected by interlacing tubes of animal substance (cœnosarc). The polyps of the madrepore colonies are small in comparison with the connecting structure, which becomes very massive; but, although large, the corallum is fragile, on account of its perforated character and the exceeding delicacy of its parts.

In species which form incrustations, new polyps arise from tissue which spreads beyond the corallites. In some species certain polyps and corallites increase in length, growing longitudinally, and continually form buds around the base. This manner of growth leads to the formation of branches, while the former manner gives lateral extension. Both of these forms of budding may take place at the same time in the same colony. The madrepores are among the most common of the reef-builders. They form reefs which extend for miles around the Florida Keys.

M. cervicornis, the stag-horn coral. This is a branching species which attains large size. Its manner of growth is as follows: At the tip of each branch is an individual polyp, which is larger than those which surround the branch. This is the original animal which started the branch, and is the parent from which all the others on the branch have budded. The large terminal polyp buds around the base; a surplus of lime also collects at the base and clogs its tissues, so that it no longer can perform the functions of life, and after a certain period the base becomes dead matter. The polyp on the upper end continues to live and rises above the excess of solid matter. At the same time it continues to form new buds. The buds become independent corallites and secrete an excess of calcareous matter at their bases, which cements them to the parent stock and increases the thickness of the branch. Thus, as the original polyp constantly rises and buds, the colony assumes a stem-like form, covered with numerous individuals. Certain polyps on the main stem have the attributes of the parent animal. These start branches, and so the process goes on, and in time the colony becomes much branched and arborescent in form. In the living coral each little polyp is like a minute sea-anemone, having a colored cylindrical body surrounded on its upper disk with numerous tentacles. (Plate XLV.)

M. palmata. This madrepore grows like the one described above, except that the branches do not remain separated, but unite or grow together, giving broad, flat surfaces which resemble fronds. When carefully examined these surfaces show striations which indicate the course of the branches. The strictures forming the lobes are caused by the failure of the branches to unite. On the Carysfort Reef of the Florida Keys this species covers the top of the reef for several miles, nearly reaching the surface, and appears like a vast bed of low yellow shrubbery. (Plate XLV.)

Genus *Astrangia*

A. danaë. A small coral found on the New England coast. It lives in the clefts of rocks in small patches, sometimes two to three inches across and one quarter of an inch or more high. Frequently it is like a thin crust of lime covered with star-like divisions. Sometimes it forms branches. The living animals are white, and when expanded rise above the cells and resemble a cluster of small sea-anemones.

SUBCLASS **ALCYONARIA** or **HALCYONOIDA**

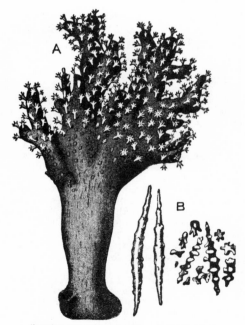

Alcyonium palmatum : A, entire colony; *B,* spicules.

In this subclass—the actinoid corals—the polyps are of two kinds. The smaller are without tentacles and are called *siphonozoöids.* The larger have but eight radial partitions and eight tentacles. This limitation of parts places them in a higher rank than the corals of the first subclass. Another characteristic of these polyps is the presence of symmetrical branchlets on the tentacles, which give them a feather-like appearance. These corals are called halcyonoids.

Some of them may easily be fancied to have been selected for halcyons' nests, as the name suggests—the sea-fans, for example.

ORDER **ALCYONACEA**

GENUS *Alcyonium*

A. palmatum. This coral community is found sometimes at low-water mark, but usually in deeper water, attached to shells and stones. It is commonly known as dead-men's-fingers, an unpleasant name given it by fishermen because of a fancied resemblance to a human hand with only the stumps of the fingers. The substance of the coral is semi-cartilaginous, with scattered spicules of lime which give it stability. When the polyps are fully extended the colony is rather attractive in appearance, but not so when contracted. It is found in abundance on the New England coast. An immense *Alcyonium, Paragorgia arborea*, grows on the fishing-banks off Newfoundland, and is sometimes brought up on the fishing-lines. It is tree-like in form, and measures six feet or more in length.

GENUS *Tubipora*

The organ-pipe coral. This genus, which is deep red in color and very fragile, consists of many tubes slightly separated from

Tubipora, organ-pipe coral, natural size.

one another, but connected by horizontal platforms at short intervals.   The form of reproduction, by budding, in this colony is
peculiar to itself.   The spicules of lime secreted in the polyp
unite or fuse into a tube or cylindrical skeleton.   At certain
stages of development the polyp sends out a horizontal expansion, which unites with the expansions of other polyps and becomes calcified, forming a shelf which binds the tubes together.
From the top of the platforms other corallites are formed, and
thus a colony is made, which broadens as it rises in its growth.
The body of the polyp is green, the skeleton red.   It belongs to
the East Indian seas and is given here only as an example of a
peculiar manner of growth.

ORDER **GORGONACEA**

SEA-FANS, SEA-WHIPS, AND SEA-FEATHERS

These are compound, tree-like *Alcyonaria*, with a calcareous or
horny skeleton which forms a branched axis and is covered with a
layer of united polyps having spicules of lime distributed through
the mass, which give some firmness to the bark-like covering.
Gorgonias, in great variety, grow in abundance on the coral reefs
and mud-flats of Florida, forming masses of low shrubbery, pink,
yellow, brown, or purple in color.

The sea-whips and sea-feathers are varieties of gorgonias,
which are named from their forms.   Some have shapes which
resemble branching shrubs; others are long unbranched rods,
either straight or spiral.   They attain a height of several feet and
are of various colors.   The colony has a horny axis surrounded
by a living mass which resembles a sheet of animal matter.   This
mass consists of polyps closely united, and has throughout its substance spicules of carbonate of lime, making it a kind of calcareous crust or bark.   In dried specimens this becomes very brittle
and is easily broken from the horny axis. (Plates XLVI, XLVII.)

The sea-fans are colonies with a central, horny, flexible, and
much-branched axis, covered, as in the sea-whips, with a layer of
united polyps containing spicules of lime, which make a some-

PLATE XLVI.

GORGONIAS.

Eugorgia aurantica.
Pterogorgia acerosa.

Muricea specifera.
Gorgonia anceps.

PLATE XLVII.

Leptogorgia rigida (a gorgonia).
Gorgonia flabellum (a gorgonia).

Eunicea lugubris (a gorgonia).
Leptogorgia Agassizii (a gorgonia).
Pennatula borealis and P. aculeata
  (sea-pens).

what firm crust. This, in dried specimens, breaks off readily. The colony branches profusely, or rather separates by fission, in one plane, the large and small branches making a network of fan-like shape and often of great fineness and intricacy. These fans attain a length of several feet and a corresponding breadth, and are abundant in semi-tropical as well as in more southern waters. In color they are red, yellow, brown, or purple.

ORDER **PENNATULACEA**

SEA-PENS

These singular colonies resemble quill-feathers, such as are used for pens, and are named for this reason. The long, horny central axis is naked below, and is partly buried in the sand, but is not permanently attached. The upper portion of the axis has two rows of short, opposite, lateral branches; on the upper side of the branches the polyps live in separate inclosures. Spicules of lime are present in the substance of the branches, which gives them stability. Sea-pens are found at moderate depths and are widely distributed. They are highly colored and phosphorescent.

TABLE SHOWING THE CLASSIFICATION OF THE CTENOPHORA DESCRIBED IN THIS CHAPTER

Class
CTENOPHORA

Orders	Genera	Species
CYDIPPIDA *(Two tentacles, retractile into sheaths)*	*Pleurobrachia*	*P. rhododaciyla*
LOBATA *(Numerous lateral tentacles contained in a groove; body compressed; two large oral lobes)*	*Bolina* *Mnemiopsis*	*B. alata* *B. septentrionalis* *B. vitrea* *M. Leidyii*
CESTIDA *(Ribbon-like form, from body being extremely compressed in the vertical plane)*	*Cestum*	*C. veneris*
BEROÏDA *(No tentacles; mouth very wide; gullet occupies greater part of body)*	*Idyia*	*I. roseola* *I. cyanthina*

CLASS **CTENOPHORA**

COMB-JELLIES

THESE are delicate, free-swimming, generally spherical bodies, resembling jellyfishes in outline, transparency, and gelatinous consistency, but differing from them widely in the manner of locomotion. They are called "comb-jellies" from the rows of flat cilia, arranged like the teeth of a comb, which run in eight meridional lines over the surface. It is by means of these cilia that the animal moves through the water. The little paddles are worked in unison, in single lines, or each one of them can be moved independently, and they give the animal varying and peculiar motions. The *Ctenophora* are nearly transparent, but have a prismatic coloring, caused by the waving cilia, and at night they are phosphorescent. They are widely distributed, being found in all seas.

The mouth of the animal opens into a gullet which extends two thirds through the length of the body. On each side of the gullet is a vertical tube. The two tubes unite at the base of the gullet, and from there run as a single canal to the end opposite the mouth, and open to the outside through two excretory pores. From the base of the gullet, where the tubes unite, two other tubes extend laterally, which divide and subdivide in a horizontal plane, becoming eight in number, and connect at the surface with the lines of cilia; then, dividing, run in opposite directions to the poles of the spherical body. The animal derives its nourishment and air through this circulatory system. A nervous system is situated at the pole opposite the mouth, in a small area surrounded by cilia, in the center is an eye-speck, or lithocyst.

ORDER **CYDIPPIDA**

Genus *Pleurobrachia*

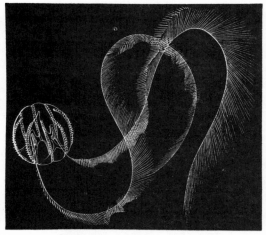

Pleurobrachia rhododactyla, in motion.

P. rhododactyla. A transparent spherical body, one inch to one and a half inches in diameter, with eight combs or plates of flat cilia extending from pole to pole. At one pole is the mouth, like a slit, at the other a small area in the center of which is an eye-spot. From the body hang two tentacles, half a yard or more in length, fringed with cilia. The tentacles are very contractile and can be rolled up or expanded with great rapidity; they take graceful curves as the animal moves rapidly through the water. *Pleurobrachia* has a pink tint, and prismatic colors play over it from the vibrating cilia. It is a beautiful and interesting creature to watch. Found along the shores of Massachusetts and Maine.

ORDER **LOBATA**

Genus *Bolina*

B. alata. Slightly oval in form; lower part of the body divided into two large lobes which hang below the mouth. Four of the swimming-plates are shorter than the other four and terminate in curious processes or short appendages called auricles. *Bolina* is about two inches in length, and is very delicate, transparent, and phosphorescent. Its contractile power enables it to vary in outline to a considerable extent. It has a slow undulating motion, and sometimes carries its lobes uppermost and open. Usu-

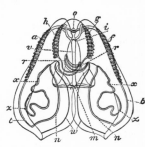

Bolina alata, seen from the broad side: *o*, eye-speck; *m*, mouth; *r*, auricles; *v*, digestive cavity; *g, h*, short rows of flappers; *a, f*, long rows of flappers; *b, n, x, t, z*, tubes winding in the larger lobes; *i*, base of gullet. About half natural size.

ally found associated with *Pleurobrachia* from Massachusetts northward.

B. septentrionalis. Found on the northern Pacific coast.

B. vitrea. A species found in Florida.

Genus *Mnemiopsis*

M. Leidyii. Resembles *Bolina* in general form; often six to eight inches in length; gregarious, thousands often being collected together; exceedingly phosphorescent.

ORDER **CESTIDA**

Genus *Cestum*

C. veneris, Venus's girdle. This singular animal, although not an inhabitant of our seas, has its place in this group, and is shown here because of its very curious shape. In form it is flat and ribbon-like. Sometimes it attains a length of five feet, while in breadth it is but one or two inches. The mouth is midway in its length and is opposite the sense-organ or eye-spot. On each side of the mouth is a short tentacle which protrudes from a sac. Four of the swimming-plates are small; the other four extend along the edge of the body. *Cestum* moves by contractions of the body more than by the combs which fringe its edges. It is very transparent, with a violet hue, and is so delicate that it is difficult to capture it uninjured. Its habitat is the Mediterranean Sea. It may be seen among the zoölogical specimens in almost any museum.

ORDER **BEROÏDA**

Genus *Idyia*

I. roseola. This species has an ovate body three to four inches in height and about half as broad. Some individuals are larger. It has

Cestum veneris.

an eye-spot on the upper rounded side, and at the other end a very large mouth opening into a digestive cavity, which occupies the greater

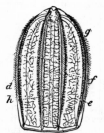

Idyia roseola, half natural size: *d, e, f, g, h,* rows of locomotive flappers.

part of the body. A delicate fringe surrounds the area about the eye-spot, and eight rows of cilia run from there to the oral end. It has no tentacles. *Idyia* is pink and especially highly colored at the spawning-time. Like other jellyfishes, their part in life is finished when they have discharged their spawn, and the first September storms break them to pieces. In July and August they are plentiful on the New England coast. They appear at the surface of the water in the hottest part of the day, but disappear entirely when the water is in the least rough or the weather is cold or the sun overcast. Their movements are slow and graceful, the long axis being carried in a nearly horizontal position. They are exceedingly voracious, feeding chiefly on other *Ctenophora,* and often swallowing animals as large as themselves.

I. cyanthina. This species, found on the northern Pacific coast, broadens near the center, making it somewhat vase-shaped. *Idyopsis Clarkii,* a similar genus, found in Florida, is globular. All these species are very beautiful, the rapid movement of the cilia giving them a brilliant iridescence.

III

WORMS
(PLATYHELMINTHES
NEMATHELMINTHES
ANNULATA)

TABLE SHOWING THE CLASSIFICATION OF THE WORMS
DESCRIBED IN THIS CHAPTER

Phylum
PLATYHELMINTHES

Class
TURBELLARIA

Orders	Genera	Species
POLYCLADIDA	*Planocera*	*P. nebulosa*
	Stylochopsis	*S. littoralis*
	Leptoplana	*L. folium*
TRICLADIDA	*Planaria*	*P. grisea*
	Procerodes	*P. frequens*
	Bdelloura	*B. rustica*
		B. candida
	Fovia	*F. Warrenii*
RHABDOCŒLIDA		

Class
TREMATODA
(External and internal parasites)

Class
CESTODA
(Internal parasites)

Class
NEMERTINEA

Tetrastemma	*T. arenicola*
Nemertes	*N. socialis*
	N. viridis
Meckelia	*M. ingens*
	M. rosea
Cerebratulus	*C. angulatus*
Cosmocephala	*C. ochracea*
Polina	*P. glutinosa*

160

Phylum
NEMATHELMINTHES
Class
NEMATODA

Genus	Species
Pontonema	*P. marinum*

Phylum
ANNULATA
Class
CHÆTOPODA
Subclass
Polychæta

Orders	Families	Genera	Species
ERRANTIA			
	SYLLIDÆ		
	APHRODITIDÆ	*Polynoë*	{ *P. squamata* / *P. sublevis*
		Harmothoë	*H. imbricata*
		Aphrodite	*A. aculeata*
	PHYLLODOCIDÆ	*Phyllodoce*	*P. gracilis*
	NEREIDÆ	*Nereis*	{ *N. virens* / *N. pelagica* / *N. limbata*
	NEPHTHYDIDÆ	*Nephthys*	{ *N. ingens* / *N. picta*
	EUNICIDÆ	*Marphysa*	*M. sanguinea*
		Diopatra	*D. cuprea*
		Arabella	*A. opalina*
		Lumbriconereis	*L. tenuis*
	GLYCERIDÆ	*Glycera*	{ *G. americana* / *G. dibranchiata*
SEDENTARIA or TUBICOLA			
	SPIONIDÆ	*Nerine*	{ *N. agilis* / *N. coniocephala*
	CIRRATULIDÆ	*Cirratulus*	*C. grandis*
	TEREBELLIDÆ	*Thelepsus*	*T. cincinnatus*
		Amphitrite	*A. ornata*
		Polycirrus	*P. eximius*
		Chætobranchus	*C. sanguineus*

Orders	Families	Genera	Species
	AMPHICTENIDÆ	*Cistenides*	*C. Gouldii*
	MALDANIDÆ	{ *Clymenella* *Maldane*	*C. torquata* *M. elongata*
	ARENICOLIDÆ	*Arenicola*	*A. marina*
	SABELLIDÆ	*Sabella*	*S. microphthalma*
	SERPULIDÆ	{ *Serpula* *Spirorbis*	*S. dianthus* *S. borealis*

Subclass

Oligochæta

(Mostly terrestrial or fresh-water forms)

Class

GEPHYREA

SIPUNCULOIDEA	{ *Sipunculus* *Phascolosoma*	*S. nudus* *P. Gouldii*

Class

HIRUDINEA

(Leeches)

WORMS

BURROWING in sand and mud, lying under stones and in crevices of rocks, concealed in various kinds of tubular cases which are free or attached to stones or shells, crawling over the ground or seaweeds, swimming free or attached to other animals, is found in abundance a class of animals commonly known as " worms," and generally regarded as repulsive creatures unworthy of attention.

To the biologist, however, worms are among the most interesting forms of lower animal life. The amateur collector, if he stops to give them careful consideration, will probably find them unexpectedly interesting, and will be surprised to find how many varieties of them there are, and how different they are from his preconceived notion of them. Worms are varied in structure, their habits are strange, and their form and color often beautiful. Although plentiful, they are not conspicuous, but are easily found if search is made for them, and so large a class of shore animals should not be passed by unnoticed. Unusual biological interest is attached to this group because, in the different types, affinities with other classes of animals are found, suggesting, perhaps, connecting-links with higher organizations. They are the first animals to show definite bilateral symmetry, or two similar sides, and to carry the same part of the body always in front. Formerly one division, called *Vermes*, comprised all the worms. To-day they are separated into four divisions, or phyla. The most careless observer easily recognizes the basis of separation, for the flatworms, the round- or threadworms, the wheel-like animalcules, and the jointed worms have very obvious differences. The names given the phyla express these distinctions, the termination meaning "worm"; the prefixes *Platy-*, *Nemat-*, *Troc-*, meaning "flat," "thread," "wheel," respectively; while *Annulata*, meaning "ringed," describes the segmented forms belonging to that phylum.

There are vast numbers of parasitic worms, which live internally or externally on their hosts, there being no animal of land or sea, of high or low degree, which is not subject to the affliction of these visitors. The parasitic worms are degenerate, some being without digestive organs, or without eyes, or without locomotor organs, and so on, as the case may be, the host supplying the missing function. The life-history of these low forms is interesting; but parasitic worms do not come within the scope of this book, and are mentioned only to mark their place in the series.

PHYLUM **PLATYHELMINTHES**

FLATWORMS

The flatworms have a flattened body, more or less compressed in the different classes. Ordinarily the body is very thin, and, when short, has a leaf-like form; when long it is ribbon-like. Some species are thick in the middle and thin at the edges. They have a dorsal, or upper, and a ventral, or under, surface; a right and a left side; an anterior and a posterior end. The anterior end is carried forward and has some of the characteristics of a head, though a distinct head is not apparent. The mouth is on the ventral surface. In some species it is in the middle of the length of the body; in others it is before or behind this point.

The flatworms are the first animals to assume pronounced bilateral symmetry. They are soft-bodied, having no supporting skeleton, and they have no segments, or divisions, such as are found in higher types, as in *Annulata*. They have no body-cavity, the space between the organs and the body-wall being filled with tissue. The alimentary canal has no anal aperture, the excretions being carried off by a water-vascular system consisting of branching vessels which end in minute bundles of vibrating cilia, called ciliary flames. These flames communicate with the exterior through small pores or flame-cells. Their sense-organs are eyes and otocysts. The latter are sacs containing crystals of carbonate of lime, and their function is supposed to be that of hearing.

The flatworms are hermaphroditic, and their propagation is by means of eggs. They are numerous and very generally distributed, occurring in fresh and salt water, on land and shore, on the surface and in the depths of the sea. A vast number also are parasites and infest, internally or externally, nearly every living creature. The parasitic forms differ anatomically from the free-living worms. The internal parasites, living by absorption of the digested food of their hosts, have no digestive organs; they are also devoid of organs of sense and of defense. The external parasites, being carried about by their hosts, are without organs of locomotion.

CLASS **TURBELLARIA**

The turbellarians are the simplest group of bilateral animals and occupy the lowest place among worms. They owe their name to the fact that they are covered with cilia, which are constantly in motion and cause a slight turbulence in the water around them.

ORDER **POLYCLADIDA**

(" Many-branched ")

The polyclads are found below half-tide mark on the under side of stones and on seaweeds. Sometimes they are found swimming about at night. They are leaf-like in form, one inch to two inches in length, and are very thin and delicate. They adapt themselves to the inequalities of the surfaces to which they attach themselves, and often are of the same color, and therefore are so inconspicuous that they are apt to escape notice. They move with a gliding motion over surfaces, and often swim when in search of food.

The intestine is much branched and has no anal aperture. From the mouth, which is placed in the center of the ventral surface, a pharynx, or muscular fold, is protruded in some species, which enables the worm to attach itself to and consume prey of considerable size. After digestion has taken place, the fecal matter collects in the main intestine and is forcibly ejected by the pharynx. Numerous eyes are collected in groups on the anterior dorsal surface, or arranged around the margin of the body. The eggs are laid in shell-like cases, and cemented together in plate-like masses or in spirals, and attached to shells or stones. (Plate XLVIII.)

Genus *Planocera*

P. nebulosa. One half of an inch wide and three quarters of an inch long, circular or elliptical in shape; very flat and thin; olive-green on the dorsal surface, with a line of darker color on the posterior end, and whitish retractile tentacles on the back. Found creeping on under side of stones in tide-pools.

Genus *Stylochopsis*

S. littoralis. About one half of an inch long; changeable in form, from broad oval to elliptical; color pale green, veined with a lighter shade on the dorsal side, flesh-colored on the ventral surface; numerous eyes arranged in irregular rows near the margin and in groups in front of the tentacles, also clusters of eyes on the tentacles. Found under stones between tide-marks.

Genus *Leptoplana*

L. folium. Body flat; margin thin and undulated; shape leaf-like, but changeable; about one inch long and one half of an inch wide; color pale yellow, veined with a deeper shade; eyes in four groups near the anterior end.

ORDER **TRICLADIDA**

(" Three-branched ")

The triclads are divided into three groups: those of the fresh-water ponds and streams, those of the land and sea, known as planarians, and those of the sea. The planarians are the most interesting worms in the order. The triclads differ from the polyclads in being elongate in form and in having the intestine in three branches instead of in many. The mouth is midway in the length of the body, on the ventral side, and from it protrudes a pharynx, which is cylindrical or bell-shaped, and is capable of great dilatation. With the pharynx the worm, which is wholly carnivorous, envelops other worms, crustaceans, or any animal food. Several species are found on the under side of stones in tide-pools.

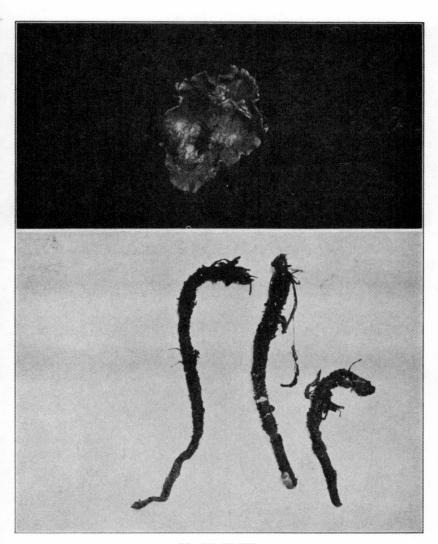

PLATE XLVIII.

Polyclad worm.
Worm-tubes of Diopatra.

GENUS *Planaria*

P. grisea. Oval or elliptical in form; anterior end truncate : posterior end rounded; color yellow or gray, with a light stripe; two black eyes surrounded with white; length one half to three quarters of an inch; width about one eighth of an inch. Found under stones between tide-marks.

GENUS *Procerodes*

P. frequens. One eighth of an inch long; brown or black above, gray below; has two kidney-shaped eyes; active and abundant. Found under stones near high-water mark.

GENUS *Bdelloura*

B. rustica. Body milk-white, smooth, thin. Found on *Ulva latissima* (sea-lettuce).
B. candida. Parasitic on the gills of the horseshoe-crab.

GENUS *Fovia*

F. Warrenii. Bright red, narrow, oblong. Found on eel-grass.

ORDER **RHABDOCŒLIDA**

Minute, active worms found among the red seaweeds. They are brown in color, and are marked by one or more transverse white bars.

CLASS **NEMERTINEA**

The nemerteans are long, narrow, flat, smooth worms, and vary from one half of an inch to many feet in length. They are exceedingly contractile, and when alarmed can shrink to less than half their normal length. They are very generally distributed, and are to be found between tide-marks, in loose coils like a string, under stones on sandy and muddy shores. The very long species, like *Lineus marinus*, are solitary, but other smaller species are gregarious, many worms being coiled together in tangled masses. Some species are to be found in empty shells, and others live among the seaweeds. They are very slimy, the epidermis secreting an abundance of mucus, and they can often be tracked by the trail of slime they leave behind them. This mucus sometimes hardens, forming for some species a tubu-

lar covering; others remain naked.   All are covered with vibrating cilia, which is a universal feature of flatworms.   In color
they may be white, yellow, green, red, purple, etc., and sometimes they are banded or striped with a contrasting color.   The
ventral is usually lighter than the dorsal surface.

The principal characteristic of the nemertean worms is a long
thread-like organ, known as the *proboscis*.   This lies in a sheath
along the center of the dorsal surface, and is quickly thrown
out to a great length, and as quickly completely withdrawn within
the body.   The proboscis is slender, hollow, muscular, and full
of nerves.   It reaches the outside through a pore at the anterior end of the body, and has no connection with the alimentary system.   It is used as a feeler and as a weapon.   Some
species have a sharp spine at the end of the proboscis, others
have stinging-cells.   The proboscis is sometimes so forcibly
ejected that it breaks off, in which case it retains its vitality for
some time, and seems as if it were itself a worm.   A new proboscis is quickly grown by the worm to take the place of a lost
one.   The head is a little broader than the body, and has eyes
arranged in one or several pairs on each side.   The mouth is on
the ventral surface, near the anterior end, has thick lips, and is
very dilatable.   Through the mouth the animal ejects a part of
the esophagus and envelops its prey, which is often of considerable size.   Chætopod worms they often swallow whole; the soft
parts, after being digested, are carried off through the regular
passages, ending in the ciliary flames (page 164), while the indi-
gestible parts are ejected at the anus.   Often the spines and
bristles find their way out by perforating the intestine and the
body-wall, without apparently doing the worm any injury.   The
perforated parts quickly heal.

These worms have the strange power of regenerating lost parts;
mutilated portions are soon repaired.   The anterior end, when
severed from the rest of the body, grows again into a complete
individual, while the posterior end continues to perform part of
its functions and retains its vitality for a considerable time before dying.   One species, *Lineus sanguineus*, is capable, after being
broken in pieces, of regenerating each section into a perfect worm.

The nemerteans are carnivorous, voracious, and often canniba-listic. They will live for some time in confinement, losing, how-ever, their bright color, and the smaller worms will gradually dis-appear, as they are devoured by the larger ones. The mode of locomotion varies with the order. Some species attach their long proboscis to a distant object, then drag the body to it; some glide rapidly along by means of the muscles of the body and the cilia which cover it; others swim. The swimming forms have thin edges which have a wave-like motion, and this, together with a lateral movement of the tail, propels them through the water. In some species the worm develops directly from the egg; others pass through a larval stage before reaching maturity.

GENUS *Tetrastemma*

T. arenicola. Dark flesh-color or purplish; slender, cylindrical, four to five inches long when extended; head changeable in form and partly distinct from body because of slight constriction at the neck. It lives in sand at low-water mark.

GENUS *Nemertes*

N. socialis. Individuals very slender, five to six inches long when extended; color brown or black, a little lighter underneath; three or four eyes in lines on each side the head. It is abundant under stones on rocky shores, many coiled together, forming large masses.

N. viridis. Color olive-green or brown, crossed by faint pale lines; body changeable in form; when extended, six to eight inches long, one eighth of an inch or less in breadth; row of dark eyes on each side of flat head. Common under stones between tide-marks on northern rocky shores.

GENUS *Meckelia*

M. ingens. One of the largest nemertean worms; found on sandy and muddy shores near low-water mark. The young, from several inches to a foot long, are common. When full-grown some attain the length of twelve or thirteen feet, and are an inch in breadth and quite flat when extended, but can contract to two or three feet in length, and are then nearly cylindrical. This worm, although so soft, penetrates the sand with great rapidity. Its head changes shape constantly and assists the proboscis when burrowing. It is also able to swim. Its color is yel-lowish or flesh-color, with whitish edges and a central band.

M. rosea. The largest specimens are six to eight inches long and one quarter of an inch broad; lives in burrows on sandy beaches; color red or pink; often covered with sand, which adheres to the mucus which the worm secretes.

Genus *Cerebratulus*

C. angulatus.   Olive-green, with light dorsal stripe.

Genus *Cosmocephala*

C. ochracea.   Two to three inches long when extended; gray or yellowish-white, and mottled by the internal organs showing through the translucent body; line of lighter color down the back; anterior end often orange-colored.   It is common near low-water mark under stones and in the dead tubes of *Serpula*.

Genus *Polina*

P. glutinosa.   One to two inches long; color orange or light yellow, with a faint line of deeper color down the center of the dorsal surface; very slimy; eyes numerous, in oblique lines on the head.   Found in tide-pools on algæ.

PHYLUM NEMATHELMINTHES

ROUNDWORMS

The worms of this phylum have the general name of roundworms, which distinguishes them from the flatworms of the preceding division and from the segmented worms of the *Annulata*. The body is elongated, cylindrical, smooth, and pointed at both ends.   With few exceptions, they are parasitic.

A few of the nematode species are free, living under stones and among seaweeds at about low-water mark.

CLASS NEMATODA

Genus *Pontonema*

P. marinum.   Slender, white, smooth, active, cylindrical; constantly coiling and uncoiling itself.

PHYLUM ANNULATA

SEGMENTED WORMS

The name of this phylum expresses the principal characteristic of the group of worms which have elongated bodies composed of series of short parts, or ring-like divisions.   Each one of these segments contains a separate and similar set of internal organs.

The annelids are divided into four classes, one of which, the *Gephyrea*, has not the characteristics which distinguish the group. The classes are easily recognized by conspicuous features. Some have bristles; others have scales; others have tentacles around the head and inclose themselves in tubes. Many are highly colored, and all are of great interest to the naturalist from the diversity of their habits, form, and structure, and from the analogies they bear to other and higher types of animals.

The annelids are the highest type of worms, their organs having attained more special functions. The sense-organs of eye and ear are more developed, and the nervous system has distinct centers, or ganglia, the first and largest ganglion being a part of the head. They are found in abundance everywhere. Some species grow to the length of one foot or two feet. Some are carnivorous, others vegetarian, and many are mud-eaters, swallowing sand and mud for the sake of the organisms they contain. They themselves are food for fishes, which devour them in vast quantities, rooting them out of their burrows or capturing them at night, at which time they swim about.

CLASS **CHÆTOPODA**
(" Bristle-footed ")

The bristle-worms. This class of worms has bunches of bristles on both sides of each segment of the body, which serve as organs of locomotion, or bristle-feet. The bristles emanate from outgrowths of the body known as *parapodia*, which are practically limbs. The parapodia are sometimes divided into distinct lobes or branches. The bristles are of various shapes and often of brilliant color. They are usually horny, sometimes

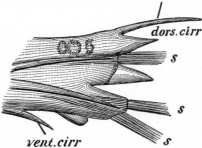

A magnified parapodium of *Nereis dumerilii: dors. cirr.*, dorsal cirrus; *vent. cirr.*, ventral cirrus; *s*, setæ.

simple, sometimes divided into joints, and vary in shape in different genera. The parapodia have, besides the bristles, a second set of hair-like appendages, called *cirri*. These are sense-organs and also have a respiratory function. The cirri too vary in shape in different genera. Generally they are hair-like, but sometimes conical; again they are broadened into scales, as in the *Aphroditidæ*.

The body-cavity in chætopod worms is divided into a series of chambers or segments. These divisions seem on the exterior like constrictions, and give the body the appearance of a series of rings. The internal organs are repeated in each segment, so that each of the latter contains a portion of the alimentary canal, a pair of *nephridia*, a pair of nerve-ganglia, and blood-vessels which connect the main blood-vessels running along the dorsal and ventral surfaces. The alimentary canal runs through the body, but is constricted at each joint. The nephridia are curved tubes, which are excretory organs, opening to the outside and carrying off the waste products which have passed into the fluid of the body-cavity.

The chætopod worms have a well-developed nervous system, beginning with a two-lobed ganglion forming a brain and head, then extending through the worm in a double ventral chain and series of ganglia. They have also a blood-vascular system. The blood is either colored or colorless. Sometimes it is a bright red or green, and is often visible through the body-wall. The circulation is effected, not by means of a heart, but by wave-like (perisaltic) contractions of the dorsal blood-vessel. The body is cylindrical, but in many cases is somewhat flattened. There are two layers of muscles, one of which encircles the body, while the other extends parallel with its length. Respiration is effected by *gills*, which may be simple, hair-like appendages to the parapodia, or branched, or comb-like in form. Sometimes they are confined to the middle segments, as in *Arenicola;* sometimes to the segments near the head, as in *Tubicola;* or they may be extended over the whole dorsal surface.

SUBCLASS **POLYCHÆTA**
("Many-bristled")

The polychæte worms have one or two well-developed parapodia, or limbs, on each side of every segment of the body, and on each parapodium is a bunch of bristles, or *chætæ*. There are hundreds of species of this class of worms, the species being based on the shape and the lobes of the parapodia, the relative length of the cirri, the form and arrangement of the chætæ, and so on. They are abundant on the shore everywhere, but abound where rocks and stones afford them some shelter. Many burrow in the sand and mud. In doing this the worm eats his way into the hole, swallowing the mud and sand. He assimilates the organic or vegetable matter the mud contains, and ejects the rest in cylindrical coils, known as castings, which lie in heaps at the mouth of the burrow. By these castings they may be traced. Others secrete tubes.

The polychæte worms are divided into *Errantia*, which are wandering, free-swimming forms, and *Sedentaria* or *Tubicola*, which live in tubes permanently. These distinctions are not strictly correct, since some species of errant polychætes form tubes (*Eunicidæ*), and some *Sedentaria* form no tubes.

Many polychætes are beautifully colored, some in vivid reds and greens, with various markings; some are iridescent; some are phosphorescent.

ORDER **ERRANTIA**

Carnivorous, free *Polychæta*, with protrusible pharynx armed with a horny jaw. "They are active, fierce beasts of prey."

FAMILY **SYLLIDÆ**

This family is the highest in organization of the worms. They are small, the majority being less than an inch in length, and many are minute. They are often highly colored. Many have long cirri on the feet; some have alternation of generation. They are common everywhere along the coast, but are not seen unless searched for. Sponges sometimes are alive with them. They are interesting subjects for microscopic study.

FAMILY **APHRODITIDÆ**

The scale-bearing annelids. This family of worms is distinguished from all others by having scales on the back. The scales, called *elytra*, are flattened dorsal cirri carried on the upper parapodia, and generally on alternate segments and in a double row down the back. The elytra are the breathing-organs, and, although of a horny texture, are richly supplied with nerves. The worms are short and have a large protrusible pharynx armed with a double pair of horny jaws.

Genus *Polynoë*

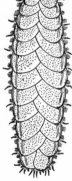

Polynoë squamata.

The species of *Polynoë* are determined by the number of scales they bear. They have a flattened short body with nearly parallel sides. The bristles are of a bright golden color. The proboscis is large and has four powerful jaws at the end and a circle of papillæ at the top. They are sluggish in movement and are found under stones and in the crevices of rocks. When disturbed they roll themselves into a ball.

P. squamata. Twelve pairs of rough scales; color sandy-brown, speckled; one inch to one and a half inches long; the broad, oval scales overlap and entirely cover the body and head. Some *Polynoë* when disturbed throw off every scale. Very common north of Cape Cod.

P. sublevis. Twelve pairs of smooth scales; usually grayish-brown in color, speckled with dark spots; iridescent; last pair of scales more slender than the others; length one and a quarter inches, breadth about one quarter of an inch.

Genus *Harmothoë*

H. imbricata. Sixteen pairs of smooth scales; variable in color; usually gray, speckled, or striped.

Genus *Aphrodite*

A. aculeata. This polychæte, sometimes called the sea-mouse, is one of the most beautiful of worms. It is brightly iridescent in color, from its setæ, which form a fur-like coating over the dorsal surface. It has fifteen pairs of scales, but they are hidden by the numerous setæ. These bristles cover its sides and back. Some are coarse and nearly an inch long, with sharp points, and are barbed near the ends. They curve over the back like the quills of a porcupine. The body is three to six inches long. It is broadest in the middle and tapers to a point. They live in mud below tide-mark, and may be found washed upon the beach after storms.

FAMILY **PHYLLODOCIDÆ**

These animals are commonly known as "paddle-worms," on account of having leaf-like cirri, which they use in locomotion. The head is long and bears four pairs of short and four pairs of long tentacles. The body is long and depressed, sometimes two feet in length, usually eight to twelve inches long. The general color is bright green and iridescent. Found in tide-pools. Specimens are often found by digging in sandy mud, or they may be obtained by placing old shells and other material in a dish of sea-water. When the water becomes a little stale, the worms of this and other families make their way to the sides of the dish, where they secrete a colorless slime which holds mud or any light matter that it may come in contact with.

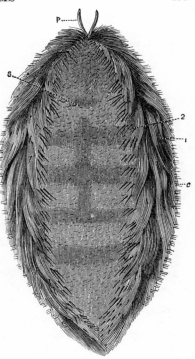

Aphrodite aculeata, natural size : *c*, neuropodial chætæ; *p*, palps; 1, iridescent bristles; 2, stiff chætæ; 3, felting bristles of notopodium.

In this condition, when lifted or disturbed, they crawl rapidly out of the slime, and show to good advantage their elongate body, which is often beautifully colored.

GENUS *Phyllodoce*

P. gracilis. Three inches or more long and one sixteenth of an inch wide ; large proboscis, with twelve longitudinal rows of prominent pro-

Phyllodoce paretii.

jections on the swollen base, its terminal end smooth, with a circle of round projections at the orifice; color green, with a row of dark spots down the center of the dorsal surface and a fainter line of spots on each side at the base of the parapodia. Found on the New England coast.

FAMILY NEREIDÆ

GENUS *Nereis*

Among the most common of the polychæte worms is the genus *Nereis,* various species of which are found in all parts of the world. They are abundant under stones, among seaweeds, and living in burrows between tide-marks. They are active, fierce, and voracious. Some attain a length of eighteen or more inches.

Head of *Nereis pelagica.*

They are commonly known as "clam-worms," and are used by fishermen for bait. *Nereis* has a distinct head, consisting of two parts. One, the *prostomium*, bears on its upper side four eyes and a pair of short, conical tentacles, and on the lateral sides a second pair of processes called *palps*. The palps are more conspicuous than the tentacles, and consist of two parts, a large base and a small terminal point, the latter capable of being withdrawn. The palps are sense-organs and perhaps test the food. The second part of the head, or *peristomium*, bears on the sides four pairs of long tentacles which are used as feelers. The mouth is on the ventral side, and through it *Nereis* throws out its pharynx, which contains a horny, notched jaw. It seizes its prey with this jaw, which, with the pharynx, is then withdrawn and tears the food apart, acting like a gizzard. The body of *Nereis* is rounded above and nearly flat below. Each of the segments has a pair of parapodia, bearing a bundle of bristles and cirri. The last segment of the body is elongated, cylindrical, and without parapodia, but has on the end a pair of long cirri, which give the appearance of a divided tail. Each segment of the body, except the head- and tail-segments, contains a pair of excretory tubes (*nephridia*), ganglia of nerves, and a portion of the intestine and of the vascular system. There are circular muscles by which the worm can diminish its diameter, longitu-

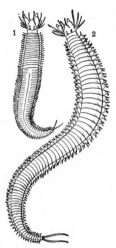

Nereis pelagica. 1, male; 2, female.

dinal muscles in four bands, and muscles to move the parapodia. Breathing is carried on over the whole surface of the body, and especially in parts of the lobes of the parapodia called gills. Its sense-organs are eyes, palps, tentacles, and cirri.

N. virens. This species is found from New York northward in muddy and shelly sand, and under rocks between tide-marks, living in burrows, which it lines with a mucous secretion. It is very active and voracious, feeding on other worms, *Crustacea*, etc., which it captures with its horny, protruded jaw. At night it leaves its burrow and swims freely about like an eel, frequently falling a prey to fishes. In color it is dull bluish-green, with some iridescence. The gills, which are leaf-like appendages on the parapodia, are green on the anterior end of the body and become bright red farther back. This species, and *N. branti* of Alaska, are the giants of polychæte worms, often measuring eighteen inches or more in length.

N. pelagica. Found in abundance on the New England shore and northern coasts under stones and on shelly bottoms. The female is four to five inches long, while the male is only two inches in length. In this species the body is widest in the middle, while in other species it is widest at the anterior end. The palps are long, and the second head-piece (peristomium) is twice as long as the next segment. The color is reddish-brown and iridescent.

N. limbata. Five to six inches long; jaws light yellow, sharp, and slender; parapodia and bristles smaller on the anterior than on the posterior end; color dark brown, with light lines on the sides and appendages, pale red on the posterior end; dorsal blood-vessel apparent, and the heart-like pulsations can be distinctly seen. The male worm is red in the middle section. Found along the middle Atlantic coast on sandy shores.

FAMILY NEPHTHYDIDÆ

In this family the worms have a long, thick, flattish body, a section of which has a quadrangular form. The lobes of the parapodia are widely separated and fringed

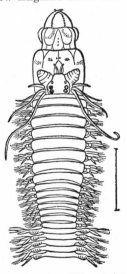

Nereis limbata. Male, anterior part of body, head and extended proboscis.

with membrane, appearing like double parapodia. The pharynx is very large and projected as in *Nereis*.

GENUS *Nephthys*

N. ingens. Sometimes six inches long and one quarter of an inch broad; usually smaller; color whitish, with red blood-vessel showing on dorsal side; appendages dark brown; moves actively and burrows quickly into the mud; when captured often breaks off a portion of the posterior end, which it is able to reproduce; proboscis large; branchiæ between the dorsal and ventral parapodia. Found burrowing in all kinds of mud on the New England coast.

N. picta. More slender than *N. ingens*; color whitish, mottled with brown on the dorsal anterior end; often a dark line down the back; head square in front and triangular in the back. Found in sandy mud at low-water mark.

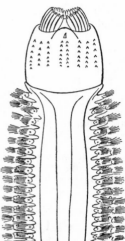

Nephthys ingens. Anterior part of body and extended proboscis; ventral view. Enlarged.

FAMILY EUNICIDÆ

These are beautiful worms, having a reddish-brown iridescent body, with bright-red branching gills, which look like feathers, along the back. They form parchment-like tubes.

GENUS *Marphysa*

M. sanguinea. Length six inches or more; color bronze or brownish-red and iridescent; has bright-red branched gills and six caudal cirri of different lengths; body flattened, except at the anterior end, where it becomes narrow and cylindrical; has powerful jaws. It is found under stones and in clefts of rocks at low-water mark, or more commonly in parchment-like tubes on shelly beaches, from Cape Cod to New Jersey.

GENUS *Diopatra*

D. cuprea. This is one of the largest and most beautiful annelids. It is found from Cape Cod to South Carolina at low-water mark, in sandy mud-flats, living in long tubes which project above the surface two or three inches and are hung with seaweeds and bits of foreign matter. *Diopatra* is twelve inches or more in length and one half of an inch in breadth. In color it is reddish-brown, specked with gray, and has a brilliant whitish or opal-like iridescence. The appendages are yellowish-brown, specked with green. The body is flattened. From the fifth segment long, dull to bright red, much-branched gills, resembling plumes,

extend nearly to the end of the worm. On the ventral side of the parapodia are whitish tubercles with a dark spot in the middle. These
papillæ secrete the long, broad tube in which the worm lives. The worm
is difficult to capture, for when pursued it retreats quickly into its tube,
which is so large that it can easily turn around within it. (Plate XLVIII.)

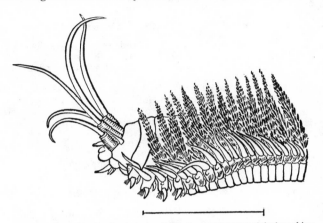

Diopatra cuprea. Head and anterior part of body, showing part of the branchiæ;
side view.

Genus *Arabella*

A. opalina. Body cylindrical, twelve to eighteen inches long, one
quarter of an inch wide in the middle, and tapers to the ends, which are
comparatively small; lateral appendages short; color bronze, with brilliant, opal-like iridescence; head small, conical, but blunt and without
tentacles; four eyes in transverse row at the base of the head; segments
well marked; coils into spirals when outside of its burrow. Found in
compact sandy mud at low-water mark on the New England coast.

Genus *Lumbriconereis*

L. tenuis. Twelve inches or more long, and slender, like a fine cord;
bright red and somewhat iridescent; very fragile. Abundant in sandy
mud on the northern New England coast, and found from New Jersey
northward.

Family GLYCERIDÆ

These worms are long and smooth, with numerous segments.
They taper at both ends. The head is small, conical, sharply
pointed, and has four very small tentacles. The proboscis, or

pharynx, when protruded, is very large and long, and appears too large for the worm. The proboscis has four hook-like jaws. These worms burrow rapidly and disappear almost instantly into the mud or sand.

GENUS *Glycera*

G. americana. Color red or purple; has branched gills on upper side of parapodia. Found from South Carolina to Cape Cod on sandy and muddy shores and flats near low-water mark.

G. dibranchiata. Has a simple gill on both sides of the parapodia; about eight inches long and one quarter of an inch wide in the middle; proboscis one inch long and wider than the body on the upper end. Abundant from New Jersey to Cape Cod.

ORDER SEDENTARIA

THE TUBICOLOUS WORMS

Many of this order construct tubes in which they live permanently. Some species of both *Sedentaria* and *Errantia* have habits pertaining to the other. These worms are without a protrusible pharynx and without jaws. The body is usually divided into two or three sections by segments and appendages of different forms. They have hair-setæ on a limited number of segments only, varying with the species; the remaining segments have *uncini*, or hooked comb-like rows of setæ, which are very small, but often crowded in bunches. Uncini exist also on segments having hair-setæ. Parapodia are often lacking on the posterior parts and are usually without cirri. The gills are usually confined to the anterior end and are sometimes represented by tentacles around the head. The different species have characteristic tubes, formed by mucus secreted by epidermal glands. Sometimes the mucus hardens, making a parchment-like tube; again it cements together grains of sand, or bits of shell, seaweeds, etc. Some species secrete

Glycera meckelii, with pharynx everted.

calcareous tubes; these are often found on rocks, in coral, and in the shells of mollusks. The anterior end of the body is more highly developed than the posterior end.

FAMILY SPIONIDÆ

GENUS *Nerine*

N. agilis. Two to three inches long; slender; somewhat flattened at the anterior end; head conical and sharp; the two tentacles about one half of an inch long; four eyes; color reddish-brown, light green on the sides; gills red; tentacles greenish-white. It burrows with extreme rapidity and lives on exposed beaches near low-water mark.

N. coniocephala. Two and a half inches long, one sixteenth of an inch in diameter; head conical; body flattened on the dorsal side, round on the ventral side; has two long tentacles turned backward and a membrane on the gills of the anterior segments; gills red; bristles long and numerous.

FAMILY CIRRATULIDÆ

Worms of this family have a cylindrical body, more or less attenuated at each end; segments similar throughout; many segments with long, filamentous cirri which act as gills; and a conical head. They live in burrows.

GENUS *Cirratulus*

C. grandis. Four to six inches long; head acute; segments numerous, short, and distinct; color dull yellow, or orange, to brown, often iridescent beneath; ventral surface somewhat flattened. Numerous long, filamentous, red to orange-colored cirri extend nearly the whole length of the body and act as gills. It is common in sand and gravel at low-water mark from Cape Cod to New Jersey.

Cirratulus grandis.

FAMILY **TEREBELLIDÆ**

The body is cylindrical and largest on the anterior end; there are one to three pairs of more or less branched gills on the anterior end, and the ventral surface of the anterior segments is thickened by glands which secrete mucus for tube-building. These gland-spaces are called *shields*.

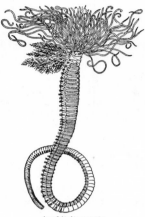

Amphitrite ornata.

GENUS *Thelepsus*

T. cincinnatus. Two to four inches long; pale red; marked like lacework on the back; gills have numerous unbranched filaments arising separately in two transverse rows; tubes thin, transparent, flexible, and hung with foreign substances; attached along the whole length.

GENUS *Amphitrite*

A. ornata. Twelve to fifteen inches long; flesh-color, reddish, or brown; three pairs of red plume-like gills and numerous flesh-colored tentacles around the anterior end; tentacles constantly in motion and sometimes extended eight or ten inches; tubes a quarter of an inch or more in diameter, and firm, being composed of sand and mud. It is found under stones in mud, gravel, and sand at low-water mark from Cape Cod to New Jersey, often associated with *Cirratulus grandis*.

GENERA *Polycirrus, Chætobranchus*

P. eximius, C. sanguineus. These are two species of bright-red, fragile worms, found under stones, in mud. They do not form tubes. The first is a small worm, the second twelve to fifteen inches long. Both have long, crowded tentacles extending in every direction and distended as the blood flows into them. *C. sanguineus* has ten-

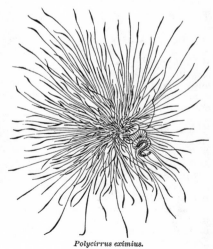

Polycirrus eximius.

tacles sixteen inches in extent, and branched gills on short pedicels on the back. They are common in mud at low-water mark from Cape Cod to New Jersey.

FAMILY AMPHICTENIDÆ

GENUS *Cistenides*

Cistenides Gouldii.

C. Gouldii constructs conical free tubes of grains of sand in a single layer; body short and a little curved; head obliquely flattened; two broad groups of golden bristles turned upward on each side of the anterior end; one to two inches long; color light red or flesh-color, mottled with red or blue. This is a common worm, and its horn-shaped tubes are so plentiful as to attract attention on sandy shores. They will repay examination with a glass, so beautifully are they built. The worm has bunches of golden bristles arranged in two rows close to the flattened anterior end, which make a kind of operculum to the tube. This feature makes the species easy to identify. The worm is transparent; the internal organs showing through give it the various bright colors. It is found on sandy and muddy shores from New Jersey northward.

FAMILY MALDANIDÆ

The tubes of these animals are formed of sand, a short portion projecting, and are very abundant in certain places. There is a horny plate on the upper surface of the head, and the skin on the sides of the head is raised in folds. There is a funnel-like process at the posterior extremity; gills are lacking. Some of the segments in the middle of the body are longer than the rest.

GENUS *Clymenella*

C. torquata. Body long, composed of twenty-two segments; the fifth segment has a collar-like fold; the caudal extremity is funnel-shaped and edged with papillæ; both

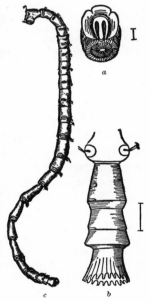

Clymenella torquata.

a, head and extended proboscis, front view; *b*, posterior end; *c*, entire animal, side view, natural size.

the first and the last three segments are bare, the rest have short bristles above and hooks below; head has a prominent convex plate with a raised border; worm pale red, with bright-red bands around the segments, sometimes brownish. It constructs nearly straight tubes of pure sand close to low-water mark in sheltered coves, and ranges from New Jersey northward.

Genus *Maldane*

M. elongata. Six to eight inches long, one eighth to one quarter of an inch in diameter; body cylindrical, cut obliquely at both ends; head bordered by a slight fold; color brown, with red blood showing through. Found in sandy mud at low-water mark, in firm, deep tubes of fine mud, on the New England coast.

Family ARENICOLIDÆ

Genus *Arenicola*

A. marina. Five to ten inches long; brownish-green; body cylindrical, thickest on the anterior end; anterior and posterior ends without chætæ; twelve to thirteen pairs of branched red gills on the central segments. It makes burrows eighteen to twenty-four inches deep on sandy southern shores, and can be traced by castings at the mouth of the burrow. Commonly known as " lugworm," and used by fishermen for bait.

Family SABELLIDÆ

In this family the gills arise from two semicircular bases forming the crown; the second lobe of the anterior extremity is reversed like a collar; the gill-filaments have secondary processes, and the tubes are flexible, composed of cemented mud or sand. Found under stones, the tube passing around the stone and opening upward.

Genus *Sabella*

S. microphthalma. Length of tube one and a quarter inches, diameter one eighth of an inch; body olive-green, specked with white; wreath of tentacles half as long as the body; tentacles pale yellowish or flesh-colored, with transverse lines of darker color. It is found on the southern New England coast.

Family SERPULIDÆ

This family forms white calcareous tubes. One of the dorsal gill-filaments is flattened, forming an operculum, or cover, with which the tube is closed when the worm has withdrawn itself inside. The tubes are commonly found attached to shells and rocks, usually solitary, but sometimes in clusters, crossing and recrossing each other on the surface of the shell or rock. Plume-like gills are attached to the anterior end of the body. The color differs in different species. These worms may easily be mistaken for the mollusks *Vermetus*, which live in similar tubes of larger size, growing in masses.

GENUS *Serpula*

S. dianthus. Tubes often three inches long and one eighth of an inch wide, the fixed end coiled and contorted, free end with circular opening; tubes often show circular ridges, marking periods of growth; operculum funnel-shaped, the exterior striated and the edge bordered with short processes; wreath of gills nearly circular and divided into two symmetrical parts; color variable. It is found in tide-pools, also on the under side of rocks at low-water mark, either solitary or congregated in masses, and ranges from Cape Cod to New Jersey.

GENUS *Spirorbis*

S. borealis. A minute calcareous tube, in a close, flat coil attached on one side; easily mistaken for a minute gasteropod shell; worm has an operculum and wreath of gills. Found on the fronds of seaweeds, on shells, etc.

CLASS **GEPHYREA**

This class of animals, once placed near the holothurians, belongs with the annelid worms on account of their mode of development, their structure being entirely dissimilar. They are without segments and without parapodia. The body-cavity is filled with fluid and is traversed by connective tissue and fine muscular fibers. They are subcylindrical animals which can retract the anterior end of the body. The mouth is surrounded by tentacles, or by tentacular folds, and is at the base of the proboscis. They live in fissures of rocks, in sand, mud, rock, or coral, and in deep gasteropod shells. Their distribution is general.

ORDER **SIPUNCULOIDEA**

GENUS *Sipunculus*

S. nudus. The body is cylindrical, a foot or more in length when extended. It is divided into two portions. The anterior end, to the extent of one sixth of the entire length of the worm, is capable of being withdrawn into the remainder of the body. This portion is called the *introvert*. The introvert is retracted by means of special muscles forming a sheath around the gullet and connected at the other end to the body-wall about half-way down the body. It is narrower than the rest of the body and is covered more or less closely with small horny papillæ which turn backward and overlap like scales. The rest of the body is divided into longitudinal furrows and circular markings, giving it the appearance of being divided into squares. These markings correspond to muscles which lie beneath. The introvert, when retracted, leaves at the opening a lobed and plaited fold of the integument, giving the appearance of tentacles. When the introvert is expanded there is a fringe-like funnel around the mouth. The body is covered with a horny cuticle and has an iridescent luster. The animal lives buried in the sand and feeds upon sand, deriving its nourishment from the organisms contained therein. The sipunculoids pass so much sand and mud through their bodies that they are said to modify the mineral substances on the bottom of the sea, as earthworms do the soil of the land.

Genus *Phascolosoma*

P. Gouldii. Body cylindrical, a foot or more in length, a quarter or half of an inch in diameter when expanded; but the body constantly changes in size and shape as it is contracted or expanded; surface of body parchment-like in texture and marked off in small squares; color dull white to light brown. It is found on the New England coast in sand and gravel at low-water mark.

IV

MOLLUSCOIDA

TABLE SHOWING THE CLASSIFICATION OF THE MOLLUSCOIDA DESCRIBED IN THIS CHAPTER

Class
POLYZOA

Subclass
Ectoprocta

(Excretory opening outside lophophore; mouth in center of circle of tentacles; tentacles retractile)

Order		Genera	Species
GYMNOLÆMATA *(Circular lophophore)*			
Suborder CYCLOSTOMATA *(Tubular calcareous zoœcia, with circular apertures devoid of closing apparatus)*	**ARTICULATA** *(Erect branches divided at intervals by chitinous joints)*	*Crisia*	*C. eburnea*
	INARTICULATA *(Erect or adherent zoarium; unjointed)*	*Tubulipora* *Diastopora*	*T. flabellaris* *D. patina*
Suborder CHEILOSTOMATA *(Calcareous or chitinous zoœcia, usually with opercula; avicularia, vibracula, and ovicells often present)*	**CELLULARINA** *(Flexible erect forms)*	*Ætea* *Eucratea* *Cellularia* *Caberea* *Bugula*	*Æ. anguinea* *E. chelata* *C. ternata* *C. Ellisii* *B. turrita* *B. Murrayana* *B. flabellata*
	FLUSTRINA *(Cells quadrate; front wall of zoœcium membranous or depressed, and has ridge-like margin)*	*Flustra* *Membranipora*	*F. membranacea* *M. pilosa* *M. lineata* *M. tenuis*
	ESCHARINA *(Zoœcium wholly calcified)*	*Escharella* *Mollia* *Cellepora*	*E. variabilis* *M. hyalina* *C. scabra* *C. ramulosa* *C. pumicosa*

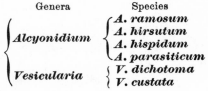

Suborder	Genera	Species
CTENOSTOMATA	*Alcyonidium*	*A. ramosum*
(Horny or gelatinous zoœcia, having tooth-like processes which close the apertures when the tentacles are retracted)		*A. hirsutum*
		A. hispidum
		A. parasiticum
	Vesicularia	*V. dichotoma*
		V. custata

Subclass

Entoprocta

(Excretory opening within lophophore ; mouth near margin of area, which is surrounded by tentacles ; tentacles roll up instead of being retracted)

Pedicellina   *P. americana*

Avicula'ria: Specifically modified zoœcia, resembling a bird's head, found only in the *Cheilostomata.*

Brown bodies: Brown pigment-masses contained in the zoœcia and derived from the breaking down of the polypides.

Lo'phophore: The disk bearing the mouth and circlet of ciliated tentacles.

Orifice: The open end of the zoœcium.

Ovicell: The receptacle in which the eggs develop.

Pe'ristome: The ridge around the orifice of cell.

Po'lypide: The parts of the animal within the zoœcium.

Vibra'cula: A lashing filament, or specifically modified zoœcia, found only in the *Cheilostomata.*

Zoa'rium: The whole colony.

Zoœ'cium: The body-wall of a single individual.

POLYZOA

AMONG the numerous objects to be found on the beach at low tide are the *Polyzoa*, of which there are said to be seventeen hundred named species of the marine forms. These little animals, although so plentiful, are inconspicuous, and it may be said that their very existence is not known to those who are not professed naturalists; yet they are easy to see, incrusting with a delicate calcareous lacework the surface of stones and shells and seaweeds in the tide-pools, and hanging from the rocks like branches of delicate seaweeds. There is hardly a frond of even the fine red algæ on which cannot be found the little tube holding shelly saucers, or the creeping stems or branches of polyzoans. Any one of these little masses, when examined with a pocket-glass, will surprise one with its delicate and beautiful structure.

This class of animals is also called *Bryozoa*, and certain species have the common names of sea-mats and corallines. They are broadly divided into two groups, namely, the erect and the incrusting forms. Those having tree- or plant-like shapes resemble seaweeds, while the colonies which spread over stones, shells, and algæ resemble moss, hence the name *Bryozoa* (moss-animals). Both groups have the general appearance of hydroids, because, like them, they are colonies having plant forms and having their organisms inclosed in cup-like sheaths. The resemblance, however, is but a superficial one, for the *Polyzoa* have a much higher organization, each animal of the colony being a separate and distinct individual. They can easily be distinguished by the hair-like processes on the tentacles. The ciliated tentacles and complete alimentary system are the conspicuous differences between these colonies and those of the hydroids.

The *Polyzoa* are very numerous and form a most attractive

191

group. They are plentiful everywhere, occurring between tide-marks and at great depths on the floor of the sea. Rocks protected from the sun are often incrusted with the calcareous forms, while branching species hang from the rocks and adorn rock pools. *Membranipora*, in lace-like sheets, will be found on the larger seaweeds as well as on various submerged objects. The beautiful little *Crisia* may be looked for on the fronds of red algæ, and *Alcyonidium*, in soft moss-like patches, on *Fucus*. On some beaches are scattered the sea-mats, *Flustra foliacea*, looking like bits of brown paper. A pocket-lens will reveal the marvelous and orderly arrangement of the two layers of cells, or zoœcia, placed back to back. There is not a more surprising object in the animal kingdom than a living branch of *Bugula*. The cells on its spiral, profusely branched clusters have appendages resembling a bird's head, with its bill constantly opening and shutting. Of the erect polyzoans some are entirely calcareous and rigid; such species live in deep water, and their colonies are called corallines, as are also the calcareous algæ. They have existed in vast numbers since early geologic times, and are plentiful in the Tertiary deposits, known as Coralline Crags. Other erect forms have a calcareous framework, which is not continuous, but has horny intervals, so that the colonies are flexible and can be swayed by the tides in shallow water where they live. Others have complete horny exoskeletons. The same differences occur in the incrusting forms, those on the seaweeds being either flexible, so that they bend with the plant, or if entirely calcareous are so small that they do not break when the plant sways to and fro. Still others are gelatinous and resemble bits of sponge. The calcareous forms are usually ornamented with ridges which form beautiful patterns.

The individuals of the polyzoan colonies are small polyp-like organisms which have a cup-like inclosure of horny or of calcareous substance, or of the two combined, as mentioned above. This inclosing sheath is the exterior or cuticle of the animal and is called the *zoœcium*, the whole colony being called the *zoarium*. The animal substance within the zoœcium is the *polypide*, and consists of the mouth, tentacles, and alimentary system. A disk at the anterior end of the body, bearing the circle of tentacles, is the *lophophore*; it is a contractile body, being, with the tentacles, protruded from the zoœcium or drawn within it at will. In some species the orifices of the zoœcia are surrounded with spines; others have lids, called *opercula*, which shut down when the polypides are retracted. A singular modification of the zoœcia is seen in the genus *Bugula*, where peculiar shapes like birds' heads, called *avicularia*, occur. In these singular appendages the upper beak is hooked, while the lower one, or mandible, is the operculum of the zoœcium. These constantly open and shut by means of muscles, and although their function is not certainly known, it is thought that they capture prey. Other modifications are whip-like processes, or flagellate filaments, called *vibracula*, which constantly beat the water. In many of the zoœcia of the colony there are dark-colored masses, called *brown bodies*. These are formed by the degeneration of the polypides, which at certain periods break down, their tentacles and alimentary system ceasing to act and becoming brown masses. The body-wall then puts out a bud internally and forms a new polypide, which absorbs, or passes out, the brown body. The term of life of a single polypide is not known, but in every colony many such transformations are constantly taking place.

The colonies originally start from larvæ produced in the *ovicells* of the zoaria. The ovicells are sometimes very large and pear-shaped, occurring at intervals on the stems; or there may be one at the top of each zoœcium. They look like pearls. A larva, when liberated, swims about for a time, then attaches itself to a fixed object, and increases, by budding, into some one of the various forms which the colonies take.

SUBCLASS **ECTOPROCTA**

ORDER **GYMNOLÆMATA**

SUBORDER **CYCLOSTOMATA**

ERECT OR CREEPING POLYZOA

The zoœcia are more or less cylindrical; the upper ends are sometimes completely free and sometimes closely adherent. The opening of the cell has no operculum. Ovicells, containing the embryos, appear like pear-shaped swellings.

Genus *Crisia*

C. eburnea. This species is found in tide-pools on algæ, especially on the red seaweeds, growing in bushy tufts from one half of an inch to an inch high. Calcareous, with horny joints; cells in two rows, semi-alternate, cylindrical, free at one end, bent; no operculum; ivory-white; ovicells large and pear-shaped. Common from Long Island Sound northward and on the Pacific coast.

Genus *Tubulipora*

T. flabellaris. This species is found attached to slender branched algæ, in coral-like masses of long, crooked, tubular cells united at the base and spreading into fan-shapes placed flat against the fronds. It is sometimes one quarter of an inch in diameter. On the same alga may often be found *Crisia*, *Mollia*, and *Cellepora*. (Plate XLIX.)

Genus *Diastopora*

Crisia eburnea; a branch bearing ovicells, highly magnified.

D. patina. Tubular cells rise from a saucer-shaped disk about a quarter of an inch in diameter; cells lie obliquely or stand erect, and are crowded toward the center; margin of disk without cells; colony white and calcareous. Found on algæ and eel-grass from Long Island Sound northward.

Suborder CHEILOSTOMATA

In this suborder the zoœcia are either horny or calcareous, and the orifices are usually surrounded with spines and have opercula. The orifices generally have raised margins, or peristomes. Ovicells form helmet-like coverings overhanging the orifices.

Genus *Ætea*

Æ. anguinea. Delicate, white, creeping, calcareous stems, from which rise numerous club-shaped cells, about one eighth of an inch high, each one with an aperture in the end. This species creeps in wavy lines along the fronds of algæ, and is frequently found on *Dasya*, *Griffithsia*, *Plocamium*, and eel-grass.

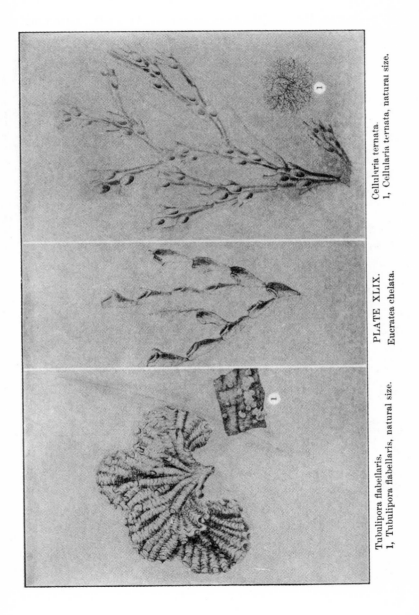

PLATE XLIX.

Tubulipora flabellaris.   Eucratea chelata.   Cellularia ternata.

1, Tubulipora flabellaris, natural size.   1, Cellularia ternata, natural size.

Caberea Ellisii.

PLATE L.
Bugula turrita.

1, Bugula Murrayana ; 2, B. Murrayana,
magnified ; 3, B. Murrayana, a few cells,
more highly magnified ; 4, B. flabellata ;
5, B. flabellata, magnified.

Genus *Eucratea*

E. chelata. A small, delicate species rising from a creeping stem. It has branches composed of single rows of horn-shaped cells having an oblique aperture on the side. Found at extreme low-water mark on hydroids, shells, stones, and *Fucus.* (Plate XLIX.)

Genus *Cellularia*

C. ternata. Zoarium filamentous, spreading, about one inch high, white, calcareous, branched in a forking manner; cells long, narrowest at base, arranged in series of three and on the same plane, apertures oblique and facing one way; horny joint between each cluster of cells. This species grows in deep water from Cape Cod northward, and is found on objects washed upon the beach. (Plate XLIX.)

Genus *Caberea*

C. Ellisii. Zoarium erect, with fibrous base, leaf-like, branches in a forking manner; branches straight, stiff, narrow, spreading; cells arranged in rows of three, adherent throughout; long bristles emanate from near base of many cells; egg-capsules globular, smooth, pearly. Common from Cape Cod northward in deep water. (Plate L.)

Genus *Bugula*

B. turrita. This is a very abundant species, found everywhere along the coast from Maine to North Carolina. Large quantities of it are

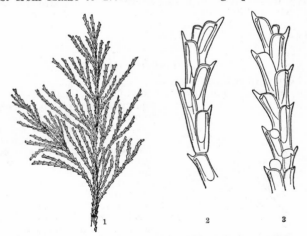

1, *Bugula turrita*, enlarged ; 2, the same, a branchlet, highly magnified;
3, the same, a branchlet, bearing ovicells.

sometimes thrown upon the beach by storms. It grows in erect tufts, sometimes a foot long, and is much branched; the branches grow around the stem in a spiral manner, forming dense clusters. The lower part of the stem is often naked (having lost the branches) and bright orange in color, while the tufts of branches at the top are pearly-white or yellowish. The cells are long, with a long, pointed spine on the upper outer angle. Like all species of *Bugula*, it has bird-head appendages, which can be seen under a powerful glass. (Plate L.)

B. Murrayana. Clusters of broad, thin, flexible fronds, one to two inches high, attached by a slender base and spreading in entangled masses; fronds wedge-shaped, flat, dividing in a forking manner; outer cells have bristle-like filaments, which constantly beat the water; all cells have avicularia, or bird-head appendages. (Plate L.)

B. flabellata. Fan-shaped fronds of flat branches, divided in a forking manner; the cells are arranged in four or five longitudinal rows, are oblong, with a spine at each side of the circular aperture, and are capped with pearl-like ovicells. This species, like others of the genus, bears the very singular structures known as avicularia, or bird-head appendages. They show, under a strong glass, a hooked beak, like that of the hawk or parrot. These beaks are attached by flexible stems and are provided internally with powerful muscles by which they are constantly opened and closed; the beak can bite with considerable force. In this species they are attached to the sides of the cells. (Plate L.)

Genus *Flustra*

F. membranacea. This species forms gauze-like incrustations on the fronds of seaweeds, and is common on *Fucus* and *Laminaria*, spreading irregularly over several inches of space. The cells are oblong, quadrangular, with a blunt, hollow spine at each angle. Many specimens have simple horny tubes, closed on top, rising from some of the cells to the height of half an inch. (Plate LI.)

Genus *Membranipora*

M. pilosa. An incrusting variety, composed of a single layer of cells spreading irregularly over the surfaces of stones, shells, and seaweeds,

sometimes completely covering the fronds of *Chondrus crispus*, *Phyllopora*, *Rhodymenia*, and other algæ. The cells are membranaceous, with a calcareous rim, and have one long hair and several small ones surrounding the large roundish apertures. It is found in abundance on the shores from Long Island Sound to the Arctic Ocean.

1, *Membranipora pilosa;* a few of the cells seen from above, magnified. 2, *Membranipora pilosa;* a single cell, seen in profile.

M. lineata. Cells oblong, crowded, closely adherent; slender spines on edge of aperture, which bend over and meet across it; incrusts rocks and shells in broad, thin, radiating patches; cells

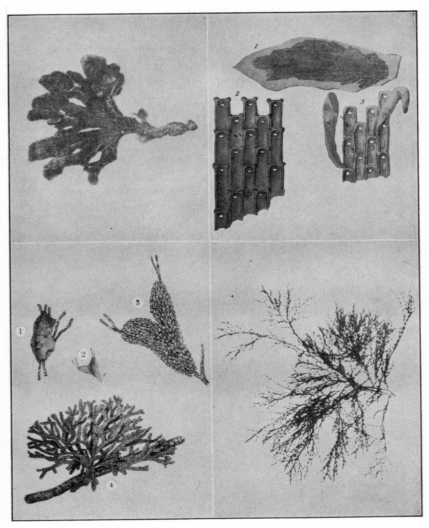

PLATE LI.

Flustra foliacea.
1, 2, Cellepora pumicosa, natural size; 3, C. pumicosa, magnified; 4, C. ramulosa.

1, Flustra membranacea; 2, 3, F. membranacea, magnified.
Vesicularia dichotoma.

much smaller and narrower than those of *M. pilosa*; easily distinguished
from that species by its manner of spreading and the absence of the one
long hair.   Common from New Jersey northward.

M. tenuis.   Common on pebbles, often covering their whole surface
with a lace-like incrustation of very small oblong cells having a three-
lobed aperture.   Found in Long Island Sound and north to Cape Cod.

Genus *Escharella*

E. variabilis.   This species forms calcareous incrustations on shells
or pebbles.   The layers are thin, but eventually overlap one another, and
the incrustation sometimes becomes an inch thick and resembles coral.
The color of the living animal is dull red.   The species ranges from Cape
Cod to South Carolina, and is abundant in Long Island Sound.

Genus *Mollia*

M. hyalina.   Cells subcylindrical, irregular, transparent, smooth,
and more or less oblique.   The species forms small circular disks on algæ
in tide-pools.

Genus *Cellepora*

C. scabra.   It forms branching, coral-like masses on slender red
algæ.

C. ramulosa.   Branches cylindrical, rough, dividing in a forking
manner, spreading, two to three inches high, calcareous; cells urn-
shaped, irregularly arranged, apertures contracted, long spine on the
outer edge.   It is found in deep water attached to shells, and in tide-
pools, where it grows chiefly on *Sertularia* and other hydroids and on
slender red algæ.   It ranges from Long Island Sound to Greenland.
(Plate LI.)

C. pumicosa.   Cells urn-shaped, irregularly crowded together, forming a conglomeration of porous, brittle masses, not exceeding an inch in
breadth, usually round when small, oblong and knobbed when large;
spine on outer margin of aperture.   It incrusts stones and the stems of
Fucus.   (Plate LI.)

Suborder CTENOSTOMATA

Genus *Alcyonidium*

A. ramosum.   Twelve to fifteen inches high; much branched;
branches smooth, cylindrical, one third of an inch in diameter, usually
crooked; branches in a forking manner; color rusty-brown.   Abundant
in shallow water, attached to rocks, from New Jersey to Cape Cod.

A. hirsutum.   A species common on seaweeds, sometimes completely
covering them, forming dirty, straw-colored, thick, cartilaginous crusts
covered with numerous conical papillæ.   These are the cells, or zoœcia;
they are surrounded with spines.   Circular yellow spots occur over the
surface, which are clusters of eggs.   A good pocket-lens will show the
cells, laid in beautiful order, and perhaps the extended tentacles.   Found
from Long Island Sound northward.

A. hispidum.   One of the most common species found incrusting the fronds of *Ascophyllum* at low-water mark.   It forms fleshy, brown, soft crusts of moderate thickness, and has spines scattered over the otherwise smooth and glistening surface.   The cells are inconspicuous, and each one has five long rigid bristles.   Habitat, Long Island Sound to Greenland.

A. parasiticum.   It forms thin, earthy crusts on algæ and hydroids. The surface is porous; the cells are distant and arranged irregularly, and seem as if composed of sand cemented with mud.

Genus *Vesicularia*

V. dichotoma (Valkeria pustulosa).   This species grows in clusters of crowded slender stems, which branch in a forking manner, the branches dividing in different planes, making a tree-like form one to three inches high.   At the points where the branches divide is a dark, opaque substance, and at these points also the cells are crowded in clusters of spiral rows and are greenish-brown in color.   The dark spots are in marked contrast to the white translucent substance of the rest of the stem, giving a spotted aspect to the whole.   (Plate LI.)

V. custata.   Delicate, thread-like, jointed stems, with slender opposite branches; cells small and elliptical, arranged mostly in clusters. Found creeping like a small dodder-plant over other polyzoans, hydroids, and seaweeds.

SUBCLASS **ENTOPROCTA**

Genus *Pedicellina*

P. americana.   A very small species.   Club-like zoœcia rise from slender, white, creeping stems; tentacles roll up instead of retracting into the cups.   Found on hydroids, other polyzoans, and algæ.

V
ECHINODERMATA

Phylum
ECHINODERMATA

Classes
ASTEROIDEA
(Starfishes)

OPHIUROIDEA
(Brittle-stars)

ECHINOIDEA
(Sea-urchins)

HOLOTHUROIDEA
(Sea-cucumbers)

CRINOIDEA
(Feather-stars and Sea-lilies)

Abo'ral surface: The side opposite the mouth.

Ambula'cra: Tubular feet used in moving.

Ambulacral zones: The five areas containing the rows of tube-feet.

Ampul'læ: Reservoirs or vesicles at the base of the tube-feet.

Auricula'ta: The larval stage of holothurians.

Bipinna'ria or *Branchiolaria:* The larval stage of starfishes.

Dorsal surface: The back of the animal, generally, but not necessarily, the upper side.

Exoskeleton: Outside framework or support, differing from a true skeleton which lies inside the body.

Interambulacral areas: The five areas between the ambulacral zones.

Larva: The animal in a stage of development from the time it leaves the egg until it reaches the complete form of the species.

Madreporic plate: A sieve-like plate of carbonate of lime.

Oral surface: The side on which the mouth is placed.

Ossicles: Calcareous plates which cover the body and form the exoskeleton.

Pedicella'riæ: Small spines which have divided ends, like scissors or forceps.

Plu'teus: The larval stage of sea-urchins.

Po'lian vessels: One to ten sacs arising from the ring-canal.

Ring-canal: The canal around the mouth.

Spines: Processes which rise from the surface of the animal.

Stone-canal: A calcareous tube leading from the madreporic plate to the ring-canal.

Suckers: Sucking-disks on the ends of the tube-feet.

Ventral surface: The side opposite the dorsal surface.

Water-vascular system: A series of canals which conduct water through the animal.

ECHINODERMATA

THE echinoderms, although their shapes are very unlike in the different classes, have the same general internal structure, and also other features which place them together in one group. They are radiates (page 113) of the highest type; they have an exoskeleton; and many of them are beset with spines, from which the name is given. They have locomotor organs, the *ambulacra*, and a *water-vascular system* peculiar to themselves. Some have the very strange power of casting off, and developing again, parts of the body.

The development from the egg to the adult is remarkable, and of unusual interest to naturalists. The larval stage of echinoderms is so unlike the mature animal that for a long time the larvæ were thought to be another class of animals, and therefore were given the names which they still retain.

In observing echinoderms it will be seen that the dorsal part is carried uppermost by some, such as the starfishes and sea-urchins. In the former the back is broad and extended; in the latter it is curved and contracted. But in crinoids the back is carried downward and is extended like a stalk; in the sea-cucumbers (holothurians) the dorsal and ventral surfaces are parallel with the long axis of the cylindrical body, instead of being on a plane with the mouth and excretory opening. Owing to the unusual positions of the dorsal and ventral surfaces, the terms *oral* (mouth side) and *aboral* (side opposite the mouth) are generally used in describing these species.

The surface of the body is divided definitely by the ambulacra, the *ambulacral zones*, and the *interambulacral spaces*, but differently in the different classes. The movement of the animals is effected by means of the tube-feet, or ambulacra. These have suckers, which are attached or released by the power of the water-vascular system. The *madreporic plate*, which can be distinctly seen in starfishes at the angle of two of the arms, is a calcareous porous plate which opens into the *stone-canal*. This canal passes through the body and opens into a circular tube which runs around the mouth. A system of canals extends from this circum-oral tube, or *ring-canal*, and eventually one canal opens into each tube-foot. Water, entering by the madreporic plate, passes through the various canals and into the tube-feet, which it dis-tends. When the feet are pressed against a substance and the water is withdrawn, a vacuum is formed, which causes the disk-ends of the feet to act like suckers. When the feet are again flooded the hold is relaxed. Thus the animal drags its body along with a slow, gliding motion. The madreporic plate, being calcareous, is said to act as a filter, purifying the water as it passes into the body, which it furnishes with oxygen as well as with locomotive power.

A curious organ found in the *Echinoidea* (sea-urchins) is called *Aristotle's lantern*. It is a complicated arrangement, not fully understood, having forty parts, and is connected with the alimen-tary system. One of the parts is the mouth, over which five teeth project. These teeth grasp and grind the food. The exoskeleton is composed of plates of carbonate of lime, called *ossicles*, which cover the surface of the body. The ossicles are of various sizes and shapes, and are one of the determining fea-tures in classification. They may be scattered spicules of lime, separated plates joined by connecting rods, or overlapping plates; or they may be fitted together so as to form a continuous shell. The starfishes are usually carnivorous, the sea-urchins usually vegetarian, while the holo-thurians, after the manner of worms, take in sand and mud, deriv-ing their nourishment from the organic particles contained in them. All echinoderms live in the sea.

Aristotle's lantern.

TABLE SHOWING THE CLASSIFICATION OF THE STARFISHES DESCRIBED IN THIS CHAPTER.

Class

ASTEROIDEA

(Starfishes)

Order PHANEROZONIA

(Ossicles not crowded; large marginal ossicles; spines only on dorsal surface; pedicellariæ sessile)

Families	Genera	Species
PORCELLANASTERIDÆ	*Ctenodiscus*	*C. corniculatus*
ASTROPECTINIDÆ	{ *Astropecten* *Psilaster* *Luidia*	*A. articularis* *P. floræ* { *L. senegalensis* { *L. clathrata* { *L. alternata*
PENTAGONASTERIDÆ	*Mediaster*	*M. æqualis*
ANTHENEIDÆ	*Hippasteria*	*H. phrygiana*
PENTACEROTIDÆ	{ *Pentaceros* { *Nidorella*	{ *P. occidentalis* { *P. reticularis* *N. armata*
ASTERINIDÆ	{ *Asterina*	{ *A. folium* { *A. miniata*

Order CRYPTOZONIA

(Ossicles crowded; pedicellariæ stalked)

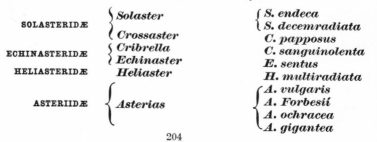

SOLASTERIDÆ	{ *Solaster* { *Crossaster*	{ *S. endeca* { *S. decemradiata* *C. papposus*
ECHINASTERIDÆ	{ *Cribrella* { *Echinaster*	*C. sanguinolenta* *E. sentus*
HELIASTERIDÆ	*Heliaster*	*H. multiradiata*
ASTERIIDÆ	{ *Asterias*	{ *A. vulgaris* { *A. Forbesii* { *A. ochracea* { *A. gigantea*

204

CLASS **ASTEROIDEA**

THE STARFISHES

THESE animals are named from their star-shaped outline. Some have five long, spreading arms diverging from a small disk, which is hardly more than their point of union; others have a large body with short arms, which are like angular projections of the body, giving a pentagonal shape. Some genera have a greater number of arms than others; *Solaster* has eleven to thirteen, and *Heliaster* (the sun-stars, found on the west tropical coast) has thirty to forty.

The mouth of the starfish is in the center of the ventral side. A ventral or *ambulacral groove* extends through each arm. In these grooves the ambulacra, or tube-feet, are arranged in rows. The *ambulacra* are hollow, cylindrical bodies, each of which has a sucker at one end, and is connected at the other end with a little globular body, the *ampulla*. The ventral groove forms a ridge in the body-cavity. It is called the *ambulacral zone*, and is formed by a double row of elongated plates, which meet and form a raised line along the middle of the inside of the arms, and appear like ribs; between them lie the ampullæ. These plates are called the *ambulacral ossicles*. Numerous other ossicles extend over the surface, buried in the integument of the body, making a calcareous network, or *exoskeleton*. The ossicles are connected by muscles so that the animal is not rigid, but is able to bend the body and even creep through comparatively small places. The ossicles are covered with *spines* of two kinds. The very minute ones are the *pedicellariæ*, and have a jointed end which opens and shuts like a pincers. Their principal use seems to be to remove waste matter or other substances from the body, keeping it free and clean. The pedicellariæ are arranged, in some species, in circles around the bases of the spines, and form groups over the dorsal surface. Examining the backs of different starfishes with a strong magnifying-glass, one will be surprised to see the varied grouping of the spines and pedicellariæ. At the extremity of each arm is a red eye-spot, which is sensitive to light, and a tube-foot, which has no sucker and which is believed to act both as an olfactory and as a feeling organ. The madreporic plate lies at the angle of two of the arms or rays. Water filters through the madreporic plate and passes by the stone-canal to the ring-canal around the mouth, and thence to the radial tubes, one of which extends through each arm and is connected by a branch with each tube-foot. At the base of each tube-foot there is a globular reservoir, or ampulla. A valve connects the tube-foot and ampulla. When the ampulla is contracted, water is forced into and distends the tube-foot; when the ampulla is distended, it withdraws the water from the tube-foot, thus acting like a suction-bulb. When water is sent into the tube-feet they are greatly extended and are then placed against an object. The water being then withdrawn through the ampullæ, a vacuum is formed, and the suckers are tightly attached. By the alternating movements of the ambulacra the animal is dragged slowly along and moves with a gliding motion. It does not deviate from a straight path, going over elevations or through depressions without turning aside; its body conforms to the irregularities of the road and never bridges over spaces. The stomach extends a little way into the arms, and a short intestine leads to the excretory opening in the center of the back. Starfishes are carnivorous and voracious, and are partic-

Diagram of water-vascular system of a starfish: *a*, madreporite; *b*, stone-canal; *c*, ring-canal; *d*, radial canals; *e*, ampullæ; *f*, ambulacra.

ularly destructive to oyster-beds. The animal fastens itself to a bivalve, and protrudes a part of its stomach, with which it envelops its prey and slowly sucks it out of its shell. When feeding on small mollusks they take them into the stomach directly. Starfishes regain by natural growth parts of the body which may be lost. Sometimes the animal throws off an arm to escape capture, and self-mutilation also occurs where unfavorable conditions exist. Oystermen formerly were ignorant of the starfish's wonderful powers of regeneration, and were in the habit of cutting up those captured in their forks and throwing them overboard, thus increasing the number instead of destroying their enemies, as each arm with a piece of the body attached to it will, it is said, become a new individual. This tenacity of life makes starfishes difficult to destroy, and they are exceedingly plentiful in all seas. One naturalist speaks of seeing on the coast of Maine a bed of starfishes which extended several miles and covered the bottom so closely that he picked sixty individuals off a small stone. On the northern shores of the Pacific coast they abound in great variety, and some are of unusual size. *Asterias gigantea* of this region measures two feet across. Another species, *Phyncopodia helianthoides*, measures a yard in diameter, and has twenty or more arms. The most common species of the Atlantic coast are *Asterias vulgaris* and *A. Forbesii;* the former ranges from Long Island northward, the latter from Massachusetts to Florida. These are the species particularly destructive to oyster-beds. *Asterias vulgaris* sometimes grows to be fifteen inches in diameter; from this, which is perhaps the largest, are found starfishes of all sizes down to the very small *Cribrella*. They inhabit all varieties of bottoms, from low-water mark to deep water. They are not always abundant in the same place, but seem to move about.

Some oystermen believe that the starfishes get into masses like a ball and are rolled along by the tide. This idea comes from the fact that an oyster-bed may be free from them one day and the next be covered by these pests. To get rid of them the beds are swept over with a tangle, which is an iron bar holding swabs of raveled rope. The spines of the starfish are caught in the tangle, and often hundreds are brought up in one haul and are then killed by steaming.

The anatomical system of the starfish is easily traced by cutting off, with scissors, the skin from the dorsal surface of the disk, and also cutting a slit down one of the arms. In the center of the body will be seen the upper part of the stomach, a small star-like spot, from which radiate five branches, which divide and lead into the much-ramified, plume-like organs which extend through the arms. These are the pyloric cæca, whose function is to secrete the digestive fluids. The much-folded stomach occupies the greater part of the central space, its large convolutions showing on top. The mouth connects with the stomach on the ventral side. By turning back the skin from the arm, small filiform processes can in some large species be seen; these are the dermal branchiæ, or breathing-organs, which may either project through pores in the skin between the ossicles or be entirely retracted. If the pyloric cæca be laid back, one can see the rib-like arrangement of the ambulacral ossicles, and also the ampullæ, which lie between the ossicles on each side of the ridge. If an ampulla be inflated and then pressed, the corresponding tube-foot will be seen to extend. To follow successfully the water-vascular system, beginning in the madreporic plate and extending through the stone-canal to the ring-canal around the mouth and thence through the arms, requires a strong glass and more skilful manipulation.

ORDER **PHANEROZONIA**

FAMILY **PORCELLANASTERIDÆ.**

GENUS *Ctenodiscus* (Plate LII)

C. corniculatus. Pentagonal; about two and a half inches in diameter; the body flat, with wide marginal plates, giving a flat edge to the rather long, pointed arms; madreporic plate large; color greenish; ambulacra without suckers, seeming to be adapted to pushing through soft mud rather than dragging over hard surfaces. It lives in deep water on muddy bottoms and ranges from Massachusetts to Greenland. When dredged the animal is usually found to be filled with soft mud.

FAMILY **ASTROPECTINIDÆ**

In this family there are only two rows of tube-feet; the rays end in sharp points and have large ossicles on the margins.

Genus *Astropecten*

A. articularis. The body is flat and smooth; the rays sharply pointed and conspicuously bordered with marginal ossicles and fringed with short spines; two rows of ambulacral feet; color rich purple. Found in shallow waters of South Atlantic coast on sandy bottoms. (Plate LII.)

Genus *Psilaster*

P. floræ. Diameter four to five inches; arms sharply pointed and conspicuously bordered with large ossicles; body flat, with smooth surface, the ossicles seeming like mosaic; bright pinkish flesh-color. It occurs in deep water off the eastern coast as far south as New Jersey.

Genus *Luidia*

This genus of starfishes is celebrated for its peculiar habit of breaking in pieces when taken from the water, and therefore good specimens are almost impossible to obtain.

L. senegalensis. Twelve to fourteen inches across; arms long and narrow, tapering to a point and fringed on the edges with spines; surface rather smooth, showing the separation of the ossicles; color almost white, with dark line running through the center of each arm; usually nine arms. Found in shallow water on the coasts of Florida and the Gulf of Mexico.

L. clathrata. Four to five inches across; light-colored; with a fringe of spines on the margins of the arms, which taper to a point; two rows of ambulacra. It is found from New Jersey southward, and is one of the most common starfishes on the sandy beaches of North and South Carolina. (Plate LII.)

L. alternata. Upper surface purplish, with irregular yellowish bands on the arms; under surface yellow. Found in shallow water on the Florida coast.

Family PENTAGONASTERIDÆ

Genus *Mediaster*

M. æqualis. Body flat; the five rays equal or exceed in length the diameter of the disk; margins have double row of large plates; surface covered with granules, which are easily rubbed off; bright red above, pale orange below; diameter four inches. Common on the coasts of Oregon and California.

Family ANTHENEIDÆ

Genus *Hippasteria*

H. phrygiana. This beautiful starfish lives in deep water, but is sometimes thrown up on the beach, and ranges from Cape Cod northward. It has a large, pentagonal, bright-scarlet disk, five to six inches in diameter, with arms rather long and pointed. The upper side is raised and cushion-like, and is covered with blunt spines; the margins have larger spines of the same shape. The pedicellariæ are sessile and so long and large as to be easily seen with the naked eye. (Plate LII.)

FAMILY PENTACEROTIDÆ

GENUS *Pentaceros*

P. occidentalis. Pentagonal; eight to twelve inches in diameter; ossicles a network of rod-like plates, with prominent spines at the points of union; body inflated in the center and running in wedge-like form to the ends of the rather long and narrow arms; the upper lines of the ridges have spines more prominent than those on the rest of the body; the spines of the larger specimens are more like large warts or small hemispheres. Found on the Lower California coast.

P. reticularis. This starfish is the largest species on our coasts. It is common in southern Florida close to the shore. The body is three to four inches thick, flat on the oral surface, but raised on the upper side, and tapers down in wedge-like form to the points of the short arms. The prominent blunt spines which cover its surface are arranged in a somewhat regular net-like order, and the sharp-edged margins have an even row of larger spines of the same form. The madreporic plate is nearly in the center of the disk, and is quite conspicuous, being bordered with a circle of small spines. Its color is dull yellow, and its size often a foot or more in diameter. It is the large starfish so often seen in curiosity-shops. (Plate LII.)

GENUS *Nidorella*

N. armata. This very curious pentagonal species, found on the California coast, is five to six inches in diameter and red in color. The upper surface is raised and covered with thick, pointed spines one half of an inch to one inch long, arranged in lines, but not crowded. The ossicles on the margins are large; some of them are hemispherical and bear large spines. Smaller spines border the under edge of the margins. (Plate LIII.)

FAMILY ASTERINIDÆ

The starfishes of this family are pentagonal, with a large body and short arms. The disk is more or less elevated in the center, and the edges are sharp. There are two rows of ambulacra. The ossicles are notched and overlapping. The family is confined to temperate and tropical waters.

GENUS *Asterina*

A. folium. Small, pentagonal, swollen (gibbous). Found on the Florida coast.

PLATE LII.

Ctenodiscus crispatus.   Astropecten articularis.
Luidia clathrata.   Hippasteria phrygiana.
              Pentaceros reticularis.

PLATE LIII.

Nidorella armata.   Asterina miniata.
Solaster decemradiata.   Crossaster papposus.

A. miniata. Pentagonal; somewhat raised in center; about one and a half inches across; edges sharp. Found on the California coast close to shore. (Plate LIII.)

ORDER **CRYPTOZONIA**

FAMILY **SOLASTERIDÆ**

GENUS *Solaster*

S. endeca. Dark red in color; nine to eleven arms, which are shorter than the breadth of the disk; diameter of disk about five inches; two rows of ambulacra; surface rather smooth. Common on the coast of Maine, and found from Cape Cod to Newfoundland below low-water mark.

S. decemradiata. This species is common on the North Pacific coast. It has ten arms, which are about twice the length of the diameter of the body, the whole body being about a foot across. (Plate LIII.)

GENUS *Crossaster*

C. papposus. Twelve to fifteen arms, half as long as the breadth of the body; upper surface an open network of calcareous rods, or ossicles; at their points of union are club-shaped tubercles bearing tufts of smaller spines; concentric lines and spots of red and purple over the spiny upper surface; color light underneath. Common on the New England coast. (Plate LIII.)

FAMILY **ECHINASTERIDÆ**

GENUS *Cribrella*

C. sanguinolenta. This species is abundant north of Cape Cod and is found of all sizes from half an inch to two inches in diameter and of various colors — purple, orange, red, yellow, flesh-color, etc. It has five round arms, generally about four times as long as the breadth of the disk. The ends are often turned upward. It is covered with crowded short spines, like little warts, which give it a nearly smooth surface. It has two rows of ambulacra. It moves with two of its arms turned forward, as if they were dragging the other three behind them. Unlike most species, the young are not free-swimming, but the eggs are carried around the mouth of the mother, and the young are retained there until they are capable of taking care of themselves. (Plate LIV.)

GENUS *Echinaster*

E. sentus. This species occurs close to shore in the waters of Florida and is perhaps the most commonly observed species on the beach. It extends as far north as New Jersey. It is purplish in color, and about four and a half inches in diameter, with two rows of ambulacra, five arms, and a surface rough with spines.

FAMILY **HELIASTERIDÆ**

GENUS *Heliaster*

H. multiradiata. Spines on the upper surface of rays in five rows, but close to the disk proper become reduced to one row. Found on the coasts of Lower California and Mexico. (Plate LIV.)

FAMILY **ASTERIIDÆ**

The *Asteriidæ* have the following characteristics : four rows of tube-feet; ossicles small and unequal; spines isolated or grouped; pedicellariæ of two forms, forceps-like and scissors-like respectively. They include the very common forms found on all beaches.

GENUS *Asterias*

A. vulgaris. The common starfish of the Atlantic coast, from Long Island Sound to Labrador. It occurs at low-water mark and extends into deep water. It has five arms, which taper to a point. Large specimens measure fifteen inches across. The upper surface is rough, being covered with short spines, which are largest and thickest at the edges of the rays, and surrounding them are the pedicellariæ. The color varies from pink, yellow, and brown to purple.

A. Forbesii. The common starfish of the Atlantic coast, from Massachusetts Bay to the Gulf of Mexico. This species resembles very closely *A. vulgaris,* but can be distinguished from it by the madreporic plate, which is bright orange, while in the former it has the same color as the animal; also the arms are a little swollen at the base and terminate more bluntly. These two species are very destructive to oyster-beds, especially where their ranges overlap. It is computed that they destroy annually two hundred thousand dollars' worth of oysters. Vast numbers congregate where the feeding-ground is good, and move in long lines from place to place. The oystermen dredge over the beds and bring them up in thousands, then steam them or throw them on the shore above high-water mark. (Plate LIV.)

A. ochracea. The common starfish of the Pacific coast, from Sitka to San Diego. Five rays, each hardly twice as long as the diameter of the body; spines running irregularly over the surface, but forming a pentagon at the middle of the disk and inclosing the madreporic plate; diameter eight inches. It is very common near San Francisco on rocks at low-water mark. (Plate LIV.)

A. gigantea. Body very large and swollen; six rays, somewhat less in length than twice the diameter of the disk; aboral surface covered with numerous short, blunt, equidistant spines of uniform size and regularly distributed; spines contracted at the base and striated; diameter two feet. Found on the California coast.

PLATE LIV.

Cribrella sanguinolenta.
Asterias Forbesii.

Heliaster multiradiata.
Asterias ochracea.

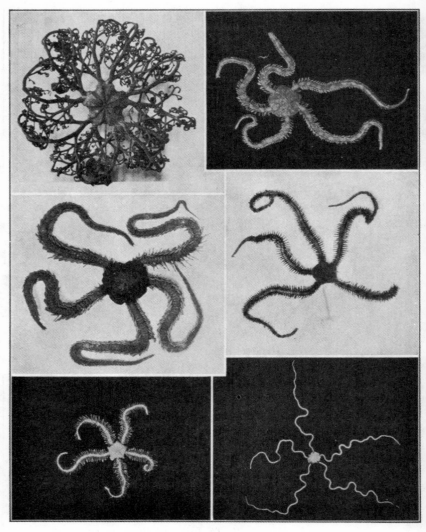

PLATE LV.

Astrophyton.
Ophiocoma œthiops.
Ophiothrix angulata.

Ophiopholis aculeata.
Ophiocoma Alexandri.
Amphiura squamata.

TABLE SHOWING THE CLASSIFICATION OF THE BRITTLE-STARS
DESCRIBED IN THIS CHAPTER.

Class
OPHIUROIDEA
(Brittle-stars)

Orders	Genera	Species
EURYALIDA *(Skin without plates; arms simple or branched, and capable of being rolled up)*	*Astrophyton*	*A. Agassizii*
OPHIURIDA *(Skin with plates)*	*Ophiopholis* *Amphiura* *Ophiocoma* *Ophiothrix*	*O. aculeata* *A. squamata* *O. riisei* *O. æthiops* *O. Alexandri* *O. angulata*

CLASS **OPHIUROIDEA**

BRITTLE-STARS

THE ophiurans, or brittle-stars, differ from the starfishes in having the arms quite distinct from the body. In starfishes the arms are extensions of the body, and the viscera extend partway into them, while in ophiurans the body is a central disk, with the five narrow arms attached to its margin. In form they suggest a spider, and sometimes are called sea-spiders. The name brittle-star is also descriptive, since they break off their limbs readily. The arms are narrow, taper to a point, usually curl at the ends, and have no ambulacral grooves, but are completely covered with bare calcareous plates (except in the first order, where they have a skin and no plates). The ambulacra are small spines without suckers, which emanate from the sides or margins of the arms and do not serve for walking. The madreporic plate is on the ventral surface, in one of the circular shields which surround the mouth. The alimentary canal ends blindly. The egg-sacs lie between the arms and open by slits on the under side, close to the arms, where they join the disk. Water flows in and out of these pouches, which are thought to have also respiratory and excretory functions. No eye-specks have been found, but they must exist, since the animal is sensible to approaching danger and quickly retreats. The ophiurans are more active than starfishes, moving by wriggling, and clambering with their arms. They are shy and hard to find, and it is difficult to capture a whole one, since they throw off pieces of their arms at the least alarm. Often they completely dismember themselves, an action which does them no permanent injury, since they reproduce lost parts. They are more commonly inhabitants of deep than of shallow waters, and are brought up from the bottom in dredges in great numbers.

Some species may be found near low-water mark under stones and in clusters of mussels, and often in seaweeds, thrown up from deep water, on the shore.

ORDER EURYALIDA

Genus *Astrophyton* (Plate LV)

A. Agassizii. This very singular ophiuran is commonly called the basket-fish, from its resemblance to a basket when the tentacles are rolled up. Its body is covered with skin instead of calcareous plates. The body is thick and somewhat circular in form, with elevated radiating ridges on the upper side, and the skin is marked off in star-like divisions. From the margin of the body extend five arms, which at once divide in a forking manner; each section again divides, and this division in pairs (dichotomous division) continues until the ends of the arms have become very numerous and attenuated. The arms are carried curled up or straight at will. In moving, the animal seems to walk on these branches as if on tiptoe, and in this position it forms a kind of net which entraps prey. The arms and prominent parts of the disk are yellow, and the depressed or membranous parts brown. *Astrophyton* is six to eighteen inches in diameter. It is found off the northern New England coast.

ORDER OPHIURIDA

Genus *Ophiopholis*

O. aculeata. This is a common species, found in shallow water on the North Atlantic coast. A similar or perhaps identical species occurs on the North Pacific coast. It is spotted purple or variegated in color. The upper surface of the body is covered with plates variously arranged, sometimes in the shape of a star, and each one is surrounded with small spines. The under side of the egg-sacs is covered with small spines. These sacs open by slits on each side next the arms, and have a rounded appearance, bulging out between the arms. The arms, which are long and attenuated at the ends, have on the upper side transverse oval plates surrounded by a border of flat, roundish granules. Sometimes the plates are divided into two or three pieces, when they are similarly bordered with granules. The arms are fringed with rows of thick, compressed, obtuse spines, generally six in each row. The under sides of the arms have large quadrangular plates slightly separated from one another and extending across the whole surface in regular, even rows. (Plate LV.)

Genus *Amphiura*

A. squamata. This very delicate species, found on shelly bottoms below low-water mark from New Jersey northward, has a body less than one quarter of an inch in diameter, with arms two inches or more in length and thread-like in size. These long, slender arms have, on both the upper and under surfaces, a row of overlapping plates, and are fringed with small spines, three in a row. The color is gray or whitish, sometimes marked with darker gray or brown. (Plate LV.)

Genus *Ophiocoma*

O. riisei, O. æthiops, O. Alexandri. These animals have long spines on the sides of the arms, which give them a bushy appearance. The surface of the body is granulated, but the arms are covered with wide plates. Their color is brown above and light beneath. *O. riisei* is found at Key West, the other two species on the coast of Lower California. (Plate LV.)

Genus *Ophiothrix*

O. angulata. Body covered with short, rough spines; egg-sacs conspicuous and extend like lobes between the arms; rays narrow and thickly beset with long spines, which are serrated on the edges and ends. Found on the Florida coast. (Plate LV.)

TABLE SHOWING THE CLASSIFICATION OF THE ECHINOIDEA DESCRIBED IN THIS CHAPTER

Class
ECHINOIDEA

Order DESMOSTICHA or REGULARIA

Shell usually globular ; mouth and anus polar ; lantern of Aristotle present)

Families	Genera	Species
CIDARIDÆ	*Cidaris*	*C. tribuloides*
	Dorocidaris	*D. papillota* / *D. Blakei*
	Porocidaris	*P. sharreri*
ARBACIADÆ	*Arbacia*	*A. punctulata*
	Cœlopleurus	*C. floridanus*
DIADEMATIDÆ	*Diadema*	*D. setosum*
ECHINOMETRIDÆ	*Echinometra*	*E. subangularis*
	Strongylocentrotus	*S. drobachiensis* / *S. purpuratus* / *S. franciscanus*
ECHINIDÆ	*Echinus*	*E. gracilis*
	Toxopneustes	*T. variegatus*

Order CLYPEASTROIDEA

(Corona or shell a more or less flattened disk; anus excentric; lantern of Aristotle present)

ECHINANTHIDÆ	*Clypeaster*	*C. ravenellii*
	Echinanthus	*E. rosaceus*
SCUTELLIDÆ	*Echinarachnius*	*E. parma* / *E. excentricus*
	Mellita	*M. testudinata*
	Encope	*E. michelini*

Order SPATANGOIDEA or PETALOSTICHA

(Heart-shaped ; mouth and excretory opening excentric; no lantern of Aristotle)

SPATANGOIDÆ	*Moira*	*M. atropos*
	Lovenia	*L. cordiformis*
	Schizaster	*S. fragilis*
	Metalia	*M. pectoralis*
	Brissopsis	*B. lyrifera*

217

CLASS **ECHINOIDEA**

ORDER **DESMOSTICHA**

SEA-URCHINS

THE shell of a sea-urchin consists of many calcareous plates, or *ossicles*, fitted closely together and forming a continuous exoskeleton. The plates are so united that externally the marks of juncture are not perceptible, but on the interior the shape of these plates is well defined. In examining such a shell, or test (they abound on the beach), it will be seen that its surface is covered with numerous hemispherical projections or knobs, which are grouped in double rows and run in meridional lines from one pole to the other of the more or less spherical body, separating it into ten divisions. Five of these divisions have perforations, or small pores in the plates of the shell, and are called the *ambulacral zones* or areas, because through these pores pass the small tubes, in the living animal, which connect the tube-feet, or *ambulacra*, with the radial water-canals and the *ampullæ* (see page 206). The wide spaces between these double rows of pores are called the *interambulacral zones* or areas. The ten spaces diverge from the *peristome*, or soft part around the mouth, in the center of the lower surface, and converge in the small area at the top or aboral side. In the center of this small circular dorsal space is the excretory opening, and surrounding it are ten plates, five of which have openings into the egg-sacs. One of them is larger than the others, and is modified to form the *madreporic plate*. The other five plates have eye-specks. The ambulacral zones terminate at these ocular plates.

The numerous spines which cover the animal are of three

kinds, and proceed from the knobs on the exoskeleton, over which they fit, forming ball-and-socket joints, which enable them to move in any direction. The long spines are ribbed, and seem to have no other function than that of protection. The second set, the *pedicellariæ*, are very peculiar small organs scattered over the surface in great numbers, and consisting of a head bearing three bill-like blades mounted on a long, flexible stalk. The office

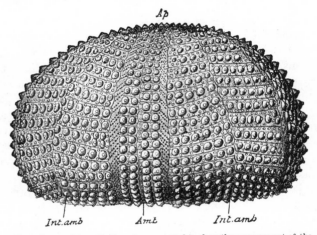

Test of sea-urchin, with the spines removed to show the arrangement of the plates, lateral view: *Amb*, ambulacral zone with its perforated plates; *Ap*, apical (aboral) pole; *Int. amb.*, interambulacral zones. (From Bronn's "Thierreich.")

of some of the pedicellariæ is to remove waste from the excretory opening; this is passed down regular lines and dropped into the water, thus keeping the body clean. Others are constantly opening and shutting their forks, reaching in all directions and grasping and removing anything which may have become entangled in the spines. They also capture floating bits of seaweed, which they drag over the body to conceal it. A third set of projections are the *sphæridia*, small globular bodies said to be connected with perception.

The spines vary greatly in size, number, and form in different species, and are such conspicuous features as to make the identification of species easy. In some the spines are solid and fluted;

in others they are hollow, sharp, and brittle; again in others they are short and silky, or very long and serrated, and so on. In one species they are so broad and flat as to resemble little sails. (See *Dorocidaris.*) (Plate LVI.)

The mouth, over which five long teeth project, is a part of Aristotle's lantern, which forms a curious and prominent feature in the center of the lower surface. Ten tentacles, like large tube-feet without suckers, lie around the mouth. The alimentary canal, starting in Aristotle's lantern, winds in two and a half coils around the inside of the shell, supported by mesenteries, and terminates in the excretory opening on the aboral surface. The sea-urchin has also a water-vascular system similar to that of starfishes (page 206). When the tube-feet are distended they project beyond the spines, and enable the animal to move slowly about; but sea-urchins are less active than starfishes, and although they are so well protected by spines and have few enemies after maturity, they lie in sluggish idleness in secluded places, and for further concealment often cover themselves with seaweeds or stones.

The sea-urchin has a nervous system, which starts in a ring around the mouth, ramifies through the body, and terminates in the eye-plates. The tube-feet and all the spines are under nervous as well as muscular control. Egg-sacs lie under the apex of the shell and open by separate ducts into the five plates on the small upper disk. Through these the eggs are discharged into the water, where they become free-swimming larvæ, called *Pluteus.* This immature sea-urchin (Pluteus) undergoes several curious transformations in the course of its development, and does not in any way resemble the mature animal. In spring the apical disk of the females will often be found covered with orange-colored ova, and that of the males with white sperms. In the growth of the animal, in its mature form, the shell enlarges by accretions of lime on the individual plates, or ossicles, of the exoskeleton, and by new plates formed around the apical disk. Sea-urchins are compared to starfishes folded over, the eye-specks on the ends of the rays meeting in a small area around the excretory opening, the ambulacra following spherical lines and leaving the mouth, as before, on the ventral side.

The *Echinoidea* present great differences in shape, being more or less spherical, oval, discoid, and heart-shaped. These variations are associated with the differences of internal structure, the openings of the digestive tract being at the opposite poles in the spherical and oval forms, but excentric in the disk- and heart-shaped species. The sea-urchins are grouped in three orders in accordance with these variations. All are characterized by the absence of arms, by having the calcareous plates immovably united to form a firm test, and by the great development of the movable spines upon the plates.

Sea-urchins are sometimes called *sea-eggs*, perhaps from their shape, but possibly from the edible quality of some species, which are eaten by the natives of the shore, who take them at the spawning season, when the egg-sacs are distended. They are gregarious, and frequently are so crowded together as literally to pave the surface of rocks and the bottoms of tide-pools in sheltered places. The following is quoted from A. Agassiz: "Many of the *Desmosticha* along coasts exposed to the action of the waves live in cavities which they hollow out of the solid rock. This they do, not by means of any solvent, but by mere mechanical action. They chisel out with their teeth the solid rock by incessant turning round and round, and keep their cave, where they are frequently prisoners for the rest of their existence, up to the size required by the growth of their test and spines, by constant gnawing. On the coast of California the common *Strongylocentrotus purpuratus* occurs in this way. We find long tracts of shore, where this sea-urchin is common, completely honeycombed and pitted by cavities and depressions in which they seek shelter against the powerful surf continually beating against the rocks. The same species does not excavate in sheltered places, where the sea-urchins can find protection between the interstices of large fragments of rock or ledges more or less sheltered from the more direct action of the open sea."

Sea-urchins in cavities of granite rock, where the openings are too small for the animal to get out, are to be seen in thousands on the coast of France at Croisic, Lower Loire. Spines of large sea-urchins are used as slate-pencils by the missionaries in the Pacific Islands.

Family CIDARIDÆ

Genus *Cidaris*

C. tribuloides. Similar to *Porocidaris sharreri*, but with thicker and stouter spines. Found from South Carolina to Brazil.

Genus *Dorocidaris*

D. papillota. A deep-water species which occurs off Chesapeake Bay and southward. It has slender spines with distinct longitudinal rows of serrations, and the spines are grouped in rosette-like forms over the small spherical body.

D. Blakei. This species is very peculiar in having broad, fan-shaped spines; vermilion in color. Found in deep water in the Bahamas and West Indies. (Plate LVII.)

Genus *Porocidaris*

P. sharreri. This species occurs, in deep water, off the coast of North Carolina and thence southward to the West Indies. The shell is light greenish-pink. The spines are white, with brownish-pink at the base, pointed, three and a half inches long, and surrounded at the base with small, flat, triangular, secondary spines. (Plate LVII.)

Family ARBACIADÆ

Genus *Arbacia*

A. punctulata. A small species found in shallow water on shelly and gravelly bottoms from Massachusetts to Mexico, and common in Long Island Sound. The shell is about one inch in diameter; the spines are rather thick and one half to three quarters of an inch long. The color varies from deep violet — almost black — to straw-color, and the spines are tipped with brown. The South Carolina species are usually brick-red in the bare interambulacral spaces, with darker sutures, and spines tipped with same color. The animal walks by means of its spines, with a tilting motion, and advances quite rapidly. (Plate LVII.)

Genus *Cœlopleurus*

C. floridanus. This beautiful sea-urchin is taken on the Florida reefs. The very brittle spines are one to four inches long, and are banded with carmine and white. The shell has zones of light chocolate-color alternating with orange and yellow.

Family DIADEMATIDÆ

Genus *Diadema*

D. setosum. Spines very brittle, and from one to two and a half inches long; jet-black. Found on the Florida reefs. (Plate LVII.)

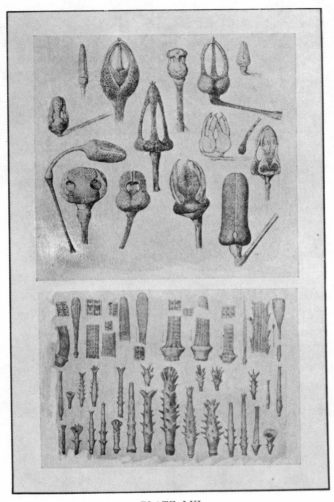

PLATE LVI.

Pedicellariæ of sea-urchins.
Spines of sea-urchins.

PLATE LVII.

Porocidaris sharreri.   Dorocidaris Blakei.
                    Arbacia punctulata.
Diadema setosum.   Strongylocentrotus franciscanus.

FAMILY ECHINOMETRIDÆ

In this family the ambulacral plates have several pairs of pores.

GENUS *Echinometra*

E. subangularis. This species, which ranges from South Carolina to Brazil, and is also found in Bermuda, is common on mud-flats and is easily distinguished by its oblong or elliptical shape. Its shell is about three inches long in its widest portion. The spines are one half of an inch to one inch long, thick at the base and tapering to a point. The color is dark purplish-green to deep violet — almost black.

GENUS *Strongylocentrotus*

S. drobachiensis. This sea-urchin (which bears, perhaps, the longest name in technical nomenclature and has no other, unless that of "sea-egg," which is applied indiscriminately to all sea-urchins) is a very common species in shallow waters of the northern temperate zones. It extends as far as New Jersey on the Atlantic and to the State of Washington on the Pacific coast. Although it is found as far south as New Jersey, it is there rare and small; but farther north, especially on the coast of Maine, it is exceedingly abundant. It is green or greenish-purple in color, and resembles somewhat a large chestnut-bur. The body is circular, somewhat depressed (but of variable thickness), and about two inches in diameter. The spines are moderately slender and longitudinally striated. It feeds partly on diatoms and other small algæ, which it cuts from the rocks with its sharp teeth. It also devours dead fishes, bones and all, and in return is swallowed whole by the wolf-fish and other large fishes. It moves by means of the tube-feet on its oral surface, slowly dragging itself along, and frequently is seen with seaweed, a stone, or some other substance on its back, which it places there with its pedicellariæ for the purpose of concealment.

S. purpuratus. The common purple sea-urchin of the west coast, from Sitka to Lower California, found in abundance on the rocks just beyond low-water mark. It is about one and a half inches in diameter, with rather thick, pointed, and fluted spines.

S. franciscanus. This is the largest species of the west coast, the shell measuring sometimes five inches across, and the thick spines one and a half inches in length. The tubercles on the naked shells are very prominent, and the zones are very clearly marked. It is purple in color and is often found in great quantities at low-water mark. It ranges from Alaska to Lower California. (Plate LVII.)

FAMILY ECHINIDÆ

In this family the ambulacral plates have but three pairs of pores.

Genus *Echinus*

E. gracilis. This is a deep-water species, which occurs from Cape Cod southward. The shell is nearly spherical, but is a little depressed on the oral side, and has twenty bands of color, alternately green and white. The spines are short and thin.

Genus *Toxopneustes*

T. variegatus. This is the common species of the Southern States, from North Carolina southward, and is found in shallow water in protected places. The shell is nearly globular; the spines vary in thickness and color, some being long, slender, and greenish, while others have stout and blunt spines of a yellowish or violet tint.

ORDER CLYPEASTROIDEA

CAKE-URCHINS

The animals of this order, commonly known as sand-cakes or sand-dollars, are flat and circular like disks. Sometimes they are cut at intervals on the margin; again they have slits through the body (*lunules*). They have a well-marked star-shaped figure on the dorsal surface. This figure is formed by the ambulacra, or tube-feet, which run in five rounded or petal-shaped lines on the under surface. The mouth, in Aristotle's lantern, is in the center of the somewhat concave ventral surface, the petal-like ambulacral zones meeting at the central space. The excretory opening is on the margin of the disk, at a point between two of the sections of the star-like figure. This marks the posterior part of the body, while the opposite arm of the star marks the front or anterior end. The spines are very fine and silky, and are spread abundantly over the whole animal. Clypeasteroids are mainly found in sand considerably below low-water mark, though some species thrive where they are exposed to the surf on open sandy beaches.

Family ECHINANTHIDÆ

Genus *Clypeaster*

C. ravenellii. This species occurs in deep water from South Carolina southward. The disk is about four inches in diameter, and is raised in the center into a large cone. The ambulacra run down the sides of the cone in straight lines, and around the base is a depressed area which emphasizes a thick border which extends around the scalloped margin. The color is light yellowish-brown. (Plate LVIII.)

Genus *Echinanthus*

E. rosaceus. This is a large species, oblong in shape, about four to five inches across and much rounded on top, the body being about two inches thick. The ambulacral zones are depressed, leaving prominent elevations which make a very conspicuous figure on the top. The color is light chocolate-brown. Found close to the shore off the coasts of Florida, South Carolina, and the West Indies.

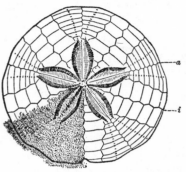

Family **SCUTELLIDÆ**

Genus *Echinarachnius*

THE SAND-DOLLARS

E. parma. This species, the shells of which are very common objects on sand-beaches from New Jersey northward, is generally known as the

Echinarachnius parma, the sand-dollar. Much smaller than natural size.

sand-dollar. The animals have flat circular disks about three inches in diameter. The ambulacral zones, in five petal-like lines, form a distinct figure on the upper surface. The mouth is in the center of the ventral surface, and the excretory opening is on the edge of the disk. In life they are covered with short, fine, silky spines, which seem like hair, and are purplish-brown in color, but turn green when taken from the water. The sand-dollars are exceedingly abundant off Nantucket Shoals, where the bottom seems paved with them. They are eaten in great numbers by flounders, cod, and haddock. When put in alcohol they stain it a dark color. Fishermen prepare an indelible ink by grinding to powder these animals and mixing it with some liquid. This species is also found on the northern Pacific coast.

E. excentricus. This is the common sand-dollar of the Pacific coast. The disk, instead of being circular as in *E. parma*, is somewhat straight across the posterior end, and the posterior ambulacral zones are shorter than the other three. The upper side of the disk is raised, forming a cone-like elevation, the apex being the center of the figure.

Genus *Mellita*

M. testudinata. The disk is rounded in front and straight in the back. Four long, narrow lunales, or cuts, occur on the sides in line with the ambulacral, petal-shaped zones, but do not extend quite to the edge of the disk; and a wide lunale occurs in the interambulacral space of the posterior end. The three anterior zones are shorter than the posterior pair. On the upper side of the disk the spines all turn toward the periphery. The color of the living animal is greenish-blue. It is very abundant from Cape Hatteras southward in shallow water, and the shells are sometimes found as far north as Cape Cod. (Plate LVIII.)

GENUS *Encope*

E. michelini. Ambulacral zones unequal in size, the posterior pair usually longer than the others; lunales like notches in the margin, with a large one opening between the posterior ambulacral zones nearly in the center of the disk; disk rounded in front and square at the back. Common on the coasts of southern Florida and the Gulf of Mexico in shallow water. (Plate LVIII.)

ORDER **SPATANGOIDEA**

HEART-URCHINS

The *Spatangoidea*, or heart-urchins, have heart-shaped or thick elliptical bodies. The mouth and excretory opening are both away from the center and on the ventral side. These animals seem deformed, so much are they out of symmetry and so different in outline from the other orders of the class. The ambulacral zones are in circles, or petaloid in outline, as in cake-urchins, but are not continuous, and the anterior one is usually unlike the others and frequently without pores. The entire body is covered with spines, and these are the chief organs of locomotion; the greater part of them turn backward, giving the living animal the semblance of a porcupine. The mouth is protected by a projecting plate, but Aristotle's lantern is absent in this order. The anatomy is in general the same as in the other orders, but the organs are turned in conformity with the inclosing shell. Most of these animals bury themselves in sand or mud and live in deep water; a few only are littoral species.

FAMILY **SPATANGOIDÆ**

GENUS *Moira*

M. atropos. Size about one inch by one and a half inches, and one inch thick; color yellowish-white, with brown spines. Found from North Carolina to Florida, from the shore to deep water.

PLATE LVIII.

Clypeaster ravenellii.   Mellita testudinata.
Encope michelini.   Test of Metalia pectoralis.
Lovenia cordiformis.

Genus *Lovenia*

L. cordiformis. About one inch by one and a half inches thick; reddish in color; resembles a little porcupine. Found on the southern California coast. (Plate LVIII.)

Genus *Schizaster*

S. fragilis. One and a half by two inches in size, and one inch thick; color brownish. Lives in deep water off the eastern coast.

Genus *Metalia*

M. pectoralis. A very large heart-urchin, found on the southern coast of Florida and in the West Indies in shallow water. It is, perhaps, the largest species found, being six to eight inches long and proportionately wide and thick. The shell is thin, more or less elliptical, and densely clothed with long reddish-gray spines. (Plate LVIII.)

Genus *Brissopsis*

B. lyrifera. A beautiful deep-water species, found off the coasts of Florida and the Gulf of Mexico. It has a red body with pale-yellowish spines. In size it is about two by two and a half inches, and is thickest on the posterior end. It is thickly clothed with long curved spines, some of which form two long tufts in the back.

TABLE SHOWING THE CLASSIFICATION OF THE HOLOTHUROIDEA
DESCRIBED IN THIS CHAPTER

Class

HOLOTHUROIDEA

Orders	Genera	Species
ELASIPODA		
(Deep-sea forms; tube-feet in zones near together)		
PEDATA	*Thyone*	*T. briareus*
(Well-developed tube-feet and false ambulacra)	*Pentacta*	*P. frondosa*
	Lophothuria	*L. fabricii*
APODA		*S. tenuis*
(Without radial canals, tube-feet, or respiratory trees)	*Synapta*	*S. roseola*
		S. rotifera
	Caudina	*C. arenata*

CLASS **HOLOTHUROIDEA**

SEA-CUCUMBERS

THE holothurians, or sea-cucumbers, although in appearance quite unlike starfishes and sea-urchins, have the characteristic ambulacral zones and other features of the group. In form they are cylindrical, and, when the tentacles and tube-feet are retracted, resemble fat worms; when fully expanded they are somewhat like sea-anemones, the tentacles forming a rosette-like top. The walls of the body are tough and muscular, with small calcareous deposits or spicules of various shapes in the skin. The mouth is at one end, the excretory opening at the other, and along the body are double rows of tube-feet. Often instead of tube-feet, or together with them, are conical processes without suckers. The ambulacra, when arranged in regular zones, are used for locomotion only in the lines running from the madreporic plate. In some species three of the zones are near together, and form a kind of sole on which the animal creeps; again the tube-feet are wholly suppressed, as in *Synapta*. Besides progressing by means of these suckers, the holothurians move, as do worms, by the extension and contraction of the body. The inner surface of the tough membrane inclosing the body is lined with powerful longitudinal and transverse muscles, by means of which the creature contracts and lengthens its body and changes its form in a wonderful manner. Around the mouth are tentacles, which are often much branched and are used as organs of touch and smell, and sometimes have an ear-sac at the base. From the mouth the food-canal, making one long coil, extends to a chamber (*cloaca*) at the other pole. The cloaca gives off a pair of much-

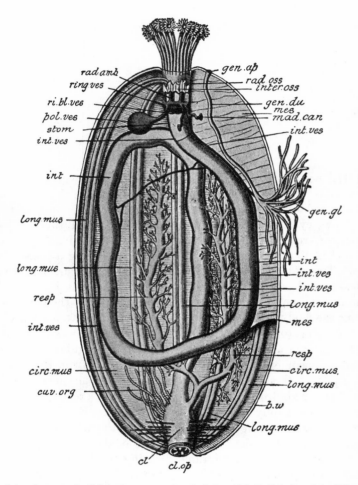

Internal organs of a *Holothurian*, as seen when the body-wall is divided along the middle of the dorsal surface: *b.w.*, body-wall; *circ. mus.*, circular layer of muscle; *cl.*, cloaca; *cl. op.*, cloacal opening with five teeth; *cuv. org.*, Cuvierian organs; *gen. ap.*, genital aperture; *gen. du.*, genital duct; *gen. gl.*, genital gland; *int.*, intestine; *inter. oss.*, interambulacral ossicles; *int. ves.*, intestinal vessels; *long. mus.*, longitudinal band of muscle; *mad. can.*, madreporic canals; *mes.*, mesentery; *pol. ves.*, Polian vesicles; *rad. amb.*, radial ambulacral vessel; *ri. bl. ves.*, ring blood-vessel; *resp.*, respiratory trees; *ring-ves.*, ring-vessel of the ambulacral system; *stom.*, stomach.

branched respiratory trees, which are constantly supplied with water by the contractions of the cloaca. At the base of one of the respiratory trees are singular structures known as *Cuvierian organs.* They are numerous, viscid, glandular tubes, which the animal can throw out, and which will adhere closely to almost anything. The holothurian has a water-vascular system, the madreporic plate being near the mouth, but not opening to the outside, and a nervous system which starts from a ring which lies around the mouth. The egg-sacs are branched tubes, often highly colored, which open to the outside, close to the wreath of tentacles surrounding the mouth.

The larvæ, when free-swimming, are called *Auricula.* In the deep-water species, *Cucumaria crocea* and *Psolus ephippiger,* the eggs, when discharged, and the young are carried on the back of the mother. In *Cucumaria lævigata* there is a brood-pouch, while in *Synapta vivipara* the young develop in the body-cavity.

The holothurians have the singular power of ejecting the whole of their internal organs and of growing them again in case they escape the enemy they have endeavored to elude by this strange method. They also turn themselves inside out, as it were, as if from *nausea,* when confined in water too stale for their uses. Often the viscera are ejected through holes in the sides of the body broken by violent muscular contractions.

Holothurians are generally distributed through all seas, but are congregated in greatest numbers in Eastern seas. Their habitat extends from shallow to very deep water. They are found in tide-pools, on rocks, and in sand or mud. Like worms, they live on organic particles contained in mud and sand, which they take into the gullet and pass through the alimentary canal.

ORDER **PEDATA**

GENUS *Thyone*

T. briareus. This is a large purple holothurian, found in shallow water from Texas to Cape Cod. It is four to five inches long and one inch or more thick, purple in color, and thickly covered over its whole surface with prominent papillæ.

GENUS *Pentacta*

P. frondosa. This animal is commonly called the sea-cucumber, and the popular name somewhat expresses its form, but it has the power of changing its shape in a most surprising manner. Sometimes it will be nearly globular, again long and thin, or it may be constricted like an hourglass. When at rest the body is ovate and somewhat pentagonal. On the angles are double lines of suckers, and in the interambulacral zones are a few scattered false ambulacra. The surface is nearly smooth, very dark purple on one side, and inclined to whitish on the other. Ten much-branched tentacles surround the mouth. The animal, when grown and expanded, measures fifteen to eighteen inches in length. This species is found throughout the whole length of both the east and the west coasts. It is very plentiful on the Maine coast in tide-pools and on the rocks at low-water mark. The genus ranges

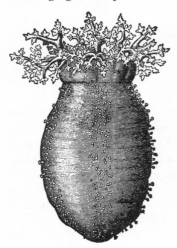

Pentacta frondosa, the sea-cucumber.

over the greater part of the globe. The tough muscular body is said to be edible, tasting somewhat like lobster, or trepang (*Holothuria edulis*), which is found on coral reefs in Eastern seas and is much valued as food by the Chinese. The internal organs of *P. frondosa* are highly colored, making its anatomy easy to trace. The muscular system is plainly defined.

GENUS *Lophothuria*

L. fabricii (Verrill), *Psolus fabricii* (Düben), *Cuvieria squamata* (D. and K.: Agassız). The body in this species is covered with rounded overlapping scales and numerous granulations, and when it is retracted is about two and a half to three inches long and about one inch thick.

Lophothuria fabricii, showing under surface with three rows of ambulacra.

rows of tube-feet lie near together, on a flat under surface, and form a kind of sole on which the animal creeps. The oral end of the body is a little raised and bears ten tentacles; these tentacles are profusely and finely branched, and when expanded are about as long as the body. The aboral end is obtuse and a little raised. Around the oral and anal openings the scales are grouped, forming circles in those regions. This holothurian is bright red in color, and when expanded is a beautiful object, perhaps the most attractive in appearance of any in the class. When retracted it has the aspect of an ascidian, and for a time was supposed to belong to that group. It is found on the New England coast on the under side of large shelving rocks.

ORDER **APODA**

GENUS *Synapta*

S. tenuis. This curious animal is long and slender, and so transparent that its internal organs are clearly visible. Around the mouth are a circular tube and a wreath of twelve branching tentacles. There are no ambulacra. Little spots scattered irregularly over the surface show, when highly magnified, small warts, each one of which has a calcareous projection shaped like a little anchor. By means of these anchors and by the contractions of its body the animal moves through the mud or sand in which it lives, near low-water mark. The sand is collected into rings at the oral end and pushed downward until the whole animal is inclosed in a sand-tube. When empty *Synapta* is white and transparent, and the digestive canal may be seen wound in a spiral throughout its length; but when gorged with food, sand, pebbles, and shells can be distinctly seen filling the food-canal, and the body then has a dark-gray color. *Synapta* grows to a length of eighteen inches or more, but is constantly breaking pieces off its posterior end by muscular contractions. When kept in confinement it soon commences to constrict its body at various points, and after a few hours there is nothing left but a mass of fragments. It is viviparous, that is, it carries its young in the body-cavity; the eggs are hatched, and the young approach maturity before they are expelled. This species ranges from Cape Cod to North Carolina, and can be found in the upper part of its burrows when the tide is out.

S. roseola. This species occurs in the same localities as *S. tenuis*, and differs from it mainly in color, which is pale red, due to minute red spots scattered through the skin.

S. rotifera. A species found in Florida. It is light purplish in color, and has eight or ten branches on each of the twelve tentacles. In this species the spicules of lime in the skin are shaped like wheels instead of anchors.

GENUS *Caudina*

C. arenata. About four inches long and tapers to the ends; the posterior end sometimes narrowed to a long, slender, tail-like extremity; tentacles around the mouth resemble cloves. It lives in sand and may be found on the New England coast, washed ashore after a storm.

Class
CRINOIDEA

Genera
Pentacrinus
Comatula

CLASS CRINOIDEA

FEATHER-STARS AND SEA-LILIES

The crinoids are inhabitants of deep water, where they grow in great numbers, forming beds of sea-lilies. Their general form, which suggests the lily, and their feather-like manner of branching, give them the two common names of sea-lilies and sea-feathers. They have a long, jointed stalk, one end of which is attached, while the other bears the disk of the animal. From the disk emanate five arms, which divide near the base, making

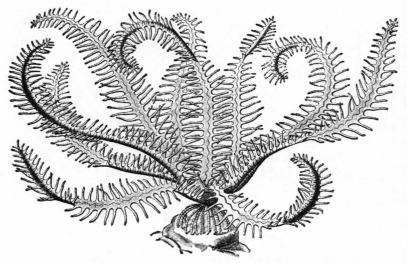

The feather-star *(Antedon)*, illustrating the *Comatula* form of crinoid.

ten arms in all. The arms have short branches along the sides. Ambulacral grooves follow the center of all the arms and branches. The mouth is in the center of the upper side, which in this case is the ventral surface. The genus *Pentacrinus* remains permanently attached, but *Comatula,* at a certain stage of development, separates from the stalk and swims freely about by means of its arms. It can attach itself temporarily by tubular processes, which are developed on the dorsal surface at the point where the stem was attached. The ossicles, or plates which cover the dorsal surface, are free, making the crinoid an animal of innumerable joints.

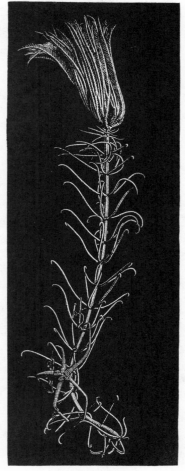

Pentacrinus asteria.

The crinoids are particularly interesting from the fact that they have existed from early geologic times, and their history is written in stone. In the early ages they were the only class of echinoderms, and their evolution into other forms can be traced through successive geologic periods. They existed in such vast numbers that the fossil forms are plentiful and are familiar to every student of geology, and are known as stone-lilies and encrinites. To-day they are decadent, there now remaining only twelve of the two hundred genera which existed formerly. A fine bed of crinoids is found off Cuba, on the slope of the coast where the water rapidly deepens from one hundred to two hundred fathoms.

Although the crinoids are deep-water forms, and are never found on the beach, they are given here because they follow in the system of classification and illustrate another curious class of echinoderms. The brief description given may add interest to the fossil forms to be seen in museums.

VI
ARTHROPODA

TABLE SHOWING THE CLASSIFICATION OF THE ARTHROPODS
DESCRIBED IN THIS CHAPTER

Phylum
ARTHROPODA

Class
CRUSTACEA

Subclass
Entomostraca
*(Crustacea of small, often of almost microscopic minuteness, and of comparatively
simple organization; appendages have little differentiation)*

Order PHYLLOPODA
(Appendages resemble leaves; mostly fresh-water species)

Suborders   Genera

EUPHYLLOPODA

*(Phyllopoda of considerable
size, bearing ten to sixty
pairs of leaf-like swim-
ming-feet)*

CLADOCERA

*(Small phyllopoda; body
laterally compressed; carapace like a bivalve shell;
four to five pairs of swimming-feet; chief organs of
locomotion are the bira-
mous antennæ; abdomen
devoid of appendages. They
abound in fresh water, are
very prolific, and afford a
large amount of food to
fresh-water fishes)*

Daphnia
Leptodora
Moina
Polyphemus

Order OSTRACODA
*(Resemble minute bivalve shells; swim by antennæ; body unsegmented;
appendages seven pairs only)*

Cypris (fresh-water)
Cypridina (marine)

238

Order **COPEPODA**

(Small size; body long, segmented; four to five pairs of once-branched appendages on thorax; abdomen without appendages; abundant in fresh and salt water; many forms parasitic)

Genera

Cyclops
Cetochilus
Sapphirina
Siphonostomata
Nicothoë

Order **CIRRIPEDIA**

(Imperfectly segmented; fixed or parasitic during adult life; inclosed in skin strengthened by calcareous plates; abdomen rudimentary; appendages biramous, usually six pairs)

Suborders	Genera	Species
	Lepas	*L. anatifera* *L. striata* *L. pectinata*
	Balanus	*B. balanoides* *B. eburneus* *B. rugosus* *B. geniculatus* *B. tintinnabulum*
RHIZOCEPHALA *(Parasitic)*	*Sacculina* (parasitic on crabs) *Peltogaster* (parasitic on hermit-crabs)	

Subclass

Malacostraca

(Highly organized Crustacea, usually of considerable size; appendages much differentiated)

Order **PHYLLOCARIDA**

(Small; covered with bivalved carapace; thoracic feet leaf-like; abdominal feet biramous; posterior segment terminates in two long spines; mostly fresh-water species)

Order **SCHIZOPODA**

(Small; transparent; shrimp-like; thorax more or less completely covered with soft carapace; thoracic appendages biramous; eyes on stalks)

Mysis   *M. sternolepis*

(Without gills or thoracic legs)

Euphausia

(With gills or thoracic legs)

Order **DECAPODA**

(Thoracic segments unite with head and form cephalothorax, which is covered by carapace; eyes stalked ; maxillipeds have exopodites ; five pairs of walking-feet without exopodites)

Suborders

MACRURA

(Abdomen usually longer than cephalothorax and commonly extended ; rostrum usually prominent ; eyes not inclosed in orbits ; antennæ and antennules large; antennæ have exopodites)

		Genera	Species
Free-swimming Forms: Shrimps and Prawns	⎧ ⎨ ⎩	*Penæus*	*P. setiferus* *P. brasiliensis*
		Palæmonetes	*P. vulgaris*
		Crangon	*C. vulgaris* *C. franciscorum*
Creeping Forms: Lobsters and Crawfish Families ASTACOIDÆ	⎧ ⎨ ⎩	*Homarus*	*H. americanus*
		Panulirus	*P. interruptus* *P. argus*
		Scyllarus	

Anomalous Forms:
Approaching the Brachyura

ANOMURA

DROMIDÆ		*Hippoconcha*	*H. arcuata*
PAGURIDÆ	⎧ ⎨ ⎩	*Pagurus*	*P. bernhardus* *P. pollicaris* *P. longicarpus*
		Clibanarius	*C. vittatus*
		Pylopagurus	
CENOBITIDÆ		*Cenobita*	*C. diogenes*
HIPPIDÆ	⎰ ⎱	*Hippa*	*H. talpoida* *H. analoga*
		Albunæa	*A. gibbesii*
PORCELLANIDÆ	⎧ ⎨ ⎩	*Porcellana*	*P. sayana*
		Petrolisthes	*P. sexspinosus* *P. armatus*
LITHODIDÆ *(Fifth pair of feet folded under the carapace)*	⎧ ⎪ ⎨ ⎪ ⎩	*Lithodes*	*L. maia*
		Echidnocerus	*E. cibarius* *E. foriminatus*
		Acantholithodes	*A. hispidus*
		Cryptolithodes	*C. sitchensis*
		Phyllolithodes	*P. papillosus*

Suborders
BRACHYURA
(Abdomen shorter than cephalothorax, and permanently folded under it; eyes inclosed in orbits; antennules and antennæ small)

Families	Genera	Species
PORTUNIDÆ *(Swimming crabs)*	{ *Carcinides* { *Callinectes* { *Ovalipes*	*C. mœnas* *C. sapidus* *O. ocellatus*
CANCROIDÆ	*Cancer*	{ *C. irroratus* { *C. borealis* { *C. magister* { *C. productus* { *C. antennarius*
	Menippe *Eupanopeus* *Eurypanopeus* *Neopanopeus* *Rhithropanopeus*	*M. mercenaria* *E. herbstii* *E. depressus* *N. texana* *R. harrisii*
GRAPSIDÆ	{ *Hemigrapsus* { *Pacygrapsus*	{ *H. nudus* { *H. oregonensis* *P. crassipes*
OCYPODIDÆ *(Sand- and fiddler-crabs)*	{ *Ocypoda* { *Uca*	*O. arenaria* { *U. minax* { *U. pugnax* { *U. pugilator*
MAIIDÆ *(Spider-crabs)*	*Libinia* *Hyas* *Loxorhynchus* *Pugettia* *Sternorhynchus* *Epialtus* *Pitho* *Lambrus*	{ *L. dubia* { *L. emarginata* { *H. coarctatus* { *H. lyratus* { *H. araneus* *L. crispatus* *P. gracilis* *S. sagittarius* *E. productus* *P. aculeata* *L. pourtalesii*
CALAPPIDÆ	*Calappa*	*C. flamma*
PINNOTHERIIDÆ	*Pinnotheres*	*P. ostreum*

(WALKING CRABS)

Order **STOMATOPODA**

(Abdomen very large; second pair of thoracic legs very large; gills borne on abdominal segments)

Squilla   *S. empusa*

Order **CUMACEA**

(Small, shrimp-like)

Suborders	Genera	Species
	Diastylis	*D. quadrispinosus*

Order **ARTHROSTRACA**

(No carapace, as a rule; six to seven pairs of walking-legs; eyes sessile)

AMPHIPODA *(Body usually compressed laterally)*	*Orchestia*	*O. agilis*
	Talorchestia	*T. longicornis*
	Gammarus	*G. locusta*
	Chelura	*C. terebrans*
	Caprella	*C. geometrica*
ISOPODA *(Body depressed or flattened)*	*Cirolana*	*C. concharum*
	Limnoria	*L. lignorum*
	Sphæroma	*S. quadridentatum*
	Idotea	*I. marina*
		I. ochotensis
		I. metallica
		I. wosnesenskii
	Chiridotea	*C. cæca*
		C. entomon

Class
MERISTOMES

Order **XIPHOSURA**

Limulus	*L. polyphemus*

Class
PANTOPODA (Lang)

Order **PYCNOGONIDA**

Phoxichilidium	*P. maxillare*

Abdomen: The posterior part of the body.

Antennæ: Articulated appendages which immediately precede the mouth.

Anten'nules: The anterior of the two pairs of feelers of the head.

Bira'mous: Having two branches.

Carapace: A thin chitinous shell covering the cephalothorax.

Cephalic: Pertaining to the head.

Cephalotho'rax: The united head and thorax.

Chela: The pair of pincers, or claw, which terminates some of the appendages.

Che'liped: A leg with chela, or claw, at the end.

Endop'odite: The inner one of the two main divisions of the limb.

Epime'ra: Divisions on the ends of the segments of amphipods and isopods, and belonging to the legs.

Epip'odite: A third branch of a limb.

Epis'toma: A triangular area in front of the mouth.

Exop'odite: The outer one of the two main branches into which the typical limb of any segment is divided.

Gastric mill: The first half of the stomach, where food is ground.

Mandibles: The pair of appendages next behind the antennæ.

Maxil'læ: The first pair of appendages after the mandibles.

Maxillipeds: The three pairs of appendages after the maxillæ.

Metame'res: Segments.

Orbits: Eye-cavities, peculiar to the higher *Crustacea*.

Prosto'mium: The region in front of the mouth; the preoral part of the head.

Rostrum: The beak in front of the head.

Segment: A part cut off or marked as separate from others.

Somite: A segment of the body.

Squame: A scale.

Telson: The last segment of the abdomen.

Thorax: The middle part of the body.

ARTHROPODA

THIS subdivision of the animal kingdom includes insects, centipedes, spiders, and crustaceans, which together constitute more than half the known species of animals. Although these animals are so unlike in general appearance, it is easy to recognize the common characteristics which place them together in one group. The name *Arthropoda*, meaning "jointed-footed," suggests perhaps one of the most obvious points of resemblance. The *Arthropoda* have bilateral symmetry, one side of the body being like the other; they are covered with a horn-like material (chitin); they are divided into segments; the segments have appendages; and the appendages are jointed so as to admit freedom of motion. Their manner of growth is peculiar; they cast off their rigid external coverings and secrete larger coats of mail, and at these periods increase in size or undergo metamorphosis.

There are such modifications of these general features as the habits of the different species demand. For instance, the appendages may be constructed for walking, swimming, boring, sucking, or the seizure and preparation of food. In some animals the appendages form a part of the breathing-organs, in others are used as organs of sense. Every detail of the organism, down to the hairs, has its special use and function.

CLASS **CRUSTACEA**

The crustaceans vary in size from microscopic minuteness to two feet or more in length. The giant crab of Japan (*Kaempferia kaempferi*) exceeds this, being commonly from eight to twelve feet across the arms, and is said to reach even greater proportions. Crustaceans live on land and sea, and in both fresh and salt water; they may be parasitic, sedentary, or free and active. There are said to be over ten thousand species, which include crabs, lobsters, shrimps, beach-fleas, wood-lice, barnacles, and water-fleas. Nine tenths of the species are marine; of these some are pelagic, and their transparent forms constitute a part of the plankton. Others live on the bottom in deep water and attain a large size. A vast number live in the littoral zone and form a considerable part of that crowded community. They are scavengers and free-booters, being great fighters, as well as predatory in their habits. As a rule, they feed on dead organic matter, which they consume in surprising quantities; some have also a vegetarian diet. They have, like starfishes, the singular power of throwing off their limbs and growing new ones.

The *Crustacea* derive their name from the nature of their crust or covering. This is earthy and brittle, not stony, like the shells of mollusks. This crust, or exoskeleton, has various degrees of firmness, from that of a delicate polished cuticle, seen in small forms, to the heavy armor of some crabs and the shell-like character of the covering of barnacles.

The lobster and crab are perhaps the most comprehensive examples as well as the largest in size of the class, the vast majority of the species being minute forms. The ocean swarms with varieties too small to be noticeable to the naked eye.

It is the province of *Crustacea* to consume decaying organic matter, both animal and vegetable, and in doing this they per-form a great service in purifying the waters of the pool, the shore, and even the sea. Not only in this are they serviceable, but to a great extent they serve as food for other animals, their flesh being palatable and preferred to that of other animals whose diet would seem to make them more wholesome. The small forms exist in such myriads, and increase so rapidly, that, although extremely small, they furnish an inexhaustible supply of food. Even some whales subsist upon these minute animals, and for man the larger species are articles of diet that are counted among the luxuries. The crustaceans are remarkable for their varied forms and for their perfect adaptation to many different conditions of life. There is no class in the animal kingdom which presents so wide a range of organization, or whose structure deviates so widely from the type form. These differences lie chiefly in the external characters and in the structure of the appendages.

Some species are solitary, like lobsters and crabs; others, like shrimps, are gregarious and live in immense shoals. In the habits of these animals there is much which excites wonder and interest.

ANATOMY OF THE HIGHER CRUSTACEA

The body of a crustacean is divided into segments, which are sometimes distinctly separated, like joints, and sometimes fused into one piece. The head part is called the *cephalic* portion, the middle section is the *thorax*, and the posterior part is the *abdomen*. The horn-like covering of the thorax is the *carapace;* where it projects over the head it is the *rostrum*. When the head and thorax are united, as in most *Crustacea*, the anterior or front portion of the animal is called the *cephalothorax*. Each segment has a pair of appendages. Each appendage has a joint attached to the body; from this arise two jointed branches, the *endopodite* and the *exopodite*, the inner and the outer foot. The appendages are modified to perform special functions. In front of the mouth are two pairs: the smaller ones are the *antennules* and have ears at the base; the larger ones are *antennæ* and are feelers. At the base of the antennæ are the *green glands*, said to have renal functions. Both the antennules and the antennæ are fringed with hairs, which aid in the sense of touch and perhaps of smell. On each side of the mouth are the *mandibles*. Then come the *maxillæ* and the *maxillipeds*, used in capturing and tearing the food and conveying it to the mouth. Thus it will be seen that some of the appendages around the head are connected with the senses, and others are used in eating. Those of the thorax are for walking; those of the abdomen for swimming, guarding the eggs, etc. The food taken into the mouth passes into the stomach through a short passage. The stomach is divided into two parts. The front one contains three long teeth which meet laterally and grind the food; this is known as the *gastric mill.*

When sufficiently fine, the food passes through a strainer of stiff bristles into the smaller portion of the stomach, where it is partially digested, and from there enters a long, straight intestine which reaches the length of the body and opens to the outside on the under side of the *telson,* or last segment. A large liver also pours its secretions into the intestine. The green substance commonly called " fat " in lobsters is the liver.

The heart consists of an elongated tube, or a short sac, which lies directly under the integument of the back. From this heart-sac, blood, which is colorless, is sent by arteries to all parts of the body; it then collects in spaces called *venous sinuses,* from which it goes to the gills, and thence back to the heart.

The nervous system begins in a large ganglion in front of the mouth, called the brain; from this two branches arise, which pass on each side of the digestive organs, meeting in ganglia in each segment and extending the whole length of the body. The gills, by which the animal breathes, are upon the limbs, or on the walls of the body immediately adjacent to them, and are generally inclosed in special chambers. In lobsters and crabs two such chambers are found under the flaps of the carapace, above the walking-legs. Gills are divided so as to present much surface to the water, from which they absorb oxygen. They are like a dense mass of little tubes arranged along a central tube. The class has two kinds of eyes, simple and compound; the latter are composed of a number of eyes. In some species the eyes are placed on the ends of movable stalks, which enable the creature to see in all directions and from a higher plane than the body occupies. As a rule, the eyes occur in the head region, but in the shrimp *Euphausia* they are on the thorax and abdomen. In barnacles simple eyes exist in the young stage, but in adult forms there are no apparent visual organs. The ear (so called) consists of a sac containing small silicious particles suspended in fluid. Numerous fine hairs on the inner surface of the sac connect with nerve-fibrils.

The organs of hearing are in various places. In decapods, or the larger *Crustacea,* they are at the base of the antennules.

The muscles are white bundles of fibers, and are in strips, which is an indication of power and activity. There are four important sets: twisted ventral muscles which bend the tail and are particularly large and strong, those which straighten the tail, those moving the appendages, and those which work the gastric mill.

Zoëa of *Cancer irroratus.* Last stage before it changes to the megalops condition.

The eggs, after being discharged, are attached to the abdominal legs of the mother by a kind of cement, or they are carried in pouches attached to the thorax. In these positions they mature, and hatch at different stages of development in different species. Some emerge with three pairs of legs, and are known as *Nauplius;* some are *Zoëa,* having a carapace and abdominal segments, but no abdominal appendages. Another stage is *Megalops,* with large stalked eyes. Others are hatched as miniature adults. These names were given when the embryo stage was not recognized and the larvæ were thought to be distinct species.

The growth of the animal is effected by moulting. The *Crustacea* are named from the crust-like covering which envelops them. It is a horny material, called chitin, in which are deposited particles of carbonate of lime, making a rigid envelop which would prevent all freedom of motion, were it not that there are spaces free from lime, and thus flexible joints are left. When the animal expands it throws off this hard covering and secretes a new and larger one. As the time of moulting approaches, the old covering becomes loosened, and a delicate new one is formed beneath it. The old shell splits open across the back just behind the

Megalops stage of *Cancer irroratus,* just after change from zoëa stage.

carapace, and the soft animal withdraws first its cephalothorax and then its abdomen, leaving the cover complete, including even the covering of the eyes and the lining of the stomach. The new shell is rapidly hardened, being already formed when the old one is cast, and the animal regains its normal condition in about a week; in the meantime it is defenseless, and lies quiet in some secluded place. Moulting is an exhausting process, and is attended with great dangers. A great mortality occurs at this time from accidents, from weakness, and also from helplessness in case of attack.

The hair-like processes scattered over the shell, often like fringes, are said to be organs of feeling.

SUBCLASS **ENTOMOSTRACA**

These are *Crustacea* of small, often microscopic size, of comparatively simple organization, and with appendages adapted to serve the purpose of respiration. These minute animals may be obtained by skimming the surface of the water with a muslin net, preferably at night, then washing off the inside of the net with a small quantity of water into a glass dish. Place the dish on a dark surface before a light, and the little creatures will gather toward the light, and may be satisfactorily observed with a glass.

ORDER **COPEPODA**

This order, though composed of minute forms, is one of great economic importance, from the fact that the little crustaceans exist in vast numbers and furnish a very considerable part of the food of many fishes. *Cyclops* is the most common of the freshwater, and *Cetochilus* of the marine genera. These, together with other genera, swarm in water wherever life exists, from the smallest pools and ditches to the broad surface of the ocean. Without having drawn a surface-net on some sheltered bay, it is difficult to have an idea of the myriads of *Entomostraca* in the sea. Although nearly transparent and of such delicate texture as to be almost jelly-like, they sometimes color the sea with a reddish tint for miles. Whales which have baleen, or fringes of whalebone, in the mouth subsist on these small organisms, which are called " brit " by the whalemen. The whales, sometimes in schools, rush through the water with open mouths, engulfing these little crustaceans, the baleen straining them from the water. Although devoured in such immense quantities, and sometimes lying dead in sheets of scum on the surface of the water, they maintain their numbers by the exceeding rapidity with which they reproduce. It has been computed that the descendants of one *Cyclops* may number in one year 4,500,000,000, provided all the young reach maturity and produce a full number of offspring.

One of the free marine forms, **Sapphirina**, is of especial interest, as it surpasses all animals in phosphorescence and sparkles by day as well as by night. It is one quarter of an inch long, and is broad and flat.

Besides the myriads of free-swimming copepods, there are parasitic forms in great number. The marine parasitic forms are commonly known as fish-lice. They have various habits, some living as commensals, others attaching themselves to animals only to be carried about; the true parasites live upon the blood and tissues of their hosts, and may fasten themselves to the external parts of the body or to the internal organs. Whales, fishes of all kinds, mollusks, starfishes, jellyfishes, and corals, all have some form of parasite, and many have several different kinds of guests. It is said that the haddock has more than a dozen which infest its external and internal membranes.

Nicothoë is found on the gills of lobsters. The truly parasitic forms are usually very degenerate and lose the characteristics of their order.

ORDER **CIRRIPEDIA**

("Curled feet")

THE BARNACLES

Barnacles of the genus *Balanus* (acorn-shells) (Plate LIX) are familiar objects on rocky shores, which they often whiten with their shells, and those of the genus *Lepas* are also widely known. The name of the order is descriptive of their curled appendages. The appendages are fringed like feathers and are drawn into or protruded from the shell at will. When extended they are constantly in motion, and create currents which carry food to the mouth of the animal, which is dependent upon such food as comes within range of its tentacles.

Their life-history is interesting. The young barnacle, called a *nauplius*, in no way resembles the adult. When it emerges from the egg it is a free and independent animal, with one eye, three

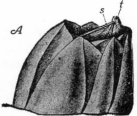

Balanus. A, external view: *s*, scutum; *t*, tergum.

pairs of legs, and a single shell. It swims about for a while and moults several times. It then has two eyes, two shells, and six pairs of legs. At this period it seeks a permanent home, and attaches its anterior end to the object it selects by means of its antennæ, which have become suckers. It makes its hold secure by secreting a cement which permanently fastens it to the spot. It

then undergoes metamorphosis, loses its bivalve shell and its eyes, and attains its characteristic *cirripeds*, or curled feathery legs, and a new shell covering. During these transformations,

from the time it becomes fixed until it attains its adult form, the barnacle fasts, living by the absorption of its own animal fat. Its food subsequently consists of the minute animal forms which abound in the sea. Its further growth is by moulting, but parts only of its covering are disengaged; the shell is permanent, and its successive stages of growth are marked

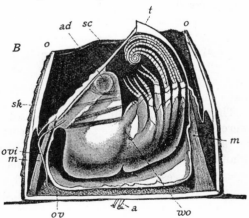

Balanus. B, anatomy: *a*, antennules; *ad*, adductor muscle; *m*, muscles of scuta and terga; *o*, edge of parapet; *ov*, ovary; *ovi*, oviduct; *sc*, scutum; *sk*, parapet; *t*, tergum; *wo*, female aperture.

upon it by lines, as in mollusks. The lining of the shell, or enveloping skin of the animal, and also the cuticle of the legs are shed, and in the spring of the year these thin, glossy casts are found in abundance floating on the surface of the water near the shore.

There are but three orders of barnacles, namely, those in which the shell is directly attached to the rocks, those which are attached to floating objects by a long stalk, and those which are parasitic on animals. A species of the third order infests the whale.

The older zoölogists classed barnacles with the *Mollusca*, but in 1829 Vaughan Thompson, in the study of their embryology, found that they should be classed with crustaceans, in company with crabs, shrimps, and water-fleas, with which their immature forms show direct relationship.

Genus *Lepas*

This genus is commonly known as the ship-barnacle, also as the goose-barnacle. It attaches itself to floating logs as well as to ships, but the latter form its principal home; consequently it is a great voyager, and, though common everywhere, is everywhere considered a stranger. The same species are found on ships coming from the most remote and widely separated regions, and so they cannot be considered native to any one locality. They are wanderers on the deep, and grow in such numbers on the bottoms of ships, especially of those which sail in warm seas, that they seriously impede the progress of the vessels. Aside from diminishing its speed, they do a ship no injury.

There was a tradition, which lasted several centuries, that geese were hatched from these shells, which somewhat resemble eggs. Gerard, in the appendix to his "Herball or Generale Historie of Plants" (1597), gives a picture of shells of *Lepas* growing on a tree, with geese falling from them and swimming about in the water below. His description is as follows: "There are founde in the North parts of Scotland and the islands adjacent called Orchades certaine trees whereon do growe certaine shell fishes of a white color, tending to russet, wherein are contiened little living creatures; which shells in time of maturitie do open, and out of them grow those little living foules whom we call barnakles, in the North of England brant geise, and in Lancashire tree geise; but the other that do fall upon the land do perish and come to nothing." He then describes in detail the various transformations, and ends with: "But what our eies have seen and hands have touched we shall declare."

The long, flexible stalk of *Lepas* is its anterior end. Generally this stalk is only half an inch long, but in some species it attains the length of a foot.

Huxley describes the barnacle as a crustacean fixed by its head and kicking food into its mouth with its legs. The mouth has a pair of small mandibles and two pairs of maxillæ, the last pair uniting to form a lower lip. The thorax has six pairs of branched appendages. The body is enveloped in a fold of skin, to which are attached five shell-like plates. One of these plates is long and narrow, and extends along the dorsal side; two are large and triangular (the terga); two are small and triangular (the scuta), the long point extending downward. These shells are on the free or posterior end.

Barnacles have a nervous system, consisting of a brain and a chain of five or more ganglia, but no special respiratory or circulatory organs are known; the cirripeds, or feet, are supposed to perform these functions. They have also a food-canal, a digestive gland, and excretory tubes. The eggs are carried under the external fold of the skin in flat cakes.

L. anatifera. The shell is bluish-white, showing lines of growth and faint radiating lines emanating from the anterior basal angle. The upper valves are narrow; the long tips point downward, and the top is blunted, leaving a space which is occupied only by a membrane. Near the apex of the shell, at the back, is a distinct angle. The dorsal valve is broad, not much compressed, and is sometimes grooved lengthwise. The cartilage of the shell and the stalk adjoining the shell are orange-colored. The stalk is grayish-brown and the cirri flesh-colored. The stalk is from one inch to six inches long. The shell is one inch long.

L. striata. Shells bluish-white; valves sharply triangular; dorsal valve compressed, forming a ridge; lines radiate from the basal angle of the lower valves and from the upper angle of the terminal valves, starting from the extreme end; the margins have a narrow edge of yellow cartilage; the stalk and cirri are of a dark slate-color; shell and stalk are each about an inch long.

L. pectinata. Shell shorter and less compressed than in the preceding species; lines of growth and radiating lines distinct; a decided line runs from anterior base to summit, a little back of the margin ; terminal end broadly obtuse (truncated) ; dorsal valve much compressed, forming a sharp edge serrated with ten to twelve teeth and distinctly striated or furrowed.

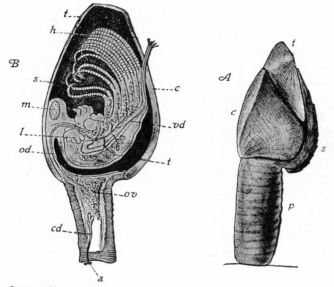

Lepas anatifera. A, the entire animal; B, anatomy. *a*, antennule; *c*, carina; *cd*, cement-gland; *l*, digestive gland; *m*, adductor muscle; *od*, oviduct; *ov*, ovary; *p*, peduncle; *s*, scutum; *t*, tergum and testis; *vd*, vas deferens; *h*, tentacles.

Genus *Balanus*

Balanus is known as the "acorn-shell," or "sea-acorn," and is found in vast numbers and of all sizes between tide-marks, incrusting rocks and the piles of piers. It also may be found attached to floating objects or to shells, or even to living animals, but its usual habitat is stationary. Unlike *Lepas*, it has no stalk, the shell being directly attached to some object. The body is surrounded by a fold of skin, to which are attached a shell consisting of six or more plates and a fourfold lid, or *operculum*, consisting of two *scuta* and two *terga*. The operculum may be called the door, as the animal opens and shuts it at will and has complete protection when it is closed. If one taps a rock incrusted with barnacles, and holds the ear near, the closing of the many doors may be distinctly heard.

The development of *Balanus* from the larval stage, as also the anatomy of the adult, is similar to that of *Lepas*. When covered with water and unmolested, there may be seen over a bed of barnacles thousands of tiny fringed feet waving to and fro. The motions look like gestures; they are perfectly regular and rapid, numbering eighty to a hundred a minute. The shell covering formed by barnacles on piles of wharves and bridges is said to be a protective agent; otherwise the barnacles seem to have no economic value in nature, as, unlike other animals, they do not serve, except in very small measure, as food to other classes. The tautog and perhaps some other fishes feed partly upon them. They are sometimes an obstacle to oyster-culture, as they fasten upon the objects intended for oyster embryos, and, growing faster than the latter, soon crowd them off. One species, *Coronula diadema*, fastens to the skin of whales. It attains the size of two inches in diameter. The shell is half an inch thick and full of cavities, into which the skin of the whale is drawn, giving the barnacle a secure hold. (Plate LIX.)

B. balanoides (Stimp.), *B. ovularis* (Gould), the rock-barnacle. This is perhaps the most conspicuous of the barnacles. It inhabits the whole northern Atlantic coast, and is so abundant that it not only whitens the rocks with a complete incrustation of shells, but the animals are so crowded that many of them lose their normal shapes and become greatly elongated. When the rocks are covered with water they seem alive, on account of the thousands of waving tentacles. This species also incrusts woodwork between tide-marks.

The shell is small, white, and variable in shape; sometimes its height is less than the diameter of its base; again the height is several times greater and the summit broader than the base. In its early stages the valves are smooth, but later the base is scalloped by four or five grooves. The summit of the plates is even and blunt. The aperture is diamond-shaped. Two valves of the operculum are pointed at the tips; two are blunt, making a deep notch in the summit. These valves are the distinctive feature by which to recognize this species, which varies so much in outward form; the species is also distinguished by its membranous base, which does not form a solid plate like that of other species.

B. eburneus, the ivory barnacle. This species, like *B. balanoides*, is a very common barnacle, and is found on all kinds of submerged woodwork, whether fixed or floating. It is also found on the carapace of crabs and *Limulus,* and on mollusks. It is chiefly found on objects below low-water mark. It ranges from Massachusetts Bay to Florida. It is easily distinguished from the preceding by its low, broad form and shelly base. The shell is smooth and circular at the base, and inclines backward, forming an oblique cone with a triangular opening; the plates terminate in points at the summit and incline backward, the last one forming a kind of beak. The operculum is pyramidal; two of its valves have both transverse and longitudinal lines well defined at the base, and are coarsely toothed at the edges; the posterior valves are slightly grooved across.

B. rugosus (Gould), *B. crenatus.* Shell white, cylindrical, somewhat conical, rugged, the summit usually as broad as the base; height often greater than diameter; aperture diamond-shaped, plates ending at the summit in acute spreading points, the posterior plate folded and curved like a beak; plates rough, with coarse, irregular ribs; valves of the operculum at the summit acute, with diverging points; the points striated. Found on shells and stones in deep water and also on bottoms of ships.

B. geniculatus. Shell dirty greenish-white, cone-shaped; aperture about the size of base; shell-plates triangular, unequal in breadth, and with alternate large and small ribs; the smaller ribs compressed and roughened on the edges by the conspicuous lines of growth which run across them; depressed areas between the plates marked with fine cross-lines; front valves of the operculum have coarse plated ridges, which incline over one another and are crossed by fine radiating lines; diameter at base one to one and a half inches; height two thirds the diameter. Found on pecten shells, and abundant off the coast of Maine.

B. tintinnabulum. Shell pink to purplish, conical, with six triangular plates, which are grooved, forming unequal ribs, and crossed by distinct lines of growth; spaces between plates crossed by lateral lines; posterior valves of the operculum longer than the others and curved forward, resembling the beak of a bird of prey; diameter at the base one inch; height one and a half inches. Found in warm waters and on vessels from the South.

SUBORDER RHIZOCEPHALA

These are parasitic forms and very degenerate. *Sacculina* lives on crabs, and its term of life is about three years, during which period the afflicted crab does not moult. Its shape is that of an ovoid sac on a stalk, which it attaches between two segments of the ventral surface of its host. The stalk divides and ramifies in a root-like manner within the body of the crab, from whose vital elements it absorbs its nourishment. The roots spread like a mycelium through the whole crab, even to the claws.

Peltogaster lives on hermit-crabs.

Different forms of Balanus.   (After Darwin.)   PLATE LIX.   Cenobita diogenes.

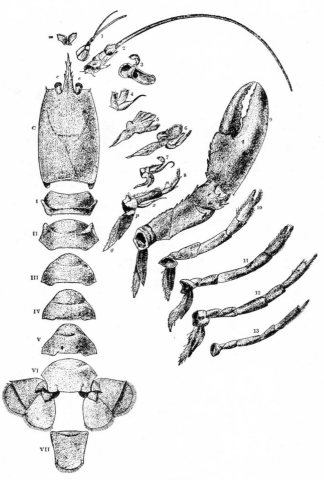

PLATE LX.

External Anatomy of a Lobster.

C, carapace; *e*, eye; *g*, gill; *m*, metastoma; *n*, endopodite; *p*, epipo-dite; *x*, exopodite; I–VII, abdominal segments; 1, antennula; 2, antenna; 3, mandibles; 4, 5, maxillæ; 6, 7, 8, maxillipeds; 9, big pincer; 10–13, walking-feet.

SUBCLASS **MALACOSTRACA**

This subclass comprises highly organized *Crustacea*, usually of considerable size, having the appendages much differentiated, the thorax with eight segments, and the abdomen with seven segments.

ORDER **SCHIZOPODA**

The name, meaning " cleft-footed," applies to the appendages of the thorax, which are once-branched (*biramous*). Gills, when present, are attached to these feet, and hang freely in the water. A delicate carapace covers the thorax; the abdomen is proportionately very large, often twice the length of the cephalothorax. In *Mysis* the eggs are carried in pouches under the thorax, giving the common name of " opossum-shrimp " to this small, transparent, phosphorescent crustacean.

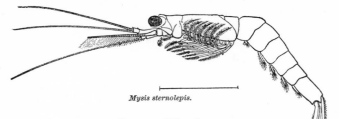

Mysis sternolepis.

GENUS *Mysis*

M. sternolepis. About one inch in length; translucent; antennæ very long; segments marked at joints with dark spots; the last two segments terminate in a stout spine; telson longer than the sixth segment; the sides are nearly straight and are armed with spines; the extremity is cleft; eyes large and prominent. Found abundantly in winter on the shores of still, muddy bays and sounds, especially among eel-grass.

ORDER **DECAPODA**

(" Ten-footed ")

The *Decapoda* are named from their ten walking-legs. The higher forms of crustaceans belong to this order. All the *Decapoda* have a similar anatomy, but are placed in two subdivisions according to their external form. In *Macrura*, the first subdivision, belong the lobsters, crawfish, shrimps, prawns, and hermit-crabs, animals having a long and more or less cylindrical body, with the abdomen extended; in *Brachyura*, the second subdivision, are placed the crabs, animals having the thorax broad and flat, and the abdomen bent under the thorax. The *Decapoda* have twenty segments, all of which, except the last one, have, at some period of life, a pair of appendages. The first two pairs of appendages, or, in the stalk-eyed forms, the first three pairs, are especially connected with the senses, and are often fringed with hairs, which are also considered to have a sense-function. The *antennules*, or first pair of appendages after the eye-stalks, are sometimes divided into two or three branches. At the base of the antennules are the ears. The *antennæ*, or second pair of appendages, are undivided, but are larger than the first pair, and are often very long. At the base of the antennæ are the renal glands. Both the antennules and the antennæ are slender, elongated, movable, and full of joints. In some species they are greatly modified, as in *Scyllarus*, where they are developed into broad swimming-plates and, perhaps, as shovels for burrowing; in some amphipods they are used as swimming-organs. (Plate LX.)

The next six pairs of appendages are grouped about the mouth. They are the *mandibles*, the *maxillæ*, and the *maxillipeds*. The mandibles are at the mouth-opening, and, being heavy and hard, are adapted to tearing and grinding; they have a jointed attachment, the *palpus*, whose office is to keep the mandibles clean. The two pairs of maxillæ are delicate and leaf-like. The three pairs of maxillipeds grow gradually larger, the last pair being very prominent and extending over the other mouth-parts. Next come five pairs of walking-feet. One or more pairs of these feet have pincer-like ends, or claws. Some species have the claws immensely developed, as in lobsters. The claws are the *chelæ*, and the feet which bear the chelæ are termed the *chelipeds*. The rest of the walking-feet have generally single, hook-like ends, but are variously modified in different species. The abdominal segments have six pairs of appendages, also variously modified. The last segment is without appendages, but often is extended into a tail, or fin-like expansion. The next to the last segment, in many forms, has appendages modified into swimming-plates, which extend on each side of the telson, forming a broad, fan-like caudal extremity.

They have, then, to correspond to the twenty segments of the body, two pairs of sensory, six pairs of mouth-, and five pairs of walking-appendages attached to the cephalothorax, and six pairs on the abdomen. The terminal segment, or telson, is without appendages. The exopodite is present on the maxillipeds, but disappears from the walking-feet in the higher forms.

In moulting the *Macrura* split in the longitudinal line down the back; in the *Brachyura* the split occurs across the body at the point between the thorax and the abdomen.

Suborder **MACRURA**

SHRIMPS, PRAWNS, LOBSTERS, CRAWFISH, AND HERMIT-CRABS

The characteristic features of the *Macrura* are an elongated body with the abdomen usually extended; a carapace, somewhat cylindrical; and the last pair of appendages of the abdomen (which are attached to the next to last segment) united with the last segment, or telson, to form a powerful caudal fin, used for swimming backward. The creeping forms in moving walk forward, but swim backward.

FREE-SWIMMING FORMS: SHRIMPS AND PRAWNS

In these animals the body is compressed and the carapace is not hard. The abdomen is very large in proportion to the cephalothorax, and has a peculiar bend. The rostrum is often longer than the thorax. The eye-stalks, antennæ, and legs sometimes attain extraordinary length, and the chelæ (claws) are not always on the first pair of legs. In some species chelæ are on two or three pairs of the legs. Above the antennæ are expanded antennal scales, which, together with the long bases of the antennules and very prominent eye-stalks, make the head a broad and conspicuous feature. The difference between shrimps and prawns is not very well defined, the small individuals seeming to be generally called shrimps, the larger full-grown ones prawns.

Prawns are known as *crevettes* in France and as *Garnelen* in Germany, where they are largely used as food. In the United States the shrimp-fishery is an industry of the South. On the California coast the fisheries are very extensive and are monopolized by the Chinese.

GENUS *Penæus*

P. setiferus. This species is about six inches in length when full-grown. A ridge or crest extends along the center of the carapace, and terminates in a long, pointed, toothed rostrum, the teeth being fringed with hair on the inner side. The antennæ are a foot or more in length; there are chelæ on the first three pairs of thoracic feet; the swimming-feet and lateral margins of the segments of the abdomen are fringed with hair; and the caudal appendages are longer than the telson. It ranges from Virginia southward, and is very abundant on the shores of the Southern States, where it is gathered for the markets. The large ones are known as prawns and the small ones as shrimps.

P. brasiliensis. This species is associated with *P. setiferus*, and, although not so abundant, forms a part of the shrimp-supply in the fisheries. It differs from the former in having a groove on each side of the ridge which runs through the center and whole length of the carapace. The first three pairs of feet are chelated. This shrimp is found as far north as Long Island, and often in brackish water, or even where the water is quite fresh.

GENUS *Palæmonetes*

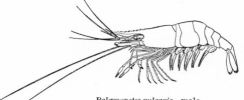

Palæmonetes vulgaris; male.

P. vulgaris (Palæmon vulgaris). Average size one half of an inch in length; body translucent, almost colorless, irregularly spotted; rostrum as long as carapace and toothed on the upper edge. It is found among eel-grass in brackish water, and also in pools and ditches on muddy shores from Massachusetts Bay to Florida. Commonly known as prawns.

GENUS *Crangon*

C. vulgaris, the common sand-shrimp. It ranges from Labrador to North Carolina on the Atlantic coast and from Alaska to southern California on the Pacific coast. It is found in abundance on sandy shores at low-water mark, and in shallow water below tide-mark; also among rocks and seaweeds. When left by the tide it buries itself in the sand. Its color varies with its location, rendering it inconspicuous. Upon the sandy shores it is translucent, pale in color, and often specked, closely resembling the sand, while on dark, muddy bottoms it is much darker. This is an edible shrimp, eagerly devoured by fishes; it is also gathered for the markets. The body of *C. vulgaris* is broad at the anterior end and tapers to a sharp point at the posterior extremity. A pair of broad, divided appendages on the cylindrical segment, which is next to the last on the abdomen, together with the sharp telson, form a fan-like swimming-tail. As in all shrimps, the antennæ are long and have plate-like antennal scales at the base, which are fringed with hairs. The mandibles are long. The movable finger of the chela is folded across the extremity of the claw.

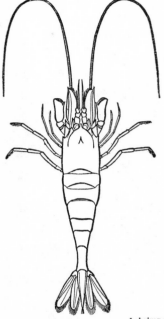

C. franciscorum, the California shrimp. This species is about three inches in length. It is distinguished from *C. vulgaris* by its larger size and by the greater length of the movable finger of the chela, which folds parallel to the side of the claw instead of across its extremity. Its color is light or dark yellowish-gray, mottled. This is the shrimp extensively gathered by the Chinese for commercial purposes. The shrimp-meat is dried and cured, and then separated by blowers very much as wheat is cleaned. It is exported to Eastern countries in great quantities, the value of the export being estimated at one hundred thousand dollars per annum.

Crangon vulgaris, the common sand-shrimp; male, natural size.

CREEPING FORMS: LOBSTERS AND CRAWFISH

FAMILY ASTACOIDÆ

GENUS *Homarus*

There are but three species of this genus, which is the most important one of all the *Crustacea*. They are *H. vulgaris* of Europe, *H. capensis* of the Cape of Good Hope, and *H. americanus*, which occurs on the eastern coast of the United States from Labrador to New Jersey. The lobster-fishery is one of great importance, and of such value that it is governed by stringent laws. The annual catch on the Atlantic coast of North America amounts to many millions of lobsters, the money value of which is very large.

H. americanus, the common lobster of the Atlantic coast. The characteristic feature of the lobster is its enormously developed chelæ,

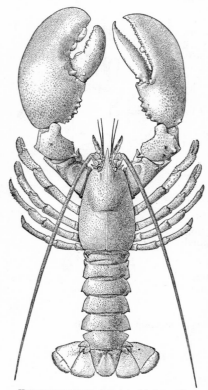

Homarus americanus, American lobster; male.

or pincer-claws, which are on the first pair of walking-feet. Small claws occur on the next two pairs, and simple hooks on the remaining two pairs. The appendages on the abdomen are divided (biramous). In the female they are used, excepting the last pair, for holding the eggs; in the male they are greatly abridged. The appendages on the next to last segment are divided and broadly flattened, forming with the telson a powerful swimming-paddle. The rostrum is very prominent, and has a long, pointed end, slightly upturned, and several spines.

The lobster belongs to the creeping forms of the order; it walks forward by means of the ten feet, but swims backward by using its caudal fin. It lives in deep water on rocky bottoms, hiding among stones, etc., but frequents sandy shores as well. It lives on dead and decaying animal matter, and it would seem strange that its flesh is so palatable, were it not that we know that chemical combinations which take place in the assimilation of food make one kind as clean, when transformed, as another. All the crustaceans have a similar dietary, being scavengers of the sea; yet fishes find them more acceptable than other animal food, and fishes capable of capturing larger prey subsist largely on the minute entomostracans described elsewhere.

The lobster is so large that it can easily be dissected, and will serve as a type of the structure of *Crustacea.* In dissecting one can follow the descriptions given of the anatomy of *Crustacea* on page 246, and will be interested in observing the beautiful arrangement of the parts and their adaptation to the uses they serve.

The female lobster carries her eggs on the abdominal legs, to which they are glued by a kind of cement. After the young emerge from the egg, the zoëæ still cling to the mother for a little time. The lobster moults eight times the first year, five times the second, and three times the third year, after which the male moults twice and the female once a year. It retires to some secluded spot for this operation, which is attended with many dangers. The back splits open longitudinally and the animal slowly withdraws, leaving the shell complete. In preparation for moulting, the lime around the contracted joints of the chelæ is absorbed, so that the soft flesh can pass through. Any injury to a limb at the time of moulting, or which results from fighting or from any accident, is repaired at successive moultings, and a lost member is replaced by a new, but not always a perfect, one.

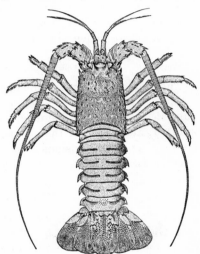

Panulirus interruptus, the spiny or rock-lobster.

Genus *Panulirus*

P. interruptus. This is the California spiny lobster, rock-lobster, or salt-water crawfish. It differs from the common lobster *Homarus* of the Atlantic coast in having no large claws, the first pair of feet being simple like the rest, also in having antennæ which are enormously long and very large at the base. The carapace is beset with spines, and the lateral margins of the abdominal segments end in spines. This species lives among the rocks on the southern California coast.

P. argus or *americanus* resembles *P. interruptus*, and is found on the coast of Florida.

Genus *Scyllarus*

Scyllarus has a broad, almost square carapace, which is uneven and coarsely granulated; the anterior corners are sharp, the posterior ones rounded. The antennæ are curiously modified into broad, flat, double plates reaching quite across the straight anterior end of the carapace. The under scales of these modified antennæ are rounded and leaf-like, the upper ones are pointed. The margins of the abdominal plates on the ventral side are toothed, and on the upper side the first three sections have knobs, the third one being the most prominent, and forming the posterior extremity when the abdomen is folded in. The walking-feet are all simple and end in points; the first pair are the longest, and the following ones gradually diminish in size. The ventral surface is rough and spiny. The abdomen is of about the same length as the carapace. These animals are found off the Florida coast and are caught in the fish-traps. They are uncommon. The very peculiar development of the antennæ makes them worthy of examination when opportunity offers.

ANOMALOUS FORMS: ANOMURA

The anomalous forms which are intermediate between the sub-orders *Macrura* and *Brachyura* were, until recently, placed in a suborder, *Anomura*. The members of this group differ from one another, and some of them resemble in external features members of the other divisions of the suborders, but there is a difference in anatomical structure which separates them in the classification.

FAMILY **DROMIDÆ**

GENUS *Hippoconcha*

H. arcuata. This curious little crab, found on the Florida coast, carries the half of a bivalve shell over its back. Its fifth pair of thoracic legs are bent over the back, and these, together with the fourth pair of legs and the spiny front edge of the carapace, enable the crab to hold the shell in position. This crab was formerly classed with the hermits, all of which were originally called *Bernhardus*, after the monk of that name.

FAMILY **PAGURIDÆ**

THE HERMIT-CRABS

In these curious animals the posterior part of the body is not protected by a crustaceous covering, and therefore the animal seeks protection by inserting its soft and defenseless abdomen into some hollow object, usually the shell of a gasteropod mollusk, as the whelk or the periwinkle (*Buccinum, Littorina*). The hermit-crabs do not always use a shell for this purpose, as they are sometimes found in the tubes of plant-stems or in sponges. Like other organisms in the animal world, they seem well fitted to make the best of their surroundings, the body becoming modified to suit the peculiar conditions under which they live. In those which inhabit shells the abdomen becomes spiral, in conformity to the convolutions of the shell. All the abdominal appendages are more or less atrophied; the sixth pair become like hooks, and these fasten to the columella of the shell, keeping the crab securely attached to it. In the female some of the abdominal appendages are hair-like and are adapted to carrying the eggs. The thorax, being protected, is protruded from the shell at will. The first pair of feet are much larger than the others, and are

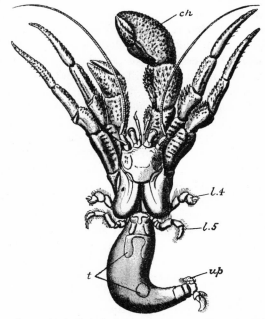

Pagurus bernhardus: *ch*, chela of first right leg; *l.*4, *l.*5, fourth and fifth legs; *t*, abdominal terga; *up*, last pair of appendages, modified to fasten to the columella of the shell in which the hermit lives.

provided with claws (chelæ). The first right foot is usually much larger than the left, and, besides the usual functions of capturing and crushing prey, the claw, or hand, serves as an operculum to close the mouth of the shell when the crab retires completely within it. The small left hand is shaped to fill out the parts of the opening not covered by the right one, thus making a close fit. The next two pairs of feet end in simple hooks, and are used for walking and dragging the crab along when he travels. These crabs move about very fast, and the houses upon their backs seem no encumbrance.

In some genera both hands are alike; in others the left one is the larger. In the case of hermits which live in tooth-shells, the right hand is cylindrical in form, fitting the circular opening of the shell. The other extreme is found in the genus *Cancellus*, where both the chelipeds and the first pair of ambulatory feet are ingeniously shaped, so that when closed they form a round operculum, or door, which closes the way into the compact sponge which this crab has for its carcinœcium, or house. It is interesting to note these differences and observe the perfection with which the feet are formed and jointed to suit the openings of different shells. Some genera show other adaptations to their twisted houses, the eye-stalks being uneven in length and the ambulatory feet unequal on the opposite sides. Besides this, some species are hairy and cover themselves with dirt for further protection. The exposed claws of some hermits have a special armature of spines, which make a fringe of points around the opening of the shell when the crab is withdrawn.

As the hermit grows he is occasionally obliged to find a new or larger shell, and there are amusing anecdotes of the troubles he experiences at these times while house-hunting. Very often he tries several shells before he finds one to fit. There is a tradition, not, however, well authenticated, that if the shell chosen happens to be occupied by its natural owner, the crab tears out and devours the unfortunate occupant. If the desired shell is occupied by another hermit inferior in strength to himself, he proceeds to take possession by violence. He then examines carefully the empty shell, inserting his legs and feelers, and if he decides to occupy it he withdraws his abdomen from the old shell and darts it so quickly into the new one that the act of transference is difficult to follow. After walking about with the new shell it sometimes proves to be unsatisfactory and further search becomes necessary. After it is well domiciled the crab never ventures outside the shell until it is obliged to change again on account of growth, or because some stronger crab dispossesses him. The shells of hermit-crabs serve frequently as the home of other animals which live with them a commensal life. The hydroid *Hydractinia polyclina* often covers the exterior of such shells with a brown, velvety growth. Some sea-anemones also are commensals with hermits. *Adamsia palliata* is always found on the shell occupied by *Eupagurus prideaux,* and never on any other. This is a European form. On our own coast a red anemone, the *Epizoanthus americanus,* found in deep water off the entire eastern shore, fastens on the shell occupied by the hermits *Eupagurus pubescens* and *E. kroyeri.* This anemone in time absorbs the shell of its host and itself becomes its protector—an advantage to the hermit, who finds room in the yielding polyp-mass for its increasing

A colony of sea-anemones *(Epizoanthus americanus)* which had completely covered and absorbed a shell occupied by a hermit-crab *(Eupagurus pubescens),* which still lived within the cavity. The polyps are not expanded.

size, and feels no longer the necessity for change of domicile. The female hermit holds its eggs in the posterior feet until they are hatched; the young are then released, pass into the water, and soon find shells for themselves.

GENUS *Pagurus*

P. bernhardus. This is a large species, bright red in color, rough and hairy. It inhabits the shells of *Fulgur carica* or of *Polynices heros.* It ranges from Cape Cod northward, and is replaced on the northern California coast by *P. alaskensis* and *P. aleuticus.*

Pagurus bernhardus, the hermit-crab.

P. pollicaris. This hermit inhabits shells similar to those occupied by the last, but is pale red in color, and its surface is granulated and not hairy. The short joint of the chela has a broad angle. It ranges from Massachusetts to Florida, and occurs at low-water mark on rocky and shelly bottoms of bays and sounds.

P. longicarpus. A quick-moving little hermit with long chelipeds, found in small shells at the water's edge in quiet places. They exist in great numbers and are eaten, shell and all, by fish. This species can be distinguished from all others by its very light color and metallic luster.

GENUS *Clibanarius*

C. vittatus. This hermit is found from North Carolina southward along the edge of the water and in tide-pools. It cannot be mistaken for any other hermit common on our coast, since it has the very distinctive feature of white longitudinal stripes on the ambulatory feet. The chelipeds are about equal, rough with tubercles, and the tips have smooth black edges. Body and feet are quite hairy. The color is brown and white.

Genus *Pylopagurus*

This genus is represented in Southern waters by several species. One of the most characteristic of them lives in *Dentalium*, the tooth-shell. The outer surface of the right hand is formed to close the shell. All the ambulatory feet and the very small left hand fold beneath, leaving only the flat surface of one hand exposed to view. Another species lives in a shell covered with polyzoans.

Family CENOBITIDÆ

Genus *Cenobita*

C. diogenes. This large hermit-crab, found in Florida and in more southern waters, inhabits the beautiful pearly shell of *Livona pica*. It lives on land a part of the year, but spends the breeding season in the water. It can be distinguished by its land-roaming habits, its large left cheliped, very stout walking-legs, and compressed eye-stalks. This species climbs the hills, but is more frequently met with in low, shaded, marshy places. (Plate LIX.)

Family HIPPIDÆ

Genus *Hippa*

Hippa talpoida, the sand-bug.

H. talpoida. This animal, commonly known as the "sand-bug," differs greatly in appearance from a crab. When the appendages are folded under the carapace it somewhat resembles an egg, the body being ovate, about half as broad as long, and the sides forming a nearly regular curve. The carapace is about one and a half inches long, convex, yellowish-white, and nearly smooth. The abdomen is long and pressed under the body, reaching nearly to the front. The eyes are minute and on the ends of long, slender stalks. The antennæ are plume-like and about as long as the carapace. *Hippa* lives on sandy beaches at or near low-water mark, exposed to the action of the waves. It burrows with great rapidity into the loose and shifting sands, using the short and stout second, third, and fourth thoracic legs and the appendages of the sixth abdominal segment for pushing and digging. Crabs of this species are gregarious and may be seen in great numbers, though but few will be captured together by digging, as they rapidly disappear beneath the sand. Sometimes they are found swimming about in the tide-pools. They seem to live upon the organic particles contained in the sand, which they swallow, the mouth not being adapted for mastication. This species ranges from Cape Cod to Florida. (Plate LXI.)

H. analoga. Similar to *H. talpoida,* but broader and flatter. It is bluish above, yellowish-white below, and the fringing hairs are black. Found on the California coast.

Genus *Albunœa*

A. gibbesii. This animal is found with *Hippa,* and, like it, burrows rapidly in the sand. Its general outline is square. The surface of the carapace is marked off with denticulated lines, which make the back appear as if composed of plates. The front edge of the carapace has a row of teeth and a prominent spine at the anterior angles. The abdomen is doubled under itself (not fitting into a groove of the thorax, as in ordinary crabs), this animal being intermediate between the long- and the short-tailed forms. The eyes are on triangular, plate-like stalks. The antennules are very long and are fringed with hair. The chelipeds have claw-like joints, which close across the straight, broad end of the hand. The first two pairs of walking-feet have curious sickle-like terminal joints. The animal is about one and a quarter inches long. *Albunœa* does not extend as far north as *Hippa,* its range being from Georgia southward. (Plate LXI.)

Family **PORCELLANIDÆ**

The crabs of this family are little more than one quarter to one half of an inch across the back. The chelipeds are broad and flattened. The first three pairs of walking-legs are well developed, and the fifth pair are very small and are doubled over the base of the carapace. The sixth segment of the abdomen has a pair of biramous appendages, which, with the telson, form a swimming-fan.

Genus *Porcellana*

P. sayana. Carapace little longer than broad; breadth about one quarter of an inch; smooth; has three acute denticulations between the eyes, the middle one the largest and depressed in the center; two denticulations on each anterior side; chelæ fringed with hair on the edges; walking-legs somewhat hairy; fifth pair of legs folded over base of carapace; color reddish, with white spots. This species was once called *occulata,* because of the eye-like spots over its entire surface. The posterior part and abdomen have longitudinal bands of color. The claws are marked like the shell. Found from South Carolina southward, often in the shells inhabited by hermit-crabs. (Plate LXI.)

Genus *Petrolisthes*

P. sexspinosus. Carapace longer than broad; breadth about one half of an inch; space between the eyes broad, but not divided into three teeth as in *Porcellana sayana ;* second joint of the cheliped has five broad teeth on its front edge and five or six small spines on its outer edge; fifth pair of legs doubled over base of carapace; whole body traversed with broken red lines. Found from South Carolina southward. (Plate LXI.)

P. armatus. Carapace longer than broad; breadth about one quarter of an inch; prominent and wide between the eyes; a small sharp spine on each anterior side; chelipeds long; second joint of cheliped twice as long as broad, with three teeth on the front edge and four or five small spines on the outer edge. Found on the Florida coast. (Plate LXI.)

Family LITHODIDÆ

The species of this family have a broad, ovate, uneven body and a prominent rostrum. The fifth pair of legs are rudimentary and are folded under the carapace in the branchial chambers, so that the crabs appear to have but four legs on each side. This is the distinguishing feature of the family, and makes them easily recognized.

Genus *Lithodes*

L. maia. The carapace is cordate (heart-shaped), and longer than broad, exclusive of the rostrum. The margin is recurved all around, and is beset with numerous very long spines. Six spines on each anterior side margin are regular and longer than the others. The surface of the carapace is covered with tubercles and spines and elevated in places. The rostrum is spiny, a third as long as the carapace, and has two spines at the base, one above the other, a spine at each side, two lateral spines near the middle, and two terminal divergent spines. The chelipeds are unequal and are covered with spines, those on the inner margin being the longer. The color is yellowish-red, lighter underneath; the spines are darker. Found on the fishing-banks off the coast of Maine. (Plate LXI.)

Genus *Echidnocerus*

E. cibarius. This curious crab has the carapace raised in front into a large cone-like elevation terminating in a long point. Three prominent but smaller cones extend across the center of the back, and two still smaller ones occur on the posterior sides and in the middle of the posterior margin. The whole surface of the carapace is covered with coarse granulations arranged in rosette-like groups. The chelipeds and legs are beset with large tubercles and fold together in such a manner that when retracted the crab is a close, compact, box-like mass, with a very rough,

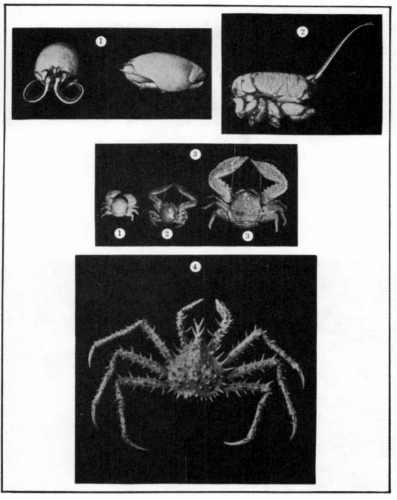

PLATE LXI.

1, Hippa talpoida.   2, Albunæa gibbesii.
3. 1, Porcellana sayana; 2, Petrolisthes armatus; 3, Petrolisthes sexspinosus.
4, Lithodes maia.

PLATE LXII.

Echidnocerus cibarius.
Echidnocerus foriminatus.

Cryptolithodes sitchensis.
Phyllolithodes papillosus.

spiny armature. The antennæ are broad at the base and covered with small spines on the sides and upper surface, and the eye-stalks are also spiny. This crab sometimes attains the size of ten inches across the carapace and a weight of seven pounds, being among the largest crabs known. It is found at the mouth of the Columbia River and along the northwest coast. (Plate LXII.)

E. foriminatus. This species resembles *E. cibarius* in the manner of closing the feet, forming a compact, box-like, spiny armature. The body is more depressed than that of the latter, and the cone-like elevations on the back are less prominent. The spines are hairy. The characteristic feature of this species is a semicircular cut in the second joints of the chelipeds, directly opposite to similar depressions in the first walking-legs, so that when the feet are folded a round hole is left, through which water flows freely to the gill-openings, which might, without these open holes, be obstructed by the close folding of the legs against the carapace. Found off the California coast near San Francisco. (Plate LXII.)

Genus *Acantholithodes*

A. hispidus. The whole body in this species, including the legs, is covered with hairy spines. The abdomen is broad, and covers about the whole under surface of the body, and is also beset with hairy spines, but they are less prominent than those on the upper side. The rostrum, terminating in spines, reaches to the tips of the eye-stalks, which are also spiny. The chelipeds are larger and longer than the walking-feet; the latter taper to a point, ending in a sharp nail. The shape of the body resembles somewhat that of a toad. This is a deep-water species, but it is sometimes brought ashore at Monterey, California, by fishermen who find it in the stomachs of fishes.

Genus *Cryptolithodes*

C. sitchensis. The most striking characteristic of this singular species is the great development of the carapace, which forms a broad, thin shield extending beyond the body and legs, and completely hiding the animal beneath it. The carapace is smooth and uneven, has a high ridge through the center of the anterior part, and the sides are broadly expanded and bluntly pointed at the extremity. The rostrum appears like a small rectangular piece cut out of the anterior side of the carapace. This species is found in the Strait of Fuca. A similar species, *C. typicus,* is found near low-water mark on the surf-washed rocks of the beach at Monterey, California. (Plate LXII.)

Genus *Phyllolithodes*

P. papillosus. The carapace is triangular, about two inches wide at the base, and narrowing to a long, pointed rostrum which terminates in a forked spine. The surface of the carapace is deeply depressed in parts, and forms a heart-shaped figure in the center. The lateral margins have four prominent spines on each side, the two at the posterior ends being thicker than the other two. The abdomen is broad, covering the whole under side of the body, and is marked off with prominent raised ridges diverging from the center line. The legs are all beset with long, rough spines. Habitat, the northwest coast. Taken from the stomachs of fishes off Monterey, California. (Plate LXII.)

Suborder **BRACHYURA**

THE CRABS

This group contains the true crabs, which are the highest of the *Crustacea*. In form they are quite the reverse of the first group. In the *Macrura*—except in the anomalous forms—the body is long and cylindrical and the abdomen extended, but in the *Brachyura* the body is flat and broad and the abdomen short and reflexed. Crabs of this suborder inhabit all seas of the globe, and are found from the shore to great depths. Some species live on land, some on the shore, some in deep water. Some forms burrow in the sand; others live under stones and boulders, or conceal themselves in crevices of rocks or in the cavities of sponges. They are divided into many families, and creep, climb, swim, or burrow, their structure being modified to their respective modes of life. There is also great variation in their shapes as well as in their color and markings. This diversity is so great and peculiar that it seems as though each one were more curious than the others.

In crabs the cephalothorax is depressed and often broader than long. The abdomen is relatively small and is folded under the thorax, lying in a groove which it fits so perfectly as to be quite hidden from above. The appendages of the abdomen are much reduced in number. The male has two pairs; the female has four pairs, which it uses for carrying its eggs. The first pair of walking-legs are comparatively large, and end in chelæ, or pinching-claws. The other eight legs terminate in simple points, except in the swimming varieties, when the fifth pair is flattened to form fins, or swimming-paddles. The eye-stalks are long and fit into sockets on the carapace. Both pairs of feelers are small. The antennules are frequently folded into small grooves. The external or third pair of maxillipeds are broad and flat, and cover the mouth-parts like a lid, or operculum.

Crabs, like other crustaceans, are scavengers, living on dead animal matter; but the land species are also vegetarian in diet. They are great fighters, but are also wily, often averting danger by resorting to stratagem. They are an interesting and curious group, as they possess a good degree of intelligence and have amusing habits.

From the time they leave the egg until they attain the adult form they pass through several complete and singular metamorphoses. The most marked forms are called the *Zoëa* and the *Megalops*. So little do these resemble the adult that originally they were classed as distinct genera far removed from the one to which they really belong. After the larva has moulted several times it appears as in the illustration on page 248—the last zoëa stage. From this it changes directly to *Megalops ;* the *Zoëa,* seeming to be attacked with violent convulsions, wriggles out of its skin a full *Megalops* (page 248). The animal then has enormous eyes, an extended abdomen, an elongated carapace, and swimming-legs. This stage is a short one, and at the first moulting changes to a form nearly approaching the adult. From this time they grow by shedding the shell at certain periods. This shedding is supposed to occur twice each summer until they have reached full growth, after which it is probable that they do not again moult; for often they are found with extraneous organisms, such as barnacles and sponges, upon them, of a size that must have required a considerable period of time for growth. The sexes of the same species sometimes differ so much that it is difficult to classify them. Even naturalists have been led into the error of assigning the male and female to separate species.

The front side margins of the carapace in many crabs are edged with a row of teeth or with spines, which vary in number and character in different species. In the spider-crabs the whole surface of the carapace is generally studded with tubercles, spines, and stiff hairs of a peculiar character. This armature is for protective purposes, and is often used to secure foreign bodies, such as algæ, hydroids, and polyzoans, which the crabs place upon their backs to disguise themselves. The burrowing crabs are usually smooth. When in motion the crab moves sideways, using the legs of one side to pull with and those of the other side to push with. As all the legs do not move at the same time, a continuous and uniform motion is kept up. Some species move with great rapidity, notably the sand-crab, *Ocypoda arenaria*. Often when pursued they will run into the surf instead of to their holes. The common edible crab, *Callinectes sapidus*, of the Atlantic coast, the fiddler-crabs, and the spider-crabs are among the well-known representatives of *Brachyura*.

FAMILY **PORTUNIDÆ**

SWIMMING CRABS

GENUS *Carcinides*

C. mœnas (M. J. Rathbun), ***Carcinus mœnas*** (Leach), the green crab. This is one of the most common species on the Atlantic coast from Cape Cod to New Jersey, and is very abundant in Vineyard Sound, Buzzard's Bay, and Long Island Sound. It is found between tide-marks, frequently well up on the beach, hiding under loose stones, also in tide-pools and in holes and cavernous places on the shore. It is from one and a half to two inches long, and a little more in breadth. It has five acute teeth on each side of the anterior part of the carapace. Its color is green,

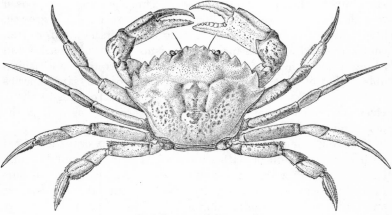

Carcinides mœnas, the green crab.

spotted with yellow, making it quite conspicuous. The surface of the carapace and limbs is more or less granulated. The posterior feet are flattened to form swimming-paddles. It is a very lively creature and has reckless audacity when brought to bay, which justifies its specific name (which implies frenzy). The French call it *crabe enragé.*

Genus *Callinectes*

C. sapidus (Mary J. Rathbun), *C. hastatus* (Stimpson), the blue crab. This is the common edible crab of the Atlantic coast. It is known at the North as the " blue crab," and at the South as the " sea-crab." It is found from Cape Cod to Florida, and after the lobster is the crustacean which has the greatest commercial value, being taken in immense quan-

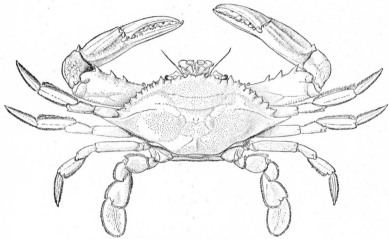

Callinectes sapidus, the blue crab.

tities for the markets, not only when the shell is hard, but immediately after moulting, before the new shell has hardened, when it is known as the " soft-shelled crab." It inhabits muddy shores, and is common in bays and at the mouths of estuaries. The carapace is about twice as broad as it is long, and has a long, sharp spine on each side which projects outward. This is a distinguishing feature. There are eight short spines on each side between the long spines and the eyes; then come recesses for the eyes, and between the eyes are four unequal teeth and a small spine underneath. The chelæ are large and somewhat unequal in size ; then come three pairs of simple feet and a fifth pair, which are flattened, forming swimming-organs. The margins of the carapace and abdomen are fringed with fine hairs, as are also most of the joints of the limbs. The upper surface of the body and claws is dark green in color, the lower surface is dingy white, the feet blue, and the tips of the spines reddish. The body is compressed, the carapace being moderately convex above, and is covered with minute granulations, which are more numerous over some portions than over others. The abdomen of the female is very broad and fills the entire space between the bases of the posterior pair of feet. During the spawning season it is so charged with eggs that often it projects out almost at right angles with the carapace. The crabs of this species are very active and can swim rapidly. They also have the habit of pushing themselves backward into the mud for concealment. They are predaceous and pugnacious, and have great strength in their claws, which they use with dexterity. They not only fight their own kind, but show a bold front to all enemies, including man. The average size is six inches across the carapace.

Genus *Ovalipes*

O. ocellatus (Rathbun), *Platyonichus ocellatus* (Latreille), the lady-crab or sand-crab. A species common on sandy shores from Cape Cod to Florida. It is found among the loose sands at low-water mark, even on the most exposed beaches, and also is abundant on sandy bottoms offshore. At low-water mark it buries itself up to the eyes and antennæ in the sand, where it watches for prey and foes, and quickly

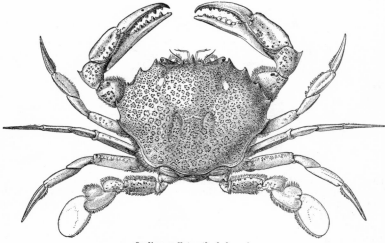

Ovalipes ocellatus, the lady-crab.

disappears beneath the sand when danger approaches. It possesses the power of burrowing in common with other marine animals which inhabit exposed beaches of loose sand. By burying itself deep in the sand it is protected from the action of the breakers. This species is easily distinguished by the color and shape of its carapace, taken in connection with its posterior swimming-feet. The body is nearly as long as it is broad, with five prominent spines on each side. The front margin is indented on each side of a three-spined rostrum, to form cavities for the eyes. The first limbs are large and have claws; the posterior ones are flattened into swimming-feet, and the intermediate three pairs are simple in structure, ending in points. In color it is white, covered with spotted rings of red and purple.

WALKING CRABS

FAMILY **CANCROIDÆ**

GENUS *Cancer*

C. irroratus, the rock-crab. This is the common crab of the New England coast. It ranges from Labrador to South Carolina, but is rare south of New Jersey. It is found on sandy as well as on rocky shores at and below low-water mark and also between tide-marks, hiding among rocks, nearly buried in sand or gravel, and in tide-pools, where sometimes amusing combats between the males may be seen. The carapace is suboval, one third broader than long, the breadth being often from three to four inches. The surface is granulated but smooth; the color is yellowish, closely dotted

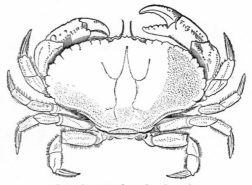

Cancer irroratus, the rock-crab; male.

with brown. The eyes are on short stalks in deep, circular holes, and between the eyes are small teeth. There are nine blunt teeth along each side of the front edge of the carapace. The first pair of legs are short and stout, and terminate in claws. The four posterior pairs are slender and end in pointed tips. This is an edible crab, and it is devoured by the larger fishes, but does not — although there seems to be no reason for it — share to any extent a place in the markets with the blue crab, *Callinectes sapidus*.

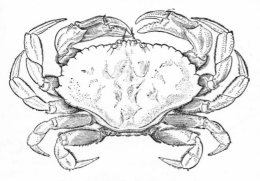

Cancer borealis, the Jonah crab; male.

C. borealis, the Jonah crab. This crab resembles, and is frequently taken for, *C. irroratus*. It is larger than the latter in full growth, and is heavier and more massive. The carapace and claws are rougher, the granules being irregular in size. The legs are proportionately shorter and heavier. The teeth on the anterior margins are rounded in front, but the posterior ones are sharply pointed. In color

it is brick-red above and yellowish beneath. It inhabits rocky shores
only and is found at low tide on the surface of the rocks, where it is exposed to the action of the waves and also to the attacks of birds of
prey, which feed upon it, while *C. irroratus,* concealed under the rocks
in the same locality, escapes their depredations. This species is supplied
to the Newport market, where it is considered preferable to the blue
crab. Its range is from the eastern end of Long Island to Nova Scotia.

   C. magister. This species inhabits the Pacific coast and ranges from
Alaska to Lower California. The adult male is from seven to nine inches
broad and from four to five inches long. The anterior margin of the
carapace is an almost regular elliptical curve with nine small teeth on
each side. At the end of the curve a large, pointed tooth projects
directly outward, and from this the carapace slopes abruptly backward,
giving a narrow posterior end. The surface of the carapace is undu-

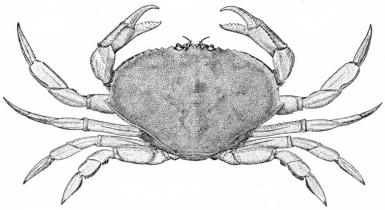

Cancer magister, the common crab of the Pacific coast; male.

lated and covered with papillæ, and is light reddish-brown, shading to
lighter color in the back. The color of the legs and under surface of the
animal is yellowish. The claws are toothed above and ribbed at the
sides. It inhabits sandy bottoms below tide-mark and is the largest and
most important edible crab of the western coast.

   C. productus, the red crab. This species, like the preceding one, is
of large size and inhabits the western coast from Alaska to the Gulf of
California. The carapace is four and a half inches in length, from five
to seven in breadth, and somewhat elliptical in outline. The teeth on
the anterior margin are distinctly separate in the adult, but in the
young appear as wrinklings of the edge of the carapace. The posterior
margins are concave. In color the animal is dark red above and yellowish beneath in the adults, but variable in the young, sometimes being
yellow spotted with red, or banded with red and yellow. It inhabits
rocky shores. This is an edible crab, but is not taken for the markets,
C. magister supplying all demands.

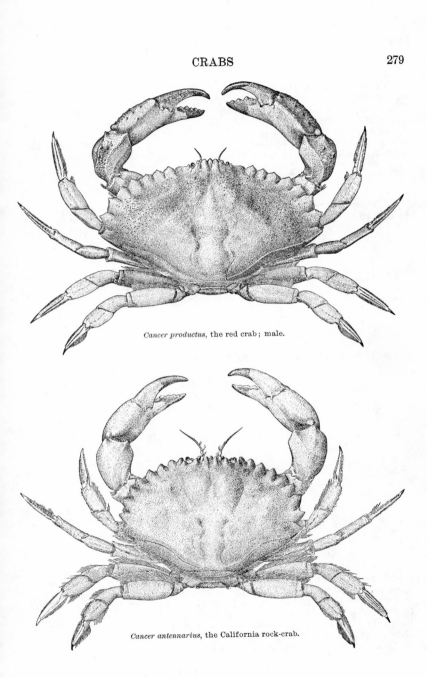

Cancer productus, the red crab; male.

Cancer antennarius, the California rock-crab.

C. antennarius, the rock-crab of the Pacific coast. This species of the California coast inhabits rocky bottoms below low-water mark. The carapace is three and a half inches long by five or six inches wide, and dark purplish-brown in color. The chelæ are marbled with purplish spots and are nearly smooth. The distinguishing features of this crab are its large and hairy antennæ, the hirsute margins of its abdomen and walking-feet, and the numerous hairs on the under side of its body.

Genus *Menippe*

M. mercenaria, the stone-crab. This species· lives in deep holes in the mud along the borders of creeks and estuaries, and also in crevices between fragments of rock, in stone-heaps and other debris, and is

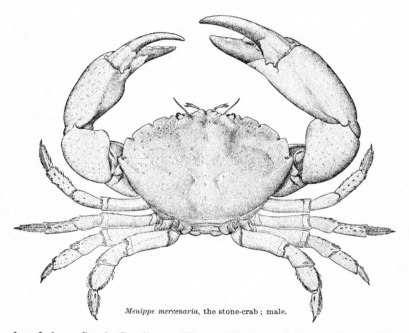

Menippe mercenaria, the stone-crab ; male.

found from South Carolina to Texas. These crabs are edible, and in some localities are hunted for food, one manner of capturing them being to thrust the hand and arm into their holes and drag them out, an operation attended with danger to the inexperienced hunter, who is likely to be badly pinched. They are withdrawn with difficulty, as they offer a strong resistance, bracing themselves with their claws against the sides of their holes, and often hold so firmly to the rocks that they are torn apart. They are also taken by a hooked iron which is thrust into the hole; the crab seizes it and is then suddenly jerked from its hole. The adult measures about three by four and a half inches, and the body is from one inch to two inches thick. One of the chelæ is larger than the other, and both are proportionately enormously large, and are tipped with black. The terminal joints of the other four pairs of legs are thickly fringed with hairs and end in points which seem like nails.

Former Genus *Panopeus*

Eupanopeus herbstii, Eurypanopeus depressus, Neopanopeus texana, Rhithropanopeus harrisii (Mary J. Rathbun). These four species, formerly all called *Panopeus*, are small crabs which live in the mud and are commonly known as mud-crabs. They are abundant under stones in muddy places, and occur on the Atlantic coast from Massachusetts Bay to Florida, though they are not commonly met with north of New Jersey. *Eupanopeus herbstii* is the largest one of the group, some of the Southern ones measuring two inches across. It is found living in mud at low-water mark, or burrowing in banks near high-tide mark. It is dark olive-brown, the claws broadly tipped with black. *Eurypanopeus depressus* is flat-tened above, and is smaller than *Neopanopeus texana*, which is somewhat convex above. The last two are com-

Eurypanopeus depressus, the mud-crab; male, natural size.

monly found together and have similar habits. *Rhithropanopeus harrisii* lives near high-water mark and also in salt-marshes, and is comparatively rare. The claws lack the dark tips of *E. herbstii,* and a distinct groove follows the edge of the carapace.

Family GRAPSIDÆ

Genus *Hemigrapsus*

H. nudus (Mary J. Rathbun), *Heterograpsus nudus* (Stimpson); *H. oregonensis* (Mary J. Rathbun), *Heterograpsus oregonensis* (Stimpson). These two species, commonly called respectively the *purple shore-crab* and the *yellow shore-crab*, are the most abundant species of the California coast. Hundreds may be found congregated under a single rock. They range from Sitka to Lower California. *H. oregonensis* literally swarms in sloughs of salt or brackish water, and hundreds of uplifted threatening claws confront the intruder who ventures on these mud-flats when the tide is out. This species, the yellow shore-crab, has a nearly square body. The anterior half of the side margins has two rather deep indentations, making two spine-like projections which bend forward. The four posterior pairs of legs are more or less hairy; the chelæ are rather large in proportion. The male is about one inch across and the female is one third less in size. The general color is yellow. *H. nudus* is found in the same localities, and differs from *H. oregonensis* in being purple in color, with mottled claws, and in having the denticulations less pronounced and the walking-feet devoid of hairs. It is also a little larger. (Plate LXIII.)

Genus *Pacygrapsus*

P. crassipes. A species very common on the California coast south of San Francisco. This crab is similar in general features to the purple and yellow ones described above, but is considerably larger, and the carapace is banded with color.

Family OCYPODIDÆ

Genus *Ocypoda*

O. arenaria, the sand- or ghost-crab. The name *Ocypoda* means "swift-footed," and, as it implies, this species is especially noted for its rapidity of movement. These crabs are the opposite of the strong-armed, thick-shelled, slow-moving *Cancroidæ.* An instance is told of a collector having great difficulty to keep up at full run with one which he chased for a considerable distance over the sand. They are also dexterous in burrowing, and live in holes, often three feet deep, dug perpendicularly into the sand. They wander far from their burrows when the tide is out, and every little while raise their stalked eyes and stand on tiptoe to look about. If alarmed, they run with great rapidity to the nearest burrow, or, if danger is close, press themselves on the sand until an attempt is made to touch them, when they again dart away rapidly, and in running hold their bodies high, and double and dodge so that it is difficult to catch them. *Ocypoda* is colored almost exactly like the sand, and this mimicry, together with its fleetness, makes it interesting to note and difficult to capture. It inhabits sandy beaches above tide-mark from Long Island to Brazil, and subsists largely upon the beach-fleas, which inhabit the same localities. It springs upon them, very much as a cat catches a mouse. The carapace of this species is almost square in outline, and on the anterior corners ends in a spine. A small portion of the carapace folds down like a band between the eyes. On each side of this band, and extending across the front, are large grooves for the eye-stalks. The body is about an inch thick; the first joints of the chelæ are toothed; one chela is a little longer than the other, and both are coarsely granulated. The other four pairs of legs are thickly fringed with hairs. (Plate LXIII.)

Genus *Uca*

U. minax (Gelasimus minax), U. pugnax (Gelasimus pugnax), U. pugilator (Gelasimus pugilator), the fiddler-crabs. These species

PLATE LXIII.

Hemigrapsus nudus.   Hyas araneus.
Ocypoda arenaria.   Pugettia gracilis.
Libinia dubia.   Pitho aculeata.

of fiddler-crabs occur on the Atlantic coast. They congregate in immense numbers, and excavate their holes in convenient localities above the reach of the tides — on salt-marshes, far up the estuaries, and along the mouths of rivers, even where the water is quite fresh. The males have one claw very largely developed; the other chela is small. The former is likened to a fiddle, the latter to a bow, and this, together with the waving motion of the large claw, gives them their popular name. This comparatively enormous claw is a distinguishing feature by which they are easily recognized without other description. The female has claws of small and equal size. These crabs burrow holes in the mud or sand half an inch to two inches in diameter and a foot or more in depth. The upper part is nearly perpendicular, becoming horizontal below, with a chamber at the end. One species, *U. minax*, constructs an archway over the mouth of its burrow, in which it sits and

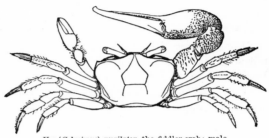

Uca (*Gelasimus*) *pugilator*, the fiddler-crab; male.

surveys the surroundings, but quickly retreats when danger approaches. The crab makes its burrow by scraping up the mud or sand and forming it into pellets, which it carries under the three anterior walking-feet on the under side, using the legs on the side moving forward, and the fourth one on the other side, to climb out of the hole. After peering cautiously about, the crab emerges, and carries its load four or five feet away before dropping it; then again looks about before quickly running back; and, finally, turning its stalked eyes, looks in all directions and suddenly disappears, soon to return with another load. The burrows cover considerable areas, and the crabs are so abundant that the marshes and shores sometimes seem to be alive with them. When alarmed, they lift the large claw and run sideways, after the manner of all crabs, to their holes, and, as many are likely to retreat into the most convenient one, the owner often finds his burrow occupied by other tenants, whom he unceremoniously proceeds to pull out. *U. minax* ranges from southern New England to Florida, and lives on salt-marshes farther away from the sea than the others, and often where the water is quite fresh. It is larger than the other species, and can be distinguished by a red patch at the joints of the legs. It is a vegetarian in diet, living on small algæ. This is the species which constructs a little observation-house over the mouth of its burrow. It can live out of water, and without food, for several days. *U. pugilator* lives on sandy and muddy flats and beaches near high-water mark, where the sand is compact and somewhat sheltered, and ranges from Cape Cod to Florida. This species, like *U. minax*, is a vegetarian. *U. pugnax* is exceedingly abundant on muddy banks and ditches of salt-marshes, the banks being sometimes completely honeycombed and undermined by them. It ranges from Cape Cod to Florida.

FAMILY MAIIDÆ

The members of this family are known as "spider-crabs." Their bodies are thick and more or less round in form, narrowing in front to a long, beak-like projection. The surface is generally rough and irregular, having tubercles, spines, prickles, and hairs. The legs are long. These crabs are often covered with seaweeds, hydroids, and other organisms, which they gather with their long and flexible chelipeds and place upon their backs, presumably to conceal themselves from their enemies. They seem to select, instinctively or with reason, such things as will bear transplanting, sometimes using sponges and polyps which are not destroyed by being torn apart, and they also select their dress with reference to its masking uses. A *Hyas* covered with bright-colored algæ was seen to remove them and replace them with sponges, when transferred to the locality of the latter, where the former did not grow. The animal takes in his claw the object he has gathered, and first holds it to his mouth, where it is moistened with a secretion of mucus or cement, and then places it on his back. If it does not hold, the operation is repeated, often several times, a new spot on the shell being selected each time. It has also been found that the coats of these crabs are covered with hairs which are differently arranged in different genera, some being hooked, others serrated, etc., and that these aid in holding the transplanted organisms in place. The crab is sometimes so covered with these growths as to be entirely concealed beneath them. It is a sluggish animal, and inhabits shallow water along the whole of the Atlantic and Pacific coasts

GENUS *Libinia*

L. dubia, L. emarginata. These two species inhabit the Atlantic coast, and are found on muddy shores and flats, among decaying seaweed, in eel-grass, and even beneath the surface of the mud. They are covered with hairs, and sometimes have planted on their backs algæ, hydroids, and even barnacles. The legs of *L. emarginata* often spread a foot or more. The males are much larger than the females. The species ranges from Maine to Florida. *L. dubia* does not extend north of Cape Cod. It is found more commonly than *L. emarginata* in very shallow water near shore.   It is not so thickly covered with spines, and has a longer rostrum, which is also more deeply divided at the end.   (Plate LXIII.)

Genus *Hyas*

H. coarctatus, the toad-crab. This species of spider-crab is found from Greenland to New Jersey, in shallow as well as in deep water.   Its body resembles strongly, both in form and size, that of a toad, hence its common name.   It forms an important part of the food of the cod.

H. lyratus.   A toad-crab of the Pacific coast, ranging from Bering Sea to Puget Sound; named from the lyre-shape of its carapace.

H. araneus.   A species which especially resembles a toad in its form.   Found off the northern New England coast.   (Plate LXIII.)

Genus *Loxorhynchus*

L. crispatus, the sheep-crab. This crab occurs on the coast of southern California.   The body is thick and about three inches across the widest portion, and tapers to a long, prominent rostrum.   It is covered with long tubercles and spines and with short, bristly hairs; the legs are long, the chelipeds stretching fully two feet.

Genus *Pugettia*

P. gracilis.   A small spider-crab found on the Pacific coast from Alaska to Puget Sound.   Its body is one half of an inch wide and

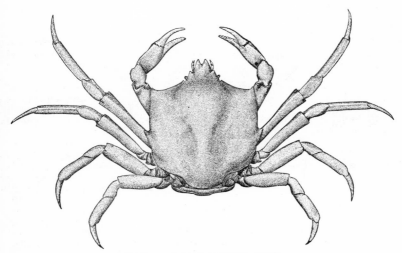

Epialtus productus, the kelp-crab; female.

one inch long, with prominent spines on the sides of the carapace, which narrows in front into a long beak ending in two spines. It is red and green above, red beneath. (Plate LXIII.)

Genus *Sternorhynchus*

S. sagittarius. This is one of the most delicately formed of the spider-crabs. The body has narrow longitudinal stripes of light and dark color. It lives offshore from Cape Hatteras southward.

Genus *Epialtus*

E. productus, the kelp-crab. This crab inhabits the coasts of California and Oregon, and is found among seaweeds on rocks just below low-water mark. The carapace is smooth, is quadrate in form, is about two inches long and broad, has two spines on each side, and has a prominent denticulated rostrum. This is the most common spider-crab of the Pacific (California) coast. It is olive-green, thus simulating in color the kelp among which it lives. (See page 285.)

Genus *Pitho*

P. aculeata. The carapace has six spines on each side, the middle two being sometimes partly united; the general outline is pentagonal; the length about one inch. Quite common on the Florida coast. (Plate LXIII.)

Genus *Lambrus*

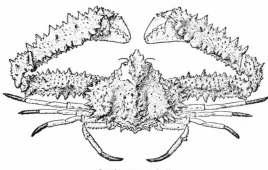

Lambrus pourtalesii.

L. pourtalesii, the long-armed spider-crab. The carapace is broader than it is long and has three elevations all covered with spines. The general surface is pitted and granulated; the rostrum points downward; the chelipeds are very long, the margins armed with spines; the breadth of the carapace is about one and a half inches; and the length of the chelipeds is about three and a half inches. Its range is from Cape Cod to Florida, and it lives among the rocks. (Plate LXIV.)

Family CALAPPIDÆ

Genus *Calappa*

C. flamma, the box-crab. This singular animal lives on sandy and muddy bottoms offshore, from North Carolina southward. The carapace is broad and straight on the posterior side, and is curved on the anterior side, narrowing to the front. The posterior side has prominent denticulations. The body is one and a half inches thick, about four to five inches wide, and two to three inches long. The chelæ are large, broad, and flattened, and are so arranged that when flexed they fit closely together across the front. When folded, and the small legs are withdrawn under the carapace, the animal is shut up as if in a box, and resembles a shell. When in danger it closes its doors, as it were, and abandons itself to the waves, which often carry it ashore. The crested claws resemble the head of a cock. (Plate LXIV.)

Family PINNOTHERIIDÆ

Genus *Pinnotheres*

P. ostreum, the oyster-crab. The female of this species lives in the gill-cavity of the oyster, and is particularly abundant in oysters from the Chesapeake. The males are seldom seen, and rarely occur in the oyster, but swim freely about. They are smaller than the female, have a firmer shell, and are dark brown above, with a dorsal stripe and two conspicuous spots. The under side of the legs is whitish. The female is commensal, at least in the adult form, and its thin, whitish, transparent carapace is tinged with pink. The species *P. maculatum* lives in *Mytilus edulis* (mussel) and in the smooth scallop, *Pecten magellanicus*. The

Pinnotheres ostreum, the oyster-crab; male, enlarged four diameters.

oyster-crab is a true messmate, and its presence in the oyster may be advantageous in helping to provide food for its host. This crab, like the rest, holds its eggs in the posterior feet until hatched, when the larvæ leave the parent and swim about for a while. The females, at the megalops stage, enter oysters — sometimes two enter the same oyster, but seldom more than one; there it remains permanently, growing to the size of an inch or more in diameter, and becomes a degenerate. The eyes become smaller; the shell never hardens, like its allies which live in open water; its limbs and chelæ are weak; and it has no pugnacity, the protection afforded by the oyster doing away with the need for the common protective features of its kind. *Pinnixa cylindrica,* a related species, lives in the tubes of large annelid worms as a commensal.

ORDER **STOMATOPODA**

Genus *Squilla*

S. empusa. This animal suggests somewhat the lobster, though very unlike it. The carapace is much smaller and softer, and leaves the last three segments of the thorax uncovered. The abdomen is larger and longer in proportion, while the legs and organs are quite different. The whole body is depressed, instead of laterally compressed. It measures from eight to ten inches in length and two inches in breadth. Instead of chelæ, the last joint of the great claw has six sharp curved spines, which fit into sockets in a groove on the second joint. By this singular organ they hold their prey securely. The abdominal feet carry the gills. The antennal scales are oblong and fringed with hair. The antennules terminate in three flagella. The caudal appendages and telson are long, strong, and armed with spines. This animal lives in burrows in the mud below low-water mark, forming large, irregular holes, but is frequently washed ashore. In color it is pale yellowish-green, each segment being bordered with darker green and edged with yellow. It is found from Cape Cod to Florida.

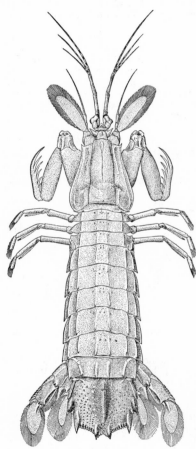

Squilla empusa, the mantis-shrimp.

ORDER **CUMACEA**

Genus *Diastylis*

D. quadrispinosus. Among the minute *Crustacea* which swim on the surface of the water, this species, with other small forms, may be captured by using a muslin net. It is a quarter of an inch or less in length. It is easily distinguished by its large carapace, the posterior portion of which is marked off in transverse ridges, the anterior end running into a sharp-pointed rostrum. It has a long, slender abdomen, the sections of which

are distinctly marked, and it terminates in long, forked spines, which **are** longer than the telson. It is found from New Jersey northward.

ORDER **ARTHROSTRACA**

SUBORDER **AMPHIPODA**

The *Amphipoda* have a laterally compressed body, with gills on the thoracic feet and an elongated abdomen. The segments of the thorax are not united, nor covered by a carapace, but the whole body is covered with a segmented, polished, flexible cuticle. The three anterior legs of the abdomen are for swimming-feet, and the posterior ones are adapted for springing. The antennæ are long and hairy. The amphipods comprise the beach-fleas and many other small crustaceans which abound between tide-marks on all beaches. Besides serving in no small measure as food for fishes, they are scavengers of the beach, and consume large quantities of waste matter. They are sometimes used in preparing skeletons for anatomical specimens. Animals to be skeletonized, being fastened to boards and anchored just below the surface of the water in sheltered places, are divested of all flesh in a few hours, and the bones are more completely cleaned than if prepared by a naturalist.

GENUS *Orchestia*

O. agilis, the beach-flea. These little crustaceans exist in countless numbers under the masses of sea-wrack on the beach. When disturbed they jump about with great agility by means of the last three pairs of abdominal feet, which are adapted to this purpose. In color the animal is brown and much resembles the decaying seaweeds among which it lives and upon which it probably feeds. The antennules are short, the antennæ long, on two long, jointed bases. The second

Orchestia agilis; male.

pair of feet in the males terminate in chelæ. The last abdominal appendages are stiff and pointed backward. The abdomen is curved under. The length of *Orchestia* is half an inch or less. Some species occur on all beaches. *O. agilis* ranges from New Jersey to Greenland.

GENUS *Talorchestia*

T. longicornis (Talitrus longicornis). This species is similar to *Orchestia agilis*, but is about an inch long when mature and of a paler color. It jumps like the latter, but not so strongly. It is found among the weeds and burrowing in the sand a little below high-water mark. The wet sand is often completely filled with its holes. It can be distinguished by its very long antennæ. Another species, *T. megalophthalma,* is distinguished by its shorter antennæ and very large eyes. Both of these species are grayish in color and closely resemble the sand. Found from Cape Cod to New Jersey.

Genus *Gammarus*

G. locusta. The animals of this genus are among the largest of the amphipods. The males are larger than the females, sometimes being one and a half inches long. They are abundant under stones and *Fucus* at and near low-water mark. Although much larger than the beach-fleas, they otherwise resemble them. They do not jump like the former, but move rapidly, lying on the side, and in water swim with the back downward. Two pairs of the thoracic feet are chelate, and three pairs are longer than the others.

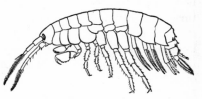

Gammarus locusta, the scud.

The feet on the last segments of the abdomen are stiff and turn sharply back, forming a part of the tail, which is used most effectively in locomotion. The antennules and antennæ are of about the same length. Several species of *Gammarus* occur in the same range, all having the same general characteristics; some have but one pair of chelate feet; the antennules are usually shorter than the antennæ; the females of all the species have no chelate feet. *G. locusta* ranges from New Jersey to Greenland. The color is generally reddish- or olive-brown. *G. annulatus* is found in the same places, but usually a little higher up on the beach; it is lighter in color, and has dark bands with red spots on the sides of the abdomen. *G. mucronatus* occurs from Cape Cod to Florida. *Melita nitida* is a smaller slate-colored amphipod found in some places; another is *Mœra levis,* which is whitish, with black eyes.

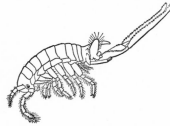

Chelura terebrans, the boring amphipod.

Genus *Chelura*

C. terebrans, the boring amphipod. This little crustacean is associated in its work on submerged timber with the isopod *Limnoria lignorum.* The excavations of the latter are narrow and cylindrical, running down into the wood, while *Chelura* makes larger burrows in oblique lines near the surface, which give the wood the appearance of having been plowed. It is very active and destructive. It feeds upon the wood into which it burrows. Its color is semi-translucent, thickly mottled above with pink.

Genus *Caprella*

C. geometrica. These very curious little animals, which are so slender as to seem like skeletons, are found in abundance clinging to hydroids, *Polyzoa*, delicate algæ, or eel-grass, or under stones in tide-pools. They resemble in color, and often in form, the objects on which they live. Holding on by the posterior feet, they extend the body out rigidly or sway it about, so that they resemble little sticks or branches, and often escape detection. In walking, they bring the hind feet up to the front ones, doubling the body

Caprella geometrica.

into a loop like the canker- or measuring-worm. The appendages on the anterior and posterior ends are furnished with chelæ and hooks; those of the middle section are rudimentary. This animal cannot be mistaken for any other. *C. geometrica* is found from Cape Cod to North Carolina. Some of the species of this genus may be found on every coast.

Suborder ISOPODA

The isopods have an elongate, flattened, but more or less arched body, composed of seven thoracic segments and a short abdomen of six segments. The six segments of the abdomen are smaller than those of the thorax, and are often more or less united, sometimes into a single piece with scarcely any trace of division above; but the number of pairs of appendages is generally six, showing the composite nature of the apparently simple organ. The last segment, or telson, is broad and has a pair of modified appendages. The seven thoracic legs are not all equal, as the name would imply, but vary greatly in different species. As a rule, they are adapted to walking or attachment, and in the female some have delicate plates which form brood-pouches. The swimming-feet fold under the abdomen, and in some species are inclosed by the first pair, which are large and plate-like, and form a complete cover for the others. The isopods are a large and widely distributed order, varying in size, and are inconspicuous because they cling closely to objects. They are retiring in habit, though extremely ferocious.

The sow-bugs or pill-bugs, common in gardens, under leaves in the woods, and under almost any pile of rubbish among decaying vegetable matter, are a land species of isopods. Other species inhabit ponds and streams of fresh water, and still others are found along the shores of all oceans, abounding among the marine vegetation of the shallow waters. Some swim free in the open sea; others are brought up from the greatest depths. Others, again, are parasites, and live in the internal organs of fishes and prawns. Sometimes a prawn is found having what appears like a very swollen throat, which actually is a little parasitic isopod of the family *Bopyridæ* attached to its gills.

GENUS *Cirolana*

C. concharum. The body consists of fourteen segments, the first being the head, the next seven the thorax, and the last six the abdomen.

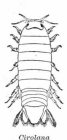

Cirolana concharum.

On the head are the triangular eyes, the antennules, and the antennæ, and underneath is the mouth, which is covered by the maxillipeds. The dorsal surface is more or less rounded. At the bases of all the segmental thoracic rings excepting the first one are sutures marking off square, scale-like pieces (*epimera*). The epimera form a border to the side margins. The legs are attached to the epimera, which are, in fact, the upper segments of the legs. The first three pairs of legs have a general resemblance to one another, and are directed forward. The last four pairs are much longer and flatter, and are directed backward. The telson, or last segment, is triangular, and the square or blunt apex is fringed with hairs. On the ventral surface of the thorax in the adult females there is a long pouch for the reception and development of the eggs. This species is usually about one and a half inches in length, but sometimes is longer. Its color is yellowish, with a brown edge on the posterior margins of the segments, somewhat translucent in the thinner parts. It is found from Cape Cod to South Carolina, swimming about in shallow water, and is especially abundant in winter.

GENUS *Limnoria*

L. lignorum, the gribble. This little isopod is very destructive in its habits, boring into submerged woodwork, like the ship-worm (*Teredo*), and doing great damage to the piles of wharves, etc. It burrows to the depth of half an inch, and completely honeycombs the surface of the wood, which then scales off or rapidly decays, and is washed away by the waves. The animal then begins anew, and in a short time, or at the rate of about an inch a year, piles diminish in diameter where *Limnoria* is plentiful, and are finally destroyed unless protected from these little crustaceans by a sheathing of metal. Although considered as pests, they have an economic value not so often recognized, as they attack all driftwood, and in time entirely destroy floating and water-

Limnoria lignorum, the gribble.

logged timber, which without their destructive agency might become
serious obstructions to navigation. *Limnoria* is only the fifth of an inch
in length, and its back is covered with minute hairs, to which dirt usually
adheres. It burrows with its mandibles, or jaws, which are chisel-like
at the ends. Its habitat extends from a little above
to a little below tide-marks throughout the whole Atlantic coast.

Genus *Sphæroma*

Sphæroma quadridentatum.

S. quadridentatum. The name of the genus
to which this species belongs is derived from the
peculiar habit of many of the species of rolling themselves into a ball when alarmed. The body is so
constructed as to admit of this singular change of
shape. The abdomen turns under, and the last
abdominal appendages, together with the narrow
epimera, shut in the legs and cover the ventral
portions with armor. The body, when extended, is an ellipse a little
over a quarter of an inch in length and half that in breadth. The legs
are hairy and adapted to walking. The anterior abdominal segments
are fused into one, but are marked at the sides with depressed lines.
The abdominal feet are plate-like and fringed with hairs. A slight
elevation runs around the margins of the animal like a border. The
color is variable. Some are a uniform slaty gray; others are marked
with a longitudinal patch of color on the
back. It is found from Cape Cod to Florida
among algæ or rocks, and is easily recognized by its habit of rolling itself into a
ball. **Sphæroma destructor** is a boring
isopod, larger than *Limnoria*, and is even
more destructive, since its holes are larger;
but its range is limited, or, at least, it has so
far been found only in the St. Johns River,
Florida.

Genus *Idotea*

I. marina (Linnæus), **I. irrorata**
(Edwards). This species is about one inch
long, and is easily recognized by the abdomen, the first three segments of which are
narrow and terminate in acute teeth, while the
other three are fused into one with straight
sides and ending in three teeth, of which
the middle one is the longest. The first pair
of abdominal feet are large, long, and plate-
like, covering the other feet and whole under
surface of the abdomen like an operculum.
The head is nearly square, the eyes are
small, and the antennæ have long peduncles.

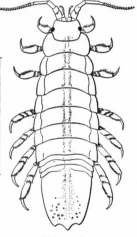

Idotea marina.

The articulations of the
thoracic feet are fringed with hair. The color of this species varies:
sometimes it is light or dark green, or brown with black spots; again

it is striped longitudinally with light color. Sometimes the stripes run transversely in bands or spots. It is found from New Jersey northward on rocky shores of bays and sounds, or in eel-grass on sandy shores.

I. ochotensis. A species very similar to the preceding, but a little larger, found on the Pacific coast.

I. metallica. This species is a little smaller than *I. marina*, and differs from it in having the end of the telson truncated, or straight, instead of dentate. The head is nearly square. The body is broadest in the middle of the thorax; the projecting epimera give a serrate appearance to the sides. The abdominal feet are inclosed in the operculum-like scales of the first pair of feet. Its color is bright blue or green, often with a metallic luster when seen in the water. It is found swimming free or floating in masses of seaweeds from Long Island northward and also on the Pacific coast.

I. wosnesenskii. A common species on the California coast, about one inch long and dark in color. The abdominal segments are united and bluntly rounded, and each has a small median tooth. The abdominal feet are inclosed by the opercular feet. Eggs and young are carried in a pouch.

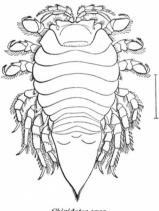

Chiridotea cæca.

GENUS *Chiridotea*

C. cæca. This species burrows beneath the surface of the sand, raising it up into a little ridge, and makes a mound at the end of the burrow, where it may be found. These trails are common on the wet sand. It imitates the sand in color, and is about half an inch in length, with a broad thorax and narrow abdomen terminating in a point. It is found on the New England coast.

C. entomon (Linnæus). This species of the northern Pacific coast is from one to three inches long. The head has the appearance of two lobes, the sides having two rounded ends. The body is broad, the abdomen narrowing to a pointed end. The last segments of the abdomen are united, and the abdominal feet are inclosed by the first pair, which extend over them like an operculum. The epimera are broad, with acute lateral angles.

CLASS **MERISTOMES**

ORDER **XIPHOSURA**

GENUS *Limulus*

L. polyphemus, the horseshoe- or king-crab. This well-known and curious animal ranges along the Atlantic coast from Maine to Mexico.

It lives on sandy and muddy shores below low-water mark, where it burrows beneath the surface. At the breeding season — May, June, and July — it comes ashore to deposit its eggs near high-water mark. The crabs come up the beach in pairs, the male being the smaller and riding on the back of the female, holding on by short feet provided with nippers, which are peculiar to the males. Sometimes the female is accompanied by several males, each one holding on to the tail of another and forming a string of animals. After the female has deposited her eggs in a hole excavated by her for the purpose, the male covers them with milt, and they then return to the water, leaving the eggs to be buried in the sand by the action of the waves. The eggs hatch in July and August, and sometimes the beach is literally alive with the young crabs,

which, however, soon disappear, and are not seen again until they are well grown. After the spawning season the adults are not very often seen, but usually their empty shells, abandoned in moulting, may be found on the shore. The horseshoe-crab, also called king-crab, is especially interesting from the fact that it is the last survivor of an otherwise extinct group of animals. Its relationships with classes which have become extinct, its nearest relatives being fossils, make it difficult to classify definitely with existing forms. Formerly it was regarded as a crustacean; now it is classed by some authors with the *Arachnida*, along with scorpions and spiders. It has the characteristics of both groups. There are only two known species of *Limulus* in the world; the other, **Limulus moluccanus,** lives on the eastern coast of Asia. *L. polyphemus* often measures a foot in diameter. The body is composed of three parts. The front portion, or cephalothorax, is broad and semicircular, with posterior angles ending in points. Near each side of its dorsal surface is a pair of large compound eyes covered with

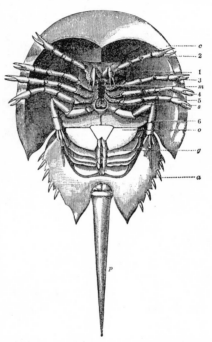

Under surface of horseshoe-crab, *Limulus polyphemus:* *a*, abdomen; *c*, cephalothorax; *g*, the first gill-bearing abdominal appendage; *m*, mouth; *o*, operculum; *p*, telson; *s*, metastoma; 1–6, cephalothoracic limbs.

thickened cuticle, and near the center line of the shell, at the base of the first spine, a pair of small, simple eyes. The second portion is the abdomen, and the third a long, movable spine attached to the last segment of the abdomen and between two terminal points of the horn-like covering.

On the cephalothorax are seven pairs of appendages. The first pair are small and lie in front of the mouth ; these and the four following pairs have chelæ, or claws. The sixth pair have no chelæ, but at the base have a peculiar process termed the flabellum. These six pairs of appendages surround the mouth, and have bristles at the base which serve as jaws. The seventh pair of thoracic appendages are broad plates called the operculum, which meet and cover the abdominal appendages to a certain extent. The abdomen has five pairs of appendages, which are plate-like and resemble the operculum in form and have an upper and an under piece. On the posterior surfaces of the abdominal feet are large, leaf-like folds, which are the gills. In front of the first pair of thoracic legs is a small tubercle supposed to have an olfactory function. *Limulus* has a blood-vascular system (the blood being bluish in color), a nervous and a digestive system. It walks with the thoracic feet and swims with the abdominal ones. It enters the sand by pushing in the rounded, anterior end. In moulting the carapace opens on the front edge. *Limulus* is edible, its meat being, it is said, as good as that of the lobster. (Plate LXIV.)

CLASS **PANTOPODA** (Lang)

ORDER **PYCNOGONIDA**

This order of animals, like *Limulus,* has no definitely determined position in the classification of marine organisms. About one hundred and fifty species of *Pycnogonida* have been described, of which thirty are found on our coast and are commonly known as sea-spiders. They are found crawling slowly over seaweeds, hydroids, and sponges, and appear to be all legs, but, like other animals, have a digestive, a circulatory, and a nervous system. They are devoid of organs of respiration. The body has a cephalothorax, which bears a conical suctorial proboscis on the anterior end, and on top a prominence containing four eyes. It has three pairs of appendages, two pairs of which are sometimes lacking; then come three free segments and a rudimentary abdomen. There is a pair of short appendages bearing claws (chelæ) and four pairs of long walking-legs. The walking-legs contain a tubular outgrowth of the body, into which the stomach extends. The egg-sacs are in the legs, and open at the basal joints. The male is provided with an extra pair of legs, for the purpose of carrying the eggs after they are deposited by the female. The

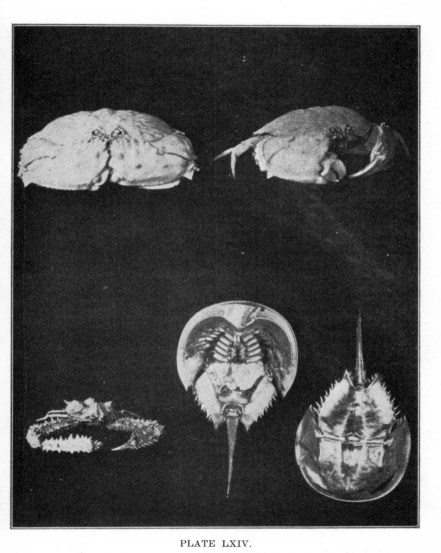

PLATE LXIV.

Calappa flamma.
Lambrus pourtalesii.

Calappa flamma, claws open, showing
form of cockscomb.
Limulus polyphemus.

ovigerous legs are run through sac-like pockets and bent under the body, and thus the eggs are carried until hatched.

GENUS *Phoxichilidium*

P. maxillare. This species is found on the New England coast creeping over hydroids and ascidians. It is purple, gray, or brown in color. Its young take shelter in the cavities of hydroids, forming galls.

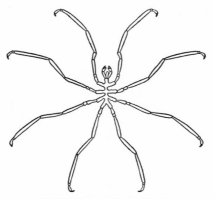

Phoxichilidium maxillare, enlarged.

VII
MOLLUSCA

TABLE SHOWING THE CLASSIFICATION OF THE MOLLUSKS DESCRIBED IN THIS CHAPTER

Phylum
MOLLUSCA

Classes	Orders	Suborders
AMPHINEURA *(Bilaterally symmetrical mollusks, having shell composed of eight plates, or devoid of shell. Including chitons and their allies)*	**POLYPLACOPHORA** *(Shell composed of eight plates)* **APLACOPHORA** *(Devoid of shell)*	
GASTEROPODA *(Unsymmetrical univalve mollusks, usually spirally coiled. Periwinkles, whelks, snails, etc.)*	**OPISTHOBRANCHIATA** *(Branchiæ, when present, behind the heart)*	**TECTIBRANCHIATA** *(Branchiæ more or less covered by mantle; shell delicate and often rudimentary)* **NUDIBRANCHIATA** *(Devoid of shell and mantle, and without true branchiæ)*
	PROSOBRANCHIATA *(Branchiæ situated in front of the heart)*	**DIATOCARDIA** *(Usually two auricles, two branchiæ, and two nephridia)* **MONOTOCARDIA** *(One auricle, one branchia, one nephridium)*
	PULMONATA *(Air-breathing mollusks)*	
SCAPHOPODA *(Mollusks without head, eyes, or heart, with tri-lobed foot and tubular shell open at both ends. The tooth-shells)*		

Classes	Orders

PELECYPODA

(Bilaterally symmetrical, headless, bivalved mollusks. Mussels, cockles, oysters, etc.)

PROTOBRANCHIATA

(Gills form a single pair of plume-like organs, each with two rows of flattened gill-filaments)

FILIBRANCHIATA

(Two pairs of plate-like gills formed of V-shaped filaments)

PSEUDOLAMELLIBRANCHIATA

(Gills plaited so as to form vertical folds)

EULAMELLIBRANCHIATA

(Firm, basket-work gills, the filaments united by vascular connections)

CEPHALOPODA

(Mollusks of high organization, having a definitely formed head surrounded by tentacles ; shell, when present, usually internal; shell, external in nautili. Cuttlefishes, squids, octopi, and nautili)

Subclasses

Tetrabranchiata

Dibranchiata **OCTOPODA**
DECAPODA

Abductor muscles : Muscles which move parts away from the axis.

Adductor muscles : Muscles which draw parts together; opposite of *abductor.*

Aperture : Opening of the spiral shell.

Bilateral symmetry : Having two equal sides, divided by a central axis.

Branchiæ : Gills, or breathing-organs; organs subservient to respiration through water.   Same as *ctenidia.*

Buccal mass : The mouth-parts as a whole; the organ of prehension and mastication of food; the pharynx: present in all mollusks except lamellibranchs.

Canal : A narrow prolongation of the aperture of a spiral shell.

Carinated : Ridged as if keeled; having a keel.

Cinereous : Ash-gray; having the color of wood-ashes.

Cirri, plural of *Cirrus :* Filamentous appendages.

Columella : An upright pillar in the center of most of the univalve shells, round which the whorls are convoluted.

Concrescent : Growing together; uniting.

Cordate : Heart-shaped.

Costæ, plural of *Costa :* Ridges of a shell.

Crenulated : Having a series of notches;   marked as with notches, as the indented margin of a shell.

Crystalline style : A transparent gelatinous substance of unknown function, which fills, at times, the stomach-parts of certain mollusks.

Ctenidia, plural of *Ctenidium :* Gills, or breathing-organs, adapted to water-respiration.

Decussated: Crossed; intersected.

Dextral: Having the aperture on the right side of the shell when the apex is upward.

Epidermis: The horny coating or outer skin of some shells.

Foot: The ventral surface of the body on which the animal rests or moves.

Fossette: A little hollow or pit.

Fuscous: Brown tinged with gray; swarthy.

Fusiform: Tapering both ways from the middle.

Lamelliform: Lamellate in structure; disposed in leaf-like layers.

Lingual ribbon: The chitinous band of teeth, or rasp, borne upon the odontophore; the radula.

Lunule: An impressed area just below the beaks of bivalve shells.

Mantle: A fleshy or membranous outgrowth of the outer body-wall; also called *pallium.*

Mantle cavity: The space between the mantle and the body.

Monomyarian: Having one adductor muscle, as an oyster.

Nephridium: The renal organ of mollusks, corresponding to kidneys in vertebrates.

Node: A knob or protuberance; also a notch in the margin.

Odon'tophore: The lingual ribbon bearing chitinous teeth.

Oper'culum: A horny or shelly plate which serves to close the aperture of the shell when the animal is retracted.

Osphra'dia, plural of *Osphradium:* Olfactory or water-testing organs.

Otocyst: The cavity, or cyst, which contains the essential parts of an organ of hearing.

Pallial line: The impression or mark made by the mantle, or pallium, on the inner surface of a bivalve shell.

Pallial sinus: A notch or recess of the pallial line; the scar of the siphon.

Papillaceous: Warty; studded with bosses; having excrescences.

Perios'tracum: Same as *epidermis.*

Per'istome: In zoölogy, mouth-parts in general; in conchology, the margin of the aperture of the shell.

Porcelanous : Resembling porcelain.

Rad'ula : Same as *lingual ribbon.*

Reticulated : Having distinct lines or veins crossing like a network; covered with netted lines.

Sculpture : Elevated or impressed marks on the surface; markings resulting from irregularity of surface; tracery.

Sinistral : Having the aperture of the shell at the left; opposite of *dextral.*

Sinuate : Curved in and out; wavy.

Siphon : A tubular fold, or prolongation of the mantle forming a tube.

Spire : All the whorls of a spiral univalve, above the first large body-whorl.

Suture : The line of junction of the successive whorls of a univalve shell, or the line of closure of the opposite valves of a bivalve shell.

Teeth : Tooth-like projections on the hinge of a bivalve shell.

Testaceous : Having a hard shell, as distinguished from crustaceous, or soft-shelled.

Turbinate : Shaped like a whipping-top; whorled from a broad base to an apex.

Umbilicus : A central, navel-like depression in the body-whorl; a circular, more or less central pit or hollow.

Umbo : The beak of a bivalve shell; the protuberance of each valve above the hinge.

Varices, plural of *Varix :* Raised marks on the shell denoting a former position of the lip of the aperture, and indicating periods of rest.

Varicose : Having prominent and tortuous formations on the shell.

Ventricose : Having the whorls of the shell swollen or strongly convex.

Whorl : One of the turns of a spiral shell. *Body-whorl,* the last whorl.

MOLLUSKS

WE now come to another large and important group of animals, with characters so peculiar to itself and differing so radically from those which distinguish any other class of living creatures, that it may be said to occupy almost a unique position in the animal kingdom. Recent investigations have demonstrated that the larval form of mollusks presents some remarkable points of similarity to the embryonic forms of the *Annelida* and to the larvæ of some other classes of lower organisms. This discovery is one of the triumphs of embryology in its patient search for that connecting-thread that weaves together all the varying forms of animal life. Aside from these subtle evidences of relationship revealed by the microscope, the mollusks appear to occupy a position of considerable isolation in the biological world.

As accepted by zoölogists to-day, this phylum is but the remnant of its former self. Aristotle considered all creatures with a testaceous covering to belong to a single family, and those later patriarchs of biology, Linnæus, Cuvier, and Lamarck, extended the group to include the greater part of all the marine invertebrate animals. Little by little the phylum has been shorn of orders and classes. First, the worms and the *Echinodermata* were separated into distinct phyla; then the barnacles were discovered to be crustaceans, and were accordingly removed from their position as "multivalves" under the *Mollusca*; then the tunicates, or ascidians, were found, through the critical examination of their larval stage, to be merely masquerading as mollusks; and lastly, the brachiopods have been somewhat reluctantly removed from their old position with the mollusks and given the distinction of a phylum almost exclusively to themselves: they retain their old associations only in the name of *Molluscoida*.

With some exceptions, all mollusks secrete from their outer skin, or mantle fold, a calcareous protective covering, or shell. This may be either "univalve" or "bivalve" according as it consists of one or two pieces. This phylum includes all the sea-shells which are so commonly found along every ocean beach, in the tide-pools, on rocks at low tide, in estuaries, and, indeed, wherever sea-water is present. The phylum also includes, as one of its large suborders, all the snails and slugs that are to be found crawling upon the land. These are true mollusks, which differ essentially from their marine brethren only in that they breathe by means of a pulmonary sac or lung instead of by gills. There are also many genera and species of mollusks that find their habitat only in the fresh water of rivers, lakes, or ponds; curiously enough, many of these fresh-water forms, like the purely terrestrial snails and slugs, are air-breathers, possessing no gills whatever, and are consequently obliged to make periodic visits to the surface of the water to obtain their necessary supply of oxygen. There are also numerous forms of mollusks that are entirely deprived of a shell covering; and, again, there are intermediate types between these two extremes that produce only more or less developed rudimentary shells. Notwithstanding these variations in the matter of a shell covering,—an important consideration in this phylum,—by reason of their anatomical features these "naked" forms are mollusks quite as much as are those that secrete the most highly developed tests.

The marvelous beauty of sea-shells and tropical land-shells, their almost infinite variety in form and coloring, has given to them an interest among collectors that is very great. There are many wonderful conchological collections in public museums and in private cabinets. It would well repay the lover of beauty as well as the more serious student of nature to examine carefully such collections when opportunity offers, for nowhere in the realm of nature can more exquisite coloring and modeling be found. The fact that shells may be preserved for all time without the expense and the vexations of preservative fluids has no doubt induced many to choose this field of natural history for special study. But the true student of zoölogy does not confine his investigations in this phylum to considerations of the shell only, for the protective armor constitutes only a portion, although an important portion, of the anatomy of the mollusk. On the same principle, it would hardly suffice to examine only the skeleton of vertebrate animals in order to become acquainted with the fishes or mammals. In a sense, the testaceous covering of a mollusk may be likened to an outer skeleton.

The older zoölogists were inclined to ignore almost entirely the animal or "soft parts" of mollusks, and their classification of the phylum into "univalve," "bivalve," and "multivalve," based upon shell-characters alone, has since been proved to be wholly artificial. The terms "univalve" and "bivalve" are, of course, often and correctly used to-day to designate mollusks possessing a single or a double shell, such as the common garden-snail, which carries upon its back a single spiral shell, and, on the other hand, the oyster or clam, which is inclosed within two valves which fit closely together. But these terms are not *technically* used, although they do indicate in a general way the more modern classification. Even among some comparatively recent conchologists a tendency to belittle the value of the "slimy creature" within the shell has led to some curious errors of grouping—mistakes which more thorough and scientific investigation has brought to light. In general, the higher classification into classes, orders, suborders, and families is exclusively based upon anatomical features, and to a large extent, also, is that of the genera; but species are always determined by their shell or conchological characteristics.

When a certain familiarity with the forms and general appearance of shells is gained, a glance at the shell alone will almost always suffice to place it at once in its true generic position, for, along with modifications of the animal itself, corresponding modifications of the shell are quite certain to take place. Hence a fairly expert zoölogist should be able to determine with considerable accuracy from an empty and dead shell the anatomical features of the animal that at one time inhabited it.

One of the main reasons for the special interest that seems to have attached to the study of conchology is derived from the fact that the durability of shells has caused their almost perfect preservation as fossils from the very earliest periods of geological time, thus furnishing the key to the solution of many problems of evolution. Upon this page of the earth's history the letters are sharp and clear, and geologists possessing a knowledge of recent forms of mollusks as well as of their geographical distribution have been enabled to read some wonderful stories of the cosmic history of islands and continents.

GEOGRAPHICAL DISTRIBUTION

Mollusks are found in every part of the world. The arctic seas possess their own characteristic faunæ, the more temperate waters of Europe and of America contain their own peculiar genera and species, and the warm waters of the tropic seas furnish the conditions favorable to the life of an immense number of characteristic forms. Again, there are the littoral species, that live only between tide-marks and are therefore exposed to the air for a number of hours each day; some of these live just about high-tide mark and have become almost terrestrial in their habits, while others must be sought at the point of lowest tide, where for only a short time each day they are deprived of their natural element. Then there are the shallow-water forms, which never appear above low-tide mark save when a neap tide surprises them; their range in depth extends to about the hundred-fathom line, more or less. Beyond this depth to several hundred fathoms other characteristic forms appear, and from the more profound depths of mid-ocean the dredge has brought to light a host of curious and interesting species.

It is the temperature of the water rather than the depth that appears to influence the distribution of marine mollusks. Thus, certain species whose natural home is in the shallow waters of the Arctic Ocean have been taken in very deep waters off the southern coast of the United States, the temperature conditions in both stations being substantially the same. This fact, however, must not be too freely accepted as establishing a principle. Some shallow-water forms have been taken at great depths, but in general the abyssal fauna is a peculiar one that cannot well be marked off into geographical provinces.

THE ARCTIC PROVINCE

The east coast of America is divided into several molluscan faunal regions. A series of very-cold-water forms belonging to a circumpolar region, called the "arctic province," are found as far south as Newfoundland. On the New England coast a number of these arctic species are also found, urged south by the influence of the cold Labrador current. The most characteristic genera belonging to this arctic fauna which are found upon the Maine and Massachusetts coasts are *Buccinum, Chrysodomus, Sipho, Trophon, Bela, Velutina, Trichotropis, Lacuna, Margarita, Pecten, Leda, Yoldia, Astarte,* and *Mya.* Examples of all these genera are encountered as far south as Cape Cod.

THE BOREAL PROVINCE

A "boreal province" corresponds with a similar faunal region upon the European shore. The mollusks which compose this fauna are about three hundred in number, and range along the New England coast from the Gulf of St. Lawrence to Cape Cod. It is a somewhat remarkable fact that many of these species are identical with English and French forms. The striking genera upon the American side are *Purpura, Littorina, Polynices (Lunatia* and *Neverita), Acmæa, Margarita, Chiton, Doris, Æolis, Mytilus, Modiola, Thracia,* and *Nucula.*

THE TRANSATLANTIC PROVINCE

Cape Cod has been regarded, until very recently, as a sharp divisional point between the boreal and the transatlantic provinces, the latter faunal area extending down the Atlantic coast of the United States to southern Florida. At Cape Cod the Labrador current is deflected from the coast, and the warmer shore waters south of that point are unfitted for the development of the boreal forms, though some of them, as we shall see, have passed the barrier and maintain themselves very successfully at Martha's Vineyard and in Long Island Sound. Some of the species whose natural habitat is south of Cape Cod are also to be found north of that point, but they do not reach their full development in the colder waters of Massachusetts Bay.

The long stretch of coast-line from Cape Cod to Florida is easily susceptible of faunal subdivision at Hatteras, below which locality a decided mixture of Antillean species is apparent. Between Long Island Sound and Hatteras the littoral molluscan fauna is disappointing to the collector, for the number of species is relatively small, and few even of these are entitled to any claims to beauty of shell. The nature of this coast, virtually a great sweep of exposed sand-beach, is not conducive to a varied or rich fauna. But if this portion of the transatlantic province is lacking in interest to the shell-collector, it is anything but disappointing to the army of men employed in the oyster- and clam-fishery. It is only within this faunal area that the American oyster, *Ostrea virginica*, the best of the edible shell-fish, finds its natural home, and here the oyster-culture is most extensively carried on.

After storms the Jersey beaches are frequently strewn with *Mactra, Tagelus, Arca,* and *Ensis ;* in more sheltered places *Fulgur* and *Polynices (Lunatia)* are commonly met. These may be accepted as the most characteristic genera of this province.

Just south of Cape Hatteras an observer is struck with the sudden change in the appearance of the shells on the beach. *Cardium, Cassis, Dolium, Arca,* and *Cancellaria* at once suggest the West Indies. About the vicinity of Hatteras the Gulf Stream approaches very near the land, bringing with its warm waters many wanderers from tropical homes. From Beaufort to Florida there is another long stretch of exposed and shifting sand-beach, which offers a scant return to the collector of mollusks.

THE CARIBBEAN PROVINCE

When Florida is reached a new world is opened to the naturalist, for there a better acquaintance is made with the great Caribbean province, which, extending from Florida to the northern shores of South America, embraces all the Bahamas, the West

Indies, the Gulf of Mexico, and the coast of Central America. Strangely enough, the mollusks of the west coast of Florida are more nearly related to those of the transatlantic province than are the shells of the east Florida coast. This remarkable fact in geographical distribution can only be explained by assuming that an open waterway once existed across the northern part of the Florida peninsula, connecting the Atlantic and the Gulf, through which a mingling of the shallow-water forms from Georgia, the Carolinas, West Florida, and the Gulf coast took place. Thus it would appear that when Florida was an island the fauna of its east coast, originally largely Antillean, was less disturbed by the southern migration of American species. The Florida Keys are essentially Antillean. The Caribbean or Antillean fauna is an exceedingly rich and varied one. Among the most prominent genera which may be encountered upon the Florida coast are *Strombus, Fasciolaria, Oliva, Marginella, Natica, Sigaretus, Littorina, Tectarius, Neritina, Melongena, Cardium, Callista, Tellina, Lucina,* and *Cyrena.* In such an extensive and rich faunal province one must not expect to find in any given locality a representation of all the characteristic genera. For instance, collections made at Havana, at Nassau, and at Vera Cruz would each contain forms more or less peculiar and local, but certain species would be found in each collection.

On the west coast of America quite the same faunal division into more or less well-marked provinces is to be found. Bering Sea belongs to the arctic province, and contains, with Labrador and Greenland, many identical forms.

THE ALEUTIAN PROVINCE

The shore waters from the southern peninsula of Alaska down to about Vancouver comprise the Aleutian province. Within this area occur some arctic species, notably the soft-shell clam, *Mya arenaria,* which the fishermen gather in such large quantities for bait along the Maine coast. An increasing number of species common to this west-coast faunal region and to the boreal province of the east coast are being recorded. Some of these have been introduced from the East by the agency of man, but others no doubt have a natural range through the icy waters north of America and down through the Bering Sea into the Pacific.

THE CALIFORNIAN PROVINCE

The Californian province extends from the neighborhood of Vancouver to Cape St. Lucas and has about five hundred species. The northern portion of this area contains some very characteristic forms, together with a good mixture of species of more northern habitat; it might properly be regarded as a subprovince. From San Diego south to the cape the character of the fauna gradually changes; this coast-line of southern California has also been considered a subregion. The main characteristic of the Californian province is a large development of *Haliotis*, of the patelliform mollusks, and of the chitons. A very few minutes on any good collecting-beach of California would convince the Eastern conchologist that he had entered upon an entirely new field of research. The most notable genera are *Calliostoma, Chlorostoma, Scurria, Acmæa*, various genera of the *Chitonidæ, Purpura, Monoceras, Amphissa, Norrisia, Olivella, Chorus,* and *Haliotis*.

THE PANAMIC PROVINCE

The warmer waters of the Gulf of California belong to the Panamic province, which extends down to South America. This is one of the richest and most interesting faunas in the world. At Panama alone, Mr. C. B. Adams, a noted collector and student of conchology, took upward of four hundred species. About eight hundred species are known in the Gulf of California alone.

It must be borne in mind that these faunal provinces relate to littoral and shallow-water species, for the present knowledge of deep-water forms is not sufficient to permit of generalization upon their distribution.

We review here only the conspicuous forms along our own coasts. It may be well to note, however, that in some other parts of the world the development of molluscan life is far in excess of anything to be found upon our shores. The veritable paradise of the naturalist is the East Indies. There the "aristocratic" genera, so called on account of their marvelous beauty, occur in their highest development — *Voluta, Mitra, Oliva, Conus,* and the various murices. There also are to be found the pearl-oysters, *Meleagrina margaritifera,* that yield their valuable harvest, and the giant clam, *Tridacna gigas,* which measures sometimes five feet in length. Over eight thousand species of mollusks are described from this surpassingly rich region, yet this vast province, as compared with the American and European shores, has been but superficially exploited by the naturalist. In whatever part of the world a naturalist may find himself, there is always a tempting array of molluscan life to attract him. Each fauna possesses features peculiar to itself, and from the point of view of the true naturalist, the more somber-hued and conventionally formed mollusks of Northern shores are no less interesting than the gorgeously tinted and fantastically shaped species of the tropics. From any faunal province of our own country one may readily gather all forms necessary to furnish ample material for study from which one may acquire an excellent idea of the biological features of the entire phylum.

STATION AND HABITS OF THE MOLLUSCA

The word "station" is used to indicate the nature of the surroundings which an animal chooses as most suited to his well-being. Some groups of mollusks, like the littorinas, the trochids, the purpuras, and the majority of those having patelliform shells, generally live on rocks above low-tide mark; other genera, like *Buccinum, Sipho,* and *Chrysodomus,* prefer rocky or gravelly ground below low-tide mark. Other mollusks burrow deep in the mud, many prefer sandy bottoms, while a host of other species seek homes upon the tangled masses of seaweed, living like arboreal creatures in the submarine forests. Nearly every conceivable character of sea-bottom or shore-line between tides harbors its own peculiar types of molluscan life. There are some very curious genera of bivalves that bore their way into the hardest rock and there find a comfortable shelter for life. A numerous class of pelagic or free-swimming mollusks supposedly never go to the bottom at all, but spend the whole of their existence on or near the surface of the sea, always in open water, where their fragile shells may not be injured by rough contact with solid substances.

The food of some is vegetable, of others, animal. The bivalves, like the clams, oysters, cockles, and mussels, feed only on microscopic organisms. They create a current of water through their siphons, or mantle openings, and then, by a process best known to themselves, catch and swallow all the animalculæ thus brought to their mouths. The univalves which possess a siphon are, for the most part, carnivorous, and are often most voracious creatures. They feed upon any animal matter they can find, while some of them are enabled by means of a sharply toothed tongue to bore through the solid shells of other mollusks and extract the succulent vitals from within. One energetic little mollusk in particular, *Urosalpinx cinerea*, is for this reason a great pest upon the oysterbeds. Univalves not possessed of a siphon may generally be considered herbivorous; they pass most of their time peacefully browsing upon algæ.

Mollusks are all oviparous or ovoviviparous; that is, they lay eggs, or, laying eggs, they retain them within their shells until the young are hatched out. As a rule, each species of mollusk has its own particular method of protecting its eggs from external injury. Some construct tough, leathery capsules which are strung together in various patterns. The egg-capsules of *Purpura lapillus*, resembling little pinkish or yellowish club-shaped stalks, may frequently be found in the crevices of rocks and under the rockweeds. The egg-cases of *Polynices* (*Lunatia*) are most peculiar, resembling inverted gelatine-bowls with the bottom knocked out; when wet they are semi-elastic translucent masses in which may be seen myriads of eggs. *Buccinum undatum* arranges its hemispherical egg-capsules in layers one above the other. The number of eggs so deposited is often very great, running well into the thousands. Egg-capsules of *Fulgur* are leathery coils of angular disks adhering by one edge to a connecting-band of a similar texture. (See Plate I.)

In bivalves the eggs are retained within the parent shell until hatched, and the young, which then escape into the water, are very different-looking creatures from the parent. Generally the young bivalve is free-swimming and exceedingly lively in its movements; sometimes by means of cilia it is enabled to attach itself to any passing host, and thus the species is widely disseminated. The fry soon lose their embryonic form and take on the characteristics of the adult.

The longevity of mollusks varies greatly with the species. Some attain an age of from ten to fifteen years, while some are only annuals. Oysters continue to grow for four or five years, after which they may survive many years more. In truth, little is known concerning the duration of life even of our better-known shore species.

In point of intelligence, mollusks must be relegated to a very low position. They give evidence of possessing no more than the most primary instincts, those of self-preservation and of reproduction. There are some forms that exercise a high degree of protective mimicry. The highest class of mollusks, the *Cephalopoda* (cuttlefishes, octopi, etc.), is widely separated from the other classes in the development of faculties that appear to correspond with intelligence. They are exceedingly crafty in the pursuit of their prey as well as in eluding capture.

STRUCTURE OF MOLLUSKS

Among the invertebrate animals, especially in the lower orders, wide physiological departures from central or typical forms are frequent. It often happens that a whole group or even suborder will differ so materially in its general characteristics from another group or suborder belonging to the same phylum that the student will be puzzled at first to understand how the two can be nearly related. In many such cases it is only when the essential features of the phylum are thoroughly understood that the relationships of its suborders can be appreciated. An example of widely divergent groups within the same phylum has already been shown in the *Echinodermata*. Who would at first suppose that the graceful *Astrophyton* could bear kinship to the inert holothurian, or that both of these have the closest family ties with the sea-urchins?

The probable reason for these startling departures from a typical form is that in the lower orders of life, where the organs and their functions are comparatively simple, the laws of evolution operate far more quickly in the adaptation of an organism to environment and changed conditions of life. A decided tendency to this departure from the type is a feature of the mollusks. It would be difficult, if not impossible, to give a general description that would fit both a common garden-snail and the common oyster, yet both are mollusks. A concise definition of the phylum is therefore practically impossible, and it seems here as if nature resented all attempts to circumscribe her living forms by rigid rules.

The most persistent characteristic of the *Mollusca* is the possession of the "mantle," a sort of outer skin which, like a bag or sack, envelops the creature above and about the sides, but is open below, permitting the animal at will to protrude or withdraw its foot. From the outer surface of this sheath-like mantle, or fold, a calcareous shell is secreted. The modifications of this mantle are infinite; indeed, in some well-marked groups it seems to have wholly disappeared, having in reality become fused to the sides of the animal, and having become therefore a mere outer skin, and no longer a tunic or cloak, as originally intended. As already noted, the mantle does not always secrete a shell, a fact which again reminds us that we cannot give a good comprehensive description of the phylum that always holds true throughout its subdivisions. The best that can be done is to give in general terms the characters which appear in a majority of the forms. A convenient method of going about this is to create, for the sake of clearness, an ideal, model, or fanciful mollusk and clothe it with all the most salient molluscan features, and from such a basis to develop, as we go on, the various types of the actual orders and suborders. There is one class of mollusks, the *Amphineura*, which conforms reasonably well in most of its features to our comprehension of the schematic mollusk. This class is sometimes referred to by biologists as the "primitive" or "original" mollusks, from which all the other classes have since been derived; but the evolutionary history of the development of the various molluscan orders through geological time does not seem to bear out the fact that an "ideal" mollusk, as we shall construct him, ever actually existed, or that his prototype, the *Amphineura*, was the first and consequently the ancestral type of the phylum. We must therefore only accept this ideal mollusk theoretically, to serve as a guide for the time being. We may profitably use it only as a lay figure—a sort of manikin, which will introduce us to the phylum. After our introduction we must forget our imaginary type and abandon any notion we may have conceived of the parental position of the *Amphineura*, its closest imitator in actual life.

THE IDEAL MOLLUSK

The ideal mollusk has a compact, somewhat elongated body, the under or ventral portion of which is thickened into a muscular disk, upon which it creeps along. This disk is called the *foot*. (Note a snail thus crawling upon his "foot.") The foot is rounded or obtusely pointed posteriorly. Forward, the body is slightly narrowed into a neck, and then expanded again into a head. Upon this head are carried two projecting, mobile, fleshy tentacles, one upon each side, that superficially resemble two horns. At the base of each tentacle, upon the inner side, is an eye. Just below and between the tentacles is a small horizontal slit,—the mouth,—the lips being slightly thickened. The visceral portion of the animal is above the foot, or *dorsal* to it, and extends the whole length of the animal from the mouth to the excretory opening, the latter being situated posteriorly. The visceral cavity is inclosed above by a thin skin; indeed, it is but the great thickening of this skin below that constitutes the foot.

The digestive tract, beginning at the mouth, opens immediately into a muscular throat, which is called the *buccal mass*. Within the buccal mass there is a long, fleshy ribbon that bears upon its upper surface numerous rows of sharp teeth; these rows of teeth run crossways on the ribbon, each row containing more or less prominent median teeth, with several laterals upon each side, and with marginal teeth on each side of the laterals. This is called the *radula*, and is used for tearing or rasping the food. When

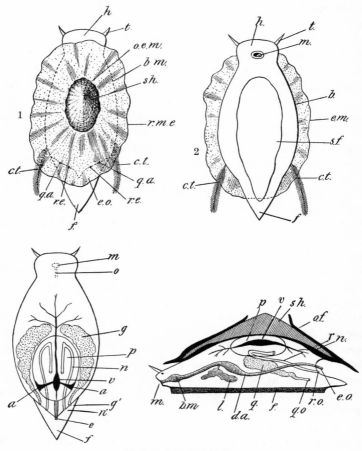

Ideal or schematic mollusk.

1, dorsal view: *h*, head; *t*, cephalic tentacle; *sh.*, shell covering visceral mass; *b. m.*, outline of body-mass; *r. m. e.*, edge of mantle; *c. t.*, ctenidia, or gills; *q. a.*, generative apertures; *r. e.*, renal openings; *e. o.*, excretory opening; *f*, posterior portion of foot; *o. e. m.*, edge of shell.

2, ventral view: *h*, head; *t*, tentacle; *m*, mouth; *b*, outline of body; *e. m.*, edge of mantle; *s. f.*, lower surface of foot; *c. t.*, ctenidia, or gills; *f*, posterior portion of foot.

3, horizontal section, showing heart, nephridia, and gonads: *m*, mouth; *o*, esophagus; *g*, gonad; *p*, pericardium; *n*, nephridium, or renal organ; *v*, ventricle; *a*, auricles; *g'*, gonad aperture; *n'*, renal opening; *e*, excretory opening; *f*, posterior portion of foot.

4, vertical median section: *m*, mouth; *b. m.*, buccal mass; *l*, liver; *d. a.*, digestive tract; *q*, gonad; *f*, foot; *q. o.*, gonad aperture, or opening of oviduct; *r. o.*, renal opening; *e. o.*, end of digestive tract, excretory opening; *n*, mantle; *r*, nephridium, or renal organ; *o. f.*, recurved portion of mantle; *sh.*, shell; *v*, ventricle; *p*, pericardium.

not in use it lies coiled up within the buccal mass. Beyond the
buccal mass, food passes into the esophagus, which widens out
into a muscular pouch or stomach; this may also be provided
with chitinous teeth or hard knobs or plates for the purpose of
further triturating the food. Above and partially surrounding
the stomach is a large reddish or brownish liver, which furnishes
to the alimentary canal the digestive juices. From the stomach
the intestine leads to the terminal anal opening. There are two
organs, serving the function of kidneys, placed dorsally one upon
each side of the body (*nephridia*). A heart lies within the median
line of the body, and consists of a ventricle and two lateral auricles. The vascular system is almost entirely closed; only in so far
as it is partially open does it essentially differ from that of higher
groups; the blood is whitish or light bluish, and receives its
oxygenation in the gills or along the free mantle surface, through
which it courses in exceedingly thin capillaries. In this manner
respiration is carried on to some extent throughout the whole
outer surface of the body. There are two *branchiæ* (gills). These
have the appearance of small feathers and are placed upon each
side of the animal posteriorly; they project slightly. Spread
over the top of this animal, fitting it perfectly, is a thin fleshy
covering attached to its dorsal portion like a skin, but hanging
free, like a flap, over the sides, the head, and the posterior end of
the animal. Upon the sides it may just cover the tips of the branchiæ, but in front the head is seen to project from under it.
The loose-hanging portion of this sac-like covering is somewhat
thickened, and perhaps recurved upward upon itself. Upon the
edge of this flap all the way around may occur a row of cilia, or
tentacular processes. This cloak-like covering is called the mantle,
and, as already noted, is the most peculiar and persistent characteristic of the *Mollusca*. The "cavity" formed between the loose-
hanging portion of the mantle and the sides of the foot is called
the *mantle cavity*, and contains posteriorly the gills, or branchiæ.
From the outer surface of this mantle a calcareous secretion takes
place, forming a shell, which, in our ideal mollusk, will be shaped
in conformity with the surface outlines of the mantle, oblong and
convex above. Over the lower portion of the shell the edge of

the mantle recurves. When the creature is disturbed or is at complete rest it may withdraw that portion of the mantle which protrudes from below the shell entirely within the edge of the shell, so that the "soft parts" may be wholly covered, and thus protected from harm. In such a state of rest nothing may be seen from above but a shell. The entire upper surface of the mantle is firmly attached to the under or inner side of the shell, except the mantle margin, this being free.

The nervous system consists of a circumesophageal ring of nerve-cells, with two cords passing along the digestive tract to the posterior end of the animal. In the head and above the buccal mass are several series of nerve-ganglia. These also communicate with the posterior portion of the animal through two parallel cords which pass along its ventral side. From these four principal branches, which traverse the entire length of the creature, minor nerve-cords are thrown off to the tentacles, the foot, the branchiæ, and the various organs of the viscera. The sexes are separate.

Reviewing our "typical mollusk," we find that it is bilaterally symmetrical—that is, uniform upon both sides of a median line from mouth to excretory opening; is unsegmented; has the ventral surface thickened into a creeping foot or disk; and is possessed of a head with tentacular processes, a radula, lateral branchiæ, a heart with a ventricle and two auricles, a well-developed mantle, and a shell.

If the reader can learn these few details of organization he knows the structure of a mollusk. In turning to the actual living forms he will find merely modifications (though sometimes confusing ones) of these various parts.

CLASSIFICATION

The *Mollusca* are divided into five great classes : *Amphineura, Gasteropoda, Scaphopoda, Pelecypoda,* and *Cephalopoda.* These names, it will be noticed, with the exception of the first, all refer to the *foot,* the modifications of the foot being selected as the basis of the first great divisions of the phylum. The *Gasteropoda* crawl upon the thickened ventral surface of their bodies (already re-

ferred to as the foot), as the common garden-snail, the periwinkles, and in general all those mollusks which have a spirally
coiled shell. The *Scaphopoda* have a long, worm-like foot, with
which they burrow in the sand or mud. Their shells are like
miniature elephant-tusks, but are open at both ends. The *Pelecypoda* have a more or less club-shaped foot, utilized, in the many
families, for a great variety of purposes. They are always inclosed in a bivalve shell. Familiar examples are the oysters,
the clams, mussels, etc. The *Cephalopoda* have the *foot* modified
into a number of *arms*, which encircle the head or the mouth.
They are the cuttlefishes, the octopi, squids, etc.

CLASS **AMPHINEURA**

ORDER **POLYPLACOPHORA**

The *Amphineura*, as already observed, approach most closely
to the ideal mollusk just described. They are bilaterally symmetrical. This fact is so important that it constitutes them a
class, notwithstanding the fact that in respect to the foot (the
basis of division into classes) they would be included with the
Gasteropoda, for (barring some exceptional instances) they creep
along upon a foot quite as our ideal mollusk would, and as the
Gasteropoda do. The head carries no tentacles, thus essentially
differing in this respect from the ideal form. The mantle is
extended down in front, completely covering the head. The
branchiæ are confined to a few pairs of *ctenidia*, or plume-like
gills, within the mantle groove or cavity, and are arranged upon
each side of the excretory opening like small feathers.

There are two orders of the *Amphineura*, the *Polyplacophora*
and the *Aplacophora* (or *Solenogastres*), the one name meaning "bearing many plates," and the other "without plates,"
the word "plate" in this sense being synonymous with "shell."
The shell of the first order consists of eight calcareous disks
arranged in a longitudinal row along the back or dorsal side of
the animal, which overlap like shingles on a roof and admit of
great variation of form in the various families.

It will be observed from the examples given that the shell plates do not entirely cover the mantle, but that a considerable portion of the upper mantle surface is left exposed along the side of the

Chiton spinosus, dorsal view.

animal. This exposed portion of the mantle is called the *girdle*. It is always very much thickened and is often exceedingly tough. In some species it is covered by a great number of calcareous spicules or granules which are embedded in the leathery mantle tissue. Strangely enough, the *Chitonidæ* (a large family of the *Polyplacophora*) possess a great number of eyes scattered over the shell plates like minute dots.

The members of this order are to be found in all parts of the world, but their greatest development is upon the west coast of America. In California

the student of marine life has a splendid opportunity to examine the chitons. They are generally to be found adhering to the under surface of stones about low-tide mark. They are very sluggish in their movements and may readily be removed from their resting-places by suddenly thrusting a knife-blade under the foot and prying them off. When thus detached they have a habit of rolling up up into a ball and so remaining indefinitely; to prevent this they should be placed at once in a jar of sea-water, where they will resume their natural position. For preservation as cabinet specimens, chitons should be tied down

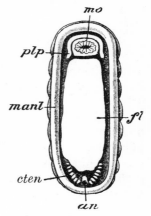

Chiton, ventral view: *an*, anus; *cten*, ctenidia; *ft*, foot; *mant*, mantle-edge; *mo*, mouth.

between two boards or flat substances, to hold them firmly extended until dried; otherwise they are apt to contract out of shape.

Six or eight species are exceedingly common upon the west

coast.   The collector who has successfully taken a number of
these will not fail to note the varying degrees of width of the
girdle in the different species.   In some
cases the girdle partially covers the overlapping shell plates.   The largest of all
the chitons inhabits the California shores
and is known as *Cryptochiton stelleri.*
It measures fully six inches in length and
three in width.   In *Cryptochiton* the gir-

Chiton ruber.   *Chiton apiculatus.*

dle is continued over the shell plates as a tough, gritty, brownish
covering.   The shell plates are white, and, as detached pieces, are
frequently to be found cast up upon the California beaches, where,
from their curious shape, they are often referred to as " butterfly-
shells."

On the east coast of America there are comparatively few
species, and these are all small and inconspicuous.   The three
commonest ones are *Chiton ruber, C. albus,* and *C. apiculatus.*
They may readily be found on stones or dead shells fished up
from below low-tide mark, or in rock-pools left by the receding
tide.

ORDER **APLACOPHORA**

This second order of the *Amphineura* is entirely destitute of
the shell plates characteristic of the first.   The outer mantle surface, however, develops a number of calcareous granules which
correspond to a shell.   The *Aplacophora* are symmetrical, having
the mouth and the excretory opening at the anterior and posterior
ends respectively.   The foot is greatly modified, being narrowed
at times to a mere slit along the ventral surface.   Some of them
have long, worm-like bodies.   This is no doubt a very primitive
form of mollusk, or, if not a primitive form, it has greatly degenerated from some higher type.   They are supposed to be commensal in habit and live in the deeper water offshore.

The *Aplacophora* are not littoral animals, and it is extremely
unlikely that one will ever encounter them upon the beach, unless, possibly, after the severest of storms.   We may therefore
leave them with this mere mention and proceed to the second
class of mollusks, the *Gasteropoda.*

TABLE SHOWING THE CLASSIFICATION OF THE GASTEROPODS
AND SCAPHOPODS DESCRIBED IN THIS CHAPTER

Phylum
MOLLUSCA

Class
GASTEROPODA

Order **OPISTHOBRANCHIATA**

Suborders	Families	Genera	Species
TECTIBRANCHIATA			
	BULLIDÆ	*Bulla*	*B. (Haminea) solitaria*
			B. occidentalis
			B. nebulosa
	APLYSIIDÆ	*Aplysia*	*A. Wilcoxii*
NUDIBRANCHIATA			
	DENDRONOTIDÆ	*Dendronotus*	*D. arborescens*
	ÆOLIDIDÆ	*Æolis*	*Æ. papillosa*
	DORIDIDÆ	*Doris*	*D. bilamellata*

Order **PROSOBRANCHIATA**

DIATOCARDIA

ACMÆIDÆ	*Acmæa*	*A. testudinalis*
		A. testudinalis, Var. *alveus*
		A. mitra
		A. patina
	Lottia	*L. gigantea*
FISSURELLIDÆ	*Fissurella*	*F. alternata*
		F. barbadensis
		F. (Glyphis) aspersa
	Lucapina	*L. crenulata*
HALIOTIDÆ	*Haliotis*	*H. splendens*
		H. rufescens
		H. cracherodii

324

Suborders	Families	Genera	Species
		Margarita	*M. cinerea*
			M. helicina
			M. undulata
			C. occidentale
		Calliostoma	*C. jujubinum*
	TROCHIDÆ		*C. annulatum*
			C. canaliculatum
			C. costatum
		Chlorostoma	*C. funebrale*
			C. brunneum
		Trochiscus	*T. norrisi*
		Livona	*L. pica*
	TURBINIDÆ	*Turbo*	*T. castaneus*
			T. castaneus, Var. *crenulatus*
	NERITIDÆ	*Nerita*	*N. peleronta*
			N. tessellata
			N. versicolor
		Neritina	*N. reclivata*
			N. viridis

MONOTOCARDIA

Suborders	Families	Genera	Species
	JANTHINIDÆ	*Janthina*	*J. fragilis*
	SCALIDÆ	*Scala*	*S. lineata*
			S. multistriata
			S. groenlandica
			S. angulata
	NATICIDÆ	*Polynices*	*P. (Lunatia) heros*
			P. (Lunatia) triseriata
			P. (Lunatia) lewisii
			P. (Neverita) duplicata
			P. (Neverita) recluziana
		Natica	*N. clausa*
			N. canrena
		Sigaretus	*S. perspectivus*
	CAPULIDÆ	*Crepidula*	*C. fornicata*
			C. plana
			C. aculeata
		Crucibulum	*C. striatum*
			C. spinosum
	LITTORINIDÆ	*Littorina*	*L. litorea*
			L. rudis
			L. palliata
			L. irrorata
			L. angulifera
			L. scutulata
			L. planaxis

Families	Genera	Species
LITTORINIDÆ	*Lacuna*	*L. vincta*
	Tectarius	*T. muricatus*
		T. nodulosus
CERITHIIDÆ	*Cerithium*	*C. floridanum*
		C. muscarum
		C. minimum
	Bittium	*B. nigrum*
	Cerithidea	*C. scalariformis*
		C. sacrata
VERMETIDÆ	*Vermicularia*	*V. spirata*
STROMBIDÆ	*Strombus*	*S. pugilis*
		S. gigas
CYPRÆIDÆ	*Cyprœa*	*C. exanthema*
		C. spurca
		C. spadacea
	Trivia	*T. pediculus*
		T. quadripunctata
		T. californica
		T. solandri
DOLIIDÆ	*Dolium*	*D. galea*
		D. perdix
	Pyrula	*P. papyratia*
CASSIDIDÆ	*Cassis*	*C. tuberosa*
		C. cameo
		C. testiculus
		C. inflata
MURICIDÆ Subfamily Muricinæ	*Murex*	*M. rufus*
		M. pomum
	Trophon	*T. clathratus*
	Urosalpinx	*U. cinerea*
	Eupleura	*E. caudata*
	Pteronotus	*P. festivus*
	Ocinebra	*O. poulsoni*
		O. lurida
		O. interfossa
	Cerostoma	*C. nuttallii*
		C. foliatum
Subfamily Purpurinæ	*Purpura*	*P. lapillus*
		P. patula
		P. hœmastoma
		P. crispata
		P. lima
		P. saxicola
	Monoceras	*M. lapilloides*
		M. engonatum
	Chorus	*C. belcheri*

Families	Genera	Species
COLUMBELLIDÆ	*Columbella*	*C. mercatoria*
		C. (Anachis) avara
		C. similis
		C. (Astyris) lunata
		C. (Amphissa) corrugata
		C. (Astyris) gausapata
NASSIDÆ	*Nassa*	*N. trivittata*
		N. obsoleta
		N. vibex
		N. fossata
		N. perpinguis
		N. tegula
		N. mendica
BUCCINIDÆ	*Buccinum*	*B. undatum*
	Chrysodomus	*C. decemcostatus*
	Sipho	*S. Stimpsoni*
		S. pygmæus
	Siphonalia	*S. kellettii*
	Tritonidea	*T. tincta*
TURBINELLIDÆ	*Fulgur*	*F. carica*
		F. canaliculata
		F. perversa
		F. pyrum
	Melongena	*M. corona*
FASCIOLARIIDÆ	*Fasciolaria*	*F. gigantea*
		F. tulipa
		F. distans
VOLUTIDÆ	*Voluta*	*V. junonia*
MARGINELLIDÆ	*Marginella*	*M. apicina*
OLIVIDÆ	*Oliva*	*O. literata*
	Olivella	*O. mutica*
		O. biplicata
		O. boetica
CONIDÆ	*Conus*	*C. floridanus*
		C. pealii
CANCELLARIIDÆ	*Cancellaria*	*C. reticulata*

Class
SCAPHOPODA

DENTALIDÆ	*Dentalium*	*D. dentale*
		D. pretiosum
		D. hexagonum
	Entalis	*E. striolata*

CLASS **GASTEROPODA**

THE class *Gasteropoda* is the largest and most comprehensive subdivision of the *Mollusca*, and within its wide range of families many differing details of organization are to be found. As a class it possesses all the most characteristic features of the phylum, though it is frequently modified in a high degree. This class includes all the univalve mollusks (except *Nautilus* and *Dentalia*), such as the snails, the whelks, and the host of spirally coiled land, fresh-water, and marine shells.

The gasteropod foot is, as has been remarked, primarily the same as in our schematic mollusk—a flat, muscular disk caused by the thickening of the ventral body-surface. The neck, head, and tentacles are also quite the same, but considerable modification of these organs will be found when we come to examine some specimens. The mantle is always present, except in the nudibranch or non-shell-bearing forms; but in few of the *Gasteropoda* is the mantle so regularly simple as in our ideal mollusk.

Perhaps the most striking feature of the *Gasteropoda*, and one that will at first surprise him who has in mind the simple structure of the ideal mollusk, is the fact that they are always asymmetrical—that is to say, a median line drawn longitudinally through a gasteropod will not divide it into halves of similar anatomical structure.

The quality of symmetry is an important one throughout the lower orders of animal life. In nearly all phyletic or class descriptions the word "symmetry" occurs, and its exact meaning must be understood. Take, for example, a human being; a median line drawn vertically would divide him into two similar halves— upon each side would be an eye, an arm, a leg, etc., of similar shape and construction. So far at least as the external features go, man is then a symmetrical creature; likewise the vertebrates in general. Cases of actual symmetry are found in the lobsters and crabs and in the segmented worms. It is usual in describing mollusks broadly and in general terms to call them symmetrical animals, yet here is the largest class within the phylum, whose representatives are none of them symmetrical. In the *Gasteropoda* the mouth is anteriorly placed in the head, just as in the ideal form, but the digestive tract, after traversing the visceral cavity in the usual fashion, suddenly turns forward and terminates in an excretory opening either on the right or on the left side of the animal, just back of the head. The various other orifices for the genital and renal glands are also placed in this unexpected anterior position. The gills, or branchiæ, are to be found upon one side only, forward of the heart, and differ somewhat in appearance from the plume-like processes of the *Amphineura.*

What, then, has become of the corresponding gill we should expect to find on the other side? The symmetrical shape of the foot is not in the least altered, but what has happened to cause this distortion of the visceral portion of the animal? And, finally, will this torsion of the body of the snail perhaps account for the spiral nature of the shell?

An evolutionary process is supposed to have taken place in mollusks, which, if real, would no doubt account for these curious conditions of torsion in the *Gasteropoda;* but the theory upon which this process is based is altogether speculative, and is not fully sustained by the facts in the case. Originally all mollusks are presumed to have been symmetrical, and are assumed to have resembled very much in form the schematic creature we have already described. Now, for some reason, certain of the primitive mollusks, but not all of them, began to develop a larger visceral mass, which, continuing to enlarge throughout many generations, began finally to protrude above and form a hump on the dorsal side of the animal. This hump, containing the liver, a portion of the intestines, and the generative glands, as it increased in bulk became so much elevated that it could no longer maintain itself in an erect position over the body, but, impelled by its own weight, began to sag over to one side. Such a process would of course tend to twist the digestive tract and bring the excretory opening constantly farther forward on one side. At the same time, this process would necessarily interfere, by the weight of the overhanging viscera and the shell covering the mass, with the development of the branchiæ lying upon that side and now crowded under the visceral mass. Thus, according to this theory, this process has continued until, in the modern gasteropod, the digestive tract has been bent upon itself and twisted from a straight course into a curve of almost 180°, bringing the excretory opening near or just over the head, where it empties into the mantle cavity; while the original right gill, by the same movement, has been brought to a position on the *left* side of the head, forward of the heart, the original left gill having been crowded out, eventually to atrophy and disappear. The same torsion is found in the nerve-cords; the heart, situated at about the pivotal position of this twisting process, has turned about upon itself, leaving an auricle in front of the ventricle, one auricle, like one of the gills, having been lost. The mantle portion covering the visceral hump naturally continued to secrete its shell, though always in conformity with the change, the result being the familiar spiral form of the usual gasteropod shell.

This theory may not be satisfactory, but the asymmetry of gasteropods is a problem to be solved, and a more interesting line of biological investigation could not be found.

Let us now take a good example of a gasteropod and locate its various organs; at the same time we may use the occasion to refer to more important modifications of these organs which will be encountered later in the various genera. The most available gasteropod on the east coast of the United States for this purpose is *Fulgur*, both on account of its large size and its abundance. *Buccinum* may be used if the student is north of Cape Cod and therefore unable to secure a good living specimen of *Fulgur;* the anatomical differences between the two are slight.

Note the siphon protruding forward from a notch in the shell. This consists merely in an elongation of a fold of the mantle, which is held in a manner to constitute a tube, through which the animal draws in water to supply the gills, lying just back of the siphon and concealed under the mantle in the cavity already spoken of as the mantle cavity.   With the exception of that portion of the mantle which constitutes the siphon, no part of its margin, it will be observed, can be seen, the edge of the shell completely hiding it from view.

In some genera the siphon is exceedingly long—in fact, longer than the body of the animal.   In these cases the mollusk is generally fond of burying itself in the sand and maintaining communication with the world above only by means of this long, fleshy tube.   In some genera the siphon is protected by an elongation of the shell, as in *Fasciolaria* (Plate LXXVI).

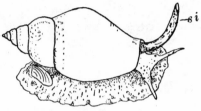

Buccinum undatum : si, siphon.

An extreme example of this is given in the figure on page 343, which represents a species of *Murex*, where the siphon is not only protected by the shell, but the shell itself is further protected by the double row of sharp spines with which it is beset.

There are some genera which possess no siphons at all, in all of which cases there is no notch in the shell opening, the aperture being round, as in *Natica* and in *Littorina* (pages 368, 371).   The mollusks of this type make a fold in the forward part of the mantle which serves as a siphon.   Such a muscular folding in the mantle would be technically called a *functional siphon.*

On the posterior dorsal side of the foot is attached a horny plate, of concentric structure about a central or subcentral point or nucleus.   This is called the *operculum,* and serves to close the entrance of the shell when the animal is withdrawn, the object no doubt being protective.   The opercula vary to a great extent in the different genera; in some cases they are calcareous, in others cartilaginous.   When the aperture of the shell is very large it often happens that the operculum does not entirely close the opening, as in *Fulgur,* but in *Buccinum* it is a close fit. The operculum is entirely wanting in the *Pulmonata,* one of the large orders of the *Gasteropoda*. The figures represent some of the commoner types of opercula.

The opercula have been utilized a great deal in the classification

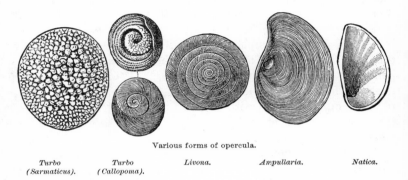

Various forms of opercula.

| Turbo | Turbo | Livona. | Ampullaria. | Natica. |
| (Sarmaticus). | (Callopoma). | | | |

of the *Gasteropoda*, and especially in some groups that have become terrestrial in habit. Often, when shell-characters utterly fail to give a clue to the proper generic position of a new or rare mollusk, the operculum may be relied upon to indicate it.

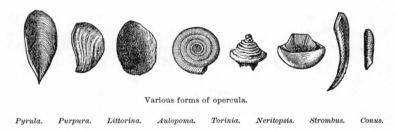

Various forms of opercula.

| Pyrula. | Purpura. | Littorina. | Aulopoma. | Torinia. | Neritopsis. | Strombus. | Conus. |

TENTACLES

Two tentacles project like fleshy horns from the sides of the head. These are not retractile, as in the land-snails, and their office appears to be that of sensory organs. In both *Fulgur* and *Buccinum* the tentacles are comparatively short and stout, and have expanded bases; in many other genera they are long and slender. Almost without exception the *Gasteropoda* possess tentacles.

EYES

In *Fulgur* the eyes are situated near the bases and upon the outer sides of the tentacles; in *Buccinum* they are extremely small and are mounted about midway between the bases and the tips of the tentacles. This is the usual position for the eyes in the marine *Gasteropoda*. Only in the pulmonates, or land-snails, are the eyes placed at the summit of the tentacles. Sight does not appear to be a very important sense in the gasteropods, although the eye in some instances becomes a highly developed organ. A number of forms that have the habit of burrowing deep into the sand or mud are quite destitute of visual organs, and certain cave-dwelling land-shells have entirely lost the sense of vision.

MOUTH AND PROBOSCIS

The mouth will easily be seen in both *Fulgur* and *Buccinum*. It is a small slit with slightly thickened, fleshy lips, and is placed on the lower forward portion of the head. In the case of both of these genera the mouth is situated at the end of a proboscis. It will be noted that *Fulgur* has a comparatively long and stout proboscis, or snout, which is not retractile. *Buccinum* has a smaller one. It is fairly safe to assume that all gasteropods that possess a proboscis are carnivorous. This organ is greatly developed in some genera, where it actually exceeds in length the rest of the animal. In such instances, no doubt, the creature is enabled to reach the interior portions of the shells of its victims and to devour every vestige of their flesh, for the mouth is most conveniently placed just at the end of this long, trunk-like organ. The genera which have no proboscis are, almost without exception, vegetable feeders.

We must now remove the animal from its shell. It is well to boil it first, for this does away with the annoying mucous secretion that is freely exuded by glands in the foot when the creature is roughly handled. Alcoholic specimens are apt to be much contracted and hardened, and are therefore less satisfactory as subjects for anatomical study. If it is not convenient to boil the specimen, break away the shell with a hammer, using care not to lacerate the soft, fleshy portion within; when this is accomplished, wash the animal carefully to remove the slimy exudation. Note the "visceral hump," which is spiral, and which formerly occupied the upper-whorl portion of the shell. The thin skin covering it is the mantle, which below is greatly thickened and free, lying about the foot like a heavy fleshy flap.

MANTLE

The mantle-edge in both of these examples is simple; that is to say, it possesses no fringe of tentacles, nor is it supplemented by extra processes, characters which mark many genera of marine *Gasteropoda*. In *Fulgur* and *Buccinum* the mantle-edge does not protrude below the edge of the shell; but in many genera, especially those which possess smooth, glossy shells, like the cowries (*Cypraea*) and the graceful *Oliva*, the mantle is proportionately very much larger. In these two genera, when the animal is extended, as in crawling about the sand, the mantle curves upward and incloses a large portion of the shell itself. Indeed, in some genera the shell is almost entirely concealed by this extension of the mantle (*Sigaretus*, *Natica*, etc.).

When the shell is removed, the folding of the mantle which constitutes the siphon can be plainly seen. The office of the siphon has already been referred to, also the fact that the presence of a siphon in the gasteropod mollusk may always be determined by merely glancing at the shell alone, for a notch at the base of the aperture indicates the place through which the siphon passed. In *Buccinum* this is merely a notch, but in *Fulgur* the siphonal canal of the shell is much longer. Just why the long siphons of some mollusks should be naked and exposed to danger, while others are so carefully protected by elongated portions of the shell, is a mystery, but nature is full of such contradictions.

THE GASTEROPOD FOOT

The foot is long, broad, and flat on the under side, like a disk. The variations in the gasteropod foot are almost infinite.

In some of the species it is amazingly large and powerful, as in *Polynices* (*Natica*), and in most of the forms which live along sandy beaches. These are sometimes provided in front with a wedge-shaped process called the *propodium*, which serves admir-

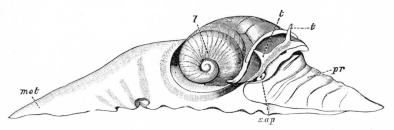

Sigaretus lævigatus, showing excessive development of the propodium (*pr.*) and metapodium (*met.*) in a mollusk living in sand (the shell, which covers only the liver and adjacent parts, has been removed): *l*, liver; *s. ap.*, aperture of proboscis, here deflected from the median line; *t, t*, tentacles; *f*, foot.

ably as a plow to push aside the heavy wet sand through which the animal forces its way. In *Nassa*, which is so common all along our coasts, the foot has two terminal appendages or points behind.

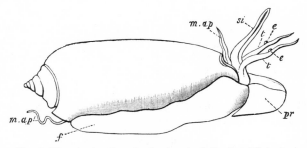

Oliva textilina showing how the front part of the foot (*f*) is developed into a sort of fender, the propodium (*pr.*): *e, e*, eyes; *m. ap.*, front appendage of mantle; *m. ap.'*, hinder appendage of mantle, folded into the suture when the animal is at rest; *si.*, siphon; *t, t*, tentacles.

There is no single feature of mollusks more important than the foot, for upon the many modifications of this organ the various molluscan classes are founded. The name *Gasteropoda* means "stomach-foot," the latter organ being merely a thickening of the ventral surface of the animal, giving to the creature, when active, the appearance of crawling upon its stomach.

If a living gasteropod is placed in a jar of sea-water and left undisturbed it will soon crawl up the side of the glass and thus afford an excellent view of the extended under surface of its foot. The majority of the gasteropods are lethargic and slow in movement, but others will be found to be exceedingly lively and able to creep up the sides of the jar and make their escape in a surprisingly short time. Further modifications of the foot will be mentioned later.

THE MANTLE CAVITY

Now let us place the animal with the foot below and the head facing us. The spiral visceral hump will point back and away from the observer. The mantle covering the visceral portion is thin and translucent like an ordinary skin, but at the base of the visceral mass the mantle suddenly thickens very greatly, and spreads over the dorsal portion of the foot or the body like a cloak. The space between the body and the loose-lying mantle is called the *mantle cavity*, and within this area are to be found several important external organs. To find these it is well to cut the mantle flap in a straight line, beginning just back of the head and ending at the point where the mantle is attached to the body. This will most easily be done with scissors. Having thus divided the mantle in front, throw back the two flaps. On the right-hand side (left of the animal), and attached to the inner side of the mantle thus exposed, will be seen the branchiæ, or gills.

THE BRANCHIÆ, OR GILLS

They consist of a row of flattened filaments bound together at the base like the leaves of a book. The blood is conveyed to these gills by a large vein, and is then forced through the thinly walled filaments, being thus brought into close contact with the water, to which it releases its carbon dioxide, and from which it receives the life-giving oxygen. In certain gasteropods there are two sets of gills, one placed upon each side of the body

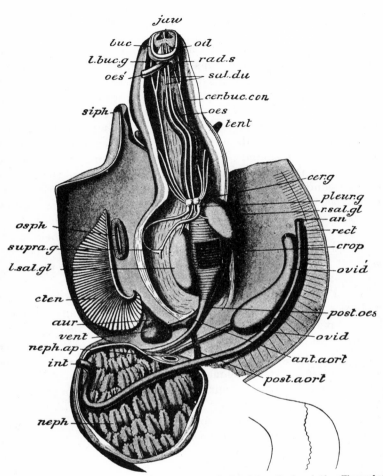

Anatomy of the internal organs of a female gasteropod, viewed from the dorsal side. The roof of the mantle cavity has been divided by a longitudinal incision and the flaps laid out, that on the left bearing the ctenidium and osphradium, and that on the right the rectum and terminal part of the oviduct. The muscular dorsal wall of the body and the introvert have been divided so as to bring into view the anterior part of the alimentary canal and a portion of the nervous system. The buccal cavity has been tilted up and opened so as to show the odontophore, and the esophagus has been cut through near the anterior end. A portion of the ventral wall of the crop has been removed so as to bring the internal folds into view, and the interior of the nephridium with the contained portion of the intestine has been exposed. The stomach is not seen, being hidden by the nephridium, and the ovary is not represented. *an.*, anus ; *ant. aort.*, anterior aorta ; *aur.*, auricle ; *buc.*, buccal cavity ; *cer. buc. con.*, cerebro-buccal connective ; *cer. g.*, cerebral ganglia ; *crop*, crop ; *cten.*, ctenidium ; *int.*, intestine ; *jaw*, jaw ; *l. buc. g.*, left buccal ganglion ; *l. sal. gl.*, left salivary gland ; *neph.*, nephridium ; *neph. ap.*, nephridial aperture ; *od.*, odontophore ; *oes.*, esophagus ; *oes'.*, anterior end of same, cut and turned aside ; *osph.*, osphradium ; *ovid.*, oviduct ; *ovid'.*, terminal thick-walled portion of oviduct ; *pleur. g.*, pleural ganglion ; *post. aort.*, posterior aorta ; *post. oes.*, posterior esophagus ; *rad. s.*, radula sac ; *r. sal. gl.*, right salivary gland ; *rect.*, rectum ; *sal. du.*, salivary duct ; *siph.*, siphon ; *supra. g.*, supra-esophageal visceral ganglion ; *tent.*, tentacle ; *vent.*, ventricle.

337

(as in the ideal mollusk); but the presence of two sets of gills only indicates, in these gasteropods, that the twisting process of the viscera, already alluded to as so remarkable a feature of this class, has not proceeded far enough to destroy the functional activity of one of the gills.

In general, it may be said that the breathing process of mollusks does not markedly differ from the respiratory methods of higher forms of animals. Whether the breathing is effected by gills or by a pulmonary sac, the essential features of the system are the same as in fishes or mammals. There are, however, some rather peculiar developments in the breathing system of gasteropods that are worthy of notice. The gills themselves differ throughout the various orders of this class both as to their structure and their relative position; in one of the orders (the *Pulmonata*) the gills have entirely disappeared, and are replaced by a pulmonary sac which fulfils the purpose of a lung.

It is a generally accepted theory that all land or air-breathing mollusks were originally marine, but by a gradual change in their habits have developed into terrestrial forms, losing their gills and acquiring in their place organs which correspond to lungs. The theory is supported by the fact that many species of marine mollusks live between tide-marks, and for several hours daily are obliged to maintain life outside of their native element. The *Littorinidæ*, which may always be found in abundance on both the east and the west American coasts, usually live high above low-tide line, and some tropical species of this genus actually live in the trees above the reach of high tide. They have gills just as in *Buccinum* or *Fulgur*, but the *Littorina* shell is strongly suggestive of certain land forms, and there is reason to believe that the genus is in course of evolution into a pulmonate. On the other hand, there are to be found in fresh water numerous genera which are true pulmonates, and which are obliged to come to the surface every few minutes to obtain air. One notable genus of marine gasteropods possesses both lungs and gills, and one marine form has entirely lost its gills and breathes only by means of lungs. It is quite likely that all mollusks are able to breathe more or less all along the exposed mantle surface, which is usually crowded with capillaries with exceedingly thin walls. This very remarkable method of surface respiration is proved to exist in the nudibranch or shell-less marine *Gasteropoda*, for they possess neither gills nor lungs.

OSPHRADIUM

Lying just under the gills, and side by side with them, is a smaller, plume-like organ having the appearance of a smaller gill; it is called the *osphradium*. The office of this organ is not definitely known, but the supposition is that it is the seat of the olfactory nerves. The osphradia are not always present, but whenever found they are placed in close conjunction with the gills, in order, probably, that the animal may best determine the quality of the water brought by the siphon to the breathing-organs. In *Buccinum* the osphradium is especially prominent. In all mollusks the sense of smell is highly developed. A dead animal anchored to the bottom will very soon attract the carnivorous *Mollusca* from every direction. This is not a bad way to trap certain species that live upon rocky stations and are otherwise difficult to secure by the dredge.

On the left-hand side (right of the animal), and adhering to the under side of the mantle flap, which has been thrown back, a somewhat inflated and convoluted tube, the rectum, will be seen. It terminates in an opening just within the mantle-edge. By the side of this are the renal and genital openings.

Having now examined the external organs, we may investigate the internal anatomy of our subject. To do this thoroughly requires considerable skill, but for the purpose of merely discovering the relative positions of the principal internal organs a little care only is necessary. The work will be greatly facilitated by boiling the animal for a few minutes, for this serves to harden the tissues and to separate the various organs in a most satisfactory manner.

To begin, open the proboscis from the mouth, cutting back so as to expose the esophagus. It will be seen that the throat is long and very muscular.

RADULA

Hidden among the red stripes of muscular fiber which line the inner surface of the throat will be found a fleshy strip covered upon one side with many transverse rows of chitinous teeth.

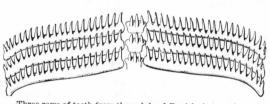

This is the *lingual ribbon,* or *radula.* Remove as much of it as possible, and examine it with a hand-glass. The radula is a most important

Three rows of teeth from the radula of *Fasciolaria trapezium.*

organ, and is a unique possession of *Mollusca,* except the pelecypods, or bivalves. Usually it lies coiled up like a spiral when not in use; its purpose is to tear and rasp food.

The radula has been the subject of much study by conchologists, and has furnished the basis for an arrangement of the numerous sections of gasteropods into somewhat well-defined groups. If the observer has a strong glass he will notice that each transverse row of teeth on the ribbon consists of a median or central tooth with several points or "cusps." *Fulgur* has a median tooth with three cusps; *Buccinum* one with six. On each side of the median tooth is a lateral tooth, which in *Fulgur* will be seen to have six cusps, and in *Buccinum* five. In many patterns of radulæ

there is, besides the median and lateral teeth, still another paired row, called the marginals. In the accompanying figures are given some examples which show small sections of lingual ribbons. While all

Portion of the radula of *Imbricaria marmorata.*

the radulæ of mollusks are capable of being grouped by their general characteristics, yet in no two species of mollusks are the radulæ quite identical.

VITAL ORGANS, STOMACH, LIVER, RENAL GLANDS, ETC.

The digestive tract will be found to widen out a short distance back into a crop or stomach, and, continuing still further, to lose itself in a soft, brownish mass within the coiled spire, which is the liver. The very large size of the liver leads one to suspect that *Fulgur* and *Buccinum* must be voracious creatures to need so large an organ for the secretion of bile. In many species of mollusks the stomach and intestines are filled quite solidly, at times, with a gelatinous transparent substance called the *crystalline stylet*. Just why the digestive tract should be clogged with this substance no one has yet been able to explain, so here again is a chance for original investigation. The intestine curves about after reaching the liver, and comes forward again to appear once more as the rectum, clinging to the inner surface of the free portion of the mantle.

Closely associated with the liver, but differing slightly in color, is the gonad, or organ in which the genital products are formed. Situated dorsally and forward of the liver and gonad is a large renal gland, which may readily be detected by its peculiar structure. In some forms the kidney is closely associated with the gonad, and seems to coöperate with the latter in the generative functions.

HEART AND VASCULAR SYSTEM

To find the heart, make an incision into the body just at the posterior end of the gills. The heart is white and round, and is inclosed within a cavity known as the *pericardium;* it has a ventricle and one or two auricles, although in *Buccinum* and *Fulgur* there is but one auricle.

There is nothing remarkable about the vascular system to distinguish it from that of many higher forms of animals. It is, however, not completely closed—by which is meant that the blood is not always contained within arteries or veins, and that it does sometimes flow into other organs and floods certain other body-cavities, although the vascular system of mollusks is by no means so completely open as is that of insects and crustaceans.

Having examined the animal which inhabits the shell and gained an idea of its anatomy, we may now turn to an inspection of the house which it has built for itself, and here we shall find a delightful subject for study.

An industrious hour of collecting upon almost any beach will provide the student with an abundance of interesting shells.

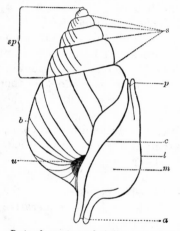

Parts of a gasteropod shell: *a*, anterior canal; *b*, body-whorl; *c*, columella; *l*, outer lip; *m*, mouth or aperture; *p*, posterior canal; *s*, sutures; *sp*, spire; *u*, umbilicus.

Putting aside the bivalves, the univalve or gasteropod shells remaining should be closely examined for the purpose of becoming acquainted with their various conchological features. The collector will see at once that he has a number of species that differ more or less widely in their general form, size, texture, and sculpture. Some shells will be long in proportion to their width, with many turns of the spire which probably terminates in a sharply pointed apex; others will be almost round, with comparatively few spiral turns which end in a blunt apex, giving to the specimen outlines suggestive of a dome. A wide range of characters will be found in the mouths or apertures of the shells, some being almost if not quite round, others oblong and with a notch cut into the lower portion of the opening, and others possibly with this notch extended into a sort of semi-inclosed channel. A first lesson in classification of the *Mollusca* may be taken by dividing the results of the first day's collecting of univalve shells into groups according to these prominent shell-characters.

A good knowledge of the parts of a gasteropod shell is essential to the student, and it can readily be acquired. Four specimens are given in the accompanying figures, representing highly divergent

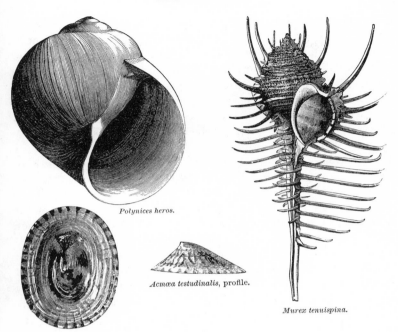

Polynices heros.

Acmœa testudinalis, profile.

Murex tenuispina.

Acmœa testudinalis, from below.

types of marine gasteropods, and their respective characteristics
may be noted by comparing them one with another: *Fasciolaria
tulipa* (Plate LXXVI), a Floridian shell; *Polynices heros*, a common species found on all the sandy shores of the American Atlantic coast; *Murex tenuispina*, an Indo-Pacific species much prized
by collectors; and *Acmœa testudinalis*, commonly found in Maine
and Massachusetts at low tide clinging to rocks.

The extreme top of the shell is called the *apex*, and it may be
either sharply pointed or obtuse. Each turn is called a *whorl;*
the last one, and always the largest, is called the *body-whorl*, the
others collectively forming the *spire* of the shell. When the animal first emerges from the egg it is always provided with one or
two whorls, which generally may be distinguished at the apex as
smoother than the rest of the spire, and a faint line may be
discovered where the shell began its growth after birth. These

first whorls of embryonic growth are usually referred to as the *nepionic whorls*. The interstices between the successive whorls are called *sutures*, and these lines of juncture may be shallow or deep according to the convexity of the whorls. The sculpturing of the whorls is often of great complexity, and exhibits *nodules*, *varices, ribs, revolving striæ, spinous processes*, and *lines of growth*. It frequently happens that there is a complete absence of any sculpturing whatever, the whole surface of the shell being perfectly smooth, save for the faint lines of growth to be detected only under a magnifying-glass. The outer edge of the mouth or aperture of the shell is called the *outer lip*. This may be more or less thickened, expanded, or simple. The inner lip is called the *columella*, and may be greatly extended anteriorly. When the mouth of the shell is round, and there is no notch or indentation either above or below, it is said to be *continuous*.

The *anterior canal* is for the accommodation of the siphon of the animal, which, as noted above, may be very long or almost entirely absent; therefore the character of the shell generally indicates whether or not the animal itself possesses a long siphon. There is in some forms a notch at the upper extremity of the mouth, which is for the accommodation of the anal discharges. When present it is called the *posterior canal*.

It will be noted that all the specimens figured as examples, save one, are spiral, the coils revolving about an imaginary axis. When the whorls are not too closely coiled there is left open to the view a hollow space throughout the entire length of the shell, which is called the *umbilicus*. When the coils of the shell are very compact there is no umbilicus to be seen. The umbilical opening may be very large, giving a clear view of the inner surfaces of all the whorls right through to the apex. The usual gasteropod shell is in reality a hollow tube wound about an imaginary axis. Since the tube increases in size as it progresses, the base of the shell is necessarily wider and larger than the apex. Thus all gasteropod shells may be reduced in shape to the single type of a cone or top, modified by the excessive length or shortness of the spire, or otherwise altered by special peculiarities. In *Polynices duplicata* (page 368), it will be observed that while the umbilicus is fairly large, its external opening, in the adult shell, has been almost completely closed by a callous process thrown off from the inner or columellar lip.

Gasteropod shells may be *sinistral* or *dextral*, according as the whorls turn to the left or right. The great majority of marine species are dextral, having the opening on the right, although a few species exhibit the curious property of being constructed upon either the one or the other plan without apparent reason. Sinistral specimens of many normally dextral species have been discovered, but they are so rare as to warrant the belief that such specimens are merely deformities or monstrosities resulting from some accident of birth.

The collector will soon learn to distinguish between young and adult specimens, for those finishing touches of wonder and beauty which the mollusk gives to his protective covering are made only by the adult. The outer lip of young gasteropod shells is usually thin and fragile; even if slightly thickened, it has an unformed or unfinished appearance.

Shells differ greatly in their *structure*, many species being porcelanous like china, others glassy, and many more are of a softer chalky composition. In the latter case the shell is usually covered with a thick membranous skin, which, when removed, leaves a dull, lusterless, white body beneath. Shells of this texture, when cast upon the beach, soon yield to the weathering action of sun and air. The porcelanous shells are composed of successive layers of carbonate of lime, throughout which is a filmy membranous framework of a substance similar to that of which the covering of the *Crustacea* is formed. The mode of deposition of the various layers of crystalline calcic carbonate and the peculiar lineation of their outer surfaces give rise to the iridescent or nacreous appearance of some shells.

With the exception of those species in which the mantle of the animal is extended over the edge of the aperture and more or less envelops the entire test, there is an outer skin of membranous or organic matter which overlies the surface of the shell. This skin is sometimes quite thick, often hairy, and is usually of a dull greenish- or brownish-yellow color. In many genera this

outer covering of the shell is excessively thin. In old specimens the epidermis is usually worn away from the apical whorls.
It often happens that the shells of the most exquisite colors and
markings are thus rendered somber and unattractive by their
tenants during life; when the animal dies, or when such specimens are kept in a cabinet for a period of time, the epidermis
dries, cracks, and falls off, revealing the wealth of color and
design beneath.

The growth of the gasteropod shell is accomplished by the
exudation from the margin of the animal's mantle of a liquid
containing the shelly matter in solution. The mantle-edge is
provided with a complicated system of glands and pores, from
which is secreted this "stony liquor." This more or less viscous
liquid, containing the carbonate of lime and the other inorganic
materials of which the shell is composed, hardens upon exposure,
and the shelly matter is then deposited in crystalline form around
the edges or lip of the shell aperture. The gasteropod shell
therefore grows by the continual building out of its aperture
through successive depositions of shelly matter at the extreme
edge of the lip. At the extreme edge of the mantle margin are
situated those glands which secrete the materials for the epidermis of the shell, and as one would therefore expect, this outer-
most layer of epidermis is first produced in the advancing growth
of the shell. There also are situated the pigment-glands, which
produce the color-secretions. The various layers of the shelly
substance are successively deposited inside the mouth of the shell
by glands situated just back of the extreme edge of the mantle
margin. Thus in the growth stage, if one could examine closely
the aperture of a gasteropod shell, one would observe at the extreme tip of the lip this projecting epidermis, just beneath it and
just inside the aperture a thin deposit of shelly matter, just beneath this, and farther in, another layer, and still farther in a
third layer.

The growth of nearly all gasteropod shells is marked by periods
of rest. During the inactive seasons the creature may thicken
the edge of the aperture to a greater or less extent by an extra
deposit of shelly matter, for otherwise the thin lip might soon be

injured or broken. These places where the lip was thickened, as a temporary protection until the young animal decided to continue building, appear on the surface of adult shells, and persist as *varices*, "raised lines of growth," "longitudinal ribs," etc. Such forms of sculptural markings generally occur at equidistant points and preserve a scheme of regularity which would indicate that the periods of rest were of seasonal occurrence. All irregularities and all surface features of the external shell simply reflect certain peculiarities of the mantle margin of the animal; all spinous processes, for instance, as in the marvelous *Murex tenuispina*, indicate the existence of finger-like processes extending from the mantle margin, which once occupied the hollow thorns projecting from the shell. When the outer surface of a shell is devoid of any sculpturing and is perfectly smooth, one may assume that the mantle margin of the animal was simple. If the edge of the lip has a crenulated appearance and the surface of the whorls is decorated with revolving ribs, the mantle margin was probably folded or wavy. There can be no doubt but that the entire mantle surface is provided to some extent with glands for the secretion of shelly matter, for if any portion of the shell is accidentally injured the animal soon repairs the break with a calcareous deposit. But such repairs are never homogeneous in texture with the other parts of the shell of normal growth; the patches are never covered externally with an epidermis, and they are always devoid of color. The function of the epidermis is to protect the calcareous shell from the corroding agents contained in sea-water. Hence it is that, when the epidermis is removed, "dead shells" exposed to the influence of the water or the weather soon lose their brilliancy and luster, and become undesirable for specimens either for the cabinet or for study. It often happens that living shells, inhabiting a region where, for one cause or another, the water is highly charged with impurities of an acid nature, are discovered to be badly corroded about the apex, where the epidermis is thin and likely to be rubbed off. For this reason specimens collected in harbors near large cities or near the mouths of rivers are apt to be poor and defective.

The inner surface of all shells, if not actually nacreous, is always perfectly smooth. When foreign substances, such as grains of sand, enter the shell and cannot be removed by the animal, the irritation caused thereby to the soft, fleshy creature induces discharges of a liquid from the glandular surface of the mantle, which hardens about the offending substance and glazes it over with a smooth, pearly deposit.

Acmæa testudinalis (page 343) presents a special type of gasteropod shell which is found in several families. Here the spire seems to be wholly absent, and the entire shell consists of but one large body-whorl. There are very many of these patelliform species, inhabiting many seas and belonging to many different genera, and in nearly all cases their embryonic shells display a spiral form. After birth the animal does not build his house upon the spiral plan, but expands the shell into one large shield-like covering. The student, however, must not presume that *Acmæa* is an ancestral type just because the simple character of the shell is suggestive of the model chosen to represent a schematic mollusk; anatomically *Acmæa* presents the complications of body-torsion which show a very considerable evolutionary change, and indicate that its simple shell is probably a degenerate form of a once more highly developed and convoluted one.

The forms, the architecture, and the painting of gasteropod shells are so infinite in variety that it would be unwise to attempt a description of their marvels. A close observer of nature's works soon becomes prepared for every surprise, but he never ceases to be charmed and fascinated by his new discoveries. The careful student alone can learn really to see and appreciate the wonders of nature, and this is especially true in the study of the *Mollusca*.

CLASSIFICATION OF GASTEROPODS

The *Gasteropoda* far exceed all the other divisions of the *Mollusca* in the number of their genera and species. Apparently this has not always been the case. There is evidence tending to show that in past geological epochs the pelecypods (the bivalve shells) outnumbered the gasteropods, but that in the course of time the increase in the genera of gasteropods has been more rapid. To judge also from the very large number of extinct families among the cephalopods, which once flourished in astonishing abundance, it would appear that they are a dying race.

The classification of the *Gasteropoda* is primarily a division into three great orders: the *Opisthobranchiata*, the *Prosobranchiata*, and the *Pulmonata*. The *Pulmonata*, which include the land and fresh-water gasteropod shells, are characterized by the presence of a breathing-sac, or lung, instead of gills. They are, therefore, essentially air-breathers, and would perish if kept too long under water. The *Opisthobranchiata* and *Prosobranchiata* are marine, and, like all animals which breathe by means of gills, soon die when removed from the water. We have already noted, however, how some genera of marine gasteropods that find their station about high-tide mark are able to live for considerable periods out of the water, notwithstanding the fact that they are fully equipped with gills and not possessed of lungs. Indeed, there is one large family of prosobranchs (the *Cyclostomatidæ*) that has become entirely terrestrial in habit, its members having lost their gills and acquired lungs, but their organization otherwise is so essentially that of the prosobranchs that they have never been considered as pulmonates.

The main difference between these two orders of marine gasteropods is that in the prosobranchs the breathing-organs (the gills) are placed in a position forward of the heart, and the degree of torsion (page 330) characteristic of this molluscan class has been continued until the auricle of the heart is in front of the ventricle. There is always a shell, usually spiral, and, with few exceptions, an operculum. In the opisthobranchs, on the other hand, the relative position of the heart and gills is reversed, and they further differ from the prosobranchs in that the sexes are always united in each individual. The opisthobranchs are not always provided with a shell. One division of the order, known as the "nudibranchs," are entirely naked. These are commonly called the " sea-slugs," and are to be found crawling about the marine vegetation in shallow water, in tide-pools, and on the piling of old docks. Curiously enough, the sea-slugs (see page 354) have no gills at all, but, having lost these apparently essential organs, are enabled to " breathe water " through their skin.   They are wonderfully beautiful creatures, and the collector must not fail to secure some specimens, put them into a jar of sea-water, and watch them expand.

There are other more superficial differences between the prosobranchs and the opisthobranchs, which will enable even a beginner to distinguish them at a glance.   When the latter are possessed of an external shell, it is bulbous, generally glassy, and with a simple lip, the aperture extending the entire length of the shell. Again, the mantle or the propodium of the foot is greatly extended and usually covers the shell almost wholly.

With the exception of the nudibranchs, which are common all along the Atlantic shore, especially north of Cape Cod, there are very few opisthobranchs to be found in American waters.   Their shells are not very abundantly found anywhere, though in Florida there are two or three species which an untrained collector might discover.

Practically all the gasteropod or univalve shells that will be taken by the ordinarily expert collector along the shore are prosobranchs.   This order includes the great majority of marine gasteropods, and is entitled to the distinction of claiming, in the great number of its genera and species, the most startling eccentricities of form and color to be found among the *Mollusca*, if not among all marine invertebrates.

Only those species which are actually abundant on the Atlantic and Pacific shores of the United States, and which are likely to be found by the untrained collector, are selected from the long list of forms which belong to the three faunal regions involved.

ORDER **OPISTHOBRANCHIATA**

SUBORDER **TECTIBRANCHIATA**

To avoid confusion, it is well to keep the systematic table in view :

Class	Orders	Suborders
GASTEROPODA	⎧ **OPISTHOBRANCHIATA** ⎨ **PROSOBRANCHIATA** ⎩ **PULMONATA**	⎰ **TECTIBRANCHIATA** ⎱ **NUDIBRANCHIATA**

PLATE LXV.

Bulla occidentalis, enlarged.   Bulla nebulosa.
Lottia gigantea, inside view.   Fissurella alternata.

As has already been remarked, shell-bearing opisthobranchs are not abundantly represented in number of species in North American waters. South of Cape Cod, in muddy bays and well-sheltered places, the little shell, *Haminea solitaria*, may, however, often be found in considerable numbers.

GENUS *Haminea*

H. solitaria. Like all external opisthobranch tests, the shell of this species is thin and fragile, and would appear to be of small importance to the creature it only partially protects. It is devoid of spire, is shining bluish-white, sometimes brownish in color, and is marked with revolving grooves, which, being cut across by irregular growth-lines, give its surface a faintly decussated appearance. The aperture is as long as the shell; the columella is incurved. This little species is especially abundant in shallow water about Vineyard Sound and in Peconic Bay.

Haminea solitaria.

GENUS *Bulla*

B. occidentalis. This species, which is found in the waters of Florida on all sandy beaches, is a relative of the Northern species just described. The shell is larger than that of *Haminea solitaria*, and has a color-pattern of mottled or clouded reddish-brown on a white foundation. There is no spire; there is a pit in place of an apex; and the aperture extends the full length of the shell. To the naked eye the surface appears smooth and shining. It is an exceedingly variable species, occurring all through the West Indies, but not north of Florida. The shores of the keys along the west coast of Florida are often strewn with these shells after storms. The animal, like all the shell-bearing opisthobranchs, is very large as compared with the shell, and the large mantle folds recurve upward, almost completely hiding the shell from view. (Plate LXV.)

B. nebulosa. This is one of the largest and finest species of the family *Bullidæ*. It is found on the coast of California south of San Francisco. The shell is much larger than that of either of the Atlantic species mentioned above, but very closely resembles them in outline, although it is built upon a more generous plan and is more richly painted. It is brownish, mottled with white and yellow patches, and is very suggestive of certain kinds of birds' eggs. The animals have a greatly extended mantle which almost completely envelops the shell. The foot is extremely large, with great wing-like developments upon each side, called parapodia. Some species of *Bulla* have been seen to swim by means of the lazy flapping of the parapodia. (Plate LXV.)

SEA-HARES

Closely allied to these outer-shell-bearing opisthobranchs is a large and important group of tectibranchs, known as "sea-hares." They have a mantle so greatly developed that it actually covers the shell, and its edges unite and fuse over the top. The shell, in consequence, having almost ceased to be of use as a protection, has degenerated into a mere horny plate, and has lost all resemblance to the ordinary gasteropod shell. Having practically lost its protective office and become a mere internal plate, it is quite probable that it will in time wholly disappear. The gills of the sea-hares are concealed under a flap of the mantle, their position being posterior to the heart. The most conspicuous representative of this type of tectibranchs in the United States is the following:

Genus *Aplysia*

A. Wilcoxii. This species appears at times in vast numbers in the waters of Florida, until the sea may truly be said to be fairly alive with them. They swim lazily with a waving motion of the parapodia. They disappear as mysteriously as they come, and for months not a specimen will be seen. There is a variety of this Floridian *Aplysia* which occurs at Cape May, but no sea-hares are to be found north of that point. The tropical Pacific furnishes an astonishing wealth of these creatures, belonging to many genera and species, and among them are some of the most beautiful of the invertebrate animals.

Suborder NUDIBRANCHIATA

The opisthobranchs are divided into two suborders, the second of which is called *Nudibranchiata*. The name is well chosen and very suggestive, for it means "naked or exposed gills"; but this anatomical feature is only one of the peculiarities of this suborder. The nudibranchs are commonly known as "sea-slugs"; for, like the land-slugs, which are also true mollusks, they possess no shell at all. That they at one time carried a shell is evident from the fact that they are born with a rudimentary testaceous covering, which soon afterward disappears.

A striking peculiarity of the nudibranchs is that the conventional molluscan mantle is not usually apparent. Instead of seeing the usual flaps or folds of the mantle which more or less encircle mollusks, and which one seems to have a right to expect, they are entirely absent, and the body of the sea-slug assumes in consequence a worm-like appearance. Other notable features of the nudibranchs are the great number of tentacular processes that usually project from the dorsal region of the animal, and, in many of the genera, an entire absence of gills. When the gills are present, as is the case in several of the nudibranch families, they are not placed along the side of the animal, where one would naturally look for them, but are arranged in the form of a rosette of plume-like processes situated in the posterior dorsal region, or, in other words, on the animal's back.

Nudibranchs are commonly to be found all along the Atlantic and Pacific coasts of North America, and more especially in the colder waters north of Cape Cod. They are essentially littoral, and live upon algæ in shallow water, upon eel-grass in sheltered places, and in tide-pools, where there is more or less vegetation. They crawl about the fronds of algæ, or swim, foot upward, with a gentle and undulating motion, or, when caught between tides, may be seen clinging to the under surface of rocks. Protective resemblances have been so remarkably developed in the nudibranchs that they are not always easy to discover; indeed, one may actually be looking at one for some time without suspecting it to be other than some torn fragment of seaweed.

There are many species belonging to several genera which frequent the Maine and Massachusetts coasts, but those most likely to be encountered are the following:

Genus *Dendronotus*

D. arborescens. This species is about one inch long and variable in color, but is usually reddish-brown or rose. There are no tentacles, but in their place are two antler-like appendages pointing forward and branched like a tree. All along the back are two rows of these curiously branched processes, which give to the animal the appearance of a plant. These *cerata*, or dorsal papillæ, are delicately transparent, contractile, and richly colored. The function of these papillæ is not fully known. As the animal has no specialized breathing-organs, it is reasonable to suppose that respiration is carried on through the outer skin and perhaps all over the surface of these branched papillæ. The liver, which in most nudibranchs is extremely large and completely surrounds the stomach, in *Dendronotus* also extends into these dorsal cerata, so that they may have some sort of digestive function.

Dendronotus arborescens.

Genus *Æolis*

Æ. papillosa. This is probably the commonest nudibranch upon the North Atlantic coast, and it occurs as frequently in European waters. It may readily be found clinging to stones, algæ, the piling of wharves, eel-grass, etc., in bays or in rocky tide-pools. The color is

Æolis papillosa.

yellowish-gray to orange, with purplish or olive spots. The cerata are very numerous, and cover the dorsal portion of the animal save for an open space along the middle of the back. There are two sets of tentacles, the two dorsal and the two simple labial tentacles. The foot tapers behind to a sharp point, and is truncate in front. As in *Dendronotus*, the liver is diffused into the cerata, which in *Æolis* are simple tubular processes without the branching character of those of the former. Both species lay their eggs in a gelatinous, bobbin-like cord, which is hung in festoons over rocks or upon zoöphytes, or at times they wind the cord in a coil upon the surfaces of stones. When the young first hatch out, they are provided with a glassy nautiloid shell, a fact which would indicate that at some remote period they were, like most mollusks, provided with a shell. *Æolis* swims in an inverted position, and is at times exceedingly active. It is very variable in coloring and in the number of cerata.

Genus *Doris*

D. bilamellata. In *Doris* we find a quite different type of nudibranch from that presented by the two genera *Dendronotus* and *Æolis*. In one there were numerous branched cerata or dorsal papillæ, in the other many plain cerata, and in neither case were there any specialized

breathing-organs. In *Doris*, however, there are no dorsal papillæ at all, the back being covered with calcareous spicules, which form a sort of secondary shell. There is a cir-
clet, or rosette, of retractile plume-like gills, or branchiæ, placed in the middle of the back posteriorly. There are various species of *Doris*, and of closely allied genera belonging to the family *Dorididæ*, which are to be found along the New England coast in tide-pools and among

rocks. Those seen by the writer never appeared to be other than very sluggish creatures, and proved to be rather unsatisfactory tenants of the aquarium.

When discovered at low tide upon moist seaweed or stones, or when disturbed in the water, nudibranchs often appear like small lumps of jelly-like tissue, without a single attractive feature. It is only when they are placed in a jar of sea-water and left un-molested for a few moments that they unfold their beauties to the view. On the Pacific coast there are numerous species of nudi-branchs, occupying corresponding shore stations and exhibiting the same degree of high coloration. There are over a thousand species of sea-slugs scattered about the various seas. They find their greatest development in tropical waters, and for brilliancy of tint and variation in form are unequaled by any other class of animal life, save perhaps the butterflies.

ORDER **PROSOBRANCHIATA**

To this exceedingly large and comprehensive order of gastero-pods belong the great majority of univalve mollusks. In point of number of genera and species and in abundance of individuals, the prosobranchs probably exceed all the other orders of mollusks combined. They may be called the typical gasteropods, the shell being univalvular and generally spiral, and the animal ex-hibiting the singular torsion of the visceral mass which has placed the breathing-organs forward of the heart. They are provided with an operculum (placed upon the posterior dorsal portion of the foot), which is used to close the aperture of the shell against enemies when the animal retires within its fortress. They are all marine except a very few families, which, supposedly of marine derivation, have become terrestrial in habit.

The prosobranchs are further subdivided into suborders according to certain peculiarities of the heart and breathing-organs. There is a group of these prosobranchs which gives evidence of an inferior degree of that visceral torsion which is always found in the gasteropods. In this group, or suborder, the heart has two auricles, and there is a pair of gills instead of only a single one. Other internal organs are paired just as they were represented to be in the schematic mollusk. This group also seems to show its primitive character in the want of a proboscis and a siphon, or, in some families, by having the ventricle of the heart traversed by the intestinal canal, just as in the lower class of mollusks, which includes the clams and oysters. For the most part the shells of this group are not typically spiral, but are patelliform, shield-like coverings, with only a suggestion of a spiral form at the very tip of the apex. This group of primitive prosobranchs is included in the following suborder:

SUBORDER **DIATOCARDIA**

This suborder is named from the presence of two auricles in the heart.

FAMILY **ACMÆIDÆ**

The first family to be noted is the *Acmæidæ*. Its principal genus, *Acmæa*, is well represented on both the east and the west coast of the United States.

GENUS *Acmæa*

A. testudinalis. This species is found in vast numbers all along the New England shore, clinging to the rocks between tides. They are usually called limpets. The shell is solid, conical, with an oval outline, and with no trace of a spiral form in the adult. When the shell is thoroughly cleaned, it generally presents a mottled coloration of pale green, brown, and white. Inside it is white and nacreous, with a large brown area under the apex. The animal has a powerful foot, by means of which it is enabled to cling to a rock with great strength. In order to dislodge it, it is necessary to approach carefully, and, taking the creature unawares, quickly slip a broad knife-blade under the foot, otherwise it is quite impossible to tear it from its resting-place. *A. testudinalis* lives entirely between tides, and ranges from the northernmost waters to New York. It feeds upon algæ and is a very sluggish animal. It has been said to leave its resting-place and wander about in search of food, returning to its original and usual spot when the tide begins to ebb. (Page 343.)

Acmœa testudinalis, var. *alveus*.

A. testudinalis, variety ***alveus.*** This variety is smaller, more fragile, and oblong. It lives upon cel-grass, its oblong shell being adapted to the narrow leaves of the grass. The coloration is brighter — reddish-brown spots on a white surface. It is exceedingly common on the New England coast.

A. mitra. On the Pacific coast there are a number of acmæas. *A. mitra* is often found dead upon the beaches. It is conical in form and pure creamy-white in color. It looks very much like a clown's pointed cap.

A. patina. This is also very abundant in California. Outside it is dark in color and is often incrusted with mineral deposits. Within there is a dark ring around the edge, then a zone of bluish-white, and a patch of brown just beneath the apex.

GENUS *Lottia*

L. gigantea. This is the largest of the California limpets. Specimens three inches long have been found. The outer surface of the shell is rough and brownish in color. The apex is near one end. Within it is almost black, shining, lustrous, with a horseshoe-shaped muscle-scar under the apex. The color is bluish and brown. (Plate LXV.)

FAMILY FISSURELLIDÆ

This is an extensive family, including several genera and a number of species, commonly known as keyhole-limpets. In the general form of the shell they closely resemble the true limpets, the *Acmœidœ*, except that they have a hole, or rather a slit, in the shell just back of the apex. Often this slit is so long that it has entirely removed the apex of the conical shell.

GENUS *Fissurella*

F. alternata, F. barbadensis. These species occur upon the southern shores of the United States, the latter, however, being confined to extreme southern Florida. *F. barbadensis* has heavy longitudinal ribs and is light green within, with a rosy circle about the apical perforation. (Plate LXV.)

GENUS *Glyphis*

G. aspersa. One of the numerous species belonging to this family which are found on the west coast of the United States. It is about one and a half inches long, grayish-white, with sharply raised longitudinal ridges, slightly rayed, crossed by revolving ribs, which give to the outer surface a decussated appearance. The apex is forward of the center, and is entirely replaced by a round perforation. The edge is wrinkled, and within smooth and white.

GENUS *Lucapina*

L. crenulata. The largest of the keyhole-limpets; the shell is often four inches in length, while the animal, with its huge yellowish foot and dark-colored mantle, which is thrown back, almost concealing the shell upon its back, is much larger. The apical perforation is very large. Shell flattened, with radiating, rounded, crowded ribs; brownish-white in color; edge crenulated; within pure white. It is found at Monterey, but live specimens are not very frequently seen near the beach. (Plate LXVI.)

FAMILY HALIOTIDÆ

GENUS *Haliotis*

This family is closely allied to the *Fissurellidæ*. The species are known on the Pacific coast by the name of abalone shells, and in England and the Channel Islands as ormers or sea-ears. There are no species of *Haliotis* on the east coast of the United States, but one has recently been dredged at a considerable depth in West Indian waters. This family, with the last, possesses the striking anatomical feature of having the heart traversed by the digestive tract. It also has two gills, the degree of torsion in the visceral mass not being sufficient to have crowded out and destroyed the original right gill. The shell is spiral, but is so greatly flattened, and the body-whorl is so greatly extended, that the shell quite loses the spiral appearance. Along the dorsal side of the shell is a row of holes, through which project numerous tentacular processes from the mantle. The outer surface of the shell, before it is polished, is usually rough and unattractive, but within, when the

animal is removed, it displays a most beautiful and highly colored
nacreous surface.   The spot near the center of the inner shell
surface where the muscles of the foot were attached is usually
most brilliantly colored.   The shell of the abalone is susceptible
of taking a very high degree of polish, and is extensively used in
commerce for colored mother-of-pearl and for inlaid work.   *Haliotis* is a vegetable-feeding genus.   They cling with great tenacity
to rocks about low tide, and it requires skill to remove them without breaking the shell.   There are several species in California.
The Chinese use the abalone for food, and have waged a persistent war upon the family along the Pacific coast until the specimens are not nearly as common as formerly.   They are also eaten
in France and in Japan.

H. splendens.   The largest and perhaps the most attractive in
appearance of the Californian species.   Speaking of this beautiful shell,
Professor Keep says: " Within, a whole rainbow is condensed in one of
the magnificent shells, though the shades of green are most conspicuous.
The coloring in the center is particularly fine, resembling a peacock's
tail.   There are about six open holes near one side of the shell, and its
length is about the same number of inches." (Plate LXVI.)
H. rufescens.   A large abalone, which sometimes attains a length of
eight or nine inches.   It is red in color, with three open holes in the
body-whorl.   The outer portion of the shell is usually incrusted with
mineral deposit and overgrown with vegetation.
H. cracherodii.   Very dark green without, with five to nine holes;
length from one to six inches; spire exceedingly short.   Common on the
Californian coast in crevices of rocks at low tide.

FAMILY **TROCHIDÆ**

This is one of the largest and most interesting families of the
Mollusca.   It contains many apparently widely separated genera
and a host of species, which for the most part are littoral, the
majority actually living between tide-marks.   The typical trochid
shell is top-shaped or pyramidal, having a broad base and many
closely wound flat whorls terminating in a sharp apex.   All the
trochids are nacreous within the aperture—a character which is
constant throughout the family.   The animal has but one gill
(the left), a short snout, and often frontal lobes on the head.
The edge of the mantle or the epipodial line of the foot is usually
ornamented with from three to five cirri.   The tentacles are

long and slender, with short peduncles for the eyes; the operculum is corneous, with a central nucleus.   The animals are herbivorous, feeding upon algæ.   The trochids are essentially tropical
shells, and the most of the genera which are comprised in the
family are only to be encountered in the warm waters of the
Pacific and Indian oceans.   Some forms are very beautiful, and
frequently are used as mantel ornaments, and the shells of one
little species, which is opalescent in its coloring, are still extensively gathered in the East Indies, to be polished and strung like
pearls in necklaces.

Genus *Margarita*

On the Atlantic coast north of Cape Cod the trochids are represented by the genus *Margarita*, with five or six species.   The
shells are small, thin, and globosely depressed, with smooth or
transversely striated whorls.   The aperture is nearly circular,
with a simple lip.

M. cinerea.   This species has several prominent revolving ridges
upon the upper side of the whorls, with finer ones on the base.   Very

Margarita cinerea.

fine growth-lines cover the entire shell.   It ranges all along
the coast north of Cape Cod, but is not usually found between
tides.   The writer has dredged many specimens in shallow
water at Eastport and Bar Harbor.

M. helicina.   A thinner and more globose species than the
last, with a translucent, shining, smooth surface of a yellowish or olive color.   *M. helicina* is very fond of the leaves of
Laminaria, and is often found clinging to them when
storms have torn these great algæ from the bottom and
cast them upon the shore.   At Bar Harbor they are common upon the eel-grass in Rodicks Weir.   This species can
generally be distinguished by its iridescent, metallic luster.

Margarita helicina.

M. undulata.   A commoner species, perhaps, than
either of the preceding, sometimes found on the rocks of sheltered

Margarita undulata.

coves at exceptionally low tides.   Judging from the number
often to be found in the stomachs of fishes, they must be considered excellent food by the cod and its allied species which
thrive along the Maine coast.   No doubt millions of *M. undulata*
are yearly destroyed in this way.   The shell is depressed,
with four rounded whorls, a flattish base, and a large umbilical
opening.   In color it varies from rose-red to brown.   The surface is decorated with numerous revolving raised lines placed at uniform distances.
Just below the suture the body-whorl is somewhat undulated with short
folds.   Height three tenths of an inch, base four tenths of an inch.

Genus *Calliostoma*

This genus is better represented on the Pacific coast of the United States than upon the Atlantic. It comprises a series of marvelously beautiful shells, often exquisitely colored. They are regularly conical or pyramidal in shape, with flattened bases. One never tires in the search for calliostomas. They are not common enough to cause one to lose interest, and whenever a good specimen is captured it seems as though one had found some gem cut and polished by nature's skilful hand and prepared for a place of honor in the cabinet.

C. occidentale. The only species of this genus found on the northeast coast. It is larger than *Margarita cinerea,* but somewhat resembles it. It is shining nacreous within and without, and has strong revolving ribs, the upper one on each whorl often being broken into a circular row of white dots. The lip is crenulated. This very pretty species is not likely to be met with upon the shore, but may be dredged in shallow water on gravelly bottoms along the Maine coast. Height about one half of an inch.

Calliostoma occidentale.

C. jujubinum. A species which occurs in the waters of Florida. Its form is almost that of a true pyramid. The sutures can scarcely be distinguished. The shell is marked by brown and purplish-red spots on a white background, and has numerous revolving ribs broken into rows of white dots like little glazed beads. The umbilicus is funnel-shaped and wide. In Tampa Bay this shell is frequently found on sponges, and may sometimes be gathered on the beach after storms, even as far north as Hatteras. There are as many as twenty species of this genus in American Atlantic waters, but they are either rare or have deep-water stations.

C. annulatum. A remarkable species of *Calliostoma,* found in California. The whorls are adorned with revolving rows of raised dots, and the sutures are frescoed in exquisite purple. This beautiful species lives upon seaweed, and on pleasant days comes to the surface of the water. It can then be collected from a boat by drawing in quantities of seaweed. It is very unlikely that the collector will ever find a specimen upon the beach, for the shell is too fragile to withstand the rough handling of the waves. Length one inch.

C. canaliculatum. The largest member of this genus to be found in American waters. It resembles the last species in form, but lacks the purple sutures. The revolving ribs are very numerous and prominent. There is no umbilicus. Length one to one and a half inches. Found on the Pacific coast.

C. costatum. A heavier shell than the preceding, with somewhat more rounded whorls. Reddish-brown in color; numerous revolving ridges; no umbilicus; about three quarters of an inch in length. It is found in rocky places, and sometimes in considerable numbers, just at low-tide mark. Found in California.

Genus *Chlorostoma*

This genus is represented in California by several species, the commonest of which is probably *C. funebrale*—a doleful name, no doubt given on account of the jet-black color.

C. funebrale. The shell is thick and strong, like most between-tide species, which are constantly exposed to the buffeting of the waves. It is to be found in countless thousands upon rocks exposed at low tide, and may be gathered at any time except full flood-tide, like the littorinas and purpuras of the east coast. Within the aperture the surface is nacreous and greenish in tint; the last whorl is drawn in, like gathers, at the suture. The umbilicus is closed. There is a white nodule at the base of the lip of the columella. Length one half of an inch to one inch. (Plate LXVII.)

C. brunneum. This species is brown, as its name would indicate, and there is greenish nacre within the aperture. It lives upon kelp, or upon rocks at very low tide. Length about an inch. (Plate LXVI.)

Genus *Trochiscus*

T. norrisi. A flattened shell with rounded, dome-like spire and obtuse apex; a fairly common species. It has a wide, deep umbilicus and a sharp lip. It is of a rich brown color, with dark chestnut about the umbilical region and greenish-white within the umbilicus; there is a band of dark olive-green about the inner margin of the lip. The shell is about two inches in diameter and of a somewhat greater height. The operculum is multispiral, with a central nucleus, and is shaggy and rough. Like all other trochids, it feeds upon algæ. It is often found upon the beach after violent storms. Found in California, south of San Francisco. (Plate LXVI.)

Genus *Livona*

L. pica. This large and interesting trochid is a West Indian species which sometimes occurs in Florida. It lives about coral reefs and rocky shores, attaching itself in vast numbers to the rocks. This shell is a favorite refuge for large hermit-crabs. It is a curious sight in certain of the West India islands to see a *Livona pica* shell scrambling up a tree, looking very much out of place upon the back of some terrestrially inclined crustacean. When well cleaned it is a beautiful shell, with black wavy lines over a greenish-white nacreous f   dation. The animal has a row of waving cirri upon each side of ⁺he mantle, and long, slender tentacles. It is largely used as an article of diet in the West Indies and Central America. (Plate LXVII.)

Family TURBINIDÆ

This family is very closely allied to the trochids, the most striking difference being in the operculum, which in the *Turbinidæ* is calcareous and usually smooth and very convex on the outside.

PLATE LXVI.

1, Lucapina crenulata.   3, Chlorostoma brunneum.
2, Haliotis splendens.   4, Neritina reclivata, enlarged.
5. Trochiscus norrisi.

PLATE LXVII.

Livona pica, reduced.
Nerita peleronta.
Nerita tessellata.

Turbo castaneus, enlarged.
Chlorostoma funebrale.

The shells are nacreous within, and the animal, with its rows of waving cirri upon each side, is very suggestive of *Trochus*. They are, for the most part, shallow-water or littoral forms.

GENUS *Turbo*

T. castaneus. This species has a range as far north as Cape Hatteras, and is especially abundant at Tampa, on the west coast of Florida. The peculiar operculum is sufficient to identify the genus at once. One variety of this species has a crenulated shoulder upon the body-whorl and is referred to as *Turbo crenulatus.* A series of intermediate forms establishes the specific identity of the two varieties. (Plate LXVII.)

FAMILY NERITIDÆ

The *Neritidæ* are strictly littoral forms, almost entirely confined to the warmer waters of tropical seas. The animal preserves the usual diatocardian features—has a short snout and long tentacles. Unlike the trochids and *Turbo*, it has no cirri along the epipodial margin. The shells are peculiarly shaped, the spire being greatly flattened and scarcely noticeable on account of the unduly large development of the body-whorl; thus the shell takes on a decidedly patelliform appearance. It is without an umbilicus. In the principal genus *Nerita* the outer lip is sharp on the edge, but greatly thickened just within.

GENUS *Nerita*

N. peleronta. This shell has two teeth on the wide, flat columellar lip, and about them is a blotch of red, suggesting blood. The common name of this shell, " bleeding-tooth," is very appropriate. Found in southern Florida. (Plate LXVII.)
N. tessellata is a smaller species, with heavy revolving ribs, and is further decorated with transverse oblique black lines. The operculum is calcareous. Both of these species have the habit of absorbing the entire inner portion of their shells. They belong to the West Indian fauna, and occur in great numbers on rocky or coral shore stations. They also may be found on the east Florida coast, well to the south. A third species, *N. versicolor,* often occurs, associated with the other two. It is somewhat smaller than the others and can easily be distinguished by the four teeth on the columellar lip, the edge of the columella being convex. (Plate LXVII.)

GENUS *Neritina*

The genus *Neritina* is very closely allied to the last, having quite the same form of shell; but it is usually more globular and variously ornamented by bright spots or zigzag lines of coloration. The neritinas have acquired the habit of ascending rivers, until they have become almost wholly a brackish- or fresh-water genus. The metropolis of this genus is in the South Sea Islands, where it attains a wonderful development in the clear running streams of the volcanic islands.

N. reclivata. A very pretty olive-green species, with very fine, wavy, longitudinal lines of coloration, found in almost all Floridian streams above the action of the tide. The nacre of the columella and within the aperture is bluish-green, and the operculum is rich olive. (Plate LXVI.)

N. viridis. A small, intensely green species, which, unlike most neritinas, is strictly marine. It belongs to the great West Indian faunal province, but is occasionally found upon the shores of Florida and of Texas.

The prosobranch gasteropods thus far considered (belonging to the suborder *Diatocardia*) all show by their anatomical structure that the process of visceral torsion, though carried very far within them, has not been complete enough to crowd out and finally destroy one of each of the paired organs. Both auricles of the heart (with some exceptions) were left intact.

Suborder MONOTOCARDIA

In this the second suborder of the prosobranch gasteropods, the twisting visceral process has been carried to the extreme. The heart has but one auricle. There is but one gill (on the left side), and this is attached to the inner side of the mantle flap. In other respects the presence of certain specialized organs would probably indicate that gasteropods belonging to this suborder are a step higher in the scale of life than those which belong to the *Diatocardia.*

Family JANTHINIDÆ

Genus *Janthina*

The genus *Janthina* has an exceedingly thin and semi-transparent shell, deep violet in color on the base and lighter blue on the spire. An interesting feature of this genus is the mode of depositing the ova. The female exudes from a gland in the foot a glutinous secretion which hardens in water, and, being filled with air-bubbles, constitutes a float. On the under side of this are deposited the eggs in rows of little capsules. While attached to this float it is impossible for a *Janthina* to sink, and hence it is that so many of these creatures are sacrificed in onshore gales of wind.

J. fragilis. The shell of this species is so brittle and fragile that it is very clearly not adapted to a life near shore. It is in reality a pelagic species which is occasionally blown ashore during easterly gales along

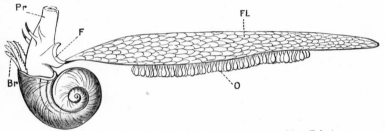

Janthina fragilis: FL, float ; O, ova ; Pr, proboscis ; Br, branchiæ ; F, foot.

the Atlantic coast of the United States. Vast numbers of these pretty creatures are sometimes encountered far out at sea, floating quietly on the surface. When storms drive them upon the beach, they become utterly helpless ; since their foot is not adapted for crawling upon the sand, they soon perish, and their brittle shells are demolished by the surf. In Florida the beaches are sometimes fairly lined with *Janthina* shells, which make a band of purple along the high-tide mark as far as the eye can reach ; then it may be years before they again appear. (Plate LXVIII.)

Family **SCALIDÆ**

Genus *Scala*

The shells of *Scala* have such a peculiar scheme of decoration that once seen they can never be mistaken. They are generally pure white, with well-rounded whorls, all of which are crossed at even distances by greatly elevated and smooth ribs. Each rib represents a rest-period, when the creature thickened the rim of the shell-aperture. The aperture is generally round, with a continuous lip. The animal has a retractile proboscis and long, slender tentacles with eyes at the outer bases, and is a predaceous, carnivorous creature. Some Asiatic species of this genus, remark-

able for their beauty and rarity, have been greatly prized by collectors.   A single specimen of the now well-known *S. pretiosa* of
China has been sold for two hundred dollars—a fancy price, indeed,
for a shell which can now be bought for a dollar!   There are
over fifty species of *Scala* on the Atlantic coast, but most of them
are either rare or belong to a zone of deeper water; there are,
however, four or five species which are exceedingly common.

*Scala line-
ata.*

S. lineata.   A species which ranges from Hatteras to New
England.   It has about eight whorls, and is slightly brownish
in color.   The ribs are robust and not greatly elevated; there
are from seventeen to nineteen on the body-whorl.   The shell
is sometimes painted with a few revolving brownish lines.

S. multistriata.   The transverse ribs are much smaller but
very numerous; the small spaces between them are
marked with many fine revolving lines.   Found
from Cape Cod southward.

S. groenlandica.   Essentially an arctic species,
which has found its way down to the New England
coast.   It is readily distinguished by the flattened,
coarsely rounded, revolving ribs, which follow
the volutions of the spire.   Over them are the usual transverse heavy ribs peculiar to this genus.

*Scala multistri-
ata.*

S. angulata.   The whorls touch one another only by the
ribs, of which there are nine to each volution.   This species
has a remarkably wide range, occurring from Cape
Cod to southern Florida.   (Plate LXVIII.)

These four species vary from one half of an inch to one inch
in length.   All of them are found on the beach after storms or
may be dredged in shallow water near the shore.

FAMILY NATICIDÆ

*Scala groen-
landica.*

This large and interesting family is well represented
in the Atlantic waters of the United States, but its more
beautiful members live in the tropics.   The New England
and New Jersey species are dull in color, but offer much of interest
to the collector and student.   The foot is enormously large, and
carries in front a great shield-like fleshy process, which curves back
over the head of the animal and serves as a plow in pushing its way
through the heavy wet sand of the beach.   When the creature is
thus seen extended in the act of crawling, one wonders how it is possible for it to withdraw so great an amount of body into its shell;
but if it is suddenly seized or irritated, it will quickly demon-

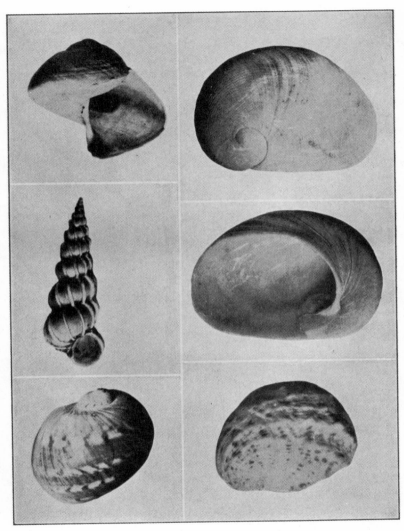

PLATE LXVIII.

Janthina fragilis.	Sigaretus perspectivus, upper side.
Scala angulata, enlarged.	Sigaretus perspectivus, under side.
Natica canrena.	Crepidula aculeata.

strate its ability to hide itself completely within its house and to close the door very effectively by means of its operculum. The eyes seem to be wanting, or they are concealed under the skin of the head. The shell is usually quite large, with a depressed spire and well-rounded whorls—especially the body-whorl, which appears to be greatly swollen. The umbilicus is usually open and moderately large, the lip simple.

GENUS *Polynices (Lunatia, Natica).*

P. heros (generally referred to as *Lunatia* or *Natica heros*). One of the commonest large shells and one of the most characteristic species of the New England and New Jersey littoral fauna. It is exceedingly common along the Long Island shore, where it may be found on the open beach, in pools with a sandy bottom left by the receding tide. It is usually partially and frequently wholly buried in the sand. The umbilicus is open and large, the operculum corneous, and the shell heavy and ashy-white to brownish, with (when young) a yellowish epidermis. Its length is from two to four inches. It has no ornamentation whatever. *P. heros* is a most voracious creature and spends its time in hunting for flesh — either alive or dead — to devour. It feeds upon dead fish, or upon other mollusks whose shell it is able to pierce by means of its radula, making a little round hole through which it sucks out the flesh from within. The curious egg-cases of this species have already been referred to. (See Plate I.) It glues together particles of sand into the form of a basin with the bottom knocked out and broken on one side. In the gelatinous substance of this basin it deposits its eggs in a regular order. These hatch out in midsummer. Egg-cases of this kind can always be found wherever *Polynices* lives. For a long time naturalists were greatly puzzled by these curious things, and their blunders are recorded in earlier works, where these egg-cases have been elaborately described as living animals belonging to various invertebrate orders. The largest and best specimens of *P. heros* are to be found south of Cape Cod. (Page 343.)

P. triseriata. A small shell of exactly the same shape as *P. heros*, but decorated with three revolving series of bluish or chestnut spots. It is pretty well determined that this so-called species is only the young of *P. heros*. It is very abundant all along the coast.

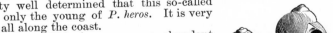

Polynices triseriata, young; *Polynices triseriata,* older specimen.

P. duplicata. This is even more abundant than *P. heros*. It has a flatter shell, with an obtuse apex and dome-like spire. The umbilicus is partly or wholly closed by a thick, callous, shelly process thrown off from the columellar lip, and is chestnut in color. The surface of the shell is smooth, often polished, ashy-white below and light chestnut above. The operculum is corneous. The length of the shell varies in different localities from one half of an inch to about two inches; the breadth slightly exceeds the length. *P. duplicata* has a very extensive range, from the Gulf of Mexico to Newfoundland. The largest and finest specimens are found in the vicinity of New York and at Hatteras. In Florida they are usually smaller. This species cannot be confounded with any other upon our coast on account of the heavy callous deposit over the umbilicus. Its habits are similar to those of *P. heros.*

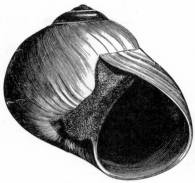

Polynices duplicata.

Natica clausa. A Northern species which is fairly abundant on the Maine coast. It has a shelly operculum, and the umbilicus is neatly closed by a pure white, shining callosity. Its length is about one half an inch, its color livid white to light brown, white within.

Natica clausa.

The calcareous operculum at once determines this shell. This species (as well as the following one) has retained the generic name of *Natica* because of the shelly operculum, as explained below.

N. canrena. One of the handsomer species of *Natica*, which occurs in Florida. Sometimes it is seen as far north as Hatteras. The shell is white, with bars of light chestnut circling the whorls, and with zigzag lines of darker purplish hue crossing them. The base of the shell is white. The aperture is large and flaring, and is purplish within. The umbilicus is partially closed by an entering callous plug. The operculum is calcareous, with eccentric, deeply cut grooves. Found in sandy stations just about low-water mark. (Plate LXVIII.)

P. lewisii. A species which occurs on the west coast of the United States. It resembles its New England relative *P. heros* very closely. *P. lewisii* is a Northern species, and does not range south of Oregon. Professor Keep mentions one specimen of the size of a six-inch globe, but such dimensions are very unusual. A good-sized specimen need not exceed four inches in height.

P. recluziana. A species well known on the southern coast of California. The umbilicus is closed by a thick, highly polished white callosity, and the general shape of the shell is strongly suggestive of the common east-coast species *P. duplicata.* A large specimen is about two inches in diameter.

[There has been much confusion in the generic nomenclature of this family. The old name *Natica* once did service for all the species; then the names *Lunatia,* *Neverita,* and *Polynices* were applied to certain special forms; but it has been wisely proposed by conchologists to use the name *Natica* for those forms having a shelly operculum, and to adopt the name *Polynices* for those having a corneous operculum. *Lunatia* and *Neverita* have become subgenera of *Polynices.*]

GENUS *Sigaretus*

A very interesting species of this genus occurs on the east coast, sparingly in New Jersey, but very abundantly south of Hatteras. *Sigaretus* is a modified *Natica*. The spire is flattened and minute. The body-whorl, being greatly expanded, gives a wide, flaring, oblique aperture. The shell is ear-shaped and white, with fine revolving lines. There is no umbilicus. The operculum is small and rudimentary. The animal is large, with an enormous foot and greatly developed propodium, and is a sand-dweller. The common east-coast form is *S. perspectivus.* (Plate LXVIII.)

FAMILY CAPULIDÆ

GENUS *Crepidula*

C. fornicata. All collectors of mollusks on the Atlantic coast sooner or later encounter this exceedingly common species adhering to oyster-shells or scallops, and often to other large live shells. It is cast upon the beach along the entire length of the Atlantic coast. The shell is obliquely oval, dull whitish in color, and either smooth or rough or even ribbed, according to the nature of the surface to which it clings. The spire is almost entirely suppressed, the little inconspicuous apex being turned to one side and closely pressed down against the body of the shell. When looking into the interior of the shell one is reminded of a boat, for the upper portion of the aperture is covered by a horizontal shelly partition, called the diaphragm, a space being left below which would correspond

Crepidula fornicata.

to the forecastle of a ship. The "stern" is round, and the "bow" is suggestively pointed.

C. plana. In this species the shell is white and flat, or slightly concave. Although it is pointed at the "bow" end and square at the "stern," the nautical resemblance stops there, because, being flat, there are no swelling sides and bow. The diaphragm is about one half the length of the shell, convex, shining, white, and translucent. *C. plana* lives generally within the aperture of large dead shells. It has a wide range, from Maine to Florida.

Crepidula plana.

C. aculeata. A common Floridian species which has a remarkable range, being found in nearly all the tropical and semi-tropical waters of the world. It is smaller than *C. fornicata*, is reddish-brown with a white diaphragm, and has several radiating ribs on the back, which are inclined to be nodulous. (Plate LXVIII.)

On the Pacific coast the following species are found: *C. adunca,* with a strongly recurved apex, and less than one inch long; *C. rugosa,* rough, brown, with the apex lying on the edge of the shell, and one inch in length; *C. navicelloides,* almost identical with the east-coast *C. plana. C. aculeata* also appears.

Genus *Crucibulum*

Crucibulum striatum, from above.

Crucibulum has a peculiar rounded shield-like form, with a very small apex on one side. Within there is a cup-shaped appendage attached by one side to the inner margin of the shell. This latter feature at once determines the genus.

Crucibulum striatum, from below.

C. striatum. This species has radiating riblets, cut by circular lines of growth. No dimension would quite reach an inch. It is a common shell on the Atlantic coast, and will be found adhering to stones and other shells, but it is not, strictly speaking, a littoral species.

C. spinosum. The shell exhibits a strong tendency to spinous processes on its back. Found along the southern part of the California shore.

Family LITTORINIDÆ

Genus *Littorina*

Littorina is probably the most characteristic genus of Northern littoral regions. Together with some of its allied genera it is also, probably, equally characteristic of various tropical littoral faunas all over the world. The family comprises strictly between-the-tides genera and species. Indeed, it is suspected that some species of *Littorina* are making very fair progress toward a terrestrial condition, for they actually live above high-tide mark,—even in the branches of overhanging trees,—and must certainly pass days at a time out of their natural element. That such a transformation is possible need not for a moment be doubted, for there are many land mollusks to-day that give abundant evidence of having been at some past time aquatic or marine species. These changes in nature are constantly going on, and the gradual substitution of a lung for a gill is no very startling metamorphosis.

The littorinas fairly swarm in favorable localities upon all shore stations. In Maine and Massachusetts the bold, rocky coast furnishes a home for several species. Often the rocks at low tide are black with them; the algæ that cling in wet masses to the exposed rocks are alive with them. One cannot walk about in such localities without crushing hundreds of specimens. Sometimes they will be found clinging in clusters upon the piling of old wharves, or crawling about the bottom at or about the low-tide mark. The best specimens of *Littorina* are found in stations where they are bathed twice a day by pure, uncontaminated sea-water; those living near the mouths of streams, or where the water is brackish or impure, are usually small and degenerate. They are vegetable feeders, and have received the common name of "periwinkles." In Great Britain they are used among the poorer classes for food. The animal has a short, broad muzzle, and eyes at the outer bases of the tentacles. The foot is longitudinally grooved, and there is a rudimentary siphonal fold in the mantle. The shells are turbinated, usually heavy, few-whorled, and with a round aperture.

L. litorea. This is supposed to be an importation from the Old World—to have come over by way of Iceland and Greenland, and then to have migrated down the Labrador coast. For many years Cape Cod formed a barrier to its advance, but now the species is abundant at Newport, and is reported at New York. It occurs on the Maine coast in astonishing numbers, living in vast colonies on the rocks exposed at low tide. The shell is thick, imperforate (no umbilicus), and usually has flat, spiral ribs. The columella is broad and white; the lip thin and black. The general color varies from black to olive or to dingy gray—sometimes reddish. The operculum is corneous, with the nucleus near the outer edge. Despite the variableness of this very common shell (the variations being chiefly in the height of the spire), it has certain unmistakable characteristics which, once seen, will enable the collector to determine it at once.

Littorina litorea.

L. rudis. A smaller species than the last. It is strong and coarse, with revolving grooves and ribs, or smooth, with interrupted whitish bands and spots. A very common variety of this species is much smaller than the typical form, being about one sixth to one fourth of an inch long, smooth, with white and yellowish spots on olive. It clings to the rocks near high-tide mark, and is usually found attached to its resting-place by a bit of hardened mucus. While the typical *L. rudis* is heavy and banded, with a moderately high spire and no color, this

Littorina rudis.

variety is thinner, with a higher spire and smoother surface, and has a color-scheme of decoration. It would be impossible to disconnect the two, for a large series of specimens will demonstrate beyond doubt, through every minute degree of variation, that the two forms belong to one and the same species. The station of *L. rudis* is much the same as that of *L. litorea*, but the smaller colored variety of *rudis* prefers quieter and more sheltered spots. It is occasionally found on reeds and grasses, on the piling of wharves, on large boulders above the line of algæ, and on algæ. It has been the writer's experience not to find *rudis* and *litorea* associated together.

L. palliata. A low-spired, globular shell with a large, tumid, smooth body-whorl. The columella is flattened, curved below, and imperforate. The color is exceedingly variable, but is usually bright, shining olive,

Littorina palliata.

and this is especially the case with those individuals that find their station in the dense masses of algæ that form so conspicuous a feature of a low-tide scene on a rocky New England coast. From pure olive-green to yellow or bright red, with revolving black bands, seems a long chromatic leap, but it is not too great for the Designer of these pretty little globular shells. As a rule, the color of the shell simulates pretty closely that of the seaweed upon which it lives, and inexperienced eyes may easily overlook hundreds of specimens, all within close reach. The banded varieties are less common. The head of the animal is somewhat orange in color, the foot slate. The distinguishing features of this species are the smooth, globular shell, the low spire, the broadly flattened columella, and the orange-colored head of the animal. It is found on *Fucus* between tides, and often associated with *L. rudis*, on the whole coast north of New Jersey. The three preceding species are distinctly boreal in their range, but their place is taken in southern Atlantic waters of the United States by the following exceedingly common species:

L. irrorata. A solid, robust shell, which attains a length of about one inch. It is in many respects suggestive of *L. litorea*, its Northern relative, but the spire is higher, with straighter outlines, and the apex is acute. The surface is ornamented with closely set, revolving ribs; the sutures are indistinct; the lip is thin, though thickened just within; and the color is whitish to pale cinereous greenish, sometimes spotted with broken brownish lines. Within it is white, with a reddish tinge on the columella, and brownish spots on the edge of the lip. This species ranges from Maryland to Texas; its station is between tides.

Littorina irrorata.

L. angulifera. As the last species resembles *L. litorea*, so this other common Southern form resembles a greatly developed and large *L. rudis* of the smoother variety. It has a high-spired shell, with an acute black tip. It has about six whorls, which are variously decorated by wavy, oblique black lines and revolving black lines broken into series of dots and larger spots near the suture. The ground-color varies from yellow to purple. None of the colors are very vivid. Within it is yellowish-white. This species has a much thinner and more delicate shell than any of the littorinas thus far considered. It is common on the piling of wharves and in sheltered nooks everywhere between tides. It is essentially a tropical species of very wide and extended range, but it does not occur north of St. Augustine. At Tampa it has been found in vast numbers. (Plate LXIX.)

The California coast furnishes two more species of *Littorina*. Their station is among the rocks between tides, and their habits are quite the same as those of the east-coast species.

L. scutulata. In this species the color is of various shades, generally dark gray, mottled with white spots. A good-sized specimen measures one half of an inch in length. The spire is high; the columella flattened, broad; the shell is purplish-white within the aperture. (Plate LXIX.)

L. planaxis. Somewhat larger than the last; wider; with a lower spire; grayish in color, sometimes speckled with white; chest nut-brown within. The columella is remarkably flattened, and a portion of the whorl next bordering the columella is excavated as though eaten away by the animal. These two species are often found associated on the rocks. (Plate LXIX.)

Genus *Lacuna*

Closely allied to *Littorina* is the genus *Lacuna*, one species of which, *L. vincta,* is very abundant on the New England coast. A curious and distinguishing feature of this genus is the umbilicus, which forms a lengthened groove along the columella. *L. vincta* rarely exceeds one half of an inch in length, and is thin, with a pointed spire of five whorls. It is either of a uniform horn-color, or purplish, or banded with chestnut. It may best be found upon marine plants in sheltered places, or may sometimes be gathered in quantity from the roots of *Laminaria* washed in by storms.

Lacuna vincta.

Genus *Tectarius*

The specific representatives of this genus are mostly tropical. *T. nodulosus* is abundant in Florida. It is about one half of an inch long, and has the flattened columella and round mouth characteristic of *Littorina*. It is decorated somewhat elaborately by revolving rows of nodules which cover the entire shell. Its station and habits are the same as those of *Littorina.*

Family CERITHIIDÆ

In this family we meet with a somewhat new type of shell— the long, turriculate shell, with many whorls and with a channeled aperture. The *Cerithiidæ* include a large number of genera, mostly tropical in distribution. Their shells are usually highly ornamented in various schemes of sculpture, but they lack beauty in color. The animal is provided with a siphon, as is indicated by the anterior canal of the shell. The operculum is corneous, with a nearly central nucleus.

GENUS *Cerithium*

C. floridanum. A very common species on the west coast of Florida, also sparingly found at Hatteras. It has eight or ten whorls, a gradually tapering spire, and a sharp apex; the aperture is oblong, with a deeply cut anterior canal projected to the left and backward (when the specimen is held apex up, with the aperture toward the observer). The sculpture is elaborate, consisting of many rows of revolving ribs, and close to the suture there are circling rows of nodes. There is a curious hump just to the left of the aperture, which is quite characteristic of the genus. The color is whitish-gray; the length one and a quarter to one and a half inches. Station, shallow water in lagoons and sheltered spots. (Plate LXIX.)

C. muscarum. Another Floridian species, somewhat smaller than the last (one inch in length). It has heavy, prominent, transverse ribs crossed by circling rows of chestnut spots, one heavy revolving rib around the base; eight or nine whorls; a high-tapering spire; and a sharp apex. The aperture is oblong, with the anterior canal projecting to the left. The columella is arched; the color shining gray to very light purplish. This very pretty little shell may be gathered literally by the shovelful all along the west Florida coast in sheltered spots, on sandy and shallow bottoms. (Plate LXIX.)

C. minimum. A still smaller Floridian shell, with jet-black aperture and anterior canal projecting horizontally to the left. The sculpture-plan is of revolving ribs and a series of white granules just below the sutures. Its station is the same as that of the last. Often the bottom of a lagoon will seem to be literally paved with these somber-hued little shells. From Tampa Bay to Charlotte Harbor they are very abundant.

GENERA *Bittium, Triforis*

These are allied genera, having numerous species upon our coasts, but the shells are so small that the inexpert collector is not likely to notice them. Hosts of these minute, turreted, decussated, blackish shells are to be found on the wiry grasses of salt-marshes. They are also found on algæ at low-water mark. In *Triforis* the whorls turn to the left. Range from Cape Cod to South Carolina.

GENUS *Cerithidea*

C. scalariformis. This species has the suggestive outlines of the family, but the aperture is simpler. The outer lip is considerably thickened, sinuous, and yellow; there is a very slight notch at the angle of the columella, and the lip serves for an anterior canal. The apex is wanting by reason of the usual truncation of two or three whorls of the spire. There are revolving ribs on the base; longitudinal ribs elsewhere. The color is a dingy drab; within, brownish-yellow. It is found in brackish water in Georgia and Florida. This species is said to suspend itself from overhanging vegetation by means of glutinous filaments. It may remain out of water for an almost indefinite time. (Plate LXIX.)

C. sacrata. A species very common on the mud-flats of San Francisco Bay. It is a high-spired shell of ten heavily ribbed whorls, with a series of revolving ribs on the body-whorl. The outer lip is sinuous, and the columella is slightly twisted. It is nacreous and brown within, dingy blue-black without. Length one inch to an inch and a quarter. (Plate LXIX.)

FAMILY **VERMETIDÆ**

GENUS *Vermicularia*

V. spirata. This is a very curious creature when considered from the point of view of the gasteropod mollusk. It seems at first as though it would be better to regard it as a worm which had created for itself a calcareous covering. But it is a true prosobranch notwithstanding the fact that it has departed widely from the conventional design in the fashioning of its shell. At first the shell starts out in a regular form, and then the whorls become separated, finally wandering about in a seemingly aimless manner. The irregular prolongation sometimes measures ten inches in length. The animal is in no way remarkable except in having the viscera greatly elongated and the foot very short and broad. The color of the animal is light brown with black spots; the shell-color is rufous or ashy-white. Shells of this genus are often found grouped together in an inextricable mass. It is found in shallow water from New England to Florida.

Vermicularia spirata.

FAMILY **STROMBIDÆ**

This is a particularly interesting family, but it is tropical, and is represented on the shores of the United States by only one genus, *Strombus*, of which we have but a few species. *Strombus* is a scavenger,—a buzzard among mollusks,—and its sense of smell is evidently very acute. Its eyes are much more highly developed than the usual gasteropod visual organs, and they are placed at the tip-ends of two very substantial eye-stalks or -pedicels. The tentacles are slender and project from the eye-pedicels. The foot is curiously developed; that portion of it which would naturally constitute the creeping-disk is exceedingly small, but the metapodium (the hinder part of the foot, upon which the operculum is situated) is very large. The corneous operculum upon its end, which is far too small to close the entrance of the shell when the creature retires within it, looks like a claw. Instead of creeping along the sand, *Strombus* proceeds by jumps or awkward leaps, turning its heavy shell first to one side, then to the other. The shell is usually heavy, with the outer lip greatly thickened.

Genus *Strombus*

S. pugilis. The very common Floridian species, often three to four inches in height, with a short spire covered with nodes or short, obtuse spines, which are also found upon the shoulder of the body-whorl (sometimes smooth). The aperture is long, with a wide notch in the outer lip and a posterior canal. Living specimens have a tough, leathery epidermis covering at least the body-whorl. The color is brownish. The columella is covered with a fairly thick callous deposit, and, as within the aperture, is highly polished, and deep purple, blackish-chestnut, or vivid carnation-red in color. The smoother varieties have gone under the name of **S. alatus,** but the identity of the two species is assured. This pugilistic *Strombus* is a very active mollusk, and when placed in a boat will sometimes effect its escape over the side in a most surprising manner. The species is very abundant in all the shallow waters of Florida. A piece of meat on a string, left overnight in some sheltered sandy spot where there are from six to eight feet of water, will surely attract them. In Florida, where the waters teem with life, unless the bait is protected in a wire cage, the chances are that the hosts of crustaceans and fish will make away with it long before the strombs can arrive on the scene. (Plate LXX.)

S. gigas. One of the largest of gasteropods, very common on the Florida Keys and also occurring in southern Florida. Hundreds of thousands of these shells have been sent to Europe from the Bahamas to be cut into cameos. This familiar shell is to be seen everywhere in the South, placed about flower-gardens and lining the paths and walks in yards. It is generally known in Florida and the West Indies as the "conch-shell." The animal is used as food in Key West, and is very generally eaten throughout the Bahamas. From their habit of eating

PLATE LXIX.

1, Littorina angulifera, twice natural size. 4, Cerithium floridanum.
2, Littorina scutulata, much enlarged. 5, Cerithium muscarum.
3, Littorina planaxis, enlarged. 6, Cerithidea scalariformis, enlarged.
7, Cerithidea sacrata.

PLATE LXX.

1, Strombus pugilis.   3, Trivia pediculus.
2, Cypræa exanthema.   4, Trivia californica.
                  5, Trivia quadripunctata.

these animals the natives of some of the Bahama Islands are themselves called "Conchs." The rich pink color of the shell is very striking.

There are perhaps seventy-five or eighty species of *Strombus* inhabiting the tropical seas, and many of them are highly prized by collectors on account of their great beauty.

FAMILY CYPRÆIDÆ

GENUS *Cyprœa*

Cyprœa is one of the "aristocratic" genera. Whether the shell or the animal itself is considered, there is probably no genus of mollusks which offers so much of beauty and interest to the collector and student. The genus is a tropical one, and finds its metropolis among the coral-fringed islands of the equatorial Pacific. Despite their brilliant colors and general attractiveness, the cowries—for such is their popular name—are very modest and shy; they prefer to hide among rocks, where they may be secure from molestation, for probably their conspicuous appearance is a real source of danger to them. In the animal of *Cyprœa* the mantle is provided with two large lateral lobes, which are reflexed and meet over the top of the shell; thus, when the mantle is fully extended, the shell is entirely concealed. These mantle lobes are often furnished with numerous forked, tufted, or ramified filaments. The foot is long; there is no operculum. The color of the animal is often very striking in its intensity. A description of the cowry-shell is hardly necessary, so familiar is every one with it. A deposit of enamel is made all over the shell, and its painting and decoration, usually very elaborate, is reserved for the adult as a final process in the artistic completion of its home. The aperture is as long as the shell, is channeled at both ends, and is toothed along both margins. The spire is insignificant and is concealed by layers of enamel. In the young the shell has a very different appearance, resembling a sharp-lipped *Oliva*, and its scheme of coloration may be entirely different from that employed by the adult.

Among the *Cyprœidœ* are many remarkable species. The splendid *Cyprœa aurantia,* a native of the Fiji Islands, is one of the shells most sought after by enthusiastic collectors. The natives learned its value long ago, and hold specimens of it at very substantial prices. It is worn as an ornament by chiefs and as a mark of distinction. The well-known *C. moneta,* also a native of the Pacific Islands, has been very extensively used as money throughout the South Seas and in Africa. There are many collectors of shells who confine their efforts almost exclusively to this and to one or two of the other "aristocratic" genera. From an esthetic point of view this is very natural, but biologically the less pretentious mollusks are quite as interesting.

Of the one hundred and fifty or more species in existence only three are to be found upon the Atlantic coast of the United States, and the chances are decidedly against the finding of any of them north of extreme southern Florida.

C. exanthema. A species not uncommon at Key West, where it may be seen slowly crawling about the mangrove roots near the water's edge. It attains a length of from four to six inches, and is so highly polished that a good specimen could be used as a mirror. In color it is shining, light chestnut, clouded with purple ; the lips are a dark, very rich chestnut ; over all are whitish spots which appear to shine forth from beneath the enamel. Lengthwise along the middle of the back is a zone of lighter color which reflects a purplish sheen. (Plate LXX.)

C. spurca. Another Floridian species, properly belonging to the West Indian fauna. It is not more than one half an inch long, and is white in color, but it is so thickly dotted with yellow spots upon the back that it would pass for a yellow shell. The base is pure white. The surface of the shell glistens in the light.

Genus *Trivia*

In the genus *Trivia* the shell is shaped in every way like that of *Cyprœa,* but its surface is never smooth. In the middle of the back is a longitudinal groove, from which run transverse ribs, which continue around to and enter into the aperture. The shells are always small, never exceeding one half of an inch in length, and their color is generally reddish or brownish, passing to pink.

T. pediculus. A Floridian species, first described by the great naturalist Linnæus. Like most of the descriptions of the earlier naturalists, this is very short and inadequate, and would apply equally well to almost any *Trivia.* The color is rose-pink, with several large brownish splashes on the back. The spire is entirely hidden. It is found in shallow water in pools, and on the beach after storms. (Plate LXX.)

T. quadripunctata. Much smaller than the preceding; rose-red, with four conspicuous reddish-brown dots on the back, two on each side of the median dorsal groove. Found in Florida. (Plate LXX.)

On the California coast are also several species of *Trivia* and one *Cypræa*, but they belong to the Southern California peninsula, and are not commonly found farther north than Santa Barbara. The cowry is called ***C. spadacea;*** it grows to a length of about two inches, is highly polished, with white base and sides, and is bright chestnut above. As is usual in the cypræas, the spire is covered with enamel.

T. californica. A species found at Monterey and thence south. It lacks the median dorsal groove, and has a whitish color-streak instead. The ribs are white, and the ground-color of the shell is dark brownish-red. These little shells, when found upon the beach, are called "coffee-shells," from their somewhat striking resemblance to the coffee-bean, being flat on one side and rounded upon the other, and otherwise resembling it in size and color. (Plate LXX.)

T. solandri. This species may be found at Santa Barbara and San Diego. It is twice as large as the last species, and has a very deep groove in the back and widely separated ribs. Color rose to brown. The groove on the back penetrates into the white portion of the shell.

FAMILY DOLIIDÆ

This small family furnishes two conspicuously handsome species belonging to the genus *Dolium*, which range from Hatteras southward into the West Indies.

GENUS *Dolium*

D. galea and ***D. perdix.*** The animal in both of these species has a relatively large foot, which spreads out while in the act of creeping and seems far too bulky ever to be withdrawn into the shell. It is square in front, and, bulging out far to each side, tapers to a blunt point behind. The most noticeable feature of the animal, however, is the great development of its proboscis, which is quite as long as the shell itself. The siphon is also long and is curved over the back of the shell. The operculum is wanting in adult specimens. The shell of *D. galea* sometimes attains a length of eight inches, with a diameter of about six inches; the other species is not quite so large. They are both ventricose, thin, inflated shells, with large body-whorls and crenulated lips. Both are slightly umbilicated and ornamented with revolving, regularly spaced ribs. The ribs of *D. perdix* are not so highly raised, but they are painted with light reddish-brown spots. *D. galea* is white, with a lower spire and deeply channeled sutures. (Plate LXXI.)

GENUS *Pyrula*

P. papyratia. One of the commonest as well as one of the handsomest of American shells. It is a Floridian species, found in shallow water and on sandy bottoms. The animal greatly resembles that of *Dolium*, except that it has two side-flaps, which, when extended, partially inclose the shell. The shell is thin, with an almost flat spire and a greatly enlarged body-whorl. The aperture is flaring, and is drawn out anteriorly into a tapering canal, which gives to the shell the outlines of a pear. The ornamentation is revolving, but not highly raised, and there are ribs with very distinct longitudinal lines of growth between. The color is pure white, or sometimes yellowish, with rufous spots; within it is golden. This attractive shell is usually from three to four inches in length, but is sometimes found considerably larger. (Plate LXXI.)

Family CASSIDIDÆ

Genus *Cassis*

The cassides, commonly known as the "helmet-shells," are carnivorous mollusks, which lead an active life in sandy stations, prowling about in search of bivalves, upon which they prey. They have a large siphon and a fairly large and extensible proboscis. The foot is broad and strong, being well adapted for plowing through the sand. The shell of *Cassis* is large, generally heavy and inflated, with a short spire and a short, recurved anterior canal. The lip is much thickened. Upon the Atlantic coast of North America there are four species of *Cassis*. They are all properly West Indian in their faunal relations, but have found lodgment on the American shore at various points. All of them have been taken in the neighborhood of Cape Hatteras, two of them in West Florida, and two in Texas.

C. tuberosa. A large, heavy shell, often from six to eight inches in length, with a flattened spire. The aperture is long and narrow, with large white teeth upon the outer lip, which is also greatly thickened. The columellar lip is ribbed. A heavy deposit of enamel to the left of the columellar lip gives the shell a triangular outline. A row of very large nodes upon the shoulder of the body-whorl and two rows of obsolete nodes below are characteristic features of this species. The color is light yellowish-brown suffused with pink. The aperture and the columellar callosity are flesh-tinted, with chestnut trimmings. The anterior canal is deep and recurved.

C. cameo. A species of about the same size as the last, but more ovate or ventricose in form. It is coarsely striated, with elevated growth-lines, and has circling rows of large, rib-like elevations, having sometimes nodes upon the body-whorl. The columella is conspicuously ribbed and greatly expanded. The outer lip is thickened, and has lamelliform teeth within. Flesh-colored; teeth white; purple-brown trimmings. A great many of these shells are sent yearly from Nassau to Italy, where they are used in cameo-cutting. It is owing to the fact that the substance of these shells is deposited in layers of different colors that they are available for this purpose. There are about fifty species of helmet-shells, the one most valued for cameo-cutting being known as the black helmet, *C. Madagascarensis.*

C. testiculus. A species found outside of the West Indies only at Key West and at Hatteras, where the Gulf Stream has brought so many West Indian forms, and left them at the point where it takes its oblique course away from the shore. This pretty species is smaller than the others just described. It has a low, depressed spire; longitudinal ribs crossing wide, flat revolving ribs; a long, narrow aperture; and a reflexed and thickened outer lip, also toothed. The columella is thickened and ribbed. The anterior canal is recurved over the back of the shell, as is usual in the genus. The color is bluish, with dark spots. There are square black spots on the reflexed lip; the aperture is pink, and the teeth and columellar ribs white. This species is exceedingly common at Nassau, and plays havoc with the more slowly moving bivalves, which it devours. (Plate LXXI.)

C. inflata. Perhaps the commonest species of *Cassis* on our coast. It is reported to be common at Beaufort, South Carolina, yet it is not so frequently met with out of the West Indies as some earlier collectors would have us believe. Beach-worn specimens, however, are not unusual all along the Florida coast. It attains a size of from three to four inches, and is a rounded, globose, ventricose shell, with a higher spire than is usual in this genus. The surface is almost smooth, the series of revolving ribs being scarcely raised on the body-whorl. The lip is thickened and reflexed, with prominent lamelliform teeth which continue as internal ribs. The lower portion of the columella is calloused and roughly granulated. The color is bluish-white, glazed, with large square brown spots. The region of the aperture is pure white. The collector should not remain content with a specimen or two of the poor beach-worn shells of this species. In general, this advice applies to the collection of all specimens. One can get no idea of the sculpturing and painting of shells from dead and worn specimens. It is quality rather than quantity that makes an interesting cabinet. (Plate LXXI.)

Family MURICIDÆ

Subfamily MURICINÆ

It seems like making a long leap to pass suddenly from the *Cassididæ* to the *Muricidæ.* In the natural biological order, as it appears in our present state of knowledge, a host of families and genera intervene between these two. But they are omitted here, either because they do not conspicuously occur upon our own shores, or because they are free-swimming pelagic mollusks, which live only far out at sea and rarely are found on the beaches. The family *Muricidæ* is an exceedingly large one, including a bewildering number of well-characterized genera. It has many representatives in every sea, but, as is apt to be the case, the finest and most striking species are tropical. The animal is not peculiar in any way, being altogether a conventional prosobranch gasteropod, with moderately long foot, and the usual tentacles placed upon a small head. There is a retractile proboscis, which suggests carnivorous habits. In reality the *Muricidæ* are perfect pirates among the *Mollusca*, attacking nearly every species they encounter, piercing its shell and devouring the unfortunate inhabitant. They live in rocky and gravelly places or about coral reefs. Their shells are seldom colored,except about the aperture. What the shells lack in color, however, they fully gain in oddness of form and in sculpturing. The anterior canal varies from a mere notch to an astonishingly long channel. The tendency to nodes, varices, spires, and varicose processes in general is a prominent feature of the family.

There are several genera, with numerous species, upon the east and west coasts of the United States, but we can do no more here than mention those which are very common.

GENUS *Murex*

Of this tropical genus there are two Floridian species—*M. rufus* and *M. pomum.* The genus has been very extensively divided into subgenera, based upon shell-characters alone. Some of these subgenera are usually accepted at full generic value, and their substitution for the old, well-established name *Murex* is to be expected. These two Floridian species fall within different subgeneric lines, and the student who goes to a museum to compare his catch with the labeled specimens on exhibition will probably be puzzled to find his two murices named *Chicoreus rufus* and *Phyllonotus pomum* respectively. But for our purposes the name *Murex* will do well enough.

M. rufus. This species scarcely ever exceeds three inches in length. Its spire is moderately high, and the aperture is oblong-ovate, with a long, slightly curved, and almost completely inclosed anterior canal. Through the end of this the fleshy siphon projects in life. The shell is most extravagantly sculptured — so intricately that it is difficult to describe it. Its most conspicuous feature is the large foliaceous varices

Dolium galea.　　　PLATE LXXI.　　　Dolium perdix.

Pyrula papyratia.

Cassis testiculus.　　　　　　　　Cassis inflata.

PLATE LXXII.

Murex rufus.
Pteronotus festivus.

Murex pomum.
Cerostoma foliatum.

Ocinebra poulsoni, enlarged.
Cerostoma nuttallii.

which cross the whorls, projecting almost one fourth of an inch from the body of the shell. Between each of these varices is a large node. There is, besides all this, a system of pronounced revolving ribs which cross the varices and nodes, giving to the shell a greatly roughened appearance. The interior is bluish-white. The operculum is corneous, with a subterminal nucleus. Unfortunately, this really handsome shell is usually incrusted with coralline or calcareous matter, which must be removed with acid before a good idea of its appearance can be had. In color it is reddish-brown to dark chestnut on the varices. It is very common on the west coast of Florida, but rarer elsewhere. (Plate LXXII.)

M. pomum. A more abundant species, found all along the coast from Hatteras to Texas. It is not so elongated as the last, and its sculptural design is much less exaggerated. Between each of the varices are two nodules. The aperture is oblong-ovate, and the anterior canal is nearly closed and recurved toward the back. Revolving ribs cross the varices and nodules. The color is ashen, with chestnut tips upon the nodes and varices, and chestnut-colored patches about the aperture. The varices are simple and not foliaceous as in *M. rufus;* the shell is more globose. Length two to three inches. (Plate LXXII.)

M. (Phyllonotus) fulvescens. The largest of the American murices. It is not commonly found except in Texas.

Genus *Trophon*

T. clathratus. A fairly common shell of the Maine coast; although it belongs to a deeper zone than that of the tides, it is occasionally found after storms upon the shore. It is a small fusiform shell, with many prominent longitudinal ribs and a produced anterior canal. *Trophon* is a boreal genus, which finds the best conditions for life in the icy waters of Labrador and Greenland.

Trophon clathratus.

Genus *Urosalpinx*

The genus *Urosalpinx* is closely allied to *Murex* and *Trophon.* Several of its species are found on the east coast of the United States.

Urosalpinx cinerea.

U. cinerea. This well-known species is regarded by Chesapeake and Long Island Sound oystermen much in the light of a plague. These active predaceous mollusks live upon bivalves, and preferably upon oysters. They bore a small round hole through the shell of their helpless victims, and then proceed to extract the succulent, fleshy animal from within. The oystermen call them by the suggestive name of " drill," and wage incessant warfare upon them. In some years these mollusks appear to go into partnership with the large starfish, *Asterias,* and the combination of the two can soon destroy any oyster-bed. The original home of this destructive little creature is presumed to be in Chesapeake Bay, but the transplanting of oyster-spat thence to Long Island Sound has introduced the enemy at the same time. The species has a wide range from Florida to Cape Cod, and locally north of that point; in fact, it may be counted upon to appear wherever there are oyster-beds. The shell is dingy gray in color, and its whorls are crossed by a dozen or more rib-like undulations, and numerous revolving striæ. The anterior canal is produced, and is yellowish-brown within. Length under an inch.

GENUS *Eupleura*

Eupleura caudata.

E. caudata. A curiously flattened shell which has close family connections with that last described. The peculiarly flat appearance is due to the fact that there is a rather wide varix upon each side of the shell. It is a small species, never more than an inch in length, dingy gray, with longitudinal undulations upon the whorls, and a long, narrow anterior canal and crenulated lip. The animal is white and yellow, and is notable for its activity. Found from Maine to Florida, about low-tide mark.

On the west coast of the United States occurs a striking development of a group of the *Muricidæ* of a curious foliaceous appearance, belonging to the genera *Pteronotus, Ocinebra,* and *Cerostoma.*

GENUS *Pteronotus*

P. festivus. The shell is marked by three well-raised varices upon each whorl, which are reflexed backward; between each varix is a rounded knob. All is covered with numerous spiral lines of sculpture, which upon crossing the varices are frilled. The aperture is oval and white within; the anterior canal is entirely closed and is reflexed slightly over the back. Length two inches; color dingy white. Found on the southern coast of California. (Plate LXXII.)

GENUS *Ocinebra*

O. poulsoni. This has the same dingy white color as the species last described. Its plan of sculpturing is somewhat different and consists of a series of rounded varices, about nine to a whorl, crossed by spiral lines. The anterior canal is open, and just within the white aperture, upon the inner side of the lip, is a series of five or six little round teeth. This species frequents the waters near San Diego, and sometimes grows to be two inches in length. (Plate LXXII.)

O. lurida. A much smaller species than the last, being not more than one half to three fourths of an inch in length. Very common at Monterey and in San Francisco Bay. It is strongly marked with spiral lines covering the longitudinal undulations usually found in this genus, but which are less prominently developed in this case.

There are several species of small ocinebras upon the California coast, but they are not easily determined without a more critical examination than we are giving our specimens. They are **O. interfossa,** a small shell with deep spiral grooves, sharp varices, and deep sutures; and **O. circumtexta,** also small, but heavy, short-spired, with scalloped or crenulated outer lip.

GENUS *Cerostoma*

C. nuttallii. A species belonging to the southern coast of California. It may be recognized at once by two prominent characters : first, a horn-like projection from near the base of the outer lip, and, second, the tumid varices alternating with rounded knobs. It has no spiral series of lines like those in *Pteronotus festivus ;* and it has a row of five or six little teeth upon the inner side of the aperture, like those in *Ocinebra poulsoni.* The anterior canal is closed. It is about two inches long. (Plate LXXII.)

C. foliatum. A shell somewhat like the last, but almost twice as large, with heavy wing-like varices (three upon each whorl), made up of overlapping plaits. The knobs between the varices are much smaller, while the revolving ribs, though fewer in number than in most of these west-coast murices, are heavy and large. The aperture is oblong, the anterior canal closed. There is a " horn " near the base of the aperture, as in *C. nuttallii,* but no row of teeth upon the under side of the lip. The color is dingy white. (Plate LXXII.)

In the waters of Oregon and Washington there are a few trophons and other forms similar to the east-coast genera. These no doubt belong to the boreal and arctic faunal provinces, and have spread over both the Atlantic and Pacific northern regions.

SUBFAMILY **PURPURINÆ**

This is considered a subfamily of the *Muricidæ,* and the group therefore bears the subfamily termination *-inæ.* There is no vital difference between it and the subfamily *Muricinæ.* The operculum in the *Purpurinæ* has a lateral nucleus instead of a subterminal one, but beyond this there are no essential differences. The shell of the purpuras is generally heavy and solid, being adapted to a life among rocks which are exposed to the beating of the surf. There is a lack of that extravagant sculptural design so characteristic of the true murices, most of the purpuras being comparatively smooth, in order, no doubt, that they may offer as little resistance as possible to the rushing, seething waters of exposed rocky shores.

The *Purpurinæ,* like some of the murices, when mutilated, exude a reddish-purple fluid. On account of this, the ancient Romans used to gather great quantities of certain Mediterranean forms belonging to these families, place them in large mortars, and grind them up, shell and all. A garment dipped in the mixture and then exposed to the sun would receive a rich purple dye. This was the basis of the famous "Tyrian purple." The process was lost, and was rediscovered many centuries later, but it was long ago abandoned in favor of the far superior modern chemical dyes.

Genus *Purpura*

P. lapillus. No one who has ever spent an observant hour among the rocks at low tide, on the shores of Massachusetts or Maine, has failed to notice the myriads of *P. lapillus* clinging to the barnacle-covered boulders, or slowly creeping about in the tide-pools. This rather pretty little

The same; a younger specimen.

Purpura lapillus.

mollusk is a native of Great Britain, and there attains its greatest development and exhibits best its marvelous range of variation. It is presumed to be an immigrant in American waters, having found its way across the sea by Iceland and Greenland, and thence down the coast. As it is a cold-water animal, and can only survive in open, rocky stations, it will probably never pass south of New York. It is difficult to describe this well-known species because it is so extremely variable. There is an individuality about the species which causes it to be recognized at once, yet its details are elusive. It is never more than one and a half inches long (in the United States), and varies in color from white through yellow to chocolate. Often it is banded in yellow or brown. Near the only sand-beach of Bar Harbor is a colony with vermilion bands. The shell varies from a smooth to an exceedingly rough exterior, the latter being caused by raised scales along the lines of growth, which make the shell even prickly to the touch. Of this latter form there is a large colony on Campobello Island. Numerous coarse revolving ridges are common. The columella is flattened and smooth, and its lower portion is a little twisted. The anterior canal is short. *P. lapillus* has been accused of attacking clams and boring their shells, as does the predaceous *Urosalpinx cinerea*, but the accusation is not well founded. *Purpura* is carnivorous, and no doubt destroys many young barnacles; but with its short and small foot it would find great difficulty in digging in the sand for clams.

In Florida waters there are several purpuras, which properly belong to the West Indian fauna, but enjoy an extensive range.

P. patula. This species has a rounded body-whorl, and sometimes a low spire, which give it much the appearance of a large limpet. Its back is decorated with rows of nodules in regular order, forming a spiral series. The chief point of distinction is the deeply excavated, broadened, and flattened columella-lip of salmon-color. A portion of the whorl itself is worn down and made smooth by being dragged over sharp coral rocks, revealing underneath the rough, incrusted exterior, a transparent colorless shelly substance. Dark and chestnut-colored patches and spots adorn the outer lip.   The shell is from two to two and a half inches long.   (Plate LXXIII.)

P. hæmastoma.   Like its relative, *P. lapillus* of Northern waters, this species is so variable as almost to defy description.   The form that usually occurs from Hatteras to Florida is of a bluish-gray color, and is indistinctly encircled with narrow yellow zones, which are crossed by somewhat vague longitudinal waves of black.   The columella and outer lip and interior are orange-yellow.   The spire is moderately high, with a sharp apex.   The whorls are noduled upon the shoulder.   There are revolving grooves throughout, even within the aperture.   A Texan variety of this species has a much more elevated spire, with channeled sutures, and small aperture of bright salmon-color.

Upon the Californian coast there are three species of *Purpura*, which markedly resemble the *P. lapillus* of the Maine shores.   Their extreme variability has given rise to much confusion in their nomenclature; the multitude of names given by numerous authors to the varietal forms of these three species constitute a list of synonyms which is appalling to the systematic student.

P. crispata.   With very few modifications, a description of *P. lapillus* would apply to this species, which occurs commonly at San Francisco and ranges north.   *Crispata* is possibly heavier, with a smaller aperture, and with four or five round teeth upon the inner white surface of the thickened outer lip.   It ranges in color from pure white to dark brown and is sometimes banded.   The surface may be smooth or rough, and is sometimes ruffled all over with wrinkled frills.   Length one and a half inches.   Its habits and station are much the same as those of *P. lapillus*, of which it is possibly a descendant, somewhat modified by changed environment.   (Plate LXXIII.)

P. lima.   A less common species, with rounded whorls and channeled suture, and about fifteen spiral grooves upon the whorls.   The color is light brown; the length from one quarter of an inch to one inch.

P. saxicola.   A shell exceedingly abundant along the whole Californian coast, living under quite the same conditions as the purpuras already described.   It is smaller than the last two, being always less than an inch in length.   It also runs through the gamut of variations as to color-scheme and sculpturing, but always preserves a certain individuality.   There is a tendency to a small umbilicus; the outer lip is sharp; the columella is flattened and slightly twisted; and anterior canal is short, and bears to the left.   A smaller aperture, with relatively thicker shell, seems to be all that distinguishes it from the smaller varieties of the east-coast species.   (Plate LXXIII.)

Genus *Monoceras*

This genus, which is very closely allied to *Purpura*, is almost wholly confined to the west coast of the United States.   The name is given on account of a peculiarity, which has, however, already been noticed in *Cerostoma*, namely, a horn-like projection from the basal portion of the outer lip.   In all other respects this genus is nothing but a true *Purpura*.

M. lapilloides. The shell in this species is about an inch in length, and has markings which give it a striking resemblance to granite. A row of small round denticles upon the inner surface of the lip is a characteristic already noticed in some of the west-coast murices. Their station is the same as that of the purpuras — between the tides on rocky, exposed shores. (Plate LXXIII.)

M. engonatum. This species has sharply ridged whorls, and revolving ribs with wavy growth-lines between them. In other respects it is almost identical with the last described. It is often found mingled with the seaweed which covers rocks between tides, and, when moist, simulates the color of its surroundings. (Plate LXXIII.)

GENUS *Chorus*

C. belcheri. This family cannot well be left without at least a mention of this large and rather handsome species. *Chorus* is a genus of but few species, confined to the Pacific shores of North and South America. This particular species does not reach as far north as San Francisco, but may be taken at low tide in the vicinity of San Diego. The prominent feature of the shell is the posterior canal, which, being abandoned as the growth of the shell continues, leaves a series of hollow, folded spiny processes upon the shoulder of the body-whorl, which appear like jagged points upon the spire. (Plate LXXIII.)

FAMILY COLUMBELLIDÆ

This is a large family of small but often exceedingly beautiful shells. Their distribution is mostly tropical, but the list of North American species is a very generous one indeed if the deeper-water forms are included. The animal is quite the same as in the *Buccinidæ*, to be described later. (See also description of *Buccinum undatum* on page 330.) The shells are usually quite solid, with a long, narrow slit for an aperture; the outer lip is thickened on the inside, especially about the middle portion, and is deeply toothed; and the lower portion of the columellar lip is also ribbed or toothed.

GENUS *Columbella*

C. mercatoria. This Antillean species is found in Florida, and is one of the gems among the American shallow-water shells. Its height is about one half of an inch. It is decorated with revolving grooves and with a variously patterned color-scheme of broken yellow or reddish

PLATE LXXIII.

1, Purpura patula.
2, Purpura crispata.
3, Purpura saxicola, enlarged.

4, Monoceras lapilloides.
5, Monoceras engonatum.
6, Chorus belcheri.

PLATE LXXIV.

1, Columbella mercatoria, enlarged.

2, Columbella (Amphissa) corrugata, enlarged.

3, Columbella (Astyris) gausapata, much enlarged.

4, Nassa fossata, about natural size.

5, Nassa mendica, enlarged.

6, Nassa perpinguis, enlarged.

7, Nassa tegula, enlarged.

8, Siphonalia kellettii, reduced.

9, Tritonidea tincta.

lines on a white background, or of white splotches on a brownish background. (Plate LXXIV.)

C. (Anachis) avara, and the variety *C. similis.* These rather slender shells, about one half to three fifths of an inch long, occur from Florida northward to Cape Cod. The upper whorls are smooth, the lower ones are undulated with vertical costæ (ten to thirteen), and the body-whorl is encircled below the middle by a series of revolving, closely set grooves. The aperture is typical of the genus, though less strongly marked by internal callosity on the outer lip and with less prominent teeth than in *C. mercatoria.* The greater development of the revolving grooves, which spread over the entire surface of the body-whorl and cross the costæ, producing a granulated surface, constitutes the variety *C. similis.* The color is brownish, with white reticulations. This species is to be found in considerable abundance in sandy mud and among stones and algæ about low-water mark. At New Bedford and Martha's Vineyard, and on Cape Cod, it may always be taken. It is also common at Norfolk and along the Virginia and Georgia coasts.

C. (Astyris) lunata. One of the characteristic eastern-coast shells, which, like the last species, ranges from Cape Ann in Massachusetts to the West Indies. It occurs about low-tide mark and just below, upon stones and algæ, or crawling about on a soft bottom. On account of its generic features, combined with the peculiar coloration, the species cannot be mistaken. The latter is a ground of reddish-brown or fawn, with encircling rows of large white or yellowish spots. The whorls are quite smooth. Length not over one fifth of an inch.

The collector soon learns to recognize the variable forms of these northern-range columbellas. They are not a difficult group, for once their generic position is established by the characters of the aperture (which are constant) the species can readily be determined, notwithstanding their tendencies to vary from the type. Californian waters also have several columbellas. The conchologists of the west coast have preferred to apply to their shells, and indeed to employ in general use, a large number of subgeneric names in place of the ordinarily accepted generic ones. The result of this is to confuse at first the student of conchology, who, though fairly familiar with the molluscan genera, finds himself perplexed when he confronts a list of west-coast shells. Thus the two common Californian columbellas are "*Amphissa*" *corrugata* and "*Astyris*" *gausapata,* these two species belonging to different subgenera of the genus *Columbella.*

C. corrugata. This shell finds its metropolis in Puget Sound, but occurs also along the Californian shore. The aperture is wider than is usual in this genus. The surface is deeply wrinkled by longitudinal costæ and is encircled by revolving grooves. Length one half of an inch; color red, or orange to light brown. It is found in shallow protected waters. (Plate LXXIV.)

C. gausapata. This species lives in great numbers about the roots of eel-grass. It is very small and smooth, with a rather high spire. The color of the spire is deep brown; the body-whorl is lighter in color. Occasionally the body-whorl is obtusely carinated just below the suture. This little shell is very common upon many beaches after heavy winds, but it should be sought for at very low tides and gathered alive. (Plate LXXIV.)

FAMILY NASSIDÆ

These are familiar, and often very characteristic, littoral shells in all parts of the world. Where they exist at all they are generally to be found in astonishingly large numbers, sometimes even crowding out all other mollusks. They are exceedingly active and predaceous, feeding upon other mollusks, whose shells they bore through by means of the sharp teeth upon their lingual ribbon. The *Nassidæ* of the east coast find a relentless enemy in the small hermit-crabs, which attack them, drag them from their coverings, and then proceed to occupy the empty shells themselves; the torn and lacerated *Nassa* animal is thereupon leisurely eaten, a retribution probably well deserved. The animal of *Nassa* (the principal genus of *Nassidæ*) is peculiar in having frequently a bifurcated tail; or, to speak more correctly, the posterior end of the foot is terminated by two appendices. It has a long siphon, and eyes placed upon the outer sides and near the base of the tentacles. The operculum has serrated edges.

GENUS *Nassa*

N. trivittata, N. obsoleta. These are the two nassas of the New England and New Jersey coasts. The first has a more northerly range, extending to the Gulf of St. Lawrence; the other is not usually found north of Cape Cod, but below that point as far as Hatteras it is probably the commonest shell of the coast. It fairly swarms in sheltered muddy reaches

Nassa trivittata, showing the animal as if crawling.

about low tide. Little pools left by the tide on the Jersey flats are sometimes so crowded with *N. obsoleta* that for lack of room the animals crawl over one another. *N. trivittata* is more commonly taken at small depths in the harbors, where it seems to live well upon all kinds of sea-bottom. Probably they exist in great numbers along the southern shore of Long Island, for the beaches are often lined with their dead and worn shells. Over half the specimens thus found will have a little round perforation upon some whorl, showing that they were victims of some cannibalistic brother. The shells of the *Nassidæ* have a short, ovate aperture, with a short anterior canal. The inner lip is smooth, and is usually coated over with a more or less heavy

Nassa trivittata.

deposit of enamel. *N. trivittata* is about one half to seven tenths of an inch long, and is yellowish-white. A series of revolving grooves cutting across a series of longitudinal lines gives the shell a decussated or granulated appearance. The whorls are somewhat shouldered at the sutures, and are white inside. *N. obsoleta* cannot be called a handsome shell by the most enthusiastic collector. Its spire is usually eroded or completely dissolved away. The color is blackish to olive, with the aperture purplish-black. The columellar lip is arched, with a twist or fold in its lower portion. It is decussated by crossing lines and grooves, though not so conspicuously as *N. trivittata;* sutures simple; length one half of an inch to one inch. Old specimens not only become eroded, but are usually covered with vegetable mould, and are not over-inspiring to the collector. They often live in brackish water, and frequent all the inlets and marine flats between Cape Cod and Hatteras. Below Hatteras both this and the last-named species occur, though not so plentifully.

*Nassa
obsoleta.*

N. vibex. This ubiquitous little mollusk seems content in any station, and swarms in all the sandy bays of Florida. It is a busybody, always on the move, and its long siphon is constantly vibrating. The shell is about one half an inch long and shining white, with brown or reddish spots. There are prominent longitudinal undulations and revolving lines upon the lower part of the body-whorl. The anterior canal is deeply cut and very short; the columellar lip arched, richly calloused, and often granulated at its base. This is probably the first live shell the collector in Florida will encounter. The animal is very graceful and prettily marked in color. The terminal cirri on the foot form a notable feature — a character belonging to the entire family.

*Nassa
vibex.*

N. fossata, N. perpinguis. On the California coast there are the huge (for this genus) *N. fossata* and the smaller but no less interesting *N. perpinguis*, also **N. tegula** and **N. mendica.** *N. fossata* grows to a length of one and a half to two inches. When adult the lip is somewhat thickened, and the entire aperture is bright orange. The color of the shell is ashen-gray, and it is marked with spiral and transverse riblets which produce a granulated surface, especially upon the upper whorls. The shell is ribbed inside the mouth. A deep groove circles the anterior canal at the base of the body-whorl. *N. perpinguis* is an especially graceful shell, smaller than the last-named and more finely decussated and darker (brown) in color. It also has a deeply channeled groove encircling the base of the body-whorl. It is often banded in chestnut. Both these species occur in the southern part of California only; *N. tegula* and *N. mendica* are of more northern range. The former resembles the Floridian *N. vibex. N. mendica* is a slender shell three quarters of an inch long, with prominent longitudinal ridges, and light brown in color, with a white aperture. (Plate LXXIV.)

FAMILY **BUCCINIDÆ**

From the number of subfamilies and genera included in this exceedingly large and comprehensive family, it would almost seem that it has served as a sort of dumping-ground for various groups of mollusks of uncertain biological affinities. Although the family has recently been reduced by the removal of several large families, it still remains a bulky one.

GENUS *Buccinum*

The animal is described at some length on page 330. It has no striking peculiarities. The siphon in *Buccinum* is fairly long; the eyes are placed about midway between the base and the end of the tentacles. It is in general a conventional prosobranch animal. The great majority of the members of this family have a boreal range and are found widely distributed within the colder waters of the world.

B. undatum. This is the most prominent representative of the *Buccinidæ* upon the North Atlantic shores of the United States. It is an

Buccinum undatum.

exceedingly common shell, ranging from Cape Cod to Greenland. It is also found in England and Scotland, where it is extensively used as food under the familiar name of " whelk." It affects every kind of station and seems to be as much at home in very considerable depths as about the low-tide mark. Upon the Maine coast it may be found almost everywhere, just below low tide. If none are in sight they may be attracted by putting a dead fish in a basket and anchoring it near shore. The American whelk is somewhat smaller than the British variety, although it attains a length of full three inches. It has revolving ribs and longitudinal oblique folds. A yellowish-brown, velvety epidermis covers the entire shell. The lip is simple, and the shell is white or golden yellow within. The columella is somewhat twisted; the operculum is corneous, with a lateral nucleus. The variations in this shell are so great as to have caused naturalists no little perplexity. Specimens taken near large cities are apt to be defective. (Plate I.)

GENUS *Chrysodomus*

C. decemcostatus. One of the most striking shells of our northeast coast. As its name indicates, it is decorated with (normally) ten costæ.

These are prominent revolving ribs or keels upon the body-whorl, the upper one being the largest, the others diminishing in size toward the base of the shell. Upon the upper whorls but two of these circling keels appear. The lip is plain, but somewhat modified by the termination of the ribs. The columella is arched above; the canal produced (sometimes to the left). The color without is dull ashen-white to horn; within, pure white. The operculum is small, with a terminal nucleus. The animal is the same as *Buccinum*. This species is not quite so common as *B. undatum*, but it is often found associated with it. At Eastport and

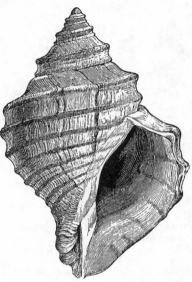

Chrysodomus decemcostatus.

Bar Harbor it is abundant just below low-water mark.

GENUS *Sipho*

S. Stimpsoni. One of the most graceful of the larger shells of our eastern coast. It is almost identical with the *S. islandicus* of northern European waters, and for a long time was considered to be the same species. *S. Stimpsoni* is not found south of Cape Cod, except possibly in deep offshore stations. North of that point it ranges to Newfoundland, but it has enjoyed the reputation of being a rare shell and has been greatly prized by local collectors in consequence. It is, in fact, not rare to any one who is provided with a dredge and rope enough to enable him to use

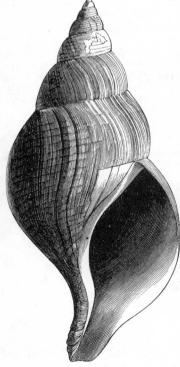

Sipho Stimpsoni.

it effectively in from twenty to one hundred feet of water. The spire is high and regular, with seven to eight slightly rounded whorls. The suture is simple, and there are faint revolving grooves. The epidermis is thick, horn-colored, and sometimes velvety; the lip simple; and the anterior canal produced. The shell is pure white within. The operculum is corneous, with a subterminal nucleus. The animal is the same as *Buccinum*, but with small irregular specks of black. This shell is found from three to five inches long.

Sipho pygmæus.

S. pygmæus. This species has the same range as that of the species just described, and often occurs associated with the young of the latter. It may be distinguished from *S. Stimpsoni* by the greater number of whorls, the more prominent revolving ridges, and the smaller aperture. The epidermis is drab-colored and strongly corrugated, inclined to hirsute. The color of the shell is pure white. Length one inch to one and a half inches. It is found from low-tide mark to very considerable depths.

GENUS *Siphonalia*

S. kellettii. *Siphonalia* is one of the Pacific genera of the *Buccinidæ*, which finds its greatest development in Japanese waters. One of these Japanese species, *S. kellettii*, is also found in California. It has the typical animal of the *Buccinidæ*, and a fusiform shell white to brownish in color, and three to five inches in length. It is conspicuously marked upon the whorls by a revolving series of large rounded knobs and indistinct revolving grooves. The operculum is corneous, the nucleus subterminal. It is found in shallow water to low-tide mark. (Plate LXXIV.)

GENUS *Tritonidea*

T. tincta. A Floridian species which ranges from Hatteras to the West Indies, and finds its station near low-tide mark, upon coralline rock or rough, stony bottom. It is about one inch in length, is of a brownish horn-color, and has an oval aperture with a crenulated outer lip and a deep anterior canal. An entering ridge of white enamel at the top of the columellar lip forms, with one of the teeth of the outer lip, a posterior canal. It is sculptured, with revolving ridges and crossing longitudinal folds. The color is bluish-white within the shell, touched with yellow about the anterior canal and along the edge of the outer lip. (Plate LXXIV.)

FAMILY TURBINELLIDÆ

GENUS *Fulgur*

Of the two genera of this family which occur in American waters, *Fulgur* may be taken as the most characteristic mollusk of the American Atlantic fauna; that is to say, *Fulgur* occurs only on the American east coast. Its range is from Cape Cod to the West Indies. The two Northern species are *F. carica* and

F. canaliculata, both of which are exceedingly common in sandy shore stations from Cape Cod southward.

F. carica. The largest univalve north of Hatteras, most easily recognized by its pear-shaped shell, with simple suture and brilliant vermilion aperture. The anterior canal is long

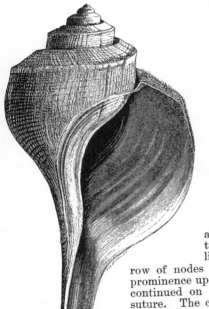

Fulgur carica.

and open; the columellar lip is twisted and arched, and the outer lip is simple. There is a revolving row of nodes or spines of various degrees of prominence upon the shoulder of the body-whorl, continued on the spiral whorls just above the suture. The color varies from ashen-gray to a dirty brown. In young specimens there are stripes and bands of violaceous brown, and the shells are striate within the aperture. The length of this shell is sometimes nine inches.

Fulgur canaliculata.

F. carica frequents almost any sort of bottom. In Long Island Sound they are common on stony ground, but they do not attain the maximum size and the high degree of aperture-coloration characteristic of those taken along the New Jersey shore, on sandy stations exposed to the surf. The string of curiously shaped capsules containing the eggs of *Fulgur* is shown in Plate I.

F. canaliculata often occurs associated with the last. It does not attain quite the same size, but specimens of both species are, on the average, about equal in cubic capacity. It is pear-shaped, like *F. carica*, and has a long anterior canal; but its distinguishing features are the flattened shoulder of the whorls and the deeply channeled sutures. The epidermis is brown, thick, and heavy. The color of the shell is whitish-gray, yellowish within. It is found in the same places as *F. carica*, and is very abundant at Atlantic City and along the entire New Jersey coast.

F. perversa. A Floridian species, immediately recognizable by the fact that it is sinistral; otherwise a description of the shell would almost fit that of *F. carica*, except in the matter of the color of the aperture, which in *F. perversa* is brownish-white. The brownish streaks upon the whorls, in young specimens, are a very noticeable feature of this shell. The shoulders of the whorls are rather flatter than in *F. carica*, but, unlike *F. canaliculata*, the sutures are simple. The row of nodes or rounded spines which encircles the body-whorl appears in the spire as nodes just above the sutures. The animal is jet-black, and frequents sandy flats, where, at low tide, it may be gathered in considerable numbers, as it plows its way along, almost wholly concealed beneath the sand. Large specimens measure quite a foot in length. In old shells the color-markings are not so brilliant, the shells being a dull, lusterless white. (Plate LXXV.)

F. pyrum. Another Floridian species, much smaller than the last (three to four inches), with a regular, pear-shaped outline, a long anterior canal, a low spire, deeply channeled sutures, flattened shoulders, and no spinous or nodose processes. It is ornamented with revolving inconspicuous ribs or striæ, alternately larger, and has a somewhat hirsute epidermis. The color is white, with transverse broad yellowish or rusty lines; the color within the aperture resembles that of the exterior color-lines. It is found on sandy stations, in shallow water. (Plate LXXV.)

Genus *Melongena*

M. corona. A Floridian species, named from the single or double row of spinous processes upon the shoulder of the body-whorl and the crenulated appearance of the spire caused by the continuations of the triangular spines. The three apical whorls are not spinous. There is also a row of hollow triangular spines obliquely encircling the base of the shell. The epidermis is heavy, rough, and brown; the aperture oval and large; the outer lip notched at points where the spines commence; the anterior canal wide and short; and the columella white and twisted, and banded within with purplish-chestnut and white. The color without is drab in older specimens, in young specimens chestnut banded with revolving striæ. Length four inches. Found in shallow water. This active predaceous animal must be the terror of the mollusks in Florida. With his sharply toothed radula he is able to pierce even the ponderous clamshell, *Venus mercenaria*, variety *mortoni*, and devour the soft fleshy parts within. No mollusk, save, perhaps, the vigorous *Strombus pugilis*, can escape the attack of this highwayman. (Plate LXXV.)

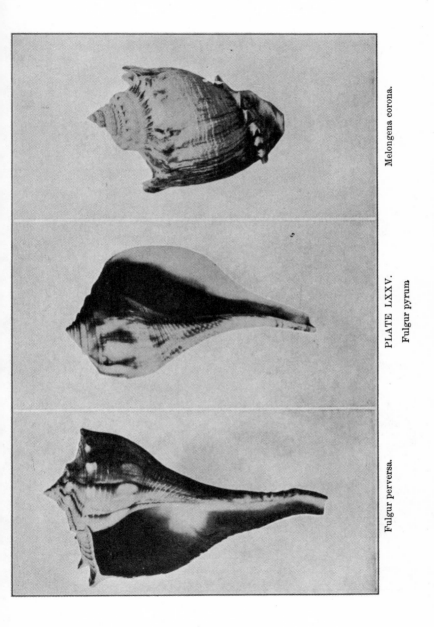

Fulgur perversa.

PLATE LXXV.
Fulgur pyrum

Melongena corona.

Fasciolaria gigantea, very much reduced.   PLATE LXXVI.   Fasciolaria distans.

Fasciolaria tulipa.

FAMILY **FASCIOLARIIDÆ**

This family comprises a number of genera of mollusks which have a fusiform shell, with a long-drawn-out spire and a long anterior canal. The animal is in no manner remarkable; no essential differences are to be noted from the usual conventional type of gasteropod mollusk, represented in the two families last described.

GENUS *Fasciolaria*

This genus is of tropical range, and contains many species of shells which are more or less conspicuous for their large size or their beauty of form. Three species occur in Floridian waters, and all of them may be taken about low-tide mark on the sandy flats which are so characteristic of Florida bays and harbors. All of them are sluggish animals which crawl very slowly along the bottom or bury themselves almost wholly in the sand, leaving only the tip of the spire projecting slightly above.

F. gigantea. This is said to be the largest gasteropod shell known. It often attains a length of sixteen inches, and specimens are reported to have been found measuring no less than two feet. This huge mollusk has a symmetrically fusiform shell, with whorls obtusely ridged and armed with large rounded nodes. The aperture is reddish-brown within. The anterior canal is long and open, and there are three "plaits," or folds, about the columella. The outer lip is more or less sinuate, the color is fleshy-white, and the shell is covered with a thick yellowish or chestnut epidermis. The animal is of a brilliant scarlet color. (Plate LXXVI.)

F. tulipa. An exceedingly common species of Floridian waters, which may justly be classed among the "show shells" of the American Atlantic fauna. It has a typically symmetrical, fusiform shape, with gracefully rounded whorls, and is spirally but not deeply grooved. The sutures are crenulated; the anterior canal is long; there are three entering folds upon the columella; and the outer lip is simple. The scheme of coloration is variable, but there are two chief patterns, which are usually followed, though they often are considerably modified. One is a light-bluish body, variegated with chestnut or olive blotches, which are more extensive upon the spire than upon the body-whorl; the other is a pinkish body, encircled with revolving black lines. The specimens of *F. tulipa*, which are found so abundantly in the shallow bays and estuaries of the Florida coast, are, for some reason, never brightly colored, as are those taken in the open sea. The length is about four to six inches. (Plate LXXVI.)

F. distans. A form almost identical with that last described. It is much smaller, varying from two to three inches in length, lacks the crenulations of the sutures, and is perfectly smooth, save for a few spiral ridges about the base. The color is bluish-white, with clouded longitudinal streaks of olive.   Encircling the shell are from four to seven black lines.   (Plate LXXVI.)

These three species of *Fasciolaria* often occur associated upon sand-banks which are exposed at unusually low tides.   It requires some force to dislodge the large *F. gigantea* from its bed of sand.   When the apex is discovered projecting an inch or less from the bottom, the collector must scrape away the sand down to the body-whorl, and then secure a good hold upon the spire and pull hard.   The stupid animal will not at once withdraw into his shell, but will hang protruded from the aperture like a great piece of vividly red meat.   To extract any of these larger fasciolarias from its shell, it is necessary to boil it for ten or fifteen minutes.   Large specimens of *F. gigantea* should remain in the pot half an hour.   The heavy corneous epidermis of *F. gigantea* will dry and crumble away unless it is rubbed with vaseline about once a year.

Family VOLUTIDÆ

Genus Voluta

Voluta junonia.

The **Volutidæ,** like the cowries, are " aristocratic " shells.   As was stated above, there are many collectors who have become so fascinated by the shells of a few of these "first families of the *Mollusca*" that they make great efforts and spend no small sums in seeking to complete their cabinet series of the rare and more beautiful forms. The *Volutidæ* certainly have very beautiful shells, and they are for the most part exceedingly rare.   The reason of their rarity has no doubt something to do with their habits.   They are probably largely dwellers upon rocky ground, where the dredge cannot reach them.   There is but one species of *Voluta* upon the American coasts which is available to the shore-collector, and this is the well-known and much-sought-after ***V. junonia.***   The animal of *Voluta* has a very broad foot, and a head curiously divided into two lobes, upon which are placed sessile eyes.   A remarkable feature of the genus is the lack of an operculum.

V. junonia. This volute has never been taken alive in shallow water near the shore, but is occasionally found cast upon the beach after violent storms. Sanibel Island is the best locality. *V. junonia* has an obtuse apex, a long aperture, and a shell from three to three and a half inches in length. The color is cream-white, painted with rows of large deep-red spots. In his " American Marine Shells," published nearly thirty years ago, Mr. Tryon says: " This is the most rare and valuable American marine shell; specimens in good condition sell for from fifty to one hundred dollars." A good specimen is probably not worth so much to-day as when Mr. Tryon wrote, but it is at least worth a careful survey of a Floridian beach after a storm.

FAMILY **MARGINELLIDÆ**

GENUS *Marginella*

This is a family of exquisite little shells. In point of beauty they would rival the volutes were they not so much handicapped by their small size. The largest *Marginella* is not more than an inch and a half in length, while the great majority of its two hundred tropical species do not exceed one half an inch. The animal is very similar to that of *Voluta;* indeed, the marginellas were until recently included in the *Volutidæ.* The shell is also suggestive of *Voluta.* It is porcelanous, highly polished, and shining like all shells which are covered by a portion of the mantle when the animal is extended. Forty-seven species of *Marginella* are recorded from the Atlantic coast of the United States. The marginellas frequent sandy or muddy sheltered spots, and may be collected between tide-marks. In California there are several species, which are so minute that it seems hardly worth while to attempt a description of them. They are white and very inconspicuous little shells. One is tempted, however, to speak of some of the fine marginellas of the Bahamas. The animals are quite as beautifully marked as the shells themselves, while the shell of one species is used in jewelry on account of its pearly luster suffused with the most delicate pink.

M. apicina. The most abundant Floridian species of this genus. It is not more than one third of an inch long, with a depressed spire, a large body-whorl, a long aperture nearly equaling the entire length of the shell, a thickened outer lip, and four very prominent plaits on the columella. The surface is smooth. The white, enlarged outer lip is glazed or highly polished, and bluish or brown in color, with red spots. (Plate LXXVII.)

FAMILY **OLIVIDÆ**

GENUS *Oliva*

The genus *Oliva* is one of the favorites among collectors. It comprises smooth, highly polished, porcelanous, and oval shells with a deeply notched, long, narrow aperture. The columellar lip is usually heavily calloused and ornamented with oblique folds. The animal's foot is very large, and extends laterally into lobes which curve back over the shell. In front the propodium is very large, forming, as in *Natica* and *Polynices*, a sort of plow. The mantle lobes almost cover the shell when extended.

O. literata. The only American example out of some sixty known species. It is found in great abundance in sandy tide-pools along the west Florida shores. It ranges from Hatteras to the West Indies, and may be looked for in stations similar to those of the naticas. It is exceedingly active, crawling rapidly over the sand or burying itself very quickly out of sight, and is carnivorous. The shell is highly polished, about two inches long, and pale yellowish-white in color, covered with longitudinal, angulated, or zigzag lines of chestnut. The spire is short, the sutures channeled, and the columella calloused with white enamel, and obliquely striated. (Plate LXXVII.)

GENUS *Olivella*

The genus *Olivella* resembles *Oliva* very closely in conchological characters, but the shells are, with few exceptions, exceedingly small, and usually have a somewhat more elongated spire than is the case in the genus *Oliva* proper. The animal of *Olivella* seems to be a degenerate, for it possesses neither tentacles nor eyes. In habit and station it resembles *Oliva*.

O. mutica. In Floridian waters this species is exceedingly common. It is not more than one fifth of an inch long, is highly polished and shining, and yellowish-white in color, with revolving pale rufous bands. It has the typical oliva-shape.

O. biplicata. A Californian species of considerable interest, the largest of the olivellas. It was evidently used by the aborigines as wampum or as ornaments, for a great many specimens are found among buried Indian relics. This species is about the size and shape of an olive. The spire is short, though longer than the typical *Oliva* spire, the shell is smooth and highly polished, and the columella is thickly calloused, and has two entering folds near the base. The color is creamy-white to dove-color, with a purple sheen over all, and purple markings

PLATE LXXVII.

1, Marginella apicina. enlarged.   3, Olivella biplicata, enlarged.
2, Oliva literata.   4. Conus floridanus.
         5, Cancellaria reticulata.

about the base. Professor Keep speaks of the vast numbers of these olivellas on sandy stations along the Pacific coast. Having found a place where a "little stream of water was oozing out from the bank of sand," he proceeded to dig with a hoe. "I found them [*O. biplicata*] by the hundreds," he continues, "and I had gathered about a thousand before the tide came in. They seemed to lie in groups just under the surface of the sand, yet wholly concealed from sight." (Plate LXXVII.)

O. boetica. A much smaller Pacific form, with a higher tapering spire. It is brown to bluish in color, and often has yellowish stripes. It is polished and shining. Found in sandy stations.

FAMILY **CONIDÆ**

GENUS *Conus*

This is a comprehensive family of several highly diversified genera. Its most prominent genus is *Conus*, a name which indicates the principal feature of the shell, for it is almost an exact cone in shape. *Conus*, along with *Voluta* and *Cypræa*, is entitled to the honor of being considered an aristocrat among mollusks. There are about three hundred and fifty species known, mostly tropical and Indo-Pacific in distribution. The shells have many points of beauty and are often of very high coloration and eccentric markings. Some of the rarer forms are famous in conchological annals for the enormous prices which they have commanded. The rare and beautiful *Conus gloria-maris* once brought £43 ($215) at an auction sale in London. In all shells of *Conus* there is a notch at the upper edge of the aperture for the accommodation of a posterior canal. In some other genera of this family this notch becomes a more prominent feature. The animal has a well-developed foot, a retractile proboscis, eyes situated upon the tentacles, and a fairly long siphon. Upon the under surface of the foot is a conspicuous pore, which opens into a water-vascular system of the foot. *Conus* is accused of having a poison-gland connected with the radula and of having shown vicious traits when captured. The animals are shy, and remain most of the time in hiding, while their pretty shells during life are generally rendered obscure by a dull, colorless epidermis. There are but few species of *Conus* upon the Atlantic shores of the United States, and these are confined to the warmer waters of Florida and the Gulf of Mexico.

C. floridanus. A not unusual shell in shallow-water stations throughout the Florida coast. It has almost the exact outlines of a cone. The flattened shoulder is marked off by an acute carina ; the spire is low, but many-whorled and pagoda-like ; the aperture is long and narrow, and the lip is simple. The coloring is yellowish, banded on a creamy-white background, or dotted in circular rows. Length two inches. (Plate LXXVII.)

C. pealii. One of the smallest species of this genus, its length never exceeding one half of an inch, whereas the majority of the cones are over two inches in length, and many of them rank as large shells. This little Floridian species is regularly cone-shaped, with carinated whorls, thin outer lip, and pagoda-like, low spire. The color is reddish-brown with sky-blue spots, or bluish-brown with lighter spots. There are encircling grooves about the base of the shell.

FAMILY **CANCELLARIIDÆ**

GENUS *Cancellaria*

The last family of the *Gasteropoda* to be considered is the *Cancellariidæ*, which has but one genus, **Cancellaria.** There are several species upon the east coast belonging to deeper-water zones, but one well-known species, **C. reticulata,** is very common on shore stations from Hatteras south. The shell is oblong and solid, with a moderate spire, and whorls slightly flattened below the sutures, and is very roughly granulated or reticulated. The aperture is narrowly ovate, and is ribbed inside. The columella has two very strong and prominent plaits. The color is white, banded and variegated with reddish-brown. Length an inch or more. (Plate LXXVII.)

CLASS **SCAPHOPODA**

FAMILY **DENTALIDÆ**

In nearly all collections of shells from the northeast coast of the United States are certain specimens about one to one and

Entalis striolata.

a half inches long, pure white, and shaped very much like an elephant's tusk. They are round, hollow tubes, slightly curved, of larger diameter at one end than at the other, and with an opening at either end. There are two very common species of these tooth-shells upon the New England coast, **Den-**

talium dentale and *Entalis striolata.* The first has a simple round
hole at the smaller end of the shell, and is faintly marked by longitudinal striæ; the other is a smooth shell which has a notch-like
fissure on the margin of the apical perforation. Neither of these
species is, strictly speaking, a littoral form, for all the *Dentalidæ*
range into deep water, many of them living only in
the profounder depths of the ocean. But these two
species are exceedingly common in the New England
coastal waters, at very moderate depths, and may
sometimes be found upon the beach cast up by storms.
They live buried in the mud, and feed upon infusorians
and all manner of microscopic organisms.

Upon the west coast *Dentalium pretiosum* is very
abundant north of California. It is almost like
the east-coast *Dentalium,* but is more slender.
The Indians used to gather these shells and string
them together upon long threads to be carried
about and used as money. In California occurs *Dentalium hexagonum,* a very delicate
little species with a slightly angulated shell.

The animal of the *Dentalidæ* is remarkable, and easily merits the rank of a separate molluscan class. It has no
head, no tentacles, no eyes, no
heart, and no gills. It is a mollusk because it has a mantle, a
foot, and a radula. Its position,
therefore, is between the *Gasteropoda,* which it resembles in
its univalve shell and radula, and

Dentalium, as seen in longitudinal section (except the foot): *S,* shell; *Mt,* mantle; *Sm,* shell
muscle; *Mh,* mantle-cavity; *F,* foot; *Mk,* cephalic prominence or oral cone; *T,* captacula;
R, radula; *D,* intestine; *L,* liver; *Af,* anus; *G,*
cerebral ganglion; *N,* kidney; *Ge,* generative
gland.

the *Pelecypoda,* to which it is related by the pointed foot and
the absence of head and tentacles, and also by the symmetry
which pervades its organization.

Upon either side of the mouth, just beneath the flap of the
mantle, are bunches of ciliated, contractile filaments (*captacula*),
flattened at the end, which are supposed to be breathing-organs,
and are perhaps exserted for the purpose of catching food.

The entire absence of such important organs as the **heart and** gills, together with the fact that they are undoubted mollusks, would indicate that the *Scaphopoda* are very degenerate animals. The circulatory and respiratory system of mollusks is typically of a high order.

A great many specimens of the *Dentalidæ* dredged in New England waters are dead shells, occupied by a worm which seals up the larger opening, leaving only a small aperture through which it protrudes its long white body. These must not mislead the collector into a vain search for a mantle and other molluscan characteristics of anatomy.

Some of the larger species of *Dentalium* from deep-sea stations are four to five inches in length.

TABLE OF THE COMMONER NORTH AMERICAN PELECYPODS
DESCRIBED IN THIS CHAPTER

Class

PELECYPODA

Orders	Families	Genera	Species
PROTOBRANCHIATA			
	NUCULIDÆ	*Nucula*	*N. proxima*
		Leda	*L. tenuisulcata*
		Yoldia	*Y. limatula*
			Y. thraciæformis
			Y. sapotilla
	SOLENOMYIDÆ	*Solenomya*	*S. velum*
			S. borealis
FILIBRANCHIATA			
	ANOMIIDÆ	*Anomia*	*A. simplex*
			A. aculeata
			A. lampe
		Placunanomia	*P. macrochisma*
	ARCIDÆ	*Arca*	*A. ponderosa*
			A. noæ
			A. pexata
	MYTILIDÆ	*Mytilus*	*M. edulis*
			M. hamatus
			M. californicus
		Modiola	*M. modiolus*
			M. plicatula
			M. tulipa
			M. recta
PSEUDOLAMELLIBRANCHIATA			
	AVICULIDÆ	*Avicula*	*A. atlantica*
		Pinna	*P. muricata*
			P. seminuda
		Perna	*P. ephippium*
	OSTREIDÆ	*Ostrea*	*O. virginica*
			O. frons
			O. lurida
	PECTINIDÆ	*Pecten*	*P. magellanicus*
			P. irradians
			P. dislocatus
			P. islandicus
			P. æquisulcatus
			P. hastatus

Orders	Families	Genera	Species
EULAMELLIBRANCHIATA			
	CARDITIDÆ	*Cardita*	*C. borealis*
			C. floridana
	ASTARTIDÆ	*Astarte*	*A. castanea*
			A. undata
	CYPRINIDÆ	*Arctica*	*A. islandica*
		Lucina	*L. tigrina*
			L. floridana
			L. pennsylvanica
	LUCINIDÆ		*L. dentata*
			L. californica
			L. nuttallii
		Loripes	*L. edentula*
		Tellina	*T. radiata*
			T. alternata
			T. bodegensis
	TELLINIDÆ		*T. tenera*
		Macoma	*M. secta*
			M. nasuta
			M. baltica
			M. proxima
			M. tenta
	DONACIDÆ	*Donax*	*D. variabilis*
			D. californicus
		Mactra	*M. solidissima*
			M. similis
	MACTRIDÆ		*M. ovalis*
			M. lateralis
		Rœta	*R. canaliculata*
		Venus	*V. mercenaria*
			Var. *mortoni*
			V. cancellata
		Cytherea	*C. (Callista) gigantea*
			C. (Callista) maculata
		Dosinia	*D. discus*
	VENERIDÆ		*D. elegans*
		Tivela	*T. crassatelloides*
		Tapes	*T. staminea*
			T. laciniata
		Chione	*C. succincta*
			C. fluctifraga
			C. simillima
		Saxidomus	*S. nuttallii*

Families	Genera	Species
PETRICOLIDÆ	*Petricola*	{ *P. pholadiformis* *P. carditoides*
CARDIIDÆ	*Cardium*	{ *C. magnum* *C. isocardia* *C. lævigatum* *C. serratum* *C. mortoni* *C. substriatum* *C. corbis* *C. quadrigenarium* *C. elatum* *C. islandicum* *C. pinnulatum*
MYIDÆ	*Mya*	*M. arenaria*
SOLENIDÆ	{ *Ensis* *Solen* *Tagelus*	*E. directus* { *S. viridis* *S. sicarius* *S. rosaceus* *T. gibbus*
GLYCIMERIDÆ	*Glycimeris*	*G. generosa*
PHOLADIDÆ	{ *Pholas* *Zirphœa*	{ *P. costata* *P. truncata* *P. californica* *Z. crispata*
TEREDINIDÆ	*Teredo*	*T. navalis*
PANDORIDÆ	*Pandora*	*P. trilineata*

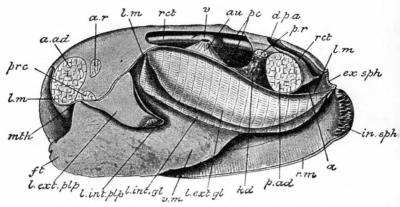

Anatomy of a pelecypod, *Anodonta cygnea.* The animal with most of the left mantle lobe removed. *a,* excretory opening; *a. ad.,* anterior adductor muscle; *a. r.,* anterior retractor muscle; *au.,* left auricle; *d. p. a.,* dorsal pallial aperture; *ex. sph.,* exhalant siphon; *ft.,* foot; *in. sph.,* inhalant siphon; *kd.,* kidney; *l. ext. gl.,* left external gill; *l. ext. plp.,* left external labial palp; *l. int. gl.,* left internal gill; *l. int. plp.,* left internal labial palp; *l. m.,* cut edge of left mantle lobe; *mth.,* mouth; *p. ad.,* posterior adductor muscle; *pc.,* pericardium; *p. r.,* posterior retractor muscle; *prc.,* protractor muscle; *rct.,* rectum; *r. m.,* right mantle lobe; *v,* ventricle; *v. m.,* visceral mass.

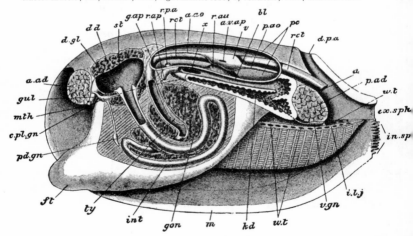

Anatomy of a pelecypod, *Anodonta cygnea.* Dissection from the left side. *a,* excretory opening; *a. ad.,* anterior adductor muscle; *a. ao.,* anterior aorta; *a. v. ap.,* auriculo-ventricular aperture; *bl.,* urinary bladder; *c. pl. gn.,* cerebropleural ganglion; *d. d.,* duct of digestive gland; *d. gl.,* digestive gland; *d. p. a.,* dorsal pallial aperture; *ex. sph.,* exhalant siphon; *ft.,* foot; *g. ap.,* genital aperture. *gon.,* gonad; *gul.,* gullet; *i. l. j.,* interlamellar junction; *in. sph.,* inhalant siphon; *int.,* intestine; *kd.* kidney; *m,* mantle; *mth.,* mouth; *p. ao.,* posterior aorta; *p. ad.,* posterior adductor muscle; *pc.,* pericardium; *pd. gn.,* pedal ganglion; *r. ap.,* renal aperture; *r. au.,* right auricle; *rct.,* rectum; *r. p. a.,* reno-pericardial aperture; *st.,* stomach; *ty.,* typhlosole; *v,* ventricle; *v. gn.,* visceral ganglion; *w. t.,* water-tubes.

CLASS **PELECYPODA**

THIS is a large and important class of the *Mollusca*, comprising an extensive group of animals, which vary widely in structure. Next to the *Gasteropoda*, it is the largest class of the phylum in number of genera and species. The name indicates a "hatchet-shaped" foot, but in many cases it is a misnomer. *Acephala*, meaning "without a head," is also employed for this class, and is, perhaps, a better term. *Lamellibranchiata*, referring to the type of gills prevalent throughout the division, is another name often used. The popular name "bivalves" is an altogether correct one, for all the animals of this class have two shells. To the *Pelecypoda* belong the oysters, clams, scallops, mussels, and, in short, all the *bivalve* mollusks (the word "valve" meaning "shell"). The organization of a pelecypod is entirely similar to that of a gasteropod or a chiton in its fundamental or essential plan, but it differs widely from both in matters of detail. If the student will keep in mind the general principles of gasteropod or the amphineuran structure when he dissects his first pelecypod, he will quickly see that the latter is about the same as a chiton would be were it folded over from a longitudinal median line as axis along its back, so that the opposite mantle-edges would meet, and its various shell-plates would unite upon either side into a single valve; or it is very like a gasteropod made symmetrical, and covered upon its two sides by separate shells instead of covered over its top by one shell. The loss of head, eyes, and tentacles, the substitution of labial palps, the extension and greater development of the gills, the modification of the foot and mantle, and the presence of certain special glands in the *Pelecypoda* become mere matters of anatomical detail.

Any large clam will serve for dissection.   In the neighborhood of New York the edible species known as the " Little Neck " clam (*Venus mercenaria*), or the larger *Mactra* of the sandy shores, will answer the purpose very well.   In Florida, *Callista*, *Venus*, and *Cardium* are all available.   On the west coast the large, heavy *Tivela crassatelloides* is probably the best subject.   The oyster (*Ostrea*) is a degenerate type; and the scallops (*Pecten*) and the mussels (*Mytilus* and *Modiola*) have certain special modifications of their organs which might prove confusing, so these genera are not recommended for dissection and study at first.

Boiling is apt to shrivel and distort the soft, fleshy animal of the bivalves, and it is far better to examine a fresh specimen. The surest way of opening a clam without injuring the animal is to break one of the shells by sharp taps of a hammer, using great care not to lacerate the body within by a too vigorous assault. Pick off the broken pieces after having separated them carefully with a knife from the mantle margin, to which they cling, and after having cut through the tough adductor muscles as close to the shell as possible.   The subject for anatomical study is then prepared " upon the half-shell."

THE MANTLE

The mantle is generally very thin, often a fleshy film of the finest tissue, and adheres to the inner side of each valve.   The outer rim of the mantle is thickened and free, i.e., is not attached to the shell.   This free portion is capable of slight extension beyond the margin of the shell when the valves are opened and the animal is off guard.   In many genera the mantle edge is highly ornate, being waved, crenulated, or fluted, or is beset with several rows of papillæ, and is often richly colored.   Mr. Hickson, a naturalist, who traveled in Celebes, says that the brilliant coloring of the mantle margins of mollusks contributed largely to the extraordinary color-effects upon the coral reefs.

It will be seen that the mantle entirely incloses the animal at the back and sides, just as the cover of a book incloses the pages or printed portion.   At the posterior end of the animal there is usually a point—or perhaps two points—at which the flaps of

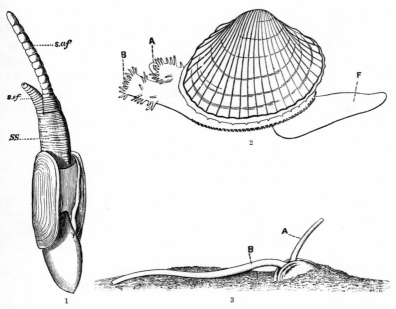

1, *Solecurtus strigillatus*, showing partly united siphons covered with leathery integument: *s. af.*, incurrent siphon ; *s. ef.*, excurrent siphon ; *SS*, the two uniting. 2, *Cardium edule*, showing partly united siphons with papillaceous orifices : *A*, excurrent ; *B*, incurrent siphon ; *F*, foot. 3, *Scrobicularia piperata*, in its natural position in the sand, showing very long tubular siphons : *A*, excurrent siphon ; *B*, incurrent siphon.

the mantle lobes unite in order to form two openings.   These openings are called the siphons.

SIPHONS

In some cases the mantle lobes do not actually unite to form regular siphonal openings, but in life the free mantle-edges have a way of adjusting themselves posteriorly to form *functional siphons* without actually coalescing.   Usually, however, the mantle flaps not only unite posteriorly to form true siphons, but are capable at that point of varying degrees of protrusion from the shell, and when extended the siphons appear as two tubes.   In some genera these siphonal tubes are very long ; in others they are fastened together and surrounded by a tough, leathery integument, which, like the siphons proper, is only an extended portion of the mantle-edge. The orifices of the siphons are generally papillaceous. These two siphons (for there are always two if there are any at all) are the *anal* or excurrent (upper) and the *branchial* or incurrent siphon. The function of the latter is to draw in the pure water to bathe the gills and to furnish food, while the office of the former is to eject waste materials and the water which has already passed over the gills.

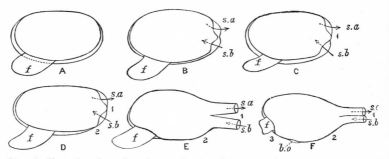

Diagram illustrating the various degrees of union of the mantle lobes : A, mantle completely open ; B, rudiments of siphons, mantle still completely open ; C, mantle closed at one point ; D, mantle closed at two points, with complete formation of siphonal apertures ; E, development of siphons, ventral closure more extended ; F, mantle closed at three points, with fourth orifice ; *f*, foot ; *s. a.*, *s. b.*, anal and branchial siphons ; 1, 2, 3, first, second, and third points of closure of mantle ; *b. o.*, byssal aperture.

MANTLE FUSION

Besides the points of juncture where the mantle-edges unite to form the siphons, the coalescence of the two mantle lobes may be extended, and they may become further united and fused together at other points. Indeed, the fusion of the mantle-edges may become almost complete ; but it always leaves the siphonal openings and a third opening through which the foot may be extended. This opening for the foot is called the *pedal opening*, or orifice. In such cases, therefore, the mantle becomes much like a bag or sac. The degree of fusion of the mantle-edges appears to correspond closely with certain changes in the organization of the animal, and this feature must be regarded as a very important character.

The figures on pages 411, 412, and 413 show the degrees of mantle fusion in various groups from the open to the almost wholly closed types. One (A, page 413) gives an example of very large siphons united together and protected by the tough, leathery integument. To the right of this cut may be seen the foot projecting from the pedal opening in the mantle. Another gives the two siphons of *Cardium*, the lower or branchial one being the longer. The mantle-edges below are fluted, and a large foot projects forward. Another shows two siphons of *Scrobicularia*, of the free and greatly extended type. Fig. B (page 413) illustrates the ventral portion of a pelecypod, which shows very well the most advanced type of mantle fusion. Besides the siphonal openings at the end of the long projection to the left, the only other opening is the very small orifice marked "2," for the accommodation of a small, insignificant foot. In the other figures different degrees of mantle fusion are indicated.

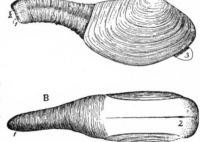

A: 1, incurrent siphon; 2, excurrent siphon; 3, foot. B: 1, siphons; 2, pedal opening.

Before removing the mantle from one side of the specimen to be examined, note the two strong muscles which are at either end of the body. These are the *anterior* and *posterior adductor* muscles, their office being to hold the valves tightly shut. They are of great strength, as any one may prove to his satisfaction by attempting to open a clam. Through a long series of forms these two muscles approach each other in position, and in the scallops and the oysters there is but one adductor muscle, occupying a central position. Morphologically it is the survival of the posterior adductor.

THE BRANCHIÆ OR GILLS

Removing carefully the thin, fleshy mantle, the gills are exposed to view—that is, of course, the gills of that side of the animal, for there are two sets, one upon each side of the body, or visceral mass, and lying between the body proper and the mantle folds. Each set consists of two plate-like bodies with a texture of reticulated or basketwork appearance. Thus there are the inner and outer right gills and the inner and outer left gills. If one gill is removed and carefully examined it will itself probably be found to be double, consisting of many filaments placed side by side and then doubled back like a row of hairpins, the filaments being united by interciliary processes, or by vascular channels together with more or less dense connective tissue.

The modifications of the pelecypod gills are difficult to follow, but the principle upon which they perform their duties is the same in all cases. The gill-filaments are all connected with a long vein, and, being hollow, admit the blood, which is aërated by close contact with the water and is then returned to another vein in immediate connection with the auricles of the heart. There is another function accomplished by the gills, which in some families seems to be quite as important as their respiratory one, namely, the office of giving lodgment to the ova while in process of development before hatching. At certain seasons the gills of a number of pelecypod genera become literally filled with eggs; sometimes this curious phenomenon extends to the mantle itself, and more or less to the entire surface of the animal. The eggs are first regularly ejected from the genital ducts and find lodgment upon the body-surface, but usually only upon the gills, where they remain as in a brood-pouch between the lamellæ of the inner and outer gills. When the eggs hatch, the free-swimming young escape from the mantle cavity. Probably not more than one individual in a million ever reaches maturity.

The figure on page 408 shows the mantle removed, exhibiting the gills, the foot, the labial palps, and the pericardium, inside of which is the heart. Removing the gills, we find exposed the body, or visceral mass, which, as in the *Gasteropoda*, is thickened below into the foot. A longitudinal section is shown on page 408, the visceral mass being sliced almost through the middle; a portion of the gills of the farther side shows below.

THE FOOT

The foot undergoes great variation, from a strong, powerful organ capable of forcing its way through heavy gravelly bottom or burrowing deeply into the sand or mud, to the merest trace of a pedal organ. In the oyster the foot has become almost entirely atrophied; the stationary life led by the animal renders such an organ quite unnecessary. Excepting in a few families, the pelecypod foot is well developed. In a number of genera the foot contains a gland for the secretion

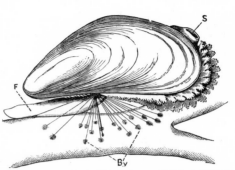

Mytilus edulis, attached by its byssus (*By*) to a piece of wood: *F*, foot; *S*, excurrent siphon, the branchial siphon being below it and not closed.

of long silk-like or horn-like fibers, which are collectively called a *byssus*. The use of a byssus is for attachment to any object to

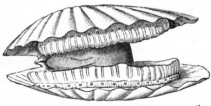

Pecten opercularis, showing the ocelli, or eyes, on the two edges of the mantle.

effect a temporary or permanent lodgment. The accompanying cut shows *Mytilus edulis*, a common east-coast pelecypod, attached by its byssus to a piece of wood. Most bivalves having a strong byssus exhibit a feeble development of the foot; nearly all bivalves, however, show traces, sometimes only in the embryo, of a byssal gland.

The visceral mass contains the liver, the exceedingly large generative glands, the kidneys, etc., and through all this soft whitish or reddish mass the alimentary canal wanders about in a tortuous fashion, finally passing through the pericardium and the ventricle of the heart, and terminating just over and back of the posterior adductor muscle.

The pelecypods have no head or tentacles, but the place of the latter is taken by two pairs of triangular flaps upon either side of the mouth. These are called the *labial palps*, and they no doubt operate by means of their ciliated surface to keep in motion the current of water over the gills and to the mouth.

As a rule, pelecypods have no eyes, but when eyes are present they are situated upon the edge of the mantle. The eyes are not highly developed organs, but they nevertheless appear to be very sensitive to light, for the bivalves which are so endowed will, when kept in aquaria, instantly close their shells when the shadow of a fish passes over them.

The heart lies in the pericardium and is situated dorsally, just in front of the posterior adductor muscle. It has a median ventricle and two lateral auricles, each connected with the branchiæ upon its respective side. It seems a curious economy that passes the intestine through the ventricle, but this is the case in the great majority of pelecypod genera. The vascular system is closed and is of a high order. It is probable that "breathing" takes place upon the inner mantle surfaces as well as in the gills themselves; for these surfaces are crowded with excessively fine and delicate capillaries, which bring the blood very near to the water. This power of "breathing by the skin" is quite characteristic of the *Mollusca* in general.

Having once familiarized one's self with the more prominent features of pelecypod organization, it becomes very interesting to examine anatomically every new form that is captured. Surprises are always in store, and sometimes the peculiar juxtaposition and relative sizes of the organs are a trifle confusing; but, upon the whole, the bivalve organization is simple and lends itself far more readily than does that of the gasteropods to satisfactory examination. Some of the more striking anatomical peculiarities are reserved for mention in the notes upon the various genera and species common upon our shores.

THE PELECYPOD SHELL

As has been seen, the testaceous covering of the *Pelecypoda* consists of two valves or shells which fit more or less closely and firmly together and are placed one upon either side of the animal. The two valves are always held together tightly along a dorsal margin by a "hinge ligament," an exceedingly tough, leathery substance, and they are usually secured the more firmly by a system of interlocking teeth, which project from the hinge. The opening and shutting of the valves is controlled by the adductor muscles of the animal, by the *ligament* which binds the valves together, and by the *cartilage*, an elastic pad of rubber-like appearance which is lodged just within the hinge, and is compressed when the valves are closed together. Thus, when the valves are closed, there is always a strain upon the adductor to overcome the elastic resistance of the cartilage. When a pelecypod dies and the pull of the adductor muscles is released, the valves gape open.

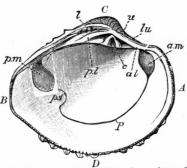

The interior characteristics of a pelecypod shell. Left valve of *Venus gnidia: A*, anterior, *B*, posterior, *C*, dorsal, *D*, ventral margin; *AB*, length, *CD*, breadth of shell; *a. m.*, anterior, *p. m.*, posterior impressions of adductor muscle; *p*, pallial line; *p. s.*, pallial sinus; *l*, ligament; *lu.*, lunule; *u*, umbo; *c*, cardinal teeth; *a. l.*, anterior lateral tooth; *p. l.*, posterior lateral tooth.

The summit or apex of the valve is called the *umbo*, or *beak*. It is usually twisted to some extent, and in certain forms develops a suggestive spiral figure. The beaks of the valves are the points where the shell-growth begins, the secretion of calcareous matter being made by the mantle margin and deposited about the edges of the valves; the growth is therefore constantly away from the umbones.

The umbones usually point forward. In many species they touch each other over the hinge-margin or approximate very closely; in other species the hinge-margin is very wide and the beaks are comparatively far apart. The hinge-margin, lying adjacent to the umbones, is known as the *dorsal margin* of the shell, in contradistinction to the *ventral margin*, opposite the umbones. The *anterior margin* is the front edge and the *posterior margin* the hinder edge of the shells, through which the siphons may project.

When the umbones are about central in respect to the posterior and anterior margins, the shells are said to be *equilateral*. When the two valves are almost exactly alike in size and shape they are called *equivalve*.

In many forms there is a heart-shaped space upon the dorsal margin of the closed valves forward of the umbones, called the *lunule*. Similarly placed back of the umbones is sometimes a more or less clearly defined space called the *escutcheon*. The outer surface of bivalve shells admits of infinite variety of sculpturing and ornamentation, ranging from a perfectly smooth to a heavily ribbed, nodose, spinous, or deeply decussated surface. The color-markings are often brilliant and eccentric.

The right and left valves may be distinguished by remembering that the siphons are always posterior, and that the umbones usually point forward.

The hinge of bivalve shells undergoes many variations in the different genera. The simplest type is a smooth edentate surface where the two valves meet and are held together only by the strong ligament. Generally, however, there is a system of interlocking teeth, those in the center of the hinge being the *cardinals* and those upon either side the *laterals*. In some forms there are rows of fine comb-like teeth along the hinge-margin, with no distinction between cardinals and laterals.

The object of these hinge-teeth is at once obvious, for they give a rigidity and increased strength to the entire mechanism, especially when closed. There is occasionally a saucer-shaped plate or platform just under the cardinal teeth and within the shell, called the *fossette*. Upon this rests the internal elastic cartilage.

Upon the smooth interior surfaces of the valves are always certain markings, which correspond to anatomical features of the animal and are consequently of considerable importance in the determination of the systematic position of the specimen. First, the well-marked impressions left by the adductor muscles will be noted; then a more or less distinct line which, describing roughly a circle, connects the two muscle scars. This line represents the points at which the mantle became detached from the shell. In other words, all the space within this *pallial line* (barring the muscle scars) was, in life, covered by the mantle, which adhered tightly to it. The space between this pallial line and the outer edge of the valve was occupied in life by the free portion of the mantle. Frequently a depression in the pallial line toward the center of the valve is seen in the posterior end. This is called the *pallial sinus*, and marks the space occupied by the siphons. The pallial sinus is absent, moderate, or deep, according as the animal possessed no siphons, or small or large ones.

The length of bivalve shells is measured from their anterior to their posterior ends, while the height indicates the greatest diameter between the umbones and the ventral margin.

The greatest possible degree of variation exists in the structure of the pelecypod shell. Every degree of thickness from the most fragile, tissue-like structure to the very heavy and ponderous tests of some of the *Veneridæ* is to be found. There is also a range in size from the very minute *Spheria* to the giant *Tridacna* of Eastern seas, which weighs several hundred pounds. As in the *Gasteropoda*, there is fortunately a very close parallelism between shell and anatomical variations. One very quickly learns to place a bivalve in its systematic position by a mere glance at the shell alone. While the higher classification into orders, suborders, etc., is based upon anatomical features, the genera often and the species always are founded upon conchological or shell characters.

The *Pelecypoda* offer one of the most interesting fields for investigation and study among the invertebrates. Although by no means neglected, they have not received as much attention on the part of biologists as has been given to other phyla, or indeed to the other classes of this same phylum.

CLASSIFICATION OF THE PELECYPODA

Nearly every systematic writer upon the mollusks has attempted to give a good classification of the bivalves, yet none of the results is wholly satisfactory. The scheme now generally adopted is one based upon modifications of the gills, or branchiæ, and has practically replaced all the older classifications, which depended upon the presence or absence of siphons, the degree of mantle fusion, the arrangement of teeth upon the hinge, the number of adductor muscles, etc. The idea of arrangement according to gill-structure is substantially this: the development of the gill from the simplest and most rudimentary type through successive stages to a higher, more complex, and presumably more efficient type, marks the natural progress or development of the pelecypod animal itself. By adopting the gill as a guide one follows, therefore, a natural method. Upon the other hand, the presence or absence of siphons, the shape of the foot, the number of adductor muscles, all depend merely upon the acquired habits of the animal, these particular features being subject to modification according to environment and changed conditions.

The five orders of the *Pelecypoda* are: *Protobranchiata, Filibranchiata, Pseudolamellibranchiata, Eulamellibranchiata, Septibranchiata.*

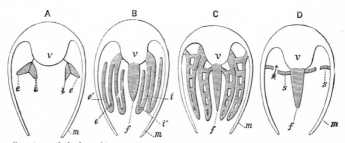

Structure of the branchiæ or gills of pelecypods, seen diagrammatically in section: A, *Protobranchiata;* B, *Filibranchiata;* C, *Eulamellibranchiata;* D, *Septibranchiata; e, e,* external row of filaments; *i, i,* internal row of filaments; *e',* external row or plate folded back; *i',* internal row folded back; *f,* foot; *m,* mantle; *s,* septum; *v,* visceral mass.

The first includes the simpler type of gill as represented in the accompanying figure (A). Its filaments are short and not reflected. The second, represented in Fig. B, has the filaments long, reflected, and connected (each filament to its adjacent ones) by means of surface cilia. The third type of gill resembles the last except that the ends of the filaments of the outer gill are attached to the mantle, and the ends of the filaments of the inner gill are attached to the foot or visceral mass. The fourth type of gill is far more highly developed. The adjacent filaments are connected, not by cilia, but by vascular channels, and the depending and recurved portions of each filament are also connected in a manner presumed to admit of the passage of blood. This gives to the organ the appearance of basketwork or network. The ends of the filaments are attached to the mantle and to the visceral mass, as in the last order, forming cavities or chambers above (see Fig. C). This order includes the great majority of the *Pelecypoda.*

The fifth and last order is confined to but two rather obscure families, in which the gill-development is carried to the point of substitution of muscular partitions which form a separate chamber connected with the mantle cavity by a narrow slit, the surface of the chamber having respiratory functions (Fig. D).

The collector of living marine objects who has become fascinated by their beauty and who derives pleasure from examining the greater beauty of their structures will find a rich field for research in the pelecypod gills. But unless he has time at his disposal and some skill with a microscope, he would do well not to venture too far into this alluring but difficult and vexatious subject.

Our coastal waters are fairly rich in bivalves, but the most strikingly handsome species of this class—and there are many of them—are inhabitants of warmer seas. Of the great number of bivalves to be found upon our own shores we can only mention briefly some of the commonest species.

ORDER **PROTOBRANCHIATA**

FAMILY **NUCULIDÆ**

In this family the gills are of the simplest and most primitive type. The mantle-edges are entirely open along the ventral margin, but they are united posteriorly in some of the *Nuculidæ* to form two short siphons. The palps are exceedingly large. The foot is also large, and by its disk-like surface is adapted to creeping, much as is a gasteropod foot ; its edges are often crenulated or scalloped, and there is no trace of a byssus. The shells are equivalve, and their most prominent feature is the hinge, which is beset with sharp, comb-like teeth in two straight rows, one upon each side of a central pit, a space reserved for the ligament.

Genus *Nucula*

N. proxima. The commonest of several species of the genus found along the New England coast. It is oblique, with a light-olive epidermis, nacreous interior, and finely crenulated margins. Its length is about one quarter of an inch. The animal has no siphons. It lives in either muddy or pebbly stations near the shore, and probably exists in countless thousands in all the bays and harbors of the New England coast.

Nucula proxima.

Genus *Leda*

L. tenuisulcata. This species has a longer shell than the preceding; it is more produced behind, and is narrowed into a blunt, slightly gaping point. The epidermis is light greenish, and the shell has a pearly luster within. The outer surface of the shell is concentrically grooved; the beaks are smooth. The foot is disk-shaped, and the animal is provided with small siphons. The length of this shell is about one inch. Its station is the muddy bottom in shoal water on the New England coast.

Leda tenuisulcata.

Genus *Yoldia*

Y. limatula. This species has the same sort of toothed hinge exhibited in the two preceding species, but the shell is considerably larger (two inches), with a smooth greenish glazed epidermis. The beaks are nearly central. The interior of the shell is light bluish and pearly. The animal has two slender, short, united siphons and a disk-shaped foot with simple margins. This species can make excellent use of its foot, for it crawls with rapidity, and also can execute leaps in an astonishing manner. Found in muddy stations in shoal water on the New England coast.

Yoldia limatula.

Y. thraciæformis. A much larger species, found on the New England coast. It may be distinguished by a rib-like wave extending obliquely from the umbones to the ventral margin of the shell. It measures over two and a half inches in length and one and a half inches in height, and is dark olive-green. The foot is like that of *Y. limatula.* The labial palps are exceedingly large.

Y. sapotilla. The shell is ovate, prolonged on one side, thin, fragile, translucent, and covered with a thin, glossy epidermis, greenish in color. The anterior half is semi-oval, the posterior portion narrowed and compressed; within it is pearly-white, with a triangular cartilage cavity, and sixteen to eighteen pointed teeth on each side. In length

Yoldia thraciæformis.

Yoldia sapotilla.

it is little less than an inch. Found from Long Island Sound northward.

FAMILY **SOLENOMYIDÆ**

GENUS *Solenomya*

Two species of this genus, which are greatly prized by collectors on account of the extraordinary development of the epidermis of the shell, occur in New England waters. The strong corneous periostracum of a deep chestnut-color projects considerably beyond the margins of the valves; the shells are exceedingly thin and fragile, and are marked with radiating lines. The two species are easily distinguished by their difference in size. *S. velum* is about one inch long and one half of an inch high. *S. borealis,* of arctic range, is quite twice that

Solenomya velum.

size. Their anatomy is similar in essentials to that of *Yoldia.* These species live near shore in sandy bottoms, and are occasionally found upon the beach between tides. Chelsea Beach, just north of Boston, is an often-quoted locality.

ORDER **FILIBRANCHIATA**

There are several families of this order which are well represented in both the Atlantic and the Pacific waters of the United States. The characteristic feature of this group of bivalves is the filamentous gill, that is, a gill with the filaments long, doubled back, and united to each other only by ciliary junctures. These junctures are so slight that they break readily when a specimen of a gill is handled, leaving the filaments free. The presence of a byssal gland in the foot, and often a well-developed byssus, is another characteristic of this order.

Family **ANOMIIDÆ**

Genus *Anomia*

This is a family of peculiar and highly specialized forms. *Anomia* has an irregularly rounded shell, with one convex and one flat or concave valve. There is no regular hinge or well-defined hinge-margin, but a raised fossette, or cartilage plate, occupies a position at the top of the valves. In the flat valve there is a large oblong hole just under the apex, through which projects a calcified byssus, by means of which the animal secures itself to oysters, dead shells, stones, or any solid object. The anomias, which have become stationary in habit, have practically lost their foot. The gills are very large and curved, while all the organs seem to be abnormally placed on account of the huge byssus and byssal muscle. For the byssus to pass, as it does, through a specially prepared hole in one of the valves is an extraordinary departure from the conventional types of byssiferous species. The heart is not traversed by the intestine. Altogether, then, *Anomia* is a very curious genus.

A. simplex. The commoner large form of New England. It varies from one to three inches in diameter, is exceedingly irregular in shape, and its surface is variously undulated and plaited in accordance with the surface of the object to which it is attached. Thousands of these valves, disjointed and separated, are cast upon the beaches all along our Atlantic coast. They are light green to salmon- or copper-color, generally fragile and scaly, and have a peculiarly dulled (as though greased) nacre.

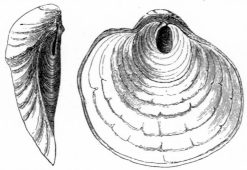

Anomia simplex, side view. *Anomia simplex*, from below.

A. aculeata is much smaller than the last species, and the surface of the convex valve is roughened by prickly scales. The smaller valve is very thin, with an almost circular aperture for the byssus. Its diameter is about half an inch. Found at-tached to stones, etc., about the holdfasts of *Fucus*.

Anomia aculeata, from above.
Anomia aculeata, from below.

A. lampe, a California species ranging more to the south, is small (half an inch), and greatly resembles the east-coast *A. aculeata*, save as regards the smooth surface of the former.

Genus *Placunanomia*

P. macrochisma. This species occurs on the Californian coast. It has the same sort of calcified byssus as *Anomia*, and also the hole to accom-modate it in the smaller valve. The scar formed by the muscle which controls the byssus is curiously rayed in this genus. The normal shape of the shell is circular; it is pearly within, and of a greenish tinge with-out. Two to four inches in diameter. (Plate LXXVIII.)

Family ARCIDÆ

Genus *Arca*

The *Arcidæ* may always be distinguished by the long row of comb-like teeth upon the hinge, the total want of siphons (a fact which may be discovered in the shell alone by its lack of a pallial sinus), and the solid trapezoidal or round shell, with its tendency to strong ribs radiating from the umbones. The periostracum, or epidermis, is heavy and often velvety or even hairy. The animal of *Arca* has the gills placed in an oblique position; the foot is large and strongly developed. No trace of mantle fusion exists. The mantle-edges bear a row of composite eyes. The gill-fila-ments are entirely free, there being even no ciliary junctions.

Arca pexata.

A. pexata. An exceedingly common species in Long Island Sound and on the coast of New Jersey. The shell is oblong, with prominent beaks directed forward. The hinge-teeth are arranged in a row posterior to the beaks, while just under the beaks are a num-ber of irregular cartilage-pits. About thirty-two to thirty-six ra-diating ribs ornament the shell. The inner margins of the shell are rather deeply scalloped; the epi-dermis is thick, shaggy, and dark

brown. Length two to two and a quarter inches; height two inches.
A. pexata is one of the few pelecypods which have red blood, a fact
which accounts for its popular name of " bloody clam."

A. ponderosa. The most prominent *Arca* upon our Atlantic coast,
especially south of Virginia. The beaks of this shell are very prominent, and do not approach each other very closely on account of the
wide dorsal margin of the shells, the large space between the beaks
being occupied by an external ligament. The hinge-teeth are smaller
in the middle. There are from twenty-five to twenty-eight ribs; the
ventral margin of the valves is somewhat contracted in the middle.
Length two and a half inches; height two inches. Very heavy and
solid. This exceedingly common species is often cast upon the beaches
south of Hatteras in numbers beyond computation. In life it is covered
with a heavy, coarse, velvety epidermis, almost jet-black in color.
(Plate LXXVIII.)

A. noæ. The well-known " Noah's-ark " shell, a common species
along the shores of the Southeastern States. It also occurs in the
Mediterranean. Unlike most arcas, it spins a byssus, by means of which
it attaches itself to the under surfaces of stones at low water. The
hinge-margin is perfectly straight and regularly toothed. The beaks
are high and are situated very far forward. The dorsal margin of the
valves is strikingly large, and is marked by lattice-like grooves; it forms
a concave surface over an inch in width between the umbones. The
shell is strongly ribbed without. The ventral margin of the valves is
sinuous and gapes slightly at a central point for the accommodation of
the byssus. (Plate LXXVIII.)

FAMILY **MYTILIDÆ**

GENERA *Mytilus, Modiola*

The *Mytilidæ* are a large family, including the mussels, so commonly found between tides upon all shores. The two ordinary
genera *Mytilus* and *Modiola*, which often occur associated together upon our eastern coast, may readily be distinguished one
from the other by the position of their beaks. In the former
genus the beak is terminal, that is, it is situated at the very tip-
end of the shell; in the latter genus it is not quite terminal.
Aside from this simple feature, the genera are practically the
same, the animals being identical. *Mytilus* and *Modiola*, commonly known as mussels, have acquired the stationary habit and
are provided with a relatively small foot (in some species amount-
ing to no more than a mere tubercle); but in place of a useful
foot is a well-developed byssogenous gland, which secretes an ex-

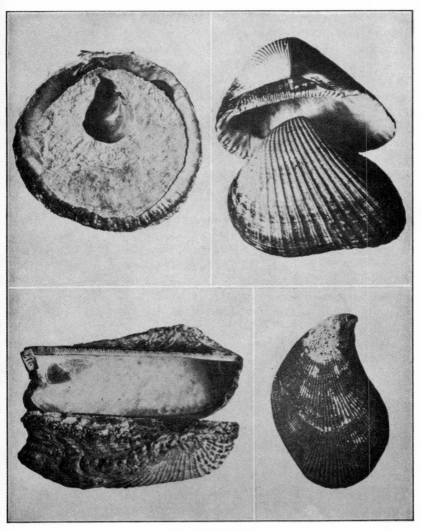

PLATE LXXVIII.

Placunanomia macrochisma.   Arca ponderosa.
Arca noæ.   Mytilus hamatus.

ceedingly tough, fibrous byssus. By means of this the animal may not only attach itself firmly to any sort of object, but may actually move about. Fibers of the byssus are thrown out, and, as though possessed of life, they seize upon objects in the direction in which

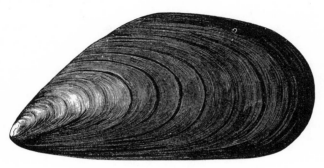

Mytilus edulis, typical form.

Mytilus desires to move, and by contraction of the muscles which control the byssus the animal is drawn forward, the operation being then repeated. It must be a very tedious method of travel. However, the *Mytilidæ* are not restless creatures. They pass their lives content to remain firmly fixed to some object, and their movements, if any, are within a very narrow circle. The animal has very long gills of the usual filamentous type. The mantle fuses at one point to form an anal siphon, the lower or branchial one being, therefore, functional. The palps are large. One curious feature of this group is the enormous extent of the genital glands, which actually appear to pervade the entire structure of the animal, gills, mantle, foot, and all. At times the whole being is a veritable receptacle for myriads of tiny yellowish eggs.

The *Mytilidæ* are of universal distribution, and are for the most part of littoral or shallow-water range. Some species are esteemed as an article of food, notably *Mytilus edulis*.

Mussel-culture has been profitably carried on in France for a long time, but the genus has not been utilized to any extent as food in this country.

Mytilus edulis is exceedingly abundant along the New England coast. It lives in colonies, often between tides, in pebbly stations among large rocks. It is always so fastened by its byssus that the beaks of the valves point downward, and the ventral margin projects above the sand or mud. The color of the epidermis in the adult form is black or a deep blue-black; the shell proper is violet. Hinge-teeth are wanting. Length two and a half inches. A variety of this species, *M. pellucidus,* is often found associated with the typical form. It is brightly rayed in green and yellow. *M. edulis* occurs in Europe, where it is quite extensively used as food. It also occurs (by importation) in San Francisco Bay.

Mytilus edulis, rayed-color variety.

M. hamatus has a more southern range than has *M. edulis*, and is found from the Chesapeake southward. Its shell is considerably twisted just below the umbonal region, while its whole surface is densely striated. Its color is dark fuscous. Length one to two inches. It is found in great numbers attached to oysters by its byssus. In Florida it is very common. (Plate LXXVIII.)

M. californicus. A common west-coast species, which finds its station among rocks exposed to the surf. It is about the same size as *M. edulis*, but has a lighter brownish glossy epidermis and several conspicuous, well-rounded, radiating ribs. The animal is orange-colored.

Modiola modiolus. After violent storms upon the New England coast, when a large *Laminaria* is wrenched from its rocky bed and washed ashore, its roots will, in many cases, be found clinging to this large mussel. The thick glossy epidermis of deep chestnut-color folds over the margin of the valves, and the outer surface, especially near the ventral margin, is covered with a tough hairy growth. Length four to five inches. The animal is orange-red. The great size and swelling fullness of this species at once distinguish it from all others upon our coast. It is not a shallow-water form, but is extremely common upon all beaches north of Hatteras. It also occurs in Alaskan waters to Puget Sound, where it is known as the "great horse-mussel." Sometimes these large modiolas may be found in rocky tide-pools which are washed by the surf at high tide. They hide far back in the crevices of boulders, and

Modiola modiolus.

are not easily detected. They are not uncommon in such stations at Mount Desert, Maine.

M. plicatula. This species of *Modiola* ranges from Canada to Hatteras, and inhabits the tidal waters of streams, sheltered muddy reaches among reeds, and tidal flats. It is a dingy-looking shell, ornamented with

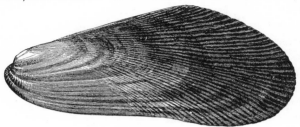

Modiola plicatula, typical form.

numerous radiating ribs, which are very fine upon the anterior portion of the shell. The epidermis is thin and of a dirty yellowish-green color. Within it is silvery-white. In the ventral margin there is an opening for the accommodation of a byssus. Length about three inches in New England; slightly larger at Norfolk. There is probably no muddy reach of land that is exposed at low tide from Maine to the Carolinas that is not inhabited by *M. plicatula*.

M. tulipa. This is the " show shell " of the genus *Modiola* in American waters. It belongs to the Southern fauna, and, like the others of its genus, it moors itself to wood or other solid objects by means of its byssus. It is of about the same size as the last species, but is perfectly smooth and of a bright-yellowish color, with dark rays over the central portion.

M. recta. A species of *Modiola* fairly abundant on the Pacific coast from Vancouver to southern California. It has a

Modiola nigra.

long, narrow shell with a dark-brown glossy epidermis; lighter posteriorly, and with a short hairy growth. The interior is white. Length three to four inches.

ORDER **PSEUDOLAMELLIBRANCHIATA**

This third order of *Pelecypoda* is made up of a number of families in which the gills are filamentous, but in which the filaments have become united at their ends to the mantle (on the outer gills) and to the body-mass (on the inner gills). Here also the first traces of the higher type of gill found in the next order appear; that is, a gill in which the filaments are connected by vascular channels instead of by cilia. This order therefore is presumed to connect the true filamentous type of gill with the fully developed lamellar type. As the filaments do not always fuse with the mantle or foot, the description of the pseudolamellibranch gill becomes somewhat vague, and there is some room for doubt whether this order should exist at all.

Most of the genera placed in it are monomyarian; that is, they have but one adductor muscle, or if two, the anterior one is very small and unimportant. The mantle-edges are entirely open, there being no regularly formed siphons. As a rule, the foot is exceedingly small or quite aborted.

FAMILY AVICULIDÆ

In this family there is an exception to the rule just stated: the foot is long. There is a byssus, and the gills (by their outer ascending filaments) are concrescent with the mantle.

The interior of all the *Aviculidæ* is of a highly polished nacre, and some of the larger species have been extensively collected for mother-of-pearl. To the *Aviculidæ* belong the pearl-oysters (*Meleagrina margaritifera*).

A delightful air of romance and adventure surrounds the pearl-fisheries, about which much has been written. The pearl is an abnormal product formed by the deposition of nacre around some foreign object, such as a grain of sand, or—usually, it is said— an egg which has failed to develop properly. They are seldom found in individuals having favorable conditions of growth, but those which are greatly crowded together and covered with various parasites and growths are most productive of them. The pearl is the same in substance as the nacreous shell of the pearl-oyster, and its iridescence is due to the fine striæ of the undulating layers of which it is composed. The pearl as well as the shell is produced by the shell-glands of the mantle. The value of the pearl is based on the brilliancy of the nacre, the size, and the form. Luster, or "orient," is to the pearl what brilliancy is to the diamond. The round form has the greatest value, next the pearshape, and lastly the oval. Pearls of inferior value are produced by other species than *Meleagrina margaritifera*, the true pearl-oyster. Many bivalves secrete similar bodies, but as they have the nature of the shell, those produced by mollusks having lusterless interiors are of no value. Beautiful pink pearls are found in the gasteropod *Strombus gigas*, the conch-shell of the West Indies. The shells of the pearl-oyster are themselves very valuable, being the "mother-of-pearl" used in the manufacture of buttons, knife-handles, inlay-work, and so on. They have three grades of commercial value; of the first are the "silver-lipped," from the South Seas, of the second the "black-lipped," from Manila and Ceylon, and of the third the "bullock-shells," from Panama.

Genus *Avicula*

A. atlantica. A Floridian species which is often found attached by its byssus to large algæ which have been washed upon the beach. The shell is reddish-brown, with many white radial lines. Its obliquely oval shape, the long wing-like extension of the dorsal margin, the inequivalve shells, and the byssal sinus placed just below the forward extension of the hinge, are characteristics which will enable one to recognize the species at once. The structure of the shell is unusual in being so largely composed of organic matter that it possesses elasticity near its thinner edges.

Genus *Pinna*

P. muricata and **P. seminuda.** Two species of this family which are very abundant in Floridian waters and are often to be found associated upon the muddy or sandy shores of bays. Like *Modiola plicatula*, they attach themselves by means of their byssus to shells or stones which lie under the surface. With the pointed end of the shell directed downward, they remain almost wholly concealed in the sand. Only about one quarter of an inch of the broad end of the shell projects above the sand. The edges of the valves are as sharp as knife-blades, and great caution must be used while walking barefooted along a beach inhabited by *Pinna*. The shells of both species are of a triangular wedge-shape and are composed of a translucent crystalline matter. *P. muricata* is beset with triangular erect scales which project out like spines. Their edges are also sharp like pieces of broken glass. *P. seminuda* also has these raised scales, but they are far more numerous and much smaller, and are arranged in closely packed radiating rows, the scales becoming obsolete near the umbones. The mantle of the animal is doubly fringed, and much decorated upon that portion which may be protruded from the shell. The posterior adductor is very large and strong; the anterior one has almost disappeared. The foot is long and slender, but is evidently a useless appendage, for the animal's habit is stationary. The byssus is large and very strong. Gloves have been made from the byssal fibers of *Pinna* mixed with silk. The gills are very long and are distinctly *not* filamentous, the adjacent filaments being clearly united by vascular channels. A very curious development of the osphradium (see page 339) into an erectile process capable of projection beyond the margin of the shell is a unique feature of *Pinna*. Sometimes thousands of pinnas are torn loose by storms and cast upon the beaches. They do not range north of Hatteras. (Plate LXXIX.)

Genus *Perna*

P. ephippium. A West Indian shell, also quite common on the east coast of Florida, and especially upon the Keys. It attaches itself by the byssus in great bunches to mangrove roots, sticks, and all manner of rubbish in brackish water. It has a very flat, irregularly shaped shell of a horn-color, and is from two to three inches across. The distinguishing feature of *Perna* is the hinge. It is straight and without teeth, but is marked by a row of transverse grooves to which the ligament is attached. These grooves constitute a row of cartilage-pits.

Family OSTREIDÆ

This family probably interests more people than any other one in the class save *Aviculidæ*. The latter furnishes the pearl-oysters, the former the edible oysters, the two thus appealing to two very strong human cravings—those of vanity and hunger.

Few realize what an enormous business the oyster trade has become in the United States. The value of it is stated to be over thirteen million dollars annually, twenty-five million bushels of oysters being taken from the Chesapeake alone. The edibility of the oyster has been known from early times, for vast heaps of empty oyster-shells, known as kitchen-middens, occur in various parts of the world. Some of them are of such size and extent as to warrant the belief that their formation must have required centuries. Shell-mounds are found along the coasts of Florida and are of some archæological value. The cultivation of oysters as recorded by Pliny dates from the first century B.C., at which

PLATE LXXIX.

Pinna muricata.
Pinna seminuda.
Pecten hastatus.

time a Roman named Sergius Orata first cultivated oysters at Baiæ. The acuteness of the gastronomic sense of a Roman epicure is thus described by Juvenal:

> He could tell
> At the first mouthful if his oysters fed
> On the Rutupian or the Lucrine bed
> Or at Circeii.

The poet Gay's opinion is expressed thus:

> The man had sure a palate cover'd o'er
> With brass or steel, that on the rocky shore
> First broke the oozy oyster's pearly coat,
> And risk'd the living morsel down his throat.

The methods employed in oyster-farming resemble those of agriculture, in that the bed is prepared, seed is sown, superfluous and foreign growths are weeded out, enemies are driven off, and the crop is harvested at stated seasons. The oyster is ovoviviparous; that is, it retains its eggs until they are partly matured. These are held in the gills and mantle folds until the time of spawning, which begins in May and lasts through the summer months. The larvæ are ejected as ciliated spheres, called spat, and swim freely about for some time, often several days, before finding a resting-spot. The oyster-grower secures many of the larvæ by placing in their way substances to which they can attach themselves. The American culturist strews his carefully prepared beds with empty oyster-shells, on which the spat settle, and the seed is thus secured; for the spat, once fastened, lose the power of locomotion and become fixed. At the end of a year the shells which hold the young oysters (now about an inch long and called "fry") are taken up, and the fry are thinned out and replanted, or are sold to other oyster-farmers.

During the period of their growth the oysters are sometimes transplanted several times. At the end of three to five years they have attained marketable size, and the beds are then harvested and prepared for another crop. Some oystermen have several acres of bottom under cultivation. These areas are obtained by purchase or grant from the State, and their limits are as defined as are the fenced-off acres of upland meadows. The business of the oyster-culturist is to plant the young oysters and watch their development, keeping the beds thinned, that the oysters may not be too crowded for their normal and symmetrical growth, and protecting them from their enemies, of which there are many. The principal enemies of the oyster are the starfish and the predaceous mollusks *Urosalpinx* and *Nassa*. Whole beds have been known to be destroyed in a single night by the visitations of starfishes, hence a constant watchfulness is required on the part of the oysterman. Policing the oyster-farms is another of his cares, for pirates abound, and a bed may be robbed in the night as easily as an orchard may be despoiled of its fruit. Oyster-culture is carried on extensively in Long Island Sound, on the coasts of New Jersey and Virginia, and in the Chesapeake Bay. The oysters from certain localities are esteemed more than others, the flavor of the oyster being very dependent upon the purity of the water and on the organisms upon which it feeds. It has been definitely shown that oysters grown in contaminated waters have been the agents of transmitting disease, notably typhoid fever and cholera.

Oyster-culture has reached the highest degree of perfection in France, where miles of muddy shores left by the ebb-tide are utilized for the purpose. The famous *parc* at Arcachon, covering ten thousand acres, illustrates the system generally practised. The spat is there collected on tiles coated with cement, piled in layers crosswise, and secured in crates. These tiles are exposed in favorable localities and collect the swimming embryos. The rough cement holding the spat is then chipped off the tiles and placed in wire trays. These *ambulances*, or *caisses ostreophiles*, placed between short posts, protect the fry from their enemies. At low tide the young oysters are carefully examined and sorted, and at the right age they are removed to open areas. The parc is divided into regular squares by canals of suitable width, some of the squares having banks and gates to retain the water of the receding tide if desired. Each man's parc is separated from that of his neighbor by canals of greater width, and often by stakes having a few branches on the ends. These *pi-*

gnons, which sway in the wind, are said to frighten away the predaceous ray which is apt to hover about the preserves. The parcs are finally thinned out by sending the oysters to other parcs to be fattened. There is a celebrated *parc d'élevage* at Marennes. It is a collection of artificial ponds, the floors of which are covered with algæ, which harbor vast numbers of diatoms and other microscopic organisms on which the oysters feed. The green diatom (*Navicula ostrearia*) gives to the oysters of Marennes the green color and peculiar flavor which is so much esteemed by the epicures of France. To the American, however, the green oyster is not acceptable.

Genus *Ostrea*

O. virginica. A description of this species, our common oyster, is hardly necessary. Every one has seen the rough, shaggy, unlovely shell. The hinge is toothless, but has a wide depression for the ligament. The animal, having stationary habits, has practically no foot at all. There is but one large adductor muscle, around which curve the gills, the latter being united to each other posteriorly. The mantle margin is finely and doubly fringed. Although *Ostrea* is a stationary mollusk, it has no byssus.

O. virginica has been introduced at San Francisco, where it lives well, but does not seem to multiply very rapidly. The native species, *O. lurida,* is about two inches long, dark in color, and stained a purplish hue. It is not very delicately flavored.

O. frons. This species has a thinner shell than *O. virginica*, with coarsely serrated margins. It occurs in beds in the neighborhood of mangroves all along our South Atlantic shores. It cannot compare with its Northern relative in flavor, but, like the European *Ostrea edulis,* it is sometimes " not bad."

Family PECTINIDÆ

Genus *Pecten*

The scallop-shells (*Pecten*) are objects too familiar to require any general description. The rounded valve, usually ornamented with radiating ribs, and the wing-like projections (called "ears"), from each side of the umbonal region, are never-failing characters. The outline of *Pecten* has been considerably employed in conventional designs for mural decorations; indeed, the figure of a well-known Mediterranean pecten (*P. jacobius*), found commonly in Palestine, became an emblem of religious significance during the middle ages. Returning crusaders fastened to their garments a specimen of "St. James's shell" as an evidence of the fact that they had been to the Holy Land, and the design of the shell came to be adopted upon many coats of arms and also in the insignia of various orders of devout and adventurous knights of the middle ages.

The animal is of the highest type of monomyarian mollusks, that is, of bivalve mollusks with only a single adductor muscle. Unlike most pelecypods, which have a very small foot, *Pecten* rarely has a byssus, and is neither a stationary nor a sluggish creature. It can propel itself through the water by spasmodically closing and opening its valves, in an eccentric, darting sort of flight, though most of the time it rests quietly upon the bottom. The mantle is entirely open and highly ornate about its margin, which is, furthermore, the seat of many eyes, capable, apparently, of no mean degree of vision. The adductor muscle is very large and strong, and occupies a central position, about which the gills circle; the latter are plainly filamentous.

P. magellanicus. The largest of the east-coast species of *Pecten*. It is a Northern species, and was long known by the name of **P. tenuiscostatus** — a name given to it on account of its very numerous radiating striæ; but it was later discovered that the North Atlantic form was in reality the same as the *P. magellanicus* of Patagonia. The latter being the older name and entitled to priority, our shell became *P. magellanicus*, the other name falling within its synonymy. The length and height of this scallop are from five to five and a half inches. One valve is more convex and slightly larger than the other, the smaller being lighter in color. The valves gape considerably along their upper margin below the hinge. The cartilage-pit is deep. North of Cape Ann this large species is of common occurrence in moderately deep water. The deeper bays and arms of the sea which everywhere penetrate the Maine coast are its favorite resorts. A good way to catch pectens is to lower a fishing-line at a spot where the fishermen report " scallop-ground," and drag it along over the bottom. Sooner or later it will enter the open shell of some pecten, which will instantly close its valves upon the string and allow itself to be drawn out of the water. In Maine these large scallops are eaten, but they have not found great favor in the city markets. In color they vary from reddish through brown to ashen.

P. islandicus. A species not so large as the last, with more prominently raised ribs (about fifty to one hundred in number), which are covered with a multitude of erect scales. The ribs persist upon the interior of the shell. The "ears" are unequal in size. The color is light orange to reddish-brown, with zones of darker and richer color. One valve is flatter than the other and more lightly colored. Greatest length about three inches; height three and a half inches. This is a Northern shell, belonging to the waters of Newfoundland, but its valves are frequently cast upon the New England beaches.

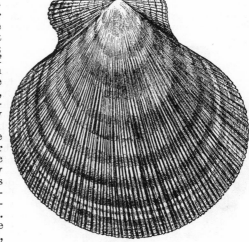

Pecten islandicus.

P. irradians. The common shallow-water species of the Atlantic coast. This exceedingly abundant species does not range north of Boston, but finds an extensive habitat to the south. Its metropolis is Cape Cod, Long Island Sound, and the Jersey coast waters. This is the true scallop of the Boston and New York markets. Only the adductor muscle is eaten. In this species there is not so marked a difference in the convexity of the two valves. There are about twenty elevated and rounded ribs, the spaces between them being also rounded. The color is variable, from a blackish horn to ashen gray. The "ears" are equal; the interior is shining, and grooved to correspond with the external ribs. Length two and three fifths inches, height two and a half inches. On clear, calm days the immature individuals of this species may often be seen in shallow water disporting themselves most gaily, skipping about and snapping their valves in great glee. Their mantle margins are very ornate in scarlet or orange, with rows of bright-blue eyes. Care must be taken in handling scallops, especially the large *P. magellanicus*, for a finger caught between the valves will be badly bruised.

P. dislocatus. South of Hatteras this species takes the place of its Northern relative, *P. irradians.* It is somewhat more globular and perhaps not quite so large, but the resemblance between the two species is very marked. It has from twenty to twenty-two rounded ribs, with very numerous concentric wrinkles between them. In color it is white, tinged with purple or yellow, with occasionally a system of blood-red lines crossing the ribs transversely. The diameter is about one and a half inches. This species has the same playful habits as *P. irradians,* and is not at all easy to capture. When pursued it dives into the mud, and sets up such a commotion by the spasmodic opening and shutting of its valves that the water at once becomes roiled, and the scallop is safely hidden in its murky depths.

P. hastatus. There are several very beautiful pectens on the Pacific coast of the United States, and two of these—one of northern and the other of southern range — resemble very closely the two Atlantic species of relatively north and south range, *P. islandicus* and *P. irradians* or *dislocatus.* The first is *P. hastatus* of Puget Sound. Valves of this exquisite shell are even occasionally found in California. It has very much the

aspect of *P. islandicus* — unequal ears and an ovate form. The most curious thing about this shell is the fact that a different system of sculpturing exists upon the two valves. Upon one the ribs are even and the whole surface is covered with raised scales; upon the other the ribs are alternately of large and small size. Color rose-pink, with deeper bands; one valve lighter-colored, suffused with delicate pink. Height two and a half inches. (Plate LXXIX.)

Pecten irradians, typical form.

P. æquisulcatus. The Southern species above referred to as resembling *P. irradians* or *dislocatus.* It has about twenty stout, well-rounded ribs, with concentric wrinkles between them. The " ears " are equal. The size and shape are as in *P. irradians.* The coloring is whitish, varying to shades of brown, and excentrically marked with spots or waving transverse lines of chestnut or horn.

ORDER **EULAMELLIBRANCHIATA**

With the pectens we leave behind all pelecypods with the true filamentous type of gill. In the order *Eulamellibranchiata* we find all the families to be possessed of the basketwork or crisscross branchial structure. Each gill is fundamentally formed of filaments which project downward, and then suddenly turn upon themselves and ascend; the ascending and descending limbs are connected, however, by processes of presumably vascular function, and adjacent filaments are connected by truly vascular channels. The closer connection of the filaments to form of each gill a sort of plate is further effected by connective tissue, which sometimes is dense enough (though always porous) to obscure the reticulated appearance of the organ. Furthermore, the edge of the outer lamella of the outer gill unites with the mantle; likewise the edge of the inner lamella of the inner gill unites with the body-mass, and *behind the body-mass* with the gills upon the other side of the animal. This union of the four gills in a straight median line behind the foot and body-mass forms a septum, which divides off from the mantle cavity a "suprabranchial" cavity. Into this cavity the excreta are discharged, and with it the anal or excurrent siphon connects. The branchial or incurrent siphon thus pours its current of water into the *lower* mantle cavity, to bathe the gills and feed the mouth, while the fresh water is not contaminated by any open and wide connection with the excretory processes. In many of the forms where the siphons are very long and united, this septum, formed by the union of the dorsal edges of the inner gills back of the foot, is continued far into the siphons, constituting the division of the two into the anal and branchial siphons.

Another feature of this order is the marked tendency to mantle fusion. As there are always siphons, the mantle-edges must necessarily have fused at two points at least, in order to have formed the siphons. The tendency, however, is for the fusion to continue, narrowing the pedal opening more and more, as though the mantle were endeavoring to envelop the entire animal in a bag or sac open only at one end (siphonal opening), but yet slightly ripped along one seam (pedal opening).

This order includes the great majority of pelecypods, and admits of many very confusing modifications in its most essential features.

FAMILY CARDITIDÆ

In this, the first family of the order, most of the characteristic features just spoken of are present. Mantle fusion, however, has not progressed beyond a degree which is just sufficient to form the siphons. There is a byssiferous gland. The name *Carditidæ* refers to the heart-shape of the shells.

Genus *Cardita*

C. borealis. A very common species north of Cape Ann, reported also in deeper water as far south as Hatteras. It is a solid, obliquely heart-shaped shell, with beaks elevated and turned forward. It has

Cardita borealis, natural size.

about eighteen to twenty rounded radiating ribs, which are broader than the grooves between them. The epidermis is rusty-brown. The hinge is strong, with two prominent teeth; the margins of the shell are strongly crenulated within. Length one inch; height about the same. This is not strictly a between-the-tides species, but its valves are often cast upon the beaches. Fine specimens may be obtained by dredging at Bar Harbor or Eastport.

C. floridana. A very common Floridian species. Its seventeen or eighteen ribs are very heavy, and are rendered nodulous by the numerous bluntly raised scales upon them. The shell is lengthened, and has a well-defined lunule and an external ligament. In color it is yellowish-white, with purple markings when young. Length one inch; height three fourths of an inch. It lives in sheltered bays; detached valves are often found cast upon the beach.

Family ASTARTIDÆ

Genus *Astarte*

Notwithstanding their rather small size, there is a trimness about the shells of *Astarte* which, taken together with their rich chestnut epidermis, makes them very interesting and desirable additions to the cabinet. The family is one of cold-water range, with a few representatives on the New England coast. Live specimens are not easily captured, for they live in deeper water than one would care to wade in, nevertheless they are frequently cast upon the beaches after storms. The animal has a very short efferent siphon, large labial palps, and very obliquely placed gills. Not more than twenty living species of *Astarte* are known, and all of them belong in, or are wanderers from, polar seas. Fully three hundred fossil species of this genus have been described from Mesozoic rocks in all parts of the world. The question naturally arises whether in these its dying days *Astarte* has sought colder waters in which to pass its remaining existence, or whether climates have changed. The fact that such strictly tropical genera as *Voluta* and *Conus* are found fossil in northern Siberia seems to be evidence in proof of great climatic variations.

A. castanea. This species has a thick and heavy shell for one so small, with round ventral margins and prominent beaks. The surface is very slightly undulated and is covered with a thick chestnut epidermis with pale and dark zones. The hinge is broad and flat, with a prominent cardinal tooth upon the right valve, which accurately fits into a pit formed by two teeth on the left valve. Length one inch; height one inch.

Astarte castanea.

A. undata. A species slightly larger than the last, with ten to twenty prominent concentric undulations.

The identification of the many species *Astarte undata.* of *Astarte* often becomes exceedingly difficult on account of the fact that the genus is a remarkably uniform one in its main characters and is infinitely variable in its minor details.

FAMILY **CYPRINIDÆ**

GENUS *Arctica*

This family is represented by one species upon the New England coast, which is much sought after by collectors. It is one of the larger clams, but is too uncommon to have received a popular name and to be generally well known by the fishermen along the shore.

A. (Cyprina) islandica. This clam has a thick though not ponderous shell, with prominent beaks and a stout, prominent ligament. Its cardinal teeth are large, but its laterals are very small. A striking feature of this species, which at once separates

Arctica (Cyprina) islandica.

it from all other shells of our coast of similar size, is the coarse, wrinkled epidermis of black to chestnut color. The shell is very suggestive of a large, overgrown *Astarte*. Length three and a half inches; height three inches. It is found of all sizes, down to one fourth of an inch in diameter, upon muddy stations in moderately deep water near the mouths of rivers; but the surest way to get it is to search the beach after a hard onshore gale.

FAMILY LUCINIDÆ

This family finds its metropolis in warmer waters, and the best representatives of it must be sought for upon the Floridian beaches or in the shallow bays of that sandy coast. A long ver-miform foot is a characteristic of the animal, as is also the fact that at times there is only a single gill upon each side of the body. In some of the *Lucinidæ*, more so than in most other pelecypods, the chief function of the gills is to furnish a brood-ing-place for the thousands of ova which the creatures generate. Sometimes a *Lucina* will be captured with the gills swollen out of all proportion, and literally stuffed with tiny, microscopic eggs. At such times the gills lose all semblance of branchial organs. The shells are orbicular, with depressed small umbones, a distinct lunule, a semi-external ligament, two cardinal teeth, and laterals (a variable feature). There is no pallial sinus. The color is white, and the outlines are rounded.

GENUS *Lucina*

L. tigrina. The largest of the group, measuring three inches across and nearly the same in height. It is flatly convex and radially ribbed by a great number of costæ which are crossed and decussated through-out with concentric ridges. The color is white. This fine shell lives only in southern Florida and is abundant in shallow water on sandy sta-tions. (Plate LXXX.)

L. floridana. One of the most abundant bivalves in Florida, often cast in thousands upon the beaches. It lives in shallow protected waters and upon sand-flats which are partly exposed at low tide. It has the usual round outlines of the genus, with exceedingly small um-bones, directed forward, and a smooth surface, save for fine growth-lines of a light straw-color. The shell is pure white. Diameter about one inch. (Plate LXXX.)

L. pennsylvanica. A species often associated with the last, but about twice as large. Its thin but tough epidermis clings to the shell in raised concentric lines, giving it a circularly ribbed appearance. The most prominent feature of this species is a depressed line upon either valve extending obliquely from the umbones to the posterior ventral margin, causing, at the margin, a pucker or break in its even continuity. The lunule is large and ribbed; the teeth are small; the color is pure white, with a light straw-tinted epidermis. (Plate LXXX.)

L. dentata. In this species the shells are thin and white, with well-marked concentric lines crossed by deep oblique narrow furrows bent at nearly right angles to the lines of growth and forming teeth around the margin. Found along the entire coast.

L. californica. The best-known California species of this genus. It is pure white, with fine concentric lines, and varies in size from one half of an inch to one and a half inches in diameter.

Lucina dentata.

The lateral teeth are the stronger, and the lunule is upon the right valve only. With these exceptions this species preserves the usual characters of this genus.

L. nuttallii, belonging to the southern shores of California, is decussated like fine wickerwork. The shell is flattened and ridged along the hinge-margin. The color is white. Diameter about one inch in large specimens. (Plate LXXX.)

Genus *Loripes*

L. edentula. A species which is seldom captured alive. Its home is in the open sea, but vast quantities of its valves are occasionally thrown upon the beaches south of Hatteras, as far as the Gulf of Mexico. On account of the weak hinge ligament, the valves become easily separated, and it is not always easy to find two that will exactly match. *Loripes* preserves the same circular outlines as *Lucina*, but is more ventricose, and the hinge and teeth are very feeble. This species is a little over two inches in length and slightly under two inches in height. It is pure white without, and is finely striated with growth-lines; bright orange within, especially about the pallial line and muscle-scars. (Plate LXXX.)

Family TELLINIDÆ

Genus *Tellina*

If we should create an aristocracy of beauty among the bivalves, as has been done by conchologists among the gasteropods, this family would deserve high rank. Most of the American species of *Tellina* are too small to impress one very greatly with their beauty, but in the West Indies and in the tropical Pacific waters are some wonderfully handsome shells belonging to this or to the allied genus *Macoma*. However, we have in Florida the very striking *T. radiata*, a truly beautiful shell, which, were it less common, would be highly prized in collections. Rarity, no doubt, adds a wonderful luster to shells as well as to gems. The animal of *Tellina* has long, slender siphons, which are separate. The gills are small, and the outer lamella or branchial fold is directed dorsally. Although the foot shows evidences of a byssogenous gland, there is no actual byssus. The shells are porcelanous and translucent, equivalve, with an external ligament, and at least two cardinal teeth in each valve.

T. radiata. This species varies from three to four inches in length, and from one and a half to one and three fourths inches in height. It is highly polished, shining white, and yellowish about the umbonal region, and has three wide rays of bright pink extending from the beaks to the ventral margin. On account of its remarkable coloration it is called the "setting-sun shell." Its surface is smooth. A common variety is of a uniform creamy-white color with carnation beaks. This shell is always offered for sale by the marine curio- and shell-dealers in Florida seaside resorts, and at Atlantic City, Cape May, and elsewhere.

T. alternata resembles the last in shape, being flattish and oblong, but it is more pointed or angulated posteriorly. There is also a slight twist in the posterior end of the shell. Its surface is decorated by numerous impressed concentric lines. The color is uniformly white or yellowish, with pink rays. Length two and a half to three inches; height two and a half inches. Found from Hatteras to the Gulf of Mexico, in shallow, sandy stations and on beaches after storms. (Plate LXXXI.)

T. bodegensis. The most striking species of *Tellina* found on the west coast, and of rather northern range. It is about two inches in length, creamy-white in color, and ornamented with very fine concentric lines. A very characteristic feature of the genus is present in this species as in the last, namely, a slight twist or bend to one side in the posterior end of the shell.

Tellina tenera, showing extended animal.

Tellina tenera.

T. tenera. A little *Tellina* found in New England waters, which, though very small, is worthy of mention on account of its abundance upon all our beaches north of Hatteras. It is only about half an inch long, and slightly over one quarter of an inch high. It may be distinguished by its general generic characters, its iridescent surface, and its delicately marked lines of growth; sometimes it is rose-tinted. Its remarkably long siphons are shown in the accompanying figure.

GENUS *Macoma*

M. secta. A very pretty thin glossy shell from two to three inches in length and about one fourth less in height, which occurs from Monterey southward. The posterior end of the shell is contracted and slightly bent; the pallial sinus is deep. There is an external ligament. (Plate LXXXI.)

M. nasuta. Another Californian species, with a less shining surface and a very thin light-brownish epidermis. The twisting of the posterior

PLATE LXXX.

1, Lucina tigrina.

2, Lucina floridana.

5, Loripes edentula.

3, Lucina pennsylvanica.

4, Lucina nuttallii.

PLATE LXXXI.

1, Tellina alternata.   3, Donax variabilis.
2, Macoma secta.   4, Donax californicus.

5, Ræta canaliculata.

margin is striking. It has very fine cardinal teeth. Length two to three inches.

M. baltica, M. proxima, M. tenta. The first two of these species are dingy in color, and are covered with a dirty-looking, thin epidermis. The first has a wide range to Norway and Scotland, and is exceedingly common all along our coast from Maine to Georgia. It occurs plentifully in the Hudson River above New York, and in all sandy or muddy bays. It is rounded in outline, while the next species (*M. proxima*) is more pointed posteriorly. When these species are buried in the sand their two long, slender siphons project above, one supplying the animal with a constant current of fresh water, and the other ejecting that which, having passed the gills and labial palps, is exhausted of its air and nutriment and contaminated by waste products. *M. tenta* is white, with very fine lines of growth, and polished and shining within. It is warped posteriorly. Length three fifths of an inch; height two fifths of an inch.

Macoma baltica.

Macoma tenta.

FAMILY DONACIDÆ

GENUS *Donax*

The *Donacidæ* are represented upon our coasts by comparatively few species, all belonging to the genus *Donax*. The shells are under an inch in length, and have a peculiarly shortened anterior portion; thus they are inequilateral. Their ventral margins are finely denticulate. The pallial sinus is deep. There are two or three cardinal teeth and a variable number of laterals.

D. variabilis. This little shell, the common Floridian form, exhibits every imaginable scheme of color-combination, and defies general or comprehensive description. Probably the most usual pattern developed is a bluish-white background with purplish radiating lines. Another is a pure-white foundation with red lines. The surface is striated longitudinally with excessively fine riblets. Length one half of an inch or slightly more. In March and April these shells are thrown alive in millions upon the Florida beaches. Each wave seems to be laden with them, and when the foaming waters of each spent breaker recede, the little shells lie still upon the sand for a moment, glittering like jewels in the sunlight; then, with a sudden protrusion of the foot and a quick turn, they all disappear like a flash, buried in the sand before the next breaker strikes them. One must be very quick to catch these active little mollusks. (Plate LXXXI.)

D. californicus. Professor Keep very aptly describes this shell, which is very common in California, as "short and stumpy, cut nearly square off at one end (anterior), and tapering to a rounded edge at the other." The same description fits both this and the Floridian *D. variabilis* so well that the two forms may be one and the same species.

If they were shells of arctic range it would be easier to connect them; but as neither is a cold-water form, it becomes more difficult to place them under one name. The increasing number of similar species being found upon the Atlantic and Pacific sides of Central America points almost conclusively to the existence of a waterway between the two oceans, somewhere between North and South America, at no very remote geological period. Possibly the closing of some such waterway through the isthmus connecting the oceans has separated these forms geographically, thus leading us to separate them specifically. (Plate LXXXI.)

Family **MACTRIDÆ**

This is a very large family of universal distribution and with a great number of genera and subgenera, rather confusedly gathered into subfamilies. The dominant genus *Mactra* comprises the largest bivalve upon the east coast of the United States.

Genus *Mactra*

The mactras live in the sand near the margin of the water, often upon the exposed open coast. The mantle is open, except where it is fused to form the siphons. These are short and united. The outer gill is dorsally directed; that is to say, it does not depend into the mantle cavity as does the inner gill, but projects just the other way; it is also smaller than the inner one. The foot is strong, bent, and tongue-shaped, and no doubt well adapted to the rough life in the surf and the heavy, shifting sands. The main characteristic of the mactra shell is the prominent triangular-shaped fossette, or cartilage plate, situated internally and just under the beaks. The shells are equivalve, and devoid of bright colors or striking sculptural features. Internally the pallial line is plain, and the sinus well marked but not deep.

Mactra solidissima.

M. solidissima is one of the very commonest, if not the commonest large bivalve of the New England, Long Island, and New Jersey beaches. It is covered with a thin brownish or straw-colored epidermis, usually more or less worn away in adult specimens and wholly absent from the dead valves found upon the beaches. There is a fragile V-shaped cardinal tooth, which is generally broken away in forcing open the valves; the lateral teeth are long and thin, and striated on their receiving surfaces. The length of this "giant clam" is from four to seven inches. This is the first shell the collector will find (north of Hatteras) when he goes to an open, sandy beach.

M. similis. A small variety of the species last described, of similar outline, but less heavy and strong. Its range is from Hatteras southward to Brazil. Passing from New Jersey to Hatteras, *Mactra solidissima* diminishes in size, and after passing that faunal barrier the Northern form is entirely replaced by this Southern variety. The shell is brighter, though not exactly bright-shining. Its habits are entirely similar to those of the Northern form. On the west coast of Florida it is the most abundant bivalve upon the beaches.

M. ovalis. A species of Northern range, which so greatly resembles *M. solidissima* as to suggest identity; but the lateral teeth are smooth and not striated, while the shell itself seldom attains a length of over four inches.

M. lateralis. An exceedingly common shell, found in all the salt-marshes and tidal estuaries of our coast. It is much smaller than the mactras just described, being not over one half of an inch in length. It is white, and is covered with a dirty brown epidermis; the hinge is strong, with deep cartilage fossette and a V-shaped marginal tooth. The laterals are long and slender. The animal has a strong foot and two slender, long siphons which are yellow in color.

Mactra lateralis.

Genus *Ræta*

R. (Labiosa) canaliculata. In this species the cartilage fossette is the same as in *Mactra* ; the marginal teeth are feeble, and there are no laterals. The shells of *Mactra* which we have examined are heavy or at least solid, but *Ræta* is thin and fragile ; it is pure white in color and is gracefully ornamented by concentric raised ribs. The shell is inflated and gapes slightly posteriorly ; it is shining white within and is deeply grooved concentrically in accordance with the external ribs. Length two and a half, height two inches. From Hatteras to Mexico, this is one of the commoner beach shells, but since, as in some other species already named, the hinge ligament and teeth are feeble, the valves become separated by the buffeting of the waves, and are cast disjointed and singly upon the beaches. (Plate LXXXI.)

Family **VENERIDÆ**

In many respects this is the most distinguished pelecypod family. It is the largest in number of genera and species, is of world-wide distribution, and supplies to hungry man a number of comestible species.   Several of its genera have been named after various goddesses and nymphs on account of the great beauty of their shells.   But from a purely biological point of view also the *Veneridæ* have claims to distinction, for they seem to represent about the highest type of shell-development among the bivalves.   The test is extremely hard and often porcelanous. It is solid without being ponderous and unwieldy in the sense of causing the animal to be helplessly overburdened by the sheer weight of its shell.   The valves are equal and have three stout cardinal teeth.   The foot is strong, the animal is active, the siphons are free or partially united, and the gills are more or less crumpled and folded.   There is a compactness and well-regulated arrangement of the organs in the *Veneridæ*, which impress one who has examined the anatomy of many pelecypods much as a well-built, efficient, and space-economizing machine would impress a mechanic.   None of the organs are weak or crowded out to furnish room for the undue or awkward development of other organs.   A good balance is preserved between them all, the result being a high type of pelecypod.

If we do not expect to find any of the more remarkable forms of the *Veneridæ* upon our shores we shall be the less disappointed when returning from collecting-expeditions.   Nevertheless, there are a few species of *Cytherea, Dosinia,* and *Tivela* in North American waters which are very handsome shells; but those of our species which are included under the generic name *Venus* are in point of beauty not worthy of their promising name.

Genus *Venus*

V. mercenaria.   This is the common "hard-shell clam," the "Little Neck" of the hotels and restaurants, with which every one in New York and New England is familiar.   The species ranges from Cape Cod to Florida, and occupies two different kinds of station: one in shallow muddy bays near low-tide mark, in estuaries, etc.; the other the sandy stations in open deeper bays or the open ocean.   Those coming from "outside" have thinner, more delicate shells, with thin, concentric ribs. They burrow in the sand or mud, or crawl quite rapidly.   The siphons are short and are united almost to their ends.   The mantle is open (save for the siphons), and the edges are delicately frilled.   In the United States this species is very extensively gathered for the markets.   When the oyster season closes in April, the hard-shell clam comes into vogue, the season lasting until September or October.   The clams are extensively gathered in the estuaries from Cape May to Cape Cod. Men armed with rakes drift about in small boats and fish the sluggish creatures up out of the mud. They will live for many days out of water if kept in a cool place. Smaller or immature clams are better for the table, since they are not so tough as their elders. A few features of the shell of this species are noticeable—the rather prominent umbones directed forward, the heart-shaped lunule, the external ligament, the concentric sculpturing of growth-lines, the pure-white interior (with occasionally violet zones about the muscle-scars and margin), the three stout cardinal teeth, the sharp-angled pallial sinus, and the ventral margin finely crenulated within. The greatest length is about three inches and the height two and a half inches, but these dimensions exceed those of the clams usually served upon the half-shell. *V. mercenaria* ranges into Florida, increasing in size and bulk as it meets the warmer waters of the Gulf Stream. The

Venus mercenaria, typical form.

Floridian form has received the varietal name of *mortoni*. This massive clam sometimes weighs five pounds, and is fully six inches in diameter. Aside from its great size and thickness, the characters of the shell are wholly those of the smaller Northern form. It is abundant in shallow, muddy, brackish bays, and is gathered by men who "tread out" the clams, feeling for them in the mud and sand with bare feet. The flesh is tough and disagreeably strong, yet the natives appear to relish it, especially when it is made into a chowder.

V. cancellata. The most abundant species of *Venus* in Florida, particularly near Tampa and on the west side. It preserves all the characteristics of the genus, and is decorated with a series of high, narrow, concentric ridges, between which are much smaller and more numerous radiating riblets. The color is dirty white to light yellow-brown without, and white and violet within. There are three cardinal teeth and no laterals. The lunule is heart-shaped; the posterior margin is broadened into a wide, concave area into which the concentric ridges do not pass. Length one to one and a fourth inches; height the same. Sometimes the beaches in Florida will in places be banked up with the valves of this very abundant *Venus*. As they live in shallow water upon sandy stations, they are easily dislodged by the heavy storms which sometimes sweep that usually placid coast. (Plate LXXXII.)

Genus *Cytherea*

C. (Callista) gigantea. One of the most beautiful Floridian shells. It is nearly or quite six inches long and about three and a fourth inches in height. The shell is porcelanous, is covered with a pinkish, livid epidermis, and is decorated with numerous longitudinal color-rays of lilac. The rays are usually broken and interrupted. Within it is china-white, and has a deep pallial sinus. It is very abundant on the west coast of Florida, at Sanibel Island, Egmont Key, Lake Worth, and on beaches. (Plate LXXXII.)

C. maculata. This species is more oval in outline than the last. It is of a fawn-color, blotched or waved with violet-brown, and is porcelanous and shining. The epidermis is also shining and corneous. Within it is china-white in color. The pallial sinus is very deep and wide. Length two and a half to three inches; height one and a half to two inches. This also is a shell to be looked for upon the beach after storms, but it will probably not be seen on the east coast of Florida, although it occurs on the Keys and also at Hatteras. Both of the species have been used as food, but not very extensively. The flesh is not lacking in tenderness, but it has a peppery taste. (Plate LXXXII.)

Genus *Dosinia*

There are two species of this very graceful genus of *Veneridæ* south of Hatteras, **D. discus** and **D. elegans.** These dosinias have united siphons. The foot is very large and strong, and the mantle margin is both papillaceous and plicated. The shells of these two species are about three or three and a half inches in length and of the same height, and are very flat. The ventral margin is almost a perfect circle, and the beaks are small and pointed. The lunule is small and cordate; the valves are very gracefully sculptured in fine, regular, impressed, concentric striæ, which are finer and less elevated in *D. discus* than in *D. elegans;* the shell is porcelanous and white, and is covered by a straw-colored, very fine, transparent epidermis. Within, the strong cardinal teeth are placed upon a long fossette. There is a deep pallial sinus. *D. discus* is characteristic of the east coast of Florida, while *D. elegans* is only found upon the west side of the State. Both may be looked for upon the beach, though living specimens must be captured with the dredge. (Plate LXXXII.)

Genus *Tivela*

The coast of California is also favored by the *Veneridæ*, a number of large species belonging to several genera being present.

T. crassatelloides. Perhaps the largest and finest of the California species. It is so common in its between-tides station that it used to be collected by plowing a furrow through the sand, the big shells being thrown out upon either side like potatoes. The shells attain a length of five and a half inches, and are porcelanous, thick, and heavy. The margins of the valves are also thick and rounded. The exterior is perfectly smooth, yellowish-white in color, and decorated

PLATE LXXXII.

Venus cancellata.
Cytherea (Callista) maculata.

Cytherea (Callista) gigantea.
Dosinia discus.

PLATE LXXXIII.

Tivela crassatelloides, one half natural
  size.
Chione succincta.

Tapes laciniata, one half natural size.
Chione simillima.

with purplish rays arranged in various groupings; over all is a glossy epidermis. The hinge-teeth are very strong, and a prominent anterior lateral tooth on the left valve is noticeable. There is an external ligament; the pallial sinus is well marked, but not very deep. (Plate LXXXIII.)

GENUS *Chione*

There are three species on the west coast. This genus is very closely allied to *Venus*, and is considered by many to be only a subgenus of the latter. All three species are white, solid, heavy shells which exhibit the same scheme of sculpturing, namely, numerous longitudinal ribs crossed by larger and less frequent concentric ridges.

C. simillima is shaped almost exactly like the east-coast *Venus cancellata*, but its concentric ridges are very numerous and sharp. There is a strongly marked cordate lunule, and hardly any pallial sinus. Length one and a half to two inches. (Plate LXXXIII.)

C. succincta has fewer concentric ridges and has a large lunule. There are purple zones within and touching the heavy cardinal teeth. Length two and a half inches. (Plate LXXXIII.)

C. fluctifraga has broad but flatter or well-rounded (not sharp) concentric ridges, no lunule, a small ligament, a fairly deep pallial sinus, and a finely crenulated margin (within) all around the valves, except when interrupted by the hinge ligament. The shell is solid and shining, and marked by deep-purple zones within. Length one to two inches. Found in southern California.

GENUS *Tapes*

This is a prominent genus of the *Veneridæ*. Its chief feature is the total want of lateral teeth. There are several large species in California.

T. staminea, T. laciniata. These are the most noticeable species. The former is sold in the San Francisco markets as the "hard-shell clam." The shell of this species is from two to three inches in length and of somewhat less height, rounded, and heavy. The sculpturing consists of radiating ribs traversed by strongly marked growth-lines. The teeth are strong, and the pallial sinus is deep. *T. laciniata* is much like the last, but its surface is reticulated by a crisscross design that is very striking. It also has a deep pallial sinus. These two species are of Southern range. They burrow in gravelly places, among stones, between tide-marks, and their presence may frequently be detected when walking along the beach at low tide by seeing a sudden jet of water ejected from a little hole in the mud or gravel. The animal, becoming alarmed at the approach of something, suddenly snaps shut its valves, and thus forces out some water through its siphons. The foot is very strong and often byssiferous in this genus. (Plate LXXXIII.)

Genus *Saxidomus*

S. nuttallii. The last of the larger west-coast *Veneridæ* which we shall examine. The genus is very closely allied to *Tapes*, and no doubt might better be considered as its subgenus. The shell is brownish-white, three to four inches in length, and heavy, rough, and coarse-looking, with irregular concentric ridges. There is no lunule, but a large external ligament is very prominent just back of the beaks. Within it is white, with a deep pallial sinus. Just below the ligament area is a zone of translucent, agate-like shell-structure. This large clam, with several others of the same genus, lives in shallow water near shore.

Family **PETRICOLIDÆ**

Genus *Petricola*

P. pholadiformis. Along the Jersey coast, especially about Atlantic City, there are small patches of clay or hard tenacious mud which lie just at the edge of the sea. As the beating of the surf gradually encroaches upon these hard fragments of once extensive clay-beds, many  specimens of this curious bivalve mollusk are washed out from their burrows in this clay and cast upon the sandy beach. The animal has long siphons which are united about one third of the way to their ends. Although this creature is allied to the *Veneridæ*, the degree of mantle fusion present is much greater, leaving in this case only a fairly long slit through which the foot may protrude. The shell is very dissimilar to that of any of the *Veneridæ*, and in many respects, judging from a conventional standard, is a remarkable form. It is exceedingly thin, is of a chalky texture, gapes widely posteriorly, and is ornamented with transverse ribs, which are feeble upon the long produced posterior portion of the shell, but strong in the anterior part, where they are crossed by the coarse lines of growth, which appear like vaulted scales upon the ribs. The color is a dull white. There are two cardinals in each valve and no laterals. Length one and a quarter to two and a half inches; height one half to three quarters of an inch. This species passes its entire life in the burrow it has made for itself in the clay. Its only motions are made in climbing to the entrance of its burrow or in retreating far out of sight within its depths. Its siphons are tipped with a dark or drab color as a measure of protection from the predaceous crabs which range about the mud surfaces near tidal marks, and are always upon the lookout for succulent bits of flesh.

Petricola pholadi-formis.

P. carditoides. A petricola of the Californian coast, very similar in its habits to the east-coast form. It bores, however, not only into clay, but also into soft rocks in order to effect a permanent lodgment. Often this species occupies a hole which it has discovered already existing ; in this case its shell grows to fit the surroundings. The hinge-teeth and sculpturing are frequently reduced and sometimes are quite obsolete ; but the shell has the chalky, thin texture that is characteristic of the genus.

There is another family of rock- and mud-boring bivalves which superficially resemble the petricolas, but their anatomical organization removes them to a little distance from the *Petricolidæ*. They are considered further on, under the name of *Pholadidæ*.

FAMILY CARDIIDÆ

GENUS *Cardium*

This is another important family of the *Pelecypoda*, which, with the *Veneridæ*, the *Mactridæ*, and the *Tellinidæ*, is entitled to distinction on account of its high organization, its high type of shell, its universal geographical distribution, and its great beauty. The dominant genus is *Cardium*—a name given on account of the fact that the shell is shaped like a heart. The animal has a very long, recurved, and surprisingly strong foot. The mantle-edges are quite freely open to the siphonal region and are highly papillate and waved. The siphons are usually very short, but have wide exterior openings and are also strongly papillate about their margins. The gills are obliquely situated, and seem to be thicker and heavier than is usual in pelecypods; they are much folded, the outer lamella being the smaller. With such a pointed foot and such short siphons *Cardium* is obviously not a deep-burrowing genus; but it does partially bury itself in soft semi-liquid sand. Its progression is effected by leaps which it is enabled to make by reaching far out with its foot, then suddenly twisting to one side and throwing the shell several inches. The shell is ventricose, is closed or gapes slightly posteriorly, and has prominent subcentral umbones and an external ligament. The sculpture-scheme of *Cardium* (if the shell is not perfectly smooth) is one of radiating ribs or ridges, which, being regular, form a perfect crenulation of the ventral margin. There are two cardinal teeth in the center, and one lateral tooth upon both the anterior and the posterior side: the latter are situated at some little distance from the beaks.

C. magnum. The largest and finest "cockle" of the east coast of the United States. It is, indeed, one of the finest cockles in the world. The almost perfect heart-shape is striking. The posterior side is somewhat flatly depressed. The thirty-three to thirty-seven regularly disposed, broad, radiating ribs; the regularly crenulated margins; the yellowish-brown color garnished with transverse rows of chestnut or purple lines or spots ; the brownish-purple posterior area—all combine to make this large *Cardium* a beautiful species. Its length is four inches; height five and a quarter inches. It is a very abundant species on the open Florida beaches, where it is often left exposed and alive at very low tides. (Plate LXXXIV.)

C. isocardia. This also is a Floridian species, of elongated heart-shape and with radiating ribs. It is not more than half as large as the last-described species. The ribs are decorated with erect vaulting scales which are exaggerated portions of growth-lines. The beaks are smaller in proportion than in *C. magnum.* The shell is brown to straw-color, stained with purplish-brown without, and has a bright salmon-red or purplish-pink interior. The margins are deeply crenulated. The teeth are arranged as in the last-described species. It is very common on the beaches of western Florida. (Plate LXXXIV.)

C. serratum, C. lævigatum. These two species have a perfectly smooth surface, and inflated, globose, heart-shaped shells, and are of a creamy-white color, suffused with a yellowish, golden tint which suggests the color of butter. Some forms are shiny, and citron-yellow and pinkish toward the margins, whence the name of "peach-shell." Height one to two inches. Not uncommon upon Florida beaches. (Plate LXXXIV.)

C. mortoni. Another of the smooth forms of *Cardium* (placed in the subgenus *Lævicardium*). It occurs in Florida and also extends up the coast to Cape Cod, being very abundant in Long Island Sound. In

Cardium mortoni, showing extended animal.

the neighborhood of Martha's Vineyard and along the north shore of Long Island this very pretty little species has been reported as occurring in soft ground even above low-tide mark, near the mouths of creeks. It is enough to say of it that it is a smaller edition of *C. lævigatum* and may be further distinguished by a purple blotch on the posterior margin, just within the valves, the general color within being bright yellow. In young specimens, zigzag lines of dark fawn-color upon the pale-yellowish background of the smooth exterior surface of the shells are a noticeable feature. The largest specimens measure an inch in length and nearly the same in height. The long cirri upon the siphons are striking.

C. substriatum. A cockle of this inflated, smooth type, which strongly resembles the east-coast form, found upon the Pacific coast. The name indicates that it is not altogether smooth, a fact only revealed, however, by a magnifying-glass. It is about one half of an inch in length, and of a light drab-color, spotted and sometimes radially lined with yellowish-brown. Professor Keep likens this species in both shape and color to a sparrow's egg. (Plate LXXXIV.)

C. elatum. A veritable giant among the cardiums. It is found on the southern Californian coast, though rarely north of the Mexican border. It is of the smooth, glossy type belonging to the subgenus *Lævicardium.* It attains a diameter of six inches, and is of a creamy-yellow appearance.

C. corbis, C. quadrigenarium. These two Californian cockles are of the ribbed type displayed in the eastern *C. magnum* and *C. isocardia.* *C. corbis* is found in the northern Californian and Puget Sound region,

PLATE LXXXIV.

1, Cardium magnum, much reduced.
2, Cardium isocardia.
3, Cardium lævigatum.

4, Cardium substriatum, enlarged.
5, Cardium corbis (young specimen).
6 Glycimeris generosa.

and *C. quadrigenarium* on the southern shores of California. The former is a full, round, heart-shaped shell with about thirty somewhat scaly ribs. The edge of the shell is deeply toothed; the color light brownish; the diameter from two to three inches. It preserves all the features of the genus as regards both shell and anatomical characters. The other species, *C. quadrigenarium*, very strongly resembles *C. magnum* in size and shape. It lacks the flattened area on the posterior portion of the shell which is characteristic of the east-coast species, and its uniform brownish-white coloration is less striking. It has about forty regularly spaced, radiating ribs, which are smooth upon the umbonal region, but elsewhere are armed with spiny processes. Diameter about six inches.(Plate LXXXIV.) *C. islandicum, C. pinnulatum.* Both of these are cold-water species and occur along the New England coast. The former has a shell

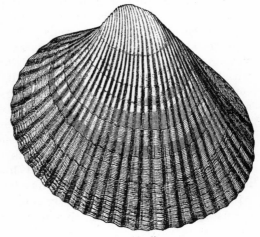

Cardium islandicum.

which varies from one half of an inch to two inches in length, and has from thirty-six to thirty-eight sharp, three-sided, radiating ribs, the furrows between them being rounded and wrinkled by growth-lines. A yellowish-brown epidermis covers the shell and bristles into a sort of fringe upon the sharp edges of the ribs. *C. islandicum* cannot be said to be a very common species in New England, although collectors have so reported it. Specimens from Massachusetts are not as large as those of more northern habitat. It does not occur south of Cape Cod. *C. pinnulatum* is one of the "small fry" among the cockles. Its largest diameter is less than one half of an inch; but what it lacks in size it seems to endeavor to make up in abundance, for it is scattered everywhere along the coast from New York northward. Specimens can nearly always be found in the stomachs of fishes, which, by the way, form an excellent hunting-ground for rare species of mollusks of small size. There are twenty-six slightly rounded ribs, with deep linear grooves between them. Upon the ribs, especially in the posterior portion of the shell, are arched scales, folded so as to appear like blunt spines. The species may easily be distinguished from the young of *C. islandicum* by the smaller number of ribs. The animal, *C. pinnulatum*, is said to be exceedingly lively and able to make rapid progress over gravelly bottom by executing sudden leaps. It has a long, recurved, very strong foot, and its movements are effected as described above. It is abundant at Bar Harbor.

Cardium pinnulatum.

FAMILY MYIDÆ

GENUS *Mya*

In this family we encounter, rather suddenly, some new features not heretofore seen in the pelecypod structure. In the first place, the siphons are enormously large, are united, and are surrounded by a leathery epidermis. The mantle-edges are fused together along the entire ventral margin, except for a small slit through which the foot may project. Although the animal may withdraw the long siphons into its shell, yet they remain to a certain extent exposed, for the valves gape widely posteriorly, and only slightly less so anteriorly. In the economy of these forms the shell seems to play a less important part than it does in the *Veneridæ*, in the *Tellinidæ*, and generally in those families whose shells are strong and, closing firmly, afford the animal within a real protection. The shell of *Mya* (the principal genus) is thin, white, and of a softer chalky texture; it gapes widely "fore and aft," and has a loosely constructed hinge apparatus, consisting of an erect projecting tooth, which fits into a pit in the opposite valve.

M. arenaria. This is the common "soft-shell clam" of New England. Its range is from Cape Cod to Greenland and Great Britain. Upon the Maine coast it is very extensively gathered and sold to the Banks fishermen for bait. Its use as food for man is probably not very great, yet it is always to be seen on sale in the markets of New England coast towns. It cannot compare in flavor with *Venus mercenaria*, the "hard-shell clam" south of Cape Cod. *M. arenaria* lives between tides in muddy, sandy, pebbly, or even rocky ground, where it can find material in which it can burrow and hide itself. It lies just below the surface, with its siphons projected into the water. When the water recedes, *Mya* draws in its siphons and awaits the return of the tide, every now and then

Mya arenaria.

ejecting a jet of water into the air. The shells vary considerably in size and thickness of valves. Large specimens are three and a half inches long and two inches high. Our forefathers were not always well posted upon the habits of mollusks, even though they may have relished them in

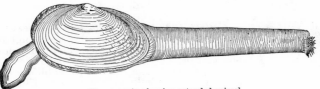

Mya arenaria, showing extended animal.

chowders and believed their flesh to possess valuable curative properties. John Winthrop, in 1634, gave a list of useful American animals, in which he remarked: "Clam, white; their broth is most excellent in all intermitting fevers, consumption, etc. These clams feed only on sand." What marvelous digestive powers!

FAMILY SOLENIDÆ

In this family are included the long, slender bivalves commonly known as "razor-shells." Every one who has been to the sea-shore has become familiar with these odd-looking mollusks, for their valves are always to be found upon every beach. Their station is upon sandy flats or bars more or less exposed at low tide. They burrow into the sand perpendicularly to a depth of two or three feet, remaining hidden most of the time. Occasionally a colony of them will be seen, each one projecting slightly from his burrow. If approached most cautiously some of them may be captured, but if the sand is jarred they all take fright and disappear in an instant. It is no easy matter to capture a "razor" when once he has taken warning, for he will dig down into the sand about as fast as one can follow with a spade. A

Ensis directus, showing extended animal: 1, foot; 2, siphons; 3, papillæ, enlarged.

good way to catch one is to approach his burrow carefully, and then plunge a spade obliquely down below him, thereby cutting off his retreat. So tenaciously will they cling to the sand by expanding the muscular foot that the shell may be pulled entirely off the body before they will let go.

Genus *Ensis*

Ensis directus.

E. directus (Solen ensis, Ensis americanus). The common species upon the New England and Jersey coasts. The foot is long, and protrudes from one end of the long shell; it is also very strong, and capable of change at will into almost any form, from a pointed bulb to a flat disk. The siphons, which project from the opposite end of the shell, are short and are not united. The gills are long. The juxtaposition of these organs is at first confusing, because the greatly elongated form of the shell and the habits of the animal in burrowing vertically into the sand have caused the foot to be pushed farther away from the posterior portion of the shell and to protrude in a direction just opposite to the siphons. The shells are bent or slightly curved; they gape at both ends; and they are fitted with very small interlocking teeth at the upper corner of the posterior end. The color is white, but a yellowish or greenish glossy epidermis covers the entire test. Length about six inches. The manner in which the animal makes its rapid descent into the sand is very interesting. First extending the foot lengthwise into a point, it plunges it into the sand; then, by forcing water into the organ it expands it, thus pushing away the sand on all sides; and still further expanding the foot at the end into a disk, it secures an anchorage which enables it to draw down its shell. By quick repetition of this process *Ensis* can get out of sight in a remarkably sudden manner.

Genus *Solen*

S. viridis. A smaller species, about two inches in length, and with a nearly straight light-green shell. It is often abundant from New Jersey southward.

S. sicarius. The common Californian species of Northern range. It is only about two inches long, and is rounded anteriorly, but is chopped off squarely behind. It is slightly curved and white, and has a glossy brown epidermis.

S. rosaceus. Another species of Southern range, very similar in form to the last, but straighter and rosy-white in color. The epidermis is glossy brown. Length two inches.

Genus *Tagelus*

T. gibbus. The extended range and shore station of this exceedingly abundant species will cause it to be among the first accessions to the cabinet of the collector south of Cape Cod. It burrows deep in sand and mud, leaving two small openings to the hole for the accommodation

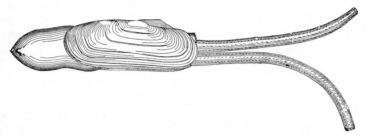

Tagelus gibbus, showing extended animal.

of its two excessively long siphons. As in *Solen* and *Ensis,* the foot is large and muscular, tongue-shaped, and capable of remarkable change of form and great freedom of movement. The long white siphons, separated from the base and each provided with orange-colored eyes (or, rather, a rudimentary sort of visual organs), are the most important feature. The apex of the hinge is not, as in *Solen* and *Ensis,* at the end of the shell, but is more conventionally placed near the middle ; the cardinal teeth are very small, two upon each valve and interlocking ; a flat, oblong, callous process serves as a fossette. The dorsal and

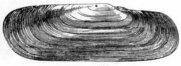

Tagelus gibbus.

ventral margins are parallel, and gape at both ends ; the shell is white, and is covered with a dense yellowish epidermis, which, passing the ventral margin, appears to become continuous with the thickened mantle-edge. There is no other species north of Hatteras with which this could be confounded. The double entrance to the burrow, which may be discovered about low-tide mark, is unique. *T. gibbus* is a good species to examine for the crystalline stylet in the digestive tract.

Family GLYCIMERIDÆ

Genus *Glycimeris*

G. generosa. A large shell of the Pacific coast, occurring most abundantly in Puget Sound waters, where it frequents muddy shallows. It is a remarkable pelecypod in respect to its siphons and the degree of mantle fusion. The appearance of the animal is that of a huge pair of united siphons, protected laterally at their larger end by two white, widely gaping valves. The very small pedal opening in the line of mantle juncture indicates a very small foot. (Plate LXXXIV.)

Family **PHOLADIDÆ**

There is a striking resemblance between the shells of this rock-boring family and those of the petricolas—a resemblance which consists principally in the texture of the shell and the tendency to different types of sculpturing upon the posterior and anterior surfaces of the valves.

Genus *Pholas*

In *Pholas* the anterior part of the hinge-margin is reflected back over the umbones, and a long rib-like tooth springs from under the umbonal region and curves out almost to the center of the valves. The shell gapes "fore and aft," and is thin, white, very hard, and brittle. The animal has a short, truncated foot and a small orifice in the mantle through which the foot may be projected. The siphons are long and are united almost to their ends. Dorsally, an exposed portion of the animal is protected by accessory calcareous plates. The habits of *Pholas* are very interesting. It is found in holes gouged out of solid rock or out of pieces of wood; sometimes, like *Petricola*, it may be found excavating in hard clay. As the anterior end of a *Pholas* shell is the larger in diameter, and is the end which is most deeply buried in the rock (the opening of the burrow being comparatively small), there was some mystery as to the way in which the creature manages to get inside its rocky dwelling. Observations in aquaria have shown that the young *Pholas* begins his process of home-building very early in life. The wearing away of the stone is effected by constantly turning the shell around, scraping with the anterior edges of the valves. A lodging-place having been secured, *Pholas* is obliged to work constantly to enlarge his burrow for the accommodation of his growing shell. The long siphons may project from the hole and draw in food and breath, but the animal is a prisoner for life. When *Pholas* has withdrawn his long siphons he is reasonably secure from his enemies, but nevertheless thousands of them are destroyed by predatory star-fishes, who know how to get at their victims. The restless crustaceans, ever on the outlook for a meal, often nip the siphons of the rock-dwellers, and a kind of worm sometimes attacks them, and, destroying the animal, proceeds to occupy the empty shell and burrow.

P. costata. This species has a wide geographical range, being found from Cape Cod to South America, but it is not abundant north of Hatteras. In Florida it burrows deep in sand as well as in wood or rock. On account of its white color and suggestive shape and sculpture, it has received the popular name of "angel's-wings." It grows to a length of seven or eight inches.

P. truncata. This has much the same range as the last, but is more commonly to be found in New England waters. It also burrows in any hard substance, or in mud above low-water mark. It is especially common in peat-banks.

Pholas costata.

P. californica. A Californian *Pholas.* The shell is about three inches in length, and resembles in all features and habits the *Pholas* of the east coast. Differences in the shell indicate that it is a distinct species.

Pholas truncata.

GENUS *Zirphœa*

Z. crispata. A species of Northern range, occurring but sparingly in New England, in hard clay or rocky burrows. It may be identified at once by the furrow which passes from the beaks across the valves to the lower edges of the shell and divides the surface of the valve into two areas. The anterior area is decorated with radiating toothed ribs; the posterior area is smooth. This conchological feature of the genus is very curious; it may be observed also in several deep-sea genera and in certain extinct fossil forms. The length of this shell is about two inches. This species also occurs in California, where its favorite station is in hard tenacious clay. Length two to four inches.

FAMILY TEREDINIDÆ

GENUS *Teredo*

Zirphœa crispata.

T. navalis. This species is worm-like in form, but it has a small bivalve shell at the larger end, and near the anterior extremity two calcareous appendages called pallets, beyond which extend two siphons. Along the surface of the mantle is secreted a continuous shelly tube which lines the burrow. This mollusk, commonly called the " ship-worm," is exceedingly destructive, perforating with its burrows submerged timber and soon rendering it useless. Various means are taken to protect ships, the piles of wharves, buoys, and the like, against its ravages; copper sheathing, large-headed nails driven close together into the wood, verdigris paint, and so on, being used with more or less effect. Vast numbers of these animals enter the wood and burrow in various directions, but they never interfere with one another, a thin partition of wood always being left between adjacent burrows. How they effect the burrowing is not determined, but it is supposed to be by means of the pallets. *Teredo* does not, like the boring isopod *Limnoria lignorum*, feed upon the wood. Its food consists of microscopic organisms which are taken in through the incurrent siphon. In temperate waters *T. navalis* grows sometimes to the length of six inches; in tropical waters it attains the length of two feet.

There are three other species of *Teredo* and one of the genus *Xylotrya* on our Northern shores; *T. navalis* is, however, the most common and most destructive. In Southern waters there are many other forms of these boring mollusks.

Teredo navalis, in a piece of timber: *P*, pallets; *SS*, siphons; *T*, tube; *V*, valve of shell.

Family **PANDORIDÆ**

Genus *Pandora*

P. trilineata. A little New England shell, remarkable on account of its extreme flatness. When looking at this shell before opening it, one naturally wonders where the animal finds room to exist between two such disk-like valves. The animal is very thin, with largely united mantle-edges, widely separated feeble adductor muscles, and a fairly large tongue-shaped foot. The shell is nacreous, rounded anteriorly, and produced posteriorly into a sort of upturned tip which gapes

Pandora trilineata.

to accommodate two little siphons. The dorsal hinge-margin is excavated and curved. Length about one inch. It is abundant at Cape Cod, in sandy stations, on oyster-beds, and is found from Maine to Florida.

TABLE SHOWING THE CLASSIFICATION OF THE CEPHALOPODS
DESCRIBED IN THIS CHAPTER

CLASS **CEPHALOPODA**

Subclasses	Orders	Genera	Species
Tetrabranchiata		*Nautilus*	
	OCTOPODA	*Octopus*	
Dibranchiata		*Argonauta*	*A. argo*
	DECAPODA	*Spirula*	
		Ommastrephes	*O. illecebrosus*
		Sepia	*L. Pealei*
		Loligo	*L. brevis*

CLASS **CEPHALOPODA**

The *Cephalopoda* form a singularly isolated group, and are so superior in organization and intelligence to all other mollusks that it is difficult to believe that they are first cousins to the lethargic gasteropod and the simply constructed bivalve. But the class bears the stamp of its origin in a mantle, a radula, and a disposition of internal organs and functions which, although highly perfected, is essentially molluscan.

Along the Atlantic coast of the United States, particularly in its northern portion, occur several examples of cephalopods belonging to the genera *Ommastrephes* and *Loligo*, all the species of which are referred to, in common parlance, as "squids." They frequent shallow water, and are often to be found in weirs, darting about with rapid, spasmodic movements, or perhaps lying motionless on the bottom. The squids enter the weirs for the purpose of capturing the young mackerel which are caught in these traps. The squid lies quietly upon the bottom, which it simulates so closely in color as to be almost invisible, and when

464

a school of fishes swims over it, darts suddenly into the midst of it, seizes a fish with its sucker-bearing arms, and kills it by the bite of its parrot-like beak or jaws. Sometimes it happens that squids, while pursuing fish too near shore, precipitate themselves upon the beach, where they flounder about, ejecting water from their siphons, which pushes them only farther away from the water, and squirting out "ink" from their ink-sacs in a vain endeavor to hide themselves from view. On bright moonlight nights squids often go ashore in vast numbers, and perish within a few inches of their native element, which they seem to be unable to regain. These creatures usually swim backward, and the theory is that, dazzled by the bright light of the moon, they continue to gaze at it while swimming, and if there happens to be a shore in the direction of their movements, they suddenly find themselves beached. The fishermen of Canada and New England take advantage of this habit and capture great quantities of squids by placing bright lights in the bows of their boats and then rowing toward shore, thus driving the squids out of the water. The Banks fishermen use them as bait for catching cod. The right claimed by American fishing-schooners to purchase squids in Newfoundland has helped to keep alive the quarrel between Canadian and American fishermen, which has vexed their respective governments for many years.

The range in size among the species of this class is very remarkable. The little sepiolas are about an inch long; the squids of our coasts vary in length from eight inches to one foot; and the giant *Architeuthis* of the North Atlantic measures, often, fifty feet from the end of its arms to the tip of its tail. Such a creature, with its long arms provided with suckers, its powerful jaws, and its rapid, alert movements, is a formidable foe. These animals have been the basis of many legends about sea-serpents and sea-monsters. A gruesome story of an octopus is told by Victor Hugo in "The Toilers of the Sea," where he gives a thrilling account of a man's encounter with a devil-fish in a cave. One who has read this tale has a vivid picture in his mind of the giant squid, and the danger of meeting one of these many-armed foes. Victor Hugo's devil-fish, however, is an animal not true to nature, but a composite, having the attributes of the polyp and of the octopus, and the name of a large ray of Southern waters, a real fish, the *Cephaloptera*, known in its localities as devil-fish. This monstrosity of the novelist's imagination has, however, done more to acquaint the general public with these interesting cephalopods than have the descriptions of scientists.

The giant squid, which is such a dangerous foe, has its own enemy in the sperm-whale. The cachalot swims through the water with its lower jaw hanging, the cephalopod grasps the jaw, and the whale then shuts his capacious mouth upon it. Whalemen describe conflicts between these enormous creatures, the whale always being the conqueror. Sperm-whales killed by man often eject great quantities of the squids in their death throes, showing this food to be almost their exclusive diet.

The name "cephalopod," meaning "feet around the head," is descriptive in part of their anatomy. The head is usually marked off by a neck-constriction, and it bears two highly organized eyes. The foot is fused in part with the head above the eyes and around the mouth; on the upper side it is divided into eight or ten long arm-like processes, bearing suckers, which act as organs of prehension. The under part of the foot forms a tube called the funnel. Through the funnel the animal expels water from the mantle cavity, and thus propels itself through the water.

The mantle covers the body of the animal, and is a cup-shaped or conical envelope, open only at the anterior end, through which project the head and siphon or funnel. It is attached to the body by a line on the dorsal side, the anterior margin being free and open, but provided with an arrangement of cartilages by which it can be hooked on to the siphon, thus completely closing the entrance to the mantle cavity. The mantle is very muscular, and is constantly expanding and contracting, taking water into the mantle cavity through the mantle opening for respiratory purposes, or expelling it through the siphon for propulsion; in the latter case the mantle opening is closed at the moment of ejecting the water. When the siphon is in its normal position the animal swims backward; but it can be turned back over the edge of the mantle, giving a forward movement.

The surface of the mantle is covered with pigment-cells (*chromatophores*). There are sets of chromatophores containing different colors. The cells are opened or closed at will by muscular action of their walls. When open the cells seem to fuse together, giving a solid color-surface, or spots of color as desired, in blue, red, yellow, or brown; when closed they seem as specks on the almost transparent tissues of the animal. Flashes of changing color follow one another with great rapidity over the living animal. In swimming it assumes the color of its surroundings.

Another curious means of protection possessed by the dibranchiate cephalopods is an ink-bag, the brown or black secretions of which are ejected through the siphon, clouding the water when the animal wishes to escape from danger. The ink taken from the ink-sac of *Sepia* is an article of commerce.

Only *Nautilus* and the female *Argonauta* have the characteristic external shell of mollusks. In all other forms the shell is internal or is invested in the integument of the mantle. Of such is the cuttlebone of commerce, which is a calcareous leaf-like body obtained from *Sepia*, the cuttlefish. The common squid *Loligo* has a horny substance situated in the dorsal side of the mantle, called the pen. *Spirula* has a spiral internal shell divided into chambers. Vast numbers of these shells are cast upon the beaches of the Pacific Islands, and they have also been found on the shore of Nantucket.

Cephalopods are separated into two subclasses. In the first, the *Tetrabranchiata*, there are four branchiæ, four nephridia, and four auricles. They are without an ink-sac, and have the foot divided into lobes bearing sheathed tentacles. *Nautilus* is the only genus.

SUBCLASS **TETRABRANCHIATA**

Genus *Nautilus*

Probably the best-known cephalopod is *Nautilus*—the pearly-shelled, chambered nautilus made immortal in the beautiful poem of Oliver Wendell Holmes. The shell of *Nautilus* is a flat spiral; the interior is divided by septa forming a series of chambers;

the septa are perforated, and through the opening runs a tube or prolongation of the body, the siphuncle, which extends to the tip of the shell. The chambers are filled with gas. The animal in the course of its growth moves forward into a newly formed chamber and builds a new septum, closing the cavity last occupied. *Nautilus* lives among the coral reefs of the southern Pacific. Its four or five species are the remnants of a once very extensive race of cephalopods. The fossil remains of many species of *Nautilus*, together with various other genera of shell-bearing cephalopods, indicate that this group has seen its best days. The dibranchiate genera, however, appear to have reached their maximum at the present day.

SUBCLASS **DIBRANCHIATA**

The second subclass, the *Dibranchiata*, is characterized by two branchiæ and two auricles. The main part of the foot is divided into eight or ten long arms provided with numerous suckers arranged in from one to four rows on the ventral side of the arms. They have also an ink-sac. The *Dibranchiata* are divided into two orders: the *Octopoda*, which have eight arms, and comprise the *Octopus* and *Argonauta;* and the *Decapoda*, which have ten arms, and comprise *Spirula, Ommastrephes, Sepia,* and *Loligo*. In these animals two of the ten arms are longer than the others, and these tentacular arms have suckers only on their broadened, club-like ends, they are kept retracted within grooves, one on each side of the head, except when needed for prehension.

Argonauta argo, female removed from shell.

Genus *Argonauta*

A. argo. In this species, the paper-nautilus, the shell, which is possessed only by the female, is not chambered. The animal rests in the shell, but has no organic connection with it other than by the membranous expansions at the extremities of the two dorsal arms, which secrete it and hold it in place. The purpose of the shell is to hold and protect the eggs.

Argonauta argo, side view of shell.

Genus *Loligo*

L. Pealei. In this species the body is cylindrical, tapers to a point, and has a flat appendage in front. The fins are terminal, half, or more than half, as long as the body, united in a point posteriorly, and obtusely rounded on the outer angles. The head is a little narrower than the mantle. There are eight sessile, subtriangular arms furnished with two series of suckers which are hemispherical and stalked, and two long retractile tentacular arms dilated at the extremities, bearing four rows of suckers. It has a pen- or quill-shaped cartilaginous substance in the dorsal integument of the mantle. Common from Cape Cod to South Carolina.

L. brevis. A small short-bodied species, with short rounded caudal fins. It is common from South Carolina to Florida, and extends as far north as Delaware Bay.

Genus *Ommastrephes*

O. illecebrosus. A species similar to *L. Pealei*, but with shorter fins. These are broad and pear-shaped, one third wider than they are long, and usually reach less than one half the length of the mantle. They are straight on the posterior end, and form nearly a right angle, while the upper margins are rounded. The head is as broad as the mantle. The arms are stout and taper to an acute point. The tentacular arms are long when expanded. The species is abundant from Cape Cod to Newfoundland, and is found as far south as Newport, Rhode Island. This is the squid which is used so extensively in the Banks fishery as bait. It

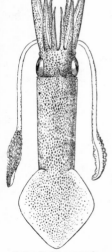

Loligo Pealei, young female ; dorsal view.

visits the shores in large schools, presumably in pursuit of prey, and often itself becomes the victim. It is a beautiful creature from its varying colors, which are truly wonderful. It changes in a moment from vivid red to deep blue, purple, orange, and so on, the colors often passing over it in flashes as it swims along.

Ommastrephes illecebrosus, young male; ventral view.

VIII

CHORDATA

TABLE SHOWING THE CLASSIFICATION OF THE CHORDATA
DESCRIBED IN THIS CHAPTER

Phylum

CHORDATA

Class

UROCHORDA or TUNICATA

Order LARVACEA

(Free-swimming, pelagic; Tunicata having caudal appendages)

Suborders   Genera

Appendicularia

Order THALIACEA

*(Free-swimming Tunicata, without caudal appendages; single or in colonies; muscles
of body-wall arranged in complete or in interrupted ring-like bands)*

CYCLOMYARIA
*(Cask-shaped bodies with complete rings
of muscular bands; oral and atrial
apertures at opposite ends of the
body)* } *Doliolum*

HEMIMYARIA
*(Spindle-shaped bodies; muscular bands
in incomplete rings; oral and atrial
apertures subterminal)* } *Salpa*

PYROSOMATA
*(Hollow cylindrical colonies; zoöids em-
bedded in a gelatinous wall; oral apertures open on the outer, atrial apertures
open on the inner surface of cylinder)* } *Pyrosoma*

Suborders	Genera	Species

Order ASCIDIACEA

(Mostly fixed Tunicata ; single or in colonies ; tests of considerable thickness)

Suborders	Genera	Species
ASCIDIA SIMPLICES *(Possess distinct tests ; usually permanently fixed)*	*Molgula*	*M. manhattensis* *M. pellucida* *M. arenata*
	Cynthia	*C. pyriformis* *C. partita* *C. carnea*
	Boltenia	*B. clavata*
	Ascidia	*A. amphora* *A. callosa*
ASCIDIA COMPOSITÆ *(Fixed colonies ; the zoöids embedded in a common gelatinous material ; without separate tests)*	*Botryllus* *Amarœcium*	*B. gouldii* *A. pellucidum*

CHORDATA

CLASS **UROCHORDA** or **TUNICATA**

THE most conspicuous animals of this class are the ascidians, which are common objects on rocky coasts. The *simple ascidians* are peculiar leathery, sac-shaped bodies which send out jets of water when touched. This habit gives them the common name of " sea-squirts." Some are highly colored, especially those of Southern waters; others are somber, unattractive bodies, often growing in masses. The *compound ascidians* are gelatinous colonies, sometimes forming thin incrustations, sometimes jelly-like masses, on seaweeds, shells, etc. This class comprises also the beautiful *Salpa*, a genus of free-swimming animals having transparent bodies encircled by rings of muscular bands, and in one stage forming chains of attached organisms which swim on the surface of the sea and of bays.

The tunicates are by some authors classed with the vertebrate animals because in the larval stage they have a notochord; this disappears, however, in the adult form, and the animals are considered degenerates. The tunicates are interesting to biologists from the remarkable changes they undergo in their life-history, and (in some genera) the marked phase of alternation of generation. One of their curious anatomical features is the blood-vascular system. The circulation is propelled by wave-like contractions of the heart, which, after forcing the blood one way for a time, stops and reverses the blood-current. The tunicates are widely distributed, and occur at all depths. (Plate LXXXV.)

474

Genus *Salpa*

The animals of this genus are transparent, subcylindrical, smooth, gelatinous bodies encircled by bands of white muscular fiber. They strikingly exemplify alternation of generations. They occur in two distinct conditions, one being solitary, the other consisting of animals united in chains. The solitary individuals are about an inch long, and have two long processes at the posterior end. These single animals reproduce by budding, and form series of individuals in small chains, the animals being arranged in two rows. The chains grow to the length of a foot or more, and contain twenty to thirty pairs of salpas. Each of these connected individuals produces in turn a single egg, which becomes a single *Salpa*, and this again, like its grandmother, reproduces by budding. Thus the animals are alike only in alternate generations. The naturalist Chamisso, who discovered the relationship between the two forms, expressed it as follows: a *Salpa* mother is not like its daughter or its mother, but resembles its sister, its grandmother, and its granddaughter.

Salpa chain.

The single zoöids liberate many colonies during the summer, which grow rapidly, and in the autumn the chains are exceedingly abundant. The *Salpa* chains swim about with a serpentine movement, and are beautiful, delicate objects with their transparent bodies banded with white, tinged with pink, and streaked with blue.

SIMPLE ASCIDIANS

These are solitary and usually fixed; they are never free-swimming, and when in colonies each animal has a distinct test. All the larger ascidians, or sea-squirts, belong to this group.

Genus *Molgula*

Body more or less globular, membranous, attached or free; orifices on very contractile tubes.

M. manhattensis. Nearly globular when the tubes are contracted; usually covered with bits of eel-grass, seaweeds, sand, etc.; surface a little rough; color olive-green. The animal is often attached to rocks, more frequently to eel-grass and seaweeds, and is sometimes so crowded as to form large clusters. Found from Maine to North Carolina.

M. pellucida. Body nearly globular, about an inch in diameter, smooth, clean, and translucent, the intestine showing through the test. The two tubes are large, swollen at the base, and divergent. The animal lives free in the sand, and is found from Massachusetts to North Carolina.

M. arenata. Body somewhat compressed laterally; test thin and covered completely with sand, which is closely adherent; about three quarters of an inch in diameter; tubes short and wide apart. Found on shelly and sandy bottoms of bays and sounds.

Genus *Cynthia*

The animal is attached, the body coriaceous, and the orifices four-lobed. Frequently associated in groups, the individuals often differing in color.

C. pyriformis. Body globular, or oblong when extended; hard, velvety, whitish surface, with pink cheeks; orifices on prominent protuberances on the upper surface. It lives in clear, deep water on rocks, and is sometimes found at low-water mark on the northern New England coast. Commonly called the sea-peach. (Plate LXXXV.)

C. partita. Body oblong; attached; test horny and wrinkled; rusty-brown; apertures square, on prominent tubes marked with triangular spots of white and purple; diameter one inch. Found on the piles of wharves and on shelly bottoms in shallow water; also on the under side of stones when they are much flattened.

C. carnea. Test low and flat, with a thin margin; adherent by a very broad base; orifices small, square, slightly prominent; red or flesh-color. Found in deep water on stones and shells on the northern New England coast.

Genus *Boltenia*

Body more or less globular, on a long stem; fixed; orifices on the side.

B. clavata. Body long, wrinkled, leathery, on a long stalk, resembling the flower of lady's-slipper (*Cypripedium*); two cross-shaped orifices wide apart on the side; yellowish in color; attached to stones in deep water, but sometimes washed ashore in storms. The stalks are often covered with polyzoans and hydroids. (Plate LXXXV.)

Genus *Ascidia*

Test gelatinous or cartilaginous; attached; it grows in bunches under stones at low-water mark. Sometimes it is variously col-

PLATE LXXXV.

ASCIDIANS.

1, Ascidia callosa.
2, Botryllus Schlosseri.
3, Cynthia pyriformis.
4, The same, enlarged.

5, Cynthia placenta.
6, Glandula fibrosa.
7, Cynthia condylomata.
8, Boltenia clavata.

9, Cynthia echinata.

ored, but otherwise it is repulsive in aspect. The apertures are wide apart; one orifice is eight-lobed, the other six-lobed.

A. amphora. Form usually globular, but more or less irregular; substance something like rubber. Found of all sizes adhering in clusters to stones, shells, and piles, and usually covered with marine growths. The color is grayish-brown.

A. callosa. Body depressed, usually oval, but varying in shape; thick, fleshy, translucent; surface uneven; apertures dark purple and prominent. Found at low tide adhering to stones and shells. (Plate LXXXV.)

COMPOUND ASCIDIANS

Ascidians of this group form fixed colonies, and are embedded in gelatinous material, the animals having a common test, but not being united by any internal union. The colonies thus formed are flat and incrusting, or are branched and lobed, or sometimes elevated on stalks. The zoöids are in some cases dotted irregularly over the entire surface, in others are in rows, or again are in groups. They have various colors—purple, yellow, blue, gray, and green. They are common on eel-grass, the piles of wharves, the bottoms of boats, and so on.

GENUS *Botryllus*

B. gouldii. This species forms thick, fleshy, translucent incrustations, often several inches in length and a quarter of an inch wide, over eel-grass, the piles of wharves, and other objects. Sometimes, at the end of summer, small objects are completely covered with the luxuriant growth of this compound ascidian. The zoöids form circular or elliptical groups, often as many as fifteen surrounding each orifice, looking like minute stars. The colonies vary in color. Often on the same stem of eel-grass will be found separate colonies varying in this respect. In some the ground-color will be olive-green specked with white, while the zoöids are purple, marked with other colors; again the arrangement is quite different.

GENUS *Amaroecium*

A. pellucidum. A massive compound ascidian, smooth, translucent, and gelatinous, which forms large, hemispherical, complex, irregular masses six inches or more in diameter. It is usually covered by adhering sand. The mass consists of club-shaped lobes, which rise from a common base. Each lobe contains a central orifice around which long, slender zoöids, sometimes an inch long, are grouped. These masses are so abundant in some places that they cover the bottom for considerable spaces. They are found in deep water from Cape Cod to North Carolina.

INDEX

Heavy-faced type is used to indicate names of classes, orders, genera, etc.; heavy-faced numerals to indicate the place where the fullest description is given

A

Abdomen, 243, **246**.
Abductor muscles, **302**.
Aboral, **202**.
 Surface, 201.
Abyssal, **23**.
Acalephs, **134**.
Acanthalithodes, 240, **271**.
 A. hispidus, 240, **271**.
Acephala, 409.
Acetabularia, 51, **57**.
 A. crenulata, 51, **57**.
Acmæa, 9, 309, **312**.
 A. mitra, 324, **357**.
 A. patina, 324, **357**.
 A. testudinalis, 41, 42, 324, 343, 348, **356**.
 A. testudinalis, var. alveus, 324, **357**.
Acmæidæ, 324, **356**.
Acontia, **145**.
Acorn-shell, **254**.
Actiniaria, 141, **142**, 143, 144.
Actinozoa, 112, 115, **141**, 142.
Adamsia palliata, 144, **267**.
Adductor muscles, **302**, 413, 417.
Æolididæ, 324.
Æolis, 41, 42, 309, 324, **354**.
 Æ. papillosa, 324, **354**.
Æquoreidæ, 116, **128**.
Ætea, 188, **194**.
 Æ. anguinea, 188, **194**.
Agarum, 36, 42, 63, 68, **69**.
Aglaophemia, **127**.
 A. struthioides, 116, **127**.
Ahnfeldtia, 76, **82**.
 A. plicata, 76, **82**.
Alaria, 63, **69**.
 A. esculenta, 41, 42, 63, **69**.
 A. gibbesii, 240, **269**.
Albunæa, 240, **269**.
Alcyonacea, 141, **151**.
Alcyonaria, 141, 142, **150**, 152.
Alcyonidium, 189, 192, **197**.
 A. hirsutum, 189, **197**.
 A. hispidum, 189, **198**.
 A. parasiticum, 189, **198**.
 A. ramosum, 189, **197**.
Alcyonium, 141, **151**.
 A. palmatum, 141, 150, 151.
Aleutian province, **311**.
Algæ, 25, 48, 62, 76.
 Botanical facts about, **25**.

Alternation of generation, **120**, 121.
Amarœcium, 473, **477**.
 A. pellucidum, 473, **477**.
Ambulacra, 201, 202, **205**, 214, 218.
Ambulacral groove, **205**.
 Ossicles, **205**.
 Zones, 201, 202, **205**, 218, 229.
American division, **24**.
Amphictenidæ, 162, **183**.
Amphineura, 300, 316, 317, 320, **321**, 323.
Amphipoda, 242, **289**.
Amphissa, 312.
 A. corrugata, 326, **389**.
Amphitrite, 161, **182**.
 A. ornata, 161, **182**.
Amphiura, 213, **215**.
 A. squamata, 213, **215**.
Ampullæ, 201, 205, 206, 218.
Anadyomene, 51, **57**.
 A. flabellata, 51, **57**.
Anatomy, 20.
 Of higher Crustacea, **246**.
Anemone Cave, 40.
Angel's-wings, 461.
Animal-flowers, **142**.
Animal life in its lowest forms, 21.
Annelida, 305.
Annulata, 159, 161, 164, 170.
Anomia, 405, **424**.
 A. aculeata, 405, **425**.
 A. lampe, 405, **425**.
 A. simplex, 405, **424**.
Anomiidæ, 405, **424**.
Anomura, 240, **264**.
Antennæ, 243, **246**, 258.
Antennules, 243, **246**, 258.
Antheneidæ, 204, **209**.
Anthomedusæ, **116**.
Aperture, **302**.
Apex, 343.
Aphrodite, 161, **174**.
 A. aculeata, 161, **174**.
Aphroditidæ, 161, 172, 173.
Aplacophora, 300, 321, 323.
Aplysella violacea, 105.
Aplysia Wilcoxii, 352.
Aplysiidæ, 324.
Apoda, 228, **233**.
Appendicularia, 472.
Arabella, 161, **179**.
 A. opalina, 161, **179**.
Arbacia, 217, **222**.

A. punctulata, 217, **222**.
Arbaciadæ, 217, 222.
Arca, 310, 405, **425**.
 A. noæ, 405, **426**.
 A. pexata, 405, **425**.
 A. ponderosa, 405, **426**.
Arcachon, 434.
Architeuthis, 465.
Arcidæ, 405, **425**.
Arctic province, **309**.
Arctica, 406, **441**.
 A. islandica, 406, **441**.
Arenicola, 162, 172, **184**.
 A. marina, 162, **184**.
Arenicolidæ, 162, **184**.
Argonauta, 464, 467, 468.
 A. argo, 464, **469**.
Aristocratic genera, 313, 377, 398, 401.
Aristotle's lantern, **203**.
Arthrocladia, 62, **67**.
 A. villosa, 62, **67**.
Arthropoda, 238, **244**.
Arthrostraca, 242, **289**.
Articulata, 188.
Ascidia, 473, **476**.
 A. amphora, 473, **477**.
 A. callosa, 473, **477**.
 A. compositæ, 473.
 A. simplices, 473.
Ascidiacea, 473.
Ascidians, 8, **474**.
 Compound, 474, **477**.
 Simple, 474, **475**.
Ascophyllum, 63, **73**.
 A. nodosum, 43, 63, **73**.
Asperococcus, 62, **66**.
 A. echinatus, 62, **66**.
Astacoidæ, 240, **261**.
Astarte, 309, 406, **440**.
 A. castanea, 406, **441**.
 A. undata, 406, **441**.
Astartidæ, 406, **440**.
Asterias, 204, **212**.
 A. Forbesii, 204, 207, **212**.
 A. gigantea, 204, 207, **212**.
 A. ochracea, 204, **212**.
 A. vulgaris, 43, 204, 207, **212**.
Asteriidæ, 204, **212**.
Asterina, 204, **210**.
 A. folium, 204, **210**.
 A. miniata, 204, **211**.
Asterinidæ, 204, **210**.
Asteroidea, 200, 204, **205**.
Astræa, 141, 146, 147, **148**.

479

A CATALOGUE OF SELECTED DOVER BOOKS
IN ALL FIELDS OF INTEREST

A CATALOGUE OF SELECTED DOVER BOOKS
IN ALL FIELDS OF INTEREST

AMERICA'S OLD MASTERS, James T. Flexner. Four men emerged unexpectedly from provincial 18th century America to leadership in European art: Benjamin West, J. S. Copley, C. R. Peale, Gilbert Stuart. Brilliant coverage of lives and contributions. Revised, 1967 edition. 69 plates. 365pp. of text.

21806-6 Paperbound $3.00

FIRST FLOWERS OF OUR WILDERNESS: AMERICAN PAINTING, THE COLONIAL PERIOD, James T. Flexner. Painters, and regional painting traditions from earliest Colonial times up to the emergence of Copley, West and Peale Sr., Foster, Gustavus Hesselius, Feke, John Smibert and many anonymous painters in the primitive manner. Engaging presentation, with 162 illustrations. xxii + 368pp.

22180-6 Paperbound $3.50

THE LIGHT OF DISTANT SKIES: AMERICAN PAINTING, 1760-1835, James T. Flexner. The great generation of early American painters goes to Europe to learn and to teach: West, Copley, Gilbert Stuart and others. Allston, Trumbull, Morse; also contemporary American painters—primitives, derivatives, academics—who remained in America. 102 illustrations. xiii + 306pp. 22179-2 Paperbound $3.00

A HISTORY OF THE RISE AND PROGRESS OF THE ARTS OF DESIGN IN THE UNITED STATES, William Dunlap. Much the richest mine of information on early American painters, sculptors, architects, engravers, miniaturists, etc. The only source of information for scores of artists, the major primary source for many others. Unabridged reprint of rare original 1834 edition, with new introduction by James T. Flexner, and 394 new illustrations. Edited by Rita Weiss. 6⅝ x 9⅝.

21695-0, 21696-9, 21697-7 Three volumes, Paperbound $13.50

EPOCHS OF CHINESE AND JAPANESE ART, Ernest F. Fenollosa. From primitive Chinese art to the 20th century, thorough history, explanation of every important art period and form, including Japanese woodcuts; main stress on China and Japan, but Tibet, Korea also included. Still unexcelled for its detailed, rich coverage of cultural background, aesthetic elements, diffusion studies, particularly of the historical period. 2nd, 1913 edition. 242 illustrations. lii + 439pp. of text.

20364-6, 20365-4 Two volumes, Paperbound $6.00

THE GENTLE ART OF MAKING ENEMIES, James A. M. Whistler. Greatest wit of his day deflates Oscar Wilde, Ruskin, Swinburne; strikes back at inane critics, exhibitions, art journalism; aesthetics of impressionist revolution in most striking form. Highly readable classic by great painter. Reproduction of edition designed by Whistler. Introduction by Alfred Werner. xxxvi + 334pp.

21875-9 Paperbound $2.50

VISUAL ILLUSIONS: THEIR CAUSES, CHARACTERISTICS, AND APPLICATIONS, Matthew Luckiesh. Thorough description and discussion of optical illusion, geometric and perspective, particularly; size and shape distortions, illusions of color, of motion; natural illusions; use of illusion in art and magic, industry, etc. Most useful today with op art, also for classical art. Scores of effects illustrated. Introduction by William H. Ittleson. 100 illustrations. xxi + 252pp.

21530-X Paperbound $2.00

A HANDBOOK OF ANATOMY FOR ART STUDENTS, Arthur Thomson. Thorough, virtually exhaustive coverage of skeletal structure, musculature, etc. Full text, supplemented by anatomical diagrams and drawings and by photographs of undraped figures. Unique in its comparison of male and female forms, pointing out differences of contour, texture, form. 211 figures, 40 drawings, 86 photographs. xx + 459pp. 5⅜ x 8⅜.

21163-0 Paperbound $3.50

150 MASTERPIECES OF DRAWING, Selected by Anthony Toney. Full page reproductions of drawings from the early 16th to the end of the 18th century, all beautifully reproduced: Rembrandt, Michelangelo, Dürer, Fragonard, Urs, Graf, Wouwerman, many others. First-rate browsing book, model book for artists. xviii + 150pp. 8⅜ x 11¼.

21032-4 Paperbound $2.50

THE LATER WORK OF AUBREY BEARDSLEY, Aubrey Beardsley. Exotic, erotic, ironic masterpieces in full maturity: Comedy Ballet, Venus and Tannhauser, Pierrot, Lysistrata, Rape of the Lock, Savoy material, Ali Baba, Volpone, etc. This material revolutionized the art world, and is still powerful, fresh, brilliant. With *The Early Work*, all Beardsley's finest work. 174 plates, 2 in color. xiv + 176pp. 8⅛ x 11.

21817-1 Paperbound $3.00

DRAWINGS OF REMBRANDT, Rembrandt van Rijn. Complete reproduction of fabulously rare edition by Lippmann and Hofstede de Groot, completely reedited, updated, improved by Prof. Seymour Slive, Fogg Museum. Portraits, Biblical sketches, landscapes, Oriental types, nudes, episodes from classical mythology—All Rembrandt's fertile genius. Also selection of drawings by his pupils and followers. "Stunning volumes," *Saturday Review*. 550 illustrations. lxxviii + 552pp. 9⅛ x 12¼.

21485-0, 21486-9 Two volumes, Paperbound $10.00

THE DISASTERS OF WAR, Francisco Goya. One of the masterpieces of Western civilization—83 etchings that record Goya's shattering, bitter reaction to the Napoleonic war that swept through Spain after the insurrection of 1808 and to war in general. Reprint of the first edition, with three additional plates from Boston's Museum of Fine Arts. All plates facsimile size. Introduction by Philip Hofer, Fogg Museum. v + 97pp. 9⅜ x 8¼.

21872-4 Paperbound $2.00

GRAPHIC WORKS OF ODILON REDON. Largest collection of Redon's graphic works ever assembled: 172 lithographs, 28 etchings and engravings, 9 drawings. These include some of his most famous works. All the plates from *Odilon Redon: oeuvre graphique complet,* plus additional plates. New introduction and caption translations by Alfred Werner. 209 illustrations. xxvii + 209pp. 9⅛ x 12¼.

21966-8 Paperbound $4.00

DESIGN BY ACCIDENT; A BOOK OF "ACCIDENTAL EFFECTS" FOR ARTISTS AND DESIGNERS, James F. O'Brien. Create your own unique, striking, imaginative effects by "controlled accident" interaction of materials: paints and lacquers, oil and water based paints, splatter, crackling materials, shatter, similar items. Everything you do will be different; first book on this limitless art, so useful to both fine artist and commercial artist. Full instructions. 192 plates showing "accidents," 8 in color. viii + 215pp. 8⅜ x 11¼. 21942-9 Paperbound $3.50

THE BOOK OF SIGNS, Rudolf Koch. Famed German type designer draws 493 beautiful symbols: religious, mystical, alchemical, imperial, property marks, runes, etc. Remarkable fusion of traditional and modern. Good for suggestions of timelessness, smartness, modernity. Text. vi + 104pp. 6⅛ x 9¼. 20162-7 Paperbound $1.25

HISTORY OF INDIAN AND INDONESIAN ART, Ananda K. Coomaraswamy. An unabridged republication of one of the finest books by a great scholar in Eastern art. Rich in descriptive material, history, social backgrounds; Sunga reliefs, Rajput paintings, Gupta temples, Burmese frescoes, textiles, jewelry, sculpture, etc. 400 photos. viii + 423pp. 6⅜ x 9¾. 21436-2 Paperbound $4.00

PRIMITIVE ART, Franz Boas. America's foremost anthropologist surveys textiles, ceramics, woodcarving, basketry, metalwork, etc.; patterns, technology, creation of symbols, style origins. All areas of world, but very full on Northwest Coast Indians. More than 350 illustrations of baskets, boxes, totem poles, weapons, etc. 378 pp. 20025-6 Paperbound $3.00

THE GENTLEMAN AND CABINET MAKER'S DIRECTOR, Thomas Chippendale. Full reprint (third edition, 1762) of most influential furniture book of all time, by master cabinetmaker. 200 plates, illustrating chairs, sofas, mirrors, tables, cabinets, plus 24 photographs of surviving pieces. Biographical introduction by N. Bienenstock. vi + 249pp. 9⅞ x 12¾. 21601-2 Paperbound $4.00

AMERICAN ANTIQUE FURNITURE, Edgar G. Miller, Jr. The basic coverage of all American furniture before 1840. Individual chapters cover type of furniture—clocks, tables, sideboards, etc.—chronologically, with inexhaustible wealth of data. More than 2100 photographs, all identified, commented on. Essential to all early American collectors. Introduction by H. E. Keyes. vi + 1106pp. 7⅞ x 10¾. 21599-7, 21600-4 Two volumes, Paperbound $11.00

PENNSYLVANIA DUTCH AMERICAN FOLK ART, Henry J. Kauffman. 279 photos, 28 drawings of tulipware, Fraktur script, painted tinware, toys, flowered furniture, quilts, samplers, hex signs, house interiors, etc. Full descriptive text. Excellent for tourist, rewarding for designer, collector. Map. 146pp. 7⅞ x 10¾. 21205-X Paperbound $2.50

EARLY NEW ENGLAND GRAVESTONE RUBBINGS, Edmund V. Gillon, Jr. 43 photographs, 226 carefully reproduced rubbings show heavily symbolic, sometimes macabre early gravestones, up to early 19th century. Remarkable early American primitive art, occasionally strikingly beautiful; always powerful. Text. xxvi + 207pp. 8⅜ x 11¼. 21380-3 Paperbound $3.50

ALPHABETS AND ORNAMENTS, Ernst Lehner. Well-known pictorial source for decorative alphabets, script examples, cartouches, frames, decorative title pages, calligraphic initials, borders, similar material. 14th to 19th century, mostly European. Useful in almost any graphic arts designing, varied styles. 750 illustrations. 256pp. 7 x 10.   21905-4 Paperbound $4.00

PAINTING: A CREATIVE APPROACH, Norman Colquhoun. For the beginner simple guide provides an instructive approach to painting: major stumbling blocks for beginner; overcoming them, technical points; paints and pigments; oil painting; watercolor and other media and color. New section on "plastic" paints. Glossary. Formerly *Paint Your Own Pictures*. 221pp.   22000-1 Paperbound $1.75

THE ENJOYMENT AND USE OF COLOR, Walter Sargent. Explanation of the relations between colors themselves and between colors in nature and art, including hundreds of little-known facts about color values, intensities, effects of high and low illumination, complementary colors. Many practical hints for painters, references to great masters. 7 color plates, 29 illustrations. x + 274pp.
20944-X Paperbound $2.75

THE NOTEBOOKS OF LEONARDO DA VINCI, compiled and edited by Jean Paul Richter. 1566 extracts from original manuscripts reveal the full range of Leonardo's versatile genius: all his writings on painting, sculpture, architecture, anatomy, astronomy, geography, topography, physiology, mining, music, etc., in both Italian and English, with 186 plates of manuscript pages and more than 500 additional drawings. Includes studies for the Last Supper, the lost Sforza monument, and other works. Total of xlvii + 866pp. 7⅞ x 10¾.
22572-0, 22573-9 Two volumes, Paperbound $10.00

MONTGOMERY WARD CATALOGUE OF 1895. Tea gowns, yards of flannel and pillow-case lace, stereoscopes, books of gospel hymns, the New Improved Singer Sewing Machine, side saddles, milk skimmers, straight-edged razors, high-button shoes, spittoons, and on and on . . . listing some 25,000 items, practically all illustrated. Essential to the shoppers of the 1890's, it is our truest record of the spirit of the period. Unaltered reprint of Issue No. 57, Spring and Summer 1895. Introduction by Boris Emmet. Innumerable illustrations. xiii + 624pp. 8½ x 11⅝.
22377-9 Paperbound $6.95

THE CRYSTAL PALACE EXHIBITION ILLUSTRATED CATALOGUE (LONDON, 1851). One of the wonders of the modern world—the Crystal Palace Exhibition in which all the nations of the civilized world exhibited their achievements in the arts and sciences—presented in an equally important illustrated catalogue. More than 1700 items pictured with accompanying text—ceramics, textiles, cast-iron work, carpets, pianos, sleds, razors, wall-papers, billiard tables, beehives, silverware and hundreds of other artifacts—represent the focal point of Victorian culture in the Western World. Probably the largest collection of Victorian decorative art ever assembled—indispensable for antiquarians and designers. Unabridged republication of the Art-Journal Catalogue of the Great Exhibition of 1851, with all terminal essays. New introduction by John Gloag, F.S.A. xxxiv + 426pp. 9 x 12.
22503-8 Paperbound $4.50

A History of Costume, Carl Köhler. Definitive history, based on surviving pieces of clothing primarily, and paintings, statues, etc. secondarily. Highly readable text, supplemented by 594 illustrations of costumes of the ancient Mediterranean peoples, Greece and Rome, the Teutonic prehistoric period; costumes of the Middle Ages, Renaissance, Baroque, 18th and 19th centuries. Clear, measured patterns are provided for many clothing articles. Approach is practical throughout. Enlarged by Emma von Sichart. 464pp. 21030-8 Paperbound $3.50

Oriental Rugs, Antique and Modern, Walter A. Hawley. A complete and authoritative treatise on the Oriental rug—where they are made, by whom and how, designs and symbols, characteristics in detail of the six major groups, how to distinguish them and how to buy them. Detailed technical data is provided on periods, weaves, warps, wefts, textures, sides, ends and knots, although no technical background is required for an understanding. 11 color plates, 80 halftones, 4 maps. vi + 320pp. 6⅛ x 9⅛. 22366-3 Paperbound $5.00

Ten Books on Architecture, Vitruvius. By any standards the most important book on architecture ever written. Early Roman discussion of aesthetics of building, construction methods, orders, sites, and every other aspect of architecture has inspired, instructed architecture for about 2,000 years. Stands behind Palladio, Michelangelo, Bramante, Wren, countless others. Definitive Morris H. Morgan translation. 68 illustrations. xii + 331pp. 20645-9 Paperbound $3.50

The Four Books of Architecture, Andrea Palladio. Translated into every major Western European language in the two centuries following its publication in 1570, this has been one of the most influential books in the history of architecture. Complete reprint of the 1738 Isaac Ware edition. New introduction by Adolf Placzek, Columbia Univ. 216 plates. xxii + 110pp. of text. 9½ x 12¾. 21308-0 Clothbound $10.00

Sticks and Stones: A Study of American Architecture and Civilization, Lewis Mumford.One of the great classics of American cultural history. American architecture from the medieval-inspired earliest forms to the early 20th century; evolution of structure and style, and reciprocal influences on environment. 21 photographic illustrations. 238pp. 20202-X Paperbound $2.00

The American Builder's Companion, Asher Benjamin. The most widely used early 19th century architectural style and source book, for colonial up into Greek Revival periods. Extensive development of geometry of carpentering, construction of sashes, frames, doors, stairs; plans and elevations of domestic and other buildings. Hundreds of thousands of houses were built according to this book, now invaluable to historians, architects, restorers, etc. 1827 edition. 59 plates. 114pp. 7⅞ x 10¾. 22236-5 Paperbound $3.50

Dutch Houses in the Hudson Valley Before 1776, Helen Wilkinson Reynolds. The standard survey of the Dutch colonial house and outbuildings, with constructional features, decoration, and local history associated with individual homesteads. Introduction by Franklin D. Roosevelt. Map. 150 illustrations. 469pp. 6⅝ x 9¼. 21469-9 Paperbound $4.00

THE ARCHITECTURE OF COUNTRY HOUSES, Andrew J. Downing. Together with Vaux's *Villas and Cottages* this is the basic book for Hudson River Gothic architecture of the middle Victorian period. Full, sound discussions of general aspects of housing, architecture, style, decoration, furnishing, together with scores of detailed house plans, illustrations of specific buildings, accompanied by full text. Perhaps the most influential single American architectural book. 1850 edition. Introduction by J. Stewart Johnson. 321 figures, 34 architectural designs. xvi + 560pp.
22003-6 Paperbound $4.00

LOST EXAMPLES OF COLONIAL ARCHITECTURE, John Mead Howells. Full-page photographs of buildings that have disappeared or been so altered as to be denatured, including many designed by major early American architects. 245 plates. xvii + 248pp. 7⅞ x 10¾. 21143-6 Paperbound $3.50

DOMESTIC ARCHITECTURE OF THE AMERICAN COLONIES AND OF THE EARLY REPUBLIC, Fiske Kimball. Foremost architect and restorer of Williamsburg and Monticello covers nearly 200 homes between 1620-1825. Architectural details, construction, style features, special fixtures, floor plans, etc. Generally considered finest work in its area. 219 illustrations of houses, doorways, windows, capital mantels. xx + 314pp. 7⅞ x 10¾. 21743-4 Paperbound $4.00

EARLY AMERICAN ROOMS: 1650-1858, edited by Russell Hawes Kettell. Tour of 12 rooms, each representative of a different era in American history and each furnished, decorated, designed and occupied in the style of the era. 72 plans and elevations, 8-page color section, etc., show fabrics, wall papers, arrangements, etc. Full descriptive text. xvii + 200pp. of text. 8⅜ x 11¼.
21633-0 Paperbound $5.00

THE FITZWILLIAM VIRGINAL BOOK, edited by J. Fuller Maitland and W. B. Squire. Full modern printing of famous early 17th-century ms. volume of 300 works by Morley, Byrd, Bull, Gibbons, etc. For piano or other modern keyboard instrument; easy to read format. xxxvi + 938pp. 8⅜ x 11.
21068-5, 21069-3 Two volumes, Paperbound $10.00

KEYBOARD MUSIC, Johann Sebastian Bach. Bach Gesellschaft edition. A rich selection of Bach's masterpieces for the harpsichord: the six English Suites, six French Suites, the six Partitas (Clavierübung part I), the Goldberg Variations (Clavierübung part IV), the fifteen Two-Part Inventions and the fifteen Three-Part Sinfonias. Clearly reproduced on large sheets with ample margins; eminently playable. vi + 312pp. 8⅛ x 11. 22360-4 Paperbound $5.00

THE MUSIC OF BACH: AN INTRODUCTION, Charles Sanford Terry. A fine, nontechnical introduction to Bach's music, both instrumental and vocal. Covers organ music, chamber music, passion music, other types. Analyzes themes, developments, innovations. x + 114pp. 21075-8 Paperbound $1.25

BEETHOVEN AND HIS NINE SYMPHONIES, Sir George Grove. Noted British musicologist provides best history, analysis, commentary on symphonies. Very thorough, rigorously accurate; necessary to both advanced student and amateur music lover. 436 musical passages. vii + 407 pp. 20334-4 Paperbound $2.75

JOHANN SEBASTIAN BACH, Philipp Spitta. One of the great classics of musicology, this definitive analysis of Bach's music (and life) has never been surpassed. Lucid, nontechnical analyses of hundreds of pieces (30 pages devoted to St. Matthew Passion, 26 to B Minor Mass). Also includes major analysis of 18th-century music. 450 musical examples. 40-page musical supplement. Total of xx + 1799pp.
(EUK) 22278-0, 22279-9 Two volumes, Clothbound $17.50

MOZART AND HIS PIANO CONCERTOS, Cuthbert Girdlestone. The only full-length study of an important area of Mozart's creativity. Provides detailed analyses of all 23 concertos, traces inspirational sources. 417 musical examples. Second edition. 509pp.
(USO) 21271-8 Paperbound $3.50

THE PERFECT WAGNERITE: A COMMENTARY ON THE NIBLUNG'S RING, George Bernard Shaw. Brilliant and still relevant criticism in remarkable essays on Wagner's Ring cycle, Shaw's ideas on political and social ideology behind the plots, role of Leitmotifs, vocal requisites, etc. Prefaces. xxi + 136pp.
21707-8 Paperbound $1.50

DON GIOVANNI, W. A. Mozart. Complete libretto, modern English translation; biographies of composer and librettist; accounts of early performances and critical reaction. Lavishly illustrated. All the material you need to understand and appreciate this great work. Dover Opera Guide and Libretto Series; translated and introduced by Ellen Bleiler. 92 illustrations. 209pp.
21134-7 Paperbound $2.00

HIGH FIDELITY SYSTEMS: A LAYMAN'S GUIDE, Roy F. Allison. All the basic information you need for setting up your own audio system: high fidelity and stereo record players, tape records, F.M. Connections, adjusting tone arm, cartridge, checking needle alignment, positioning speakers, phasing speakers, adjusting hums, trouble-shooting, maintenance, and similar topics. Enlarged 1965 edition. More than 50 charts, diagrams, photos. iv + 91pp. 21514-8 Paperbound $1.25

REPRODUCTION OF SOUND, Edgar Villchur. Thorough coverage for laymen of high fidelity systems, reproducing systems in general, needles, amplifiers, preamps, loudspeakers, feedback, explaining physical background. "A rare talent for making technicalities vividly comprehensible," R. Darrell, *High Fidelity*. 69 figures. iv + 92pp. 21515-6 Paperbound $1.25

HEAR ME TALKIN' TO YA: THE STORY OF JAZZ AS TOLD BY THE MEN WHO MADE IT, Nat Shapiro and Nat Hentoff. Louis Armstrong, Fats Waller, Jo Jones, Clarence Williams, Billy Holiday, Duke Ellington, Jelly Roll Morton and dozens of other jazz greats tell how it was in Chicago's South Side, New Orleans, depression Harlem and the modern West Coast as jazz was born and grew. xvi + 429pp.
21726-4 Paperbound $2.50

FABLES OF AESOP, translated by Sir Roger L'Estrange. A reproduction of the very rare 1931 Paris edition; a selection of the most interesting fables, together with 50 imaginative drawings by Alexander Calder. v + 128pp. 6½x9¼.
21780-9 Paperbound $1.50

AGAINST THE GRAIN (A REBOURS), Joris K. Huysmans. Filled with weird images, evidences of a bizarre imagination, exotic experiments with hallucinatory drugs, rich tastes and smells and the diversions of its sybarite hero Duc Jean des Esseintes, this classic novel pushed 19th-century literary decadence to its limits. Full unabridged edition. Do not confuse this with abridged editions generally sold. Introduction by Havelock Ellis. xlix + 206pp. 22190-3 Paperbound $2.00

VARIORUM SHAKESPEARE: HAMLET. Edited by Horace H. Furness; a landmark of American scholarship. Exhaustive footnotes and appendices treat all doubtful words and phrases, as well as suggested critical emendations throughout the play's history. First volume contains editor's own text, collated with all Quartos and Folios. Second volume contains full first Quarto, translations of Shakespeare's sources (Belleforest, and Saxo Grammaticus), Der Bestrafte Brudermord, and many essays on critical and historical points of interest by major authorities of past and present. Includes details of staging and costuming over the years. By far the best edition available for serious students of Shakespeare. Total of xx + 905pp.
21004-9, 21005-7, 2 volumes, Paperbound $7.00

A LIFE OF WILLIAM SHAKESPEARE, Sir Sidney Lee. This is the standard life of Shakespeare, summarizing everything known about Shakespeare and his plays. Incredibly rich in material, broad in coverage, clear and judicious, it has served thousands as the best introduction to Shakespeare. 1931 edition. 9 plates. xxix + 792pp. (USO) 21967-4 Paperbound $3.75

MASTERS OF THE DRAMA, John Gassner. Most comprehensive history of the drama in print, covering every tradition from Greeks to modern Europe and America, including India, Far East, etc. Covers more than 800 dramatists, 2000 plays, with biographical material, plot summaries, theatre history, criticism, etc. "Best of its kind in English," New Republic. 77 illustrations. xxii + 890pp.
20100-7 Clothbound $8.50

THE EVOLUTION OF THE ENGLISH LANGUAGE, George McKnight. The growth of English, from the 14th century to the present. Unusual, non-technical account presents basic information in very interesting form: sound shifts, change in grammar and syntax, vocabulary growth, similar topics. Abundantly illustrated with quotations. Formerly Modern English in the Making. xii + 590pp.
21932-1 Paperbound $3.50

AN ETYMOLOGICAL DICTIONARY OF MODERN ENGLISH, Ernest Weekley. Fullest, richest work of its sort, by foremost British lexicographer. Detailed word histories, including many colloquial and archaic words; extensive quotations. Do not confuse this with the Concise Etymological Dictionary, which is much abridged. Total of xxvii + 830pp. 6½ x 9¼.
21873-2, 21874-0 Two volumes, Paperbound $6.00

FLATLAND: A ROMANCE OF MANY DIMENSIONS, E. A. Abbott. Classic of science-fiction explores ramifications of life in a two-dimensional world, and what happens when a three-dimensional being intrudes. Amusing reading, but also useful as introduction to thought about hyperspace. Introduction by Banesh Hoffmann. 16 illustrations. xx + 103pp. 20001-9 Paperbound $1.00

POEMS OF ANNE BRADSTREET, edited with an introduction by Robert Hutchinson. A new selection of poems by America's first poet and perhaps the first significant woman poet in the English language. 48 poems display her development in works of considerable variety—love poems, domestic poems, religious meditations, formal elegies, "quaternions," etc. Notes, bibliography. viii + 222pp.

22160-1 Paperbound $2.00

THREE GOTHIC NOVELS: THE CASTLE OF OTRANTO BY HORACE WALPOLE; VATHEK BY WILLIAM BECKFORD; THE VAMPYRE BY JOHN POLIDORI, WITH FRAGMENT OF A NOVEL BY LORD BYRON, edited by E. F. Bleiler. The first Gothic novel, by Walpole; the finest Oriental tale in English, by Beckford; powerful Romantic supernatural story in versions by Polidori and Byron. All extremely important in history of literature; all still exciting, packed with supernatural thrills, ghosts, haunted castles, magic, etc. xl + 291pp.

21232-7 Paperbound $2.50

THE BEST TALES OF HOFFMANN, E. T. A. Hoffmann. 10 of Hoffmann's most important stories, in modern re-editings of standard translations: Nutcracker and the King of Mice, Signor Formica, Automata, The Sandman, Rath Krespel, The Golden Flowerpot, Master Martin the Cooper, The Mines of Falun, The King's Betrothed, A New Year's Eve Adventure. 7 illustrations by Hoffmann. Edited by E. F. Bleiler. xxxix + 419pp. 21793-0 Paperbound $3.00

GHOST AND HORROR STORIES OF AMBROSE BIERCE, Ambrose Bierce. 23 strikingly modern stories of the horrors latent in the human mind: The Eyes of the Panther, The Damned Thing, An Occurrence at Owl Creek Bridge, An Inhabitant of Carcosa, etc., plus the dream-essay, Visions of the Night. Edited by E. F. Bleiler. xxii + 199pp. 20767-6 Paperbound $1.50

BEST GHOST STORIES OF J. S. LEFANU, J. Sheridan LeFanu. Finest stories by Victorian master often considered greatest supernatural writer of all. Carmilla, Green Tea, The Haunted Baronet, The Familiar, and 12 others. Most never before available in the U. S. A. Edited by E. F. Bleiler. 8 illustrations from Victorian publications. xvii + 467pp. 20415-4 Paperbound $3.00

MATHEMATICAL FOUNDATIONS OF INFORMATION THEORY, A. I. Khinchin. Comprehensive introduction to work of Shannon, McMillan, Feinstein and Khinchin, placing these investigations on a rigorous mathematical basis. Covers entropy concept in probability theory, uniqueness theorem, Shannon's inequality, ergodic sources, the E property, martingale concept, noise, Feinstein's fundamental lemma, Shanon's first and second theorems. Translated by R. A. Silverman and M. D. Friedman. iii + 120pp. 60434-9 Paperbound $1.75

SEVEN SCIENCE FICTION NOVELS, H. G. Wells. The standard collection of the great novels. Complete, unabridged. *First Men in the Moon, Island of Dr. Moreau, War of the Worlds, Food of the Gods, Invisible Man, Time Machine, In the Days of the Comet.* Not only science fiction fans, but every educated person owes it to himself to read these novels. 1015pp. 20264-X Clothbound $5.00

LAST AND FIRST MEN AND STAR MAKER, TWO SCIENCE FICTION NOVELS, Olaf Stapledon. Greatest future histories in science fiction. In the first, human intelligence is the "hero," through strange paths of evolution, interplanetary invasions, incredible technologies, near extinctions and reemergences. Star Maker describes the quest of a band of star rovers for intelligence itself, through time and space: weird inhuman civilizations, crustacean minds, symbiotic worlds, etc. Complete, unabridged. v + 438pp. 21962-3 Paperbound $2.50

THREE PROPHETIC NOVELS, H. G. WELLS. Stages of a consistently planned future for mankind. *When the Sleeper Wakes,* and *A Story of the Days to Come,* anticipate *Brave New World* and *1984,* in the 21st Century; *The Time Machine,* only complete version in print, shows farther future and the end of mankind. All show Wells's greatest gifts as storyteller and novelist. Edited by E. F. Bleiler. x + 335pp. (USO) 20605-X Paperbound $2.50

THE DEVIL'S DICTIONARY, Ambrose Bierce. America's own Oscar Wilde— Ambrose Bierce—offers his barbed iconoclastic wisdom in over 1,000 definitions hailed by H. L. Mencken as "some of the most gorgeous witticisms in the English language." 145pp. 20487-1 Paperbound $1.25

MAX AND MORITZ, Wilhelm Busch. Great children's classic, father of comic strip, of two bad boys, Max and Moritz. Also Ker and Plunk (Plisch und Plumm), Cat and Mouse, Deceitful Henry, Ice-Peter, The Boy and the Pipe, and five other pieces. Original German, with English translation. Edited by H. Arthur Klein; translations by various hands and H. Arthur Klein. vi + 216pp. 20181-3 Paperbound $2.00

PIGS IS PIGS AND OTHER FAVORITES, Ellis Parker Butler. The title story is one of the best humor short stories, as Mike Flannery obfuscates biology and English. Also included, That Pup of Murchison's, The Great American Pie Company, and Perkins of Portland. 14 illustrations. v + 109pp. 21532-6 Paperbound $1.25

THE PETERKIN PAPERS, Lucretia P. Hale. It takes genius to be as stupidly mad as the Peterkins, as they decide to become wise, celebrate the "Fourth," keep a cow, and otherwise strain the resources of the Lady from Philadelphia. Basic book of American humor. 153 illustrations. 219pp. 20794-3 Paperbound $1.50

PERRAULT'S FAIRY TALES, translated by A. E. Johnson and S. R. Littlewood, with 34 full-page illustrations by Gustave Doré. All the original Perrault stories— Cinderella, Sleeping Beauty, Bluebeard, Little Red Riding Hood, Puss in Boots, Tom Thumb, etc.—with their witty verse morals and the magnificent illustrations of Doré. One of the five or six great books of European fairy tales. viii + 117pp. 8⅛ x 11. 22311-6 Paperbound $2.00

OLD HUNGARIAN FAIRY TALES, Baroness Orczy. Favorites translated and adapted by author of the *Scarlet Pimpernel.* Eight fairy tales include "The Suitors of Princess Fire-Fly," "The Twin Hunchbacks," "Mr. Cuttlefish's Love Story," and "The Enchanted Cat." This little volume of magic and adventure will captivate children as it has for generations. 90 drawings by Montagu Barstow. 96pp. (USO) 22293-4 Paperbound $1.95

THE RED FAIRY BOOK, Andrew Lang. Lang's color fairy books have long been children's favorites. This volume includes Rapunzel, Jack and the Bean-stalk and 35 other stories, familiar and unfamiliar. 4 plates, 93 illustrations x + 367pp.
21673-X Paperbound $2.50

THE BLUE FAIRY BOOK, Andrew Lang. Lang's tales come from all countries and all times. Here are 37 tales from Grimm, the Arabian Nights, Greek Mythology, and other fascinating sources. 8 plates, 130 illustrations. xi + 390pp.
21437-0 Paperbound $2.50

HOUSEHOLD STORIES BY THE BROTHERS GRIMM. Classic English-language edition of the well-known tales — Rumpelstiltskin, Snow White, Hansel and Gretel, The Twelve Brothers, Faithful John, Rapunzel, Tom Thumb (52 stories in all). Translated into simple, straightforward English by Lucy Crane. Ornamented with head-pieces, vignettes, elaborate decorative initials and a dozen full-page illustrations by Walter Crane. x + 269pp.
21080-4 Paperbound $2.50

THE MERRY ADVENTURES OF ROBIN HOOD, Howard Pyle. The finest modern ver-sions of the traditional ballads and tales about the great English outlaw. Howard Pyle's complete prose version, with every word, every illustration of the first edition. Do not confuse this facsimile of the original (1883) with modern editions that change text or illustrations. 23 plates plus many page decorations. xxii + 296pp.
22043-5 Paperbound $2.50

THE STORY OF KING ARTHUR AND HIS KNIGHTS, Howard Pyle. The finest chil-dren's version of the life of King Arthur; brilliantly retold by Pyle, with 48 of his most imaginative illustrations. xviii + 313pp. 6⅛ x 9¼.
21445-1 Paperbound $2.50

THE WONDERFUL WIZARD OF OZ, L. Frank Baum. America's finest children's book in facsimile of first edition with all Denslow illustrations in full color. The edition a child should have. Introduction by Martin Gardner. 23 color plates, scores of drawings. iv + 267pp.
20691-2 Paperbound $2.50

THE MARVELOUS LAND OF OZ, L. Frank Baum. The second Oz book, every bit as imaginative as the Wizard. The hero is a boy named Tip, but the Scarecrow and the Tin Woodman are back, as is the Oz magic. 16 color plates, 120 drawings by John R. Neill. 287pp.
20692-0 Paperbound $2.50

THE MAGICAL MONARCH OF MO, L. Frank Baum. Remarkable adventures in a land even stranger than Oz. The best of Baum's books not in the Oz series. 15 color plates and dozens of drawings by Frank Verbeck. xviii + 237pp.
21892-9 Paperbound $2.25

THE BAD CHILD'S BOOK OF BEASTS, MORE BEASTS FOR WORSE CHILDREN, A MORAL ALPHABET, Hilaire Belloc. Three complete humor classics in one volume. Be kind to the frog, and do not call him names . . . and 28 other whimsical animals. Familiar favorites and some not so well known. Illustrated by Basil Blackwell. 156pp.
(USO) 20749-8 Paperbound $1.50

EAST O' THE SUN AND WEST O' THE MOON, George W. Dasent. Considered the best of all translations of these Norwegian folk tales, this collection has been enjoyed by generations of children (and folklorists too). Includes True and Untrue, Why the Sea is Salt, East O' the Sun and West O' the Moon, Why the Bear is Stumpy-Tailed, Boots and the Troll, The Cock and the Hen, Rich Peter the Pedlar, and 52 more. The only edition with all 59 tales. 77 illustrations by Erik Werenskiold and Theodor Kittelsen. xv + 418pp. 22521-6 Paperbound $3.50

GOOPS AND HOW TO BE THEM, Gelett Burgess. Classic of tongue-in-cheek humor, masquerading as etiquette book. 87 verses, twice as many cartoons, show mischievous Goops as they demonstrate to children virtues of table manners, neatness, courtesy, etc. Favorite for generations. viii + 88pp. 6½ x 9¼.
22233-0 Paperbound $1.25

ALICE'S ADVENTURES UNDER GROUND, Lewis Carroll. The first version, quite different from the final *Alice in Wonderland,* printed out by Carroll himself with his own illustrations. Complete facsimile of the "million dollar" manuscript Carroll gave to Alice Liddell in 1864. Introduction by Martin Gardner. viii + 96pp. Title and dedication pages in color. 21482-6 Paperbound $1.25

THE BROWNIES, THEIR BOOK, Palmer Cox. Small as mice, cunning as foxes, exuberant and full of mischief, the Brownies go to the zoo, toy shop, seashore, circus, etc., in 24 verse adventures and 266 illustrations. Long a favorite, since their first appearance in St. Nicholas Magazine. xi + 144pp. 6⅝ x 9¼.
21265-3 Paperbound $1.75

SONGS OF CHILDHOOD, Walter De La Mare. Published (under the pseudonym Walter Ramal) when De La Mare was only 29, this charming collection has long been a favorite children's book. A facsimile of the first edition in paper, the 47 poems capture the simplicity of the nursery rhyme and the ballad, including such lyrics as I Met Eve, Tartary, The Silver Penny. vii + 106pp. 21972-0 Paperbound $1.25

THE COMPLETE NONSENSE OF EDWARD LEAR, Edward Lear. The finest 19th-century humorist-cartoonist in full: all nonsense limericks, zany alphabets, Owl and Pussycat, songs, nonsense botany, and more than 500 illustrations by Lear himself. Edited by Holbrook Jackson. xxix + 287pp. (USO) 20167-8 Paperbound $2.00

BILLY WHISKERS: THE AUTOBIOGRAPHY OF A GOAT, Frances Trego Montgomery. A favorite of children since the early 20th century, here are the escapades of that rambunctious, irresistible and mischievous goat—Billy Whiskers. Much in the spirit of *Peck's Bad Boy,* this is a book that children never tire of reading or hearing. All the original familiar illustrations by W. H. Fry are included: 6 color plates, 18 black and white drawings. 159pp. 22345-0 Paperbound $2.00

MOTHER GOOSE MELODIES. Faithful republication of the fabulously rare Munroe and Francis "copyright 1833" Boston edition—the most important Mother Goose collection, usually referred to as the "original." Familiar rhymes plus many rare ones, with wonderful old woodcut illustrations. Edited by E. F. Bleiler. 128pp. 4½ x 6⅜. 22577-1 Paperbound $1.25

TWO LITTLE SAVAGES; BEING THE ADVENTURES OF TWO BOYS WHO LIVED AS INDIANS AND WHAT THEY LEARNED, Ernest Thompson Seton. Great classic of nature and boyhood provides a vast range of woodlore in most palatable form, a genuinely entertaining story. Two farm boys build a teepee in woods and live in it for a month, working out Indian solutions to living problems, star lore, birds and animals, plants, etc. 293 illustrations. vii + 286pp.

20985-7 Paperbound $2.50

PETER PIPER'S PRACTICAL PRINCIPLES OF PLAIN & PERFECT PRONUNCIATION. Alliterative jingles and tongue-twisters of surprising charm, that made their first appearance in America about 1830. Republished in full with the spirited woodcut illustrations from this earliest American edition. 32pp. $4\frac{1}{2}$ x $6\frac{3}{8}$.

22560-7 Paperbound $1.00

SCIENCE EXPERIMENTS AND AMUSEMENTS FOR CHILDREN, Charles Vivian. 73 easy experiments, requiring only materials found at home or easily available, such as candles, coins, steel wool, etc.; illustrate basic phenomena like vacuum, simple chemical reaction, etc. All safe. Modern, well-planned. Formerly *Science Games for Children*. 102 photos, numerous drawings. 96pp. $6\frac{1}{8}$ x $9\frac{1}{4}$.

21856-2 Paperbound $1.25

AN INTRODUCTION TO CHESS MOVES AND TACTICS SIMPLY EXPLAINED, Leonard Barden. Informal intermediate introduction, quite strong in explaining reasons for moves. Covers basic material, tactics, important openings, traps, positional play in middle game, end game. Attempts to isolate patterns and recurrent configurations. Formerly *Chess*. 58 figures. 102pp.   (USO) 21210-6 Paperbound $1.25

LASKER'S MANUAL OF CHESS, Dr. Emanuel Lasker. Lasker was not only one of the five great World Champions, he was also one of the ablest expositors, theorists, and analysts. In many ways, his Manual, permeated with his philosophy of battle, filled with keen insights, is one of the greatest works ever written on chess. Filled with analyzed games by the great players. A single-volume library that will profit almost any chess player, beginner or master. 308 diagrams. xli x 349pp.

20640-8 Paperbound $2.75

THE MASTER BOOK OF MATHEMATICAL RECREATIONS, Fred Schuh. In opinion of many the finest work ever prepared on mathematical puzzles, stunts, recreations; exhaustively thorough explanations of mathematics involved, analysis of effects, citation of puzzles and games. Mathematics involved is elementary. Translated by F. Göbel. 194 figures. xxiv + 430pp.   22134-2 Paperbound $3.00

MATHEMATICS, MAGIC AND MYSTERY, Martin Gardner. Puzzle editor for Scientific American explains mathematics behind various mystifying tricks: card tricks, stage "mind reading," coin and match tricks, counting out games, geometric dissections, etc. Probability sets, theory of numbers clearly explained. Also provides more than 400 tricks, guaranteed to work, that you can do. 135 illustrations. xii + 176pp.

20338-2 Paperbound $1.50

MATHEMATICAL PUZZLES FOR BEGINNERS AND ENTHUSIASTS, Geoffrey Mott-Smith. 189 puzzles from easy to difficult—involving arithmetic, logic, algebra, properties of digits, probability, etc.—for enjoyment and mental stimulus. Explanation of mathematical principles behind the puzzles. 135 illustrations. viii + 248pp.
20198-8 Paperbound $1.75

PAPER FOLDING FOR BEGINNERS, William D. Murray and Francis J. Rigney. Easiest book on the market, clearest instructions on making interesting, beautiful origami Sail boats, cups, roosters, frogs that move legs, bonbon boxes, standing birds, etc. 40 projects; more than 275 diagrams and photographs. 94pp.
20713-7 Paperbound $1.00

TRICKS AND GAMES ON THE POOL TABLE, Fred Herrmann. 79 tricks and games— some solitaires, some for two or more players, some competitive games—to entertain you between formal games. Mystifying shots and throws, unusual caroms, tricks involving such props as cork, coins, a hat, etc. Formerly *Fun on the Pool Table*. 77 figures. 95pp.
21814-7 Paperbound $1.00

HAND SHADOWS TO BE THROWN UPON THE WALL: A SERIES OF NOVEL AND AMUSING FIGURES FORMED BY THE HAND, Henry Bursill. Delightful picturebook from great-grandfather's day shows how to make 18 different hand shadows: a bird that flies, duck that quacks, dog that wags his tail, camel, goose, deer, boy, turtle, etc. Only book of its sort. vi + 33pp. 6½ x 9¼. 21779-5 Paperbound $1.00

WHITTLING AND WOODCARVING, E. J. Tangerman. 18th printing of best book on market. "If you can cut a potato you can carve" toys and puzzles, chains, chessmen, caricatures, masks, frames, woodcut blocks, surface patterns, much more. Information on tools, woods, techniques. Also goes into serious wood sculpture from Middle Ages to present, East and West. 464 photos, figures. x + 293pp.
20965-2 Paperbound $2.00

HISTORY OF PHILOSOPHY, Julián Marias. Possibly the clearest, most easily followed, best planned, most useful one-volume history of philosophy on the market; neither skimpy nor overfull. Full details on system of every major philosopher and dozens of less important thinkers from pre-Socratics up to Existentialism and later. Strong on many European figures usually omitted. Has gone through dozens of editions in Europe. 1966 edition, translated by Stanley Appelbaum and Clarence Strowbridge. xviii + 505pp.
21739-6 Paperbound $3.00

YOGA: A SCIENTIFIC EVALUATION, Kovoor T. Behanan. Scientific but non-technical study of physiological results of yoga exercises; done under auspices of Yale U. Relations to Indian thought, to psychoanalysis, etc. 16 photos. xxiii + 270pp.
20505-3 Paperbound $2.50

Prices subject to change without notice.
Available at your book dealer or write for free catalogue to Dept. GI, Dover Publications, Inc., 180 Varick St., N. Y., N. Y. 10014. Dover publishes more than 150 books each year on science, elementary and advanced mathematics, biology, music, art, literary history, social sciences and other areas.